Sentencing as a Human Process

John Hogarth

Published by the University of Toronto Press
in association with the Centre of Criminology
University of Toronto

©University of Toronto Press 1971

Toronto and Buffalo
Reprinted 1974

ISBN 0-8020-1750-9 (cloth)
ISBN 0-8020-6223-7 (paper)

LC 73-151374

Printed in Canada

Foreword

This book marks the inception of a series devoted to Canadian studies in criminology under the aegis of the Centre of Criminology, University of Toronto. Through the medium of this series it is hoped to present the results of research undertaken by members of the Centre of Criminology and also the work of other individual scholars whose research base, located in Canada, may be in the universities, governmental agencies, or privately supported research institutions. Criminology, for the purposes of the series, will be given a broad interpretation that encompasses the contributions of law, the social and behavioural sciences, as well as those other branches of knowledge whose potential value to the understanding and handling of crime in modern society is still relatively unrecognized or undeveloped. Furthermore, it is expected that the subject matter to be contained in the series will include the nature and scope of criminal activity, criminal law and its sanctions, correctional theories and practices, and the administration of criminal justice including the role of the police, prosecuting authorities, defence counsel and the judiciary.

During the past decade Canada has been active, in a manner reflected by many other nations, in instituting changes and experimentation of various kinds in the broad field of criminal justice. This ferment has engendered in this country a notably receptive atmosphere towards criminological research that augurs well for the future, however paradoxical might be the cautious attitude displayed by all levels of government towards the investment of public resources to support such research. That progress has been made is not open to serious questioning, and the launching of the present series may come, in retrospect, to be seen as representing another landmark in the history of dealing with the problems of crime and criminal justice in Canada.

It is most appropriate that the inaugural volume of "Canadian Studies in Criminology" should be Professor John Hogarth's interdisciplinary study of decision-making in the area of sentencing. However strong might be the claim of individual segments of the criminal justice and correctional systems to have its basic philosophy and practices investigated, or to have evaluated its past and present performance, the choice of this study on sentencing by Professor Hogarth as the first research project to be conducted in the Centre of Criminology was no accident. It is doubtful if any sector occupies so central or so pervasive a position as that associated with the discharge of sentencing responsibilities by the criminal courts. Unlike other countries, in Canada the magistrates' courts (recently re-designated in Ontario as the Criminal Division of the Provincial Courts) carry the major burden of the criminal law jurisdiction, with commensurate powers in matters of sentencing. When the co-operation of the large body of judges who preside over these courts became manifest, an unique opportunity presented itself to examine empirically the sentencing process in the normal course of the court's work, including all the factors that precede the actual disposition by the court of individual cases.

The magnitude of the task undertaken by Professor Hogarth is largely evident in the pages that follow. Those of us who have been close to the project since it was first launched will recognize also the author's special qualities, so rarely combined in the one person, but so necessary to the successful completion of this kind of interdisciplinary effort. For understandable reasons, it has not been found possible to include the substantial body of additional statistical material upon which the findings reported in this volume are based. Interested readers who would like to avail themselves of these technical appendices should write for copies to the Centre of Criminology, University of Toronto. Meanwhile, work is continuing on the remaining parts of the project which will deal with the probation officers' role in sentencing and will examine how probation officers of different backgrounds, attitudes and experience process and interpret information in the preparation of pre-sentence reports. It is also planned to conduct a series of follow-up studies of those offenders who constituted the sample of the present study.

Patently, this research has involved the participation of large numbers of individuals without whose consistent devotion to their self-imposed tasks it is certain that the project would never have reached its final goal. Indeed, it might almost be said that there existed within the framework of the study a subsidiary project worthy of detailed documentation in its own right, representing as it did the logistics of a major research exercise. I readily acknowledge the indebtedness of the Centre of Criminology to the willing array of judges, probation and police officers, and public administrators who have waited long and patiently to see the final outcome to their united efforts.

The body of outside respondents has been amply matched by the team of researchers with the Centre who have laboured steadily and persistently over the years under the inspired direction of Professor Hogarth and his able research associate, Miss Barbara Schloss. The road that they have travelled has been a long and arduous one, calling for the application of all their intellectual and human resources. They have earned the respect and appreciation of everyone associated with the Centre of Criminology.

There remains the pleasant responsibility of recording the Centre's gratitude to the Ford Foundation and to the Ontario Department of Justice and the Attorney General for their financial nurturing of this venture through all its vicissitudes.

Centre of Criminology   J. Ll. J. Edwards
University of Toronto

Preface

Ordinarily a person doing research can protect himself from criticism of his published work by claiming that he did not have the time, co-operation or funds to do everything that should be done in the course of his study. None of these protections is available to this author. This book was written under almost ideal conditions. Splendid co-operation was received from all concerned, adequate financial and human resources were made available, and a stimulating and supportive intellectual environment existed.

The research was greatly influenced by a group of people working in the field of criminology in the Toronto area. While it is both premature and pretentious to say that in Toronto a new school of criminological thought has developed, a community of intellectual concern is beginning to take place. This approach may be characterized as an attempt to apply rigorous methodology to data generated from a phenomenological perspective. Phenomenology provides a starting point for our research. It is simply a way of getting as close as possible to the subject matter of an inquiry without becoming prematurely entangled in theoretical considerations. Our approach is not a rejection of classical methodology, as appears to be the case with many social phenomenologists, but rather a conscious strategy to make both method and concept conform to the phenomenon under study. In the realm of human behaviour, it is felt that a useful starting point is the investigation of what the subjects themselves "know" about the world and themselves, rather than a description of "objectively" defined characteristics of their behaviour. It is an approach which liberates us from the necessity of determining the course of the inquiry before any of the data is in. Theoretical considerations and methodology only become relevant within the context of a constantly developing understanding of the phenomena.

Our research, like other scientific endeavours, is directed towards formulating generalizations about observed regularities in behaviour. At least that is the ultimate objective. In moving towards that goal, three questions were asked: (a) What does sentencing mean to each individual judge? (b) What common patterns of meaning exist among the judges as a group? (c) What does sentencing mean to us as students of the process? Each of these questions requires its own scheme of imagery and methodology. The sequence in which the chapters of this book are organized follows the developmental stages in our own thinking about sentencing. We start with a deliberately naive position and build a model of the decision process, straw by straw, guided primarily by an effort to understand sentencing as magistrates themselves experience it. All the data upon which the eventual model was built concerned the meanings that judges attached to the facts of the cases and those surrounding circumstances which they deemed significant, including how they defined self in relationship to those facts and circumstances. The end result is a set of testable generalizations about judicial reasoning in sentencing.

This study would not have been possible without the help of very many people, to whom the writer is greatly indebted.

I am particularly grateful to the following leading Ontario Provincial Court judges who participated from the beginning in the design and execution of this work: Judge R.G. Groom, Chairman of the Sentencing Committee of the Ontario Provincial Court Judges' Association, Chief Judge A.O. Klein, Judge J.C. Dunlap, Judge S. Tupper Bigelow, Senior Judge W.J. Tuchtie, Judge J.L. Roberts, Judge E.W. Kenrick, Judge R.B. Baxter and Judge F.K. Jasperson (since retired). These judges acted as advisors to the project and helped in the pre-testing of instruments that were eventually used. The constructive advice that was received, together with the support given in interpreting the project to other judges, made the study possible. I am also indebted to Senior Judge F.C. Hayes and Judge L.A. Sherwood, who, as presidents of the Ontario Magistrates' Association during the course of this work, gave it their unqualified support.

I also owe thanks to many people in the Ontario Probation Service. Full and consistent support was given by its Director and Assistant Director, Mr D.W.F. Couglan and Mr G.G. McFarlane, respectively. The Supervising Probation Officers and the members of the Research Committee of the Ontario Probation

Officers' Association gave particularly helpful advice regarding the design of the instruments used by probation officers.

Excellent co-operation was received from police officers in the province. The Chairman of the Ontario Police Commission, Mr R. P. Milligan QC, co-ordinated the collection of data from individual departments, and was always ready to offer help and advice. Mr E.H. Silk QC, Commissioner of the Ontario Provincial Police, ensured that all necessary data were received from provincial police officers, and Mr James P. Mackey, then Chief of the Metropolitan Toronto Police Department, did the same with respect to cases originating from his area. To these senior men, and to all individual police officers who participated in the study, I would like to express sincere thanks.

I am also grateful to the Minister of Justice of the Province of Ontario, Mr A.A. Wishart QC, the Deputy Minister of Justice, Mr A.R. Dick QC, and to Mr A.A. Russell QC, Assistant Deputy Minister, who gave their official support and helped in many other tangible ways.

The degree of co-operation extended by the provincial judges, probation officers, and police officers would not have been possible without an atmosphere of trust between the Centre of Criminology and the agencies and individuals concerned. This goodwill exists primarily because of the work of the Director of the Centre of Criminology, Professor J.Ll.J. Edwards. For his constant advice and support, and for his opening of many doors, I am extremely grateful. To my good friends and colleagues, Mr Peter McNaughton-Smith and Dr Hans Mohr, I owe a special debt of thanks. Many of the ideas underlying both the concepts and methods used in the course of this study originated from long and frequent conversations with them. Dr Malcolm Courtis and Mrs Inez Dussuyer gave helpful advice on attitude measurement and information processing. Mr Clifford Shearing, Miss Patricia Jones, and Miss Judith Mosoff worked hard and enthusiastically on several aspects of the study.

The individual to whom I owe most is my friend and colleague, Miss Barbara Schloss. As Senior Research Assistant during the course of this project, Miss Schloss took day-to-day responsibility for the enormous task of data processing, coding, and computing. If it were not for her dedication, loyalty, and competence in the face of many difficulties, this project would not have been completed.

I also wish to thank a number of individuals who assisted Miss Schloss in data processing. Miss Lois Murray and Miss Annette

Clough were employed for periods of time as research assistants, and both dealt competently and without complaint with the tedious task of coding the data as it was collected. I am grateful to those members of the Junior League of Toronto who gave voluntarily of their time and effort in dealing with some of the more routine aspects of data processing. In particular, I would like to thank Mrs Elspeth Hogg, now president of the Junior League, and Miss Rosemary Hodgins, both of whom took time from busy schedules to assist in this work.

At the very beginning, Professor Thorsten Sellin of the University of Pennsylvania gave useful advice with respect to the design of the project. Later, his colleague, Professor Marvin Wolfgang, offered constructive comments with respect to the presentation of the analysis.

I am grateful to a large number of people at the University of Cambridge. To the Director and Staff of the Institute of Criminology, I wish to express sincere appreciation. Many useful comments of a detailed nature were made by Professor Glanville Williams. Mr Keith Hawkins and Mr Hugh Barr read the drafts of the chapters as they emerged, and this resulted in numerous changes in matters of detail. Mrs Helen Liepins and Mrs Jill Abcarius worked tirelessly and patiently in various secretarial tasks during the early and middle stages of the project. Mrs Mary Stafford and Mrs M. Manning uncomplainingly typed and re-typed the final manuscript.

I am also grateful to York University and Osgoode Hall Law School for arranging my work in such a way that facilitated the completion of the study. In particular, I would like to express appreciation to Dean Gerald Le Dain and Professors Paul Weiler and Jeffrey Jowell for their useful comments.

Finally, and most importantly, I must say that I could not have completed this project without the kindness and understanding of my wife Flora. Needless to say, all weaknesses or mistakes made during the course of this project are my responsibility.

John Hogarth

Contents

SENTENCING AS A HUMAN PROCESS

1

Introduction:
The Problem of Sentencing

"There is no decision in the criminal process that is so complicated and so difficult to make as that of the sentencing judge."[1]

The Problem of Conflicting Goals

Sentencing occupies a central position in the administration of criminal justice. Decisions made at this stage have not only important consequences for offenders, but they also affect the entire criminal justice system. Judges and magistrates are given enormous power over the lives of individuals. The proper exercise of that power is a matter of concern to offenders, to the agencies and individuals responsible for law enforcement and the treatment of offenders, and to the public at large.

It is often said that the imposition of sentences is one of the more important mechanisms through which society attempts to achieve its social goals. The main difficulty arises from the fact that there is little agreement as to what these social goals are, or indeed should be. Some people would argue that the rehabilitation of convicted offenders is the best method of preventing crime.[2] There are others who believe that it is the deterrent effect of criminal sanctions that offers the greatest protection.[3] Still others maintain that the detention of dangerous or anti-social offenders is the only guarantee that they will not commit further crime, at least during the period of custody.[4] Finally, there are those who feel that criminal sanctions find their justification, not in the prevention of crime, but rather in an alleged moral right and duty invested in the courts to inflict punishment on convicted offenders as an expression of society's disapproval of their crimes.[5]

The main burden of reconciling the competing goals of the criminal justice system falls on the sentencing judge. Among judges and magistrates each approach has its advocates, and it is not difficult to discover reported cases in which the courts have emphasized one or more of them.[6]

In recent years there has been a noticeable shift in emphasis in rationale for sentencing from "looking backward" to the offence for purposes of punishment, to "looking forward" to the likely impact of a sentence on the future behaviour of the offender, and in some instances, on potential offenders in the community at large.

A shift in emphasis from punishment to control poses a host of new problems for the courts and has made sentencing an exceedingly difficult task. It is one thing to make a verbal commitment to the control of crime through reformation and deterrence, but it is quite another to demonstrate that this objective can be achieved. Estimating the likely impact of the sentence on the offender, or on potential offenders, is a most complex task. It is difficult to know with any degree of certainty whether an offender before the court is likely to pose the risk of further crime, and even more difficult to know whether that risk can be in any way altered by choosing one form of sentence over another. Still more difficult is estimating whether the imposition of a deterrent penalty is likely to prevent potential offenders from committing crime. Finally, there is the thorny problem of deciding to what extent it is morally justified to punish individuals for crimes they have not yet committed or for the potential crimes of others.

At the same time, it is widely recognized that the prevention and control of crime should be achieved with minimum interference in the liberty of the subject. The "rehabilitative ideal" can often be in contradiction with this value. The public demands a fair and even-handed administration of justice. This means that the courts may feel obliged to ensure that the sanctions they impose bear some relationship to the crime and that no penal, deterrent, or correctional measure involves a greater deprivation of liberty than the offence itself warrants.

Even if it could be agreed that the main purpose in sentencing was to prevent crime through reformation and deterrence, the ability of the courts to achieve these goals through sentencing is limited because knowledge about the deterrent or rehabilitative effect of different penal measures is limited. Magistrates and judges are not provided with evidence of the results of their decisions. Moreover, the little evidence which exists tends to show that, as far as it can be determined, penal measures are irrelevant to the chance that offenders will commit further offences. While research can demonstrate that offenders possessing certain characteristics stand different chances of being reconvicted after specified periods of time, it has not been possible to demonstrate that the chances of reconviction would in any way be altered by applying one particular measure rather than another.[7] Still more difficult is the problem of estimating whether the imposition of a sanction on the offender before the court will deter potential offenders from crime. The evidence is, at best, equivocal.[8]

Judges and magistrates in Canada cannot look to the legislature for guidance in matters of sentence. The formal law as expressed in the Criminal Code and related statutes gives enormous discretionary power to the courts without guidance as to how that power is to be exercised. Very high maximum penalties are provided in legislation leaving it to the courts alone to decide what penalties should be imposed and for what purpose. Failure of parliament to establish a criminal policy expressed in legislative criteria for the imposition of sentence is, perhaps, one of the main reasons for inconsistency in sentencing. It is not surprising, however, that our legislators have failed to address themselves seriously to this question as there are deep divisions in society as to what social purposes sentencing should serve. In the absence of legislative criteria and in an atmosphere of controversy about sentencing, it would not be surprising if the courts were inconsistent in the application of sentencing principles. This situation makes sentencing a lonely and onerous task for the courts.

Limitations imposed by scant knowledge and by lack of treatment facilities undoubtedly impose sharp restrictions on what the courts can achieve through sentencing. But judges and magistrates cannot wait for the results of research or for the improvement of treatment methods. Nor can they postpone making decisions until there is consensus in society about the principles to apply. Sentencing must take place within the framework of existing knowledge and resources. Within this framework the kinds of decisions made will, to a large extent, depend on what information is made available and how it is used. Knowledge of how courts use information, therefore, is the key to understanding the decision-making process.

The selection of valid information from the mass of data that could be used is becoming more difficult for the courts. Criminology and corrections are in the midst of a virtual "fact explosion," and the sentencer is faced with the problem of having to sift the amount of information that is available. Only a fraction of this information is immediately useful, and indeed, much of it is likely to be proved invalid. The intellectual junk-yard in criminology is piled high with discarded theories and discredited concepts. This encourages a certain scepticism on the part of judges and magistrates about using available knowledge, which will not be dispelled until it can be convincingly shown that by using this knowledge more effective sentencing decisions can be made. In the meantime there are bound to be differences among judges and magistrates in the type and amount of information that they use in sentencing.

In summary, the fundamental problems in sentencing arise from the fact that there is lack of agreement as to the social purposes that sentencing should serve, lack of evidence as to the effectiveness of penal measures to achieve these objectives, and lack of uniformity in the way present knowledge is used. In this situation it is not surprising that there is some uncertainty, confusion, and lack of agreement among judges in their approach to sentencing problems which, in turn, leads to disparity in sentencing practice. The next section will explore this problem more fully.

The Problem of Disparity

A universal criticism of sentencing is the apparent disparity of sentences imposed by different judges for cases which do not appear to be substantially different from one another. The imposition of unequal sentences for the same offence, or for offences of comparable seriousness, without a clearly visible justification, amounts, in the public mind, to judicial caprice. Accused and counsel openly "jockey" for lenient judges and the notion that the criminal justice system is fairly and evenly applied is thereby shown to be a myth.[9] The report of the President's Commission on Law Enforcement quotes, with approval, the statement made by Mr Justice Jackson, when he was Attorney- General of the United States: "It is obviously repugnant to one's sense of justice that the judgement meted out to an offender should depend in large part on a purely fortuitous circumstance; namely, the personality of the particular judge before whom the case happens to come for disposition."[10]

The report also noted that unwarranted sentencing disparity affects correctional administration.[11] Prisoners compare sentences and a prisoner who is given cause to believe that he has been the victim of what may appear to him to be a judge's prejudice is often a hostile inmate. The effect is "to create a profound disrespect for the law in the very person who the prison is charged with inculcating a greater measure of respect."[12]

The extent of disparity in sentencing may be more apparent than real. Within each offence category there may be many different combinations of facts related to the offender, the offence and the surrounding circumstances which could properly affect the selection of a penalty. Without adequate statistical control over the types of cases appearing before the courts, it would be wrong to assume that there is genuine lack of uniformity in sentencing. Apparently unequal sentences for similar offences may also result from differences in the social contexts in which the courts operate, such as differences in the crime rate, or in public opinion, or in the resources to deal with offenders available locally.

It would therefore appear that complete uniformity in sentencing is not only unrealizable, but perhaps undesirable. It would mean a return to a penal code in which sentences are fixed entirely by statute, regardless of the particular circumstances of the offender before the court. The best that can be hoped for is what Roger Hood termed "equality of consideration."[13] By this he meant that in roughly similar situations courts ought to consider similar factors and have similar reasons for selecting particular forms of sentence. The crucial problem is one of establishing agreed criteria for sentencing, and as it has already been noted, the determination of this issue is fraught with difficulty as it necessarily involves an attempt to reconcile the contradictory goals of the criminal justice system.

The extent of the apparent disparity in sentencing has been amply demonstrated in a number of studies.[14] All that will be attempted here is to comment on some of the more important ones so far reported.

In 1935, Sellin compared sentences given to natural-born whites, foreign-born whites, and negroes, and found discrepancies which he attributed to "the human equation in judicial administration."[15]

In 1940, McGuire and Holtzoff examined disparity among judges in the United States in sentencing liquor and narcotic cases. They end with the conclusion: "the differences are primarily due to the diverse attitudes on the part of individual judges towards various crimes, and the severity or lightness of the punishment depends in each instance very largely on the personality of the trial judge."[16]

Gaudet's influential study of disparity in sentencing in New Jersey came to the following conclusion: "The criteria for sentences are unevenly and capriciously applied and the primary influence upon sentences is the personality of the judge; his personality in terms of his social background, education, religion, expressive temperament, and social attitudes."[17] This is a surprising conclusion in view of the fact that no evidence was produced as to these variables.

Edward Green's survey of these and other early studies rightly points to weaknesses in their research designs which made the analyses insensitive to the scope and variety of legal factors which could have properly accounted for the apparent disparity in sentencing.[18] Green's own study of sentencing by eighteen Philadelphia judges shows that when factors such as the type and severity of the crime, the number of criminal acts charged, and the offender's past record are taken into account, some of the apparent variation in sentencing disappears. Green strongly objects to the imputing of attitudes from apparently inconsistent sentencing behaviour. He stresses the rationality of the sentencing process and he concludes with: "Certain orderly processes underline the application of criteria for sentencing ... uniformity as well as inconsistency characterize the sentences of various judges, the latter being most conspicuous in cases of intermediate gravity."[19] Despite the title of his book, Judicial Attitudes in Sentencing, Green does not provide independent evidence of the existence of judicial attitudes, but rather imputes them from consistencies in sentencing behaviour. The use of the concept "attitude" to explain consistency among judges, without supporting evidence, is vulnerable to the same criticism made by Green of those studies that employ this concept to explain inconsistency between judges. The establishment of a statistical relationship between factors such as the severity of the crime and criminal record to the pattern of sentencing decisions made does not mean that these factors were consciously or even subconsciously in the minds of judges at the time of sentence.

One would, indeed, be surprised to find that sentences bear no relationship to the facts of the cases. The important question is one of determining the amount of variation in sentencing practice that can be attributed solely to differences in the cases, and the amount that is due solely to the personal characteristics of the judges concerned. The data and statistical methods used by Green would not allow for such a comparison.[20]

Hood's study of variations in sentencing among twelve urban magistrates courts during the years 1951 to 1954 cautiously opens with the "null hypothesis" that: "differences in sentencing are not associated with variations in the types of offenders and offences confronting magistrates in different areas."[21] After demonstrating that this hypothesis is partially rebutted by the evidence, he goes on to suggest that variations in sentencing practice are the result of different "policies" of the magistrates concerned. He shows that: "middle-class magistrates dealing with working-class offenders in relatively small and stable communities, are likely to be relatively severe."[22] He concludes with the statement: "the imprisonment policies of magistrates appear to be related to the social characteristics of the areas, the social constitution of the bench, and its particular view of the crime problem."[23] Hood frankly admits that his data on social characteristics, attitudes, and views of magistrates were sketchy and incomplete. This information was obtained from "impressions noted by the field workers during the interviews with various persons connected with the court" but it was "not available for all courts in the sample."[24] The weakness in the data detracts from the otherwise significant finding that judicial attitudes and policies may not be an independent cause of judicial behaviour, but may arise partly, at least, from the social structures in which the courts are situated.

More recently, Shoham reported an evaluation of the sentencing policy of the criminal courts in Israel.[25] The material for the research was drawn from sentences imposed by nine judges in three district courts of Israel during the year 1956. Examining both the actual sentences imposed and the reasons for judgement given, Shoham concluded that there 'were great variations between one judge and another in their methods of sentencing and the degree of severity; these variations cannot be attributed altogether to the first two factors involved in the offender and the offence, but must be mainly due to a third factor, namely, the sentencing attitude and the disposition of the individual judge himself."

Turning to Canada, the only empirical study of significance that has so far been reported is that by Stuart Jaffary, *The Sentencing of Adults in Canada*.[27] The data collected were confined to public records and were limited to showing differences in sentencing practices between provinces. These data were supplemented by Jaffary's own observations of trends in other countries and he does not claim to have done more than give a description, rather than an analysis, of the sentencing problem in Canada. However, he was able to show, for example, that an offender convicted of theft was nearly twice as likely to be sent to prison in Quebec as in Canada as a whole, and almost five times as likely as in the provinces of Manitoba, Saskatchewan, or British Columbia. Jaffary stresses the "strongly punitive philosophy" of Canadian courts, supporting this conclusion with a comparison of the frequency and length of the institutional sentences imposed in Canada with that in other countries.

The difficulty with Jaffary's study, and indeed with all the studies mentioned so far, is that they have been restricted to an examination of sentencing as revealed from official statistical records, particularly police sources. The usual procedure is to use these official sources to collect as much information as possible concerning the type and severity of the offences committed, the backgrounds and characteristics of the offenders concerned and the nature of the sentencing decisions made. This type of research has been often called an "input-output" or a "stimulus-response" model, as the facts of the case constitute the input or stimulus and the sentencing behaviour of the judge, the output or response. It has also been called a "black box" model, as nothing is known about the judges or magistrates apart from the decisions they make.

In studies of this kind, differences in sentencing behaviour which cannot be explained by known differences in the kinds of cases dealt with, are usually attributed to the "policies," "attitudes," or even the "personalities" of the judge or magistrate concerned. Thus, punitive judicial attitudes are inferred from apparently punitive sentencing behaviour. Judges are said to be "tough-minded," "tender-minded," "conservative," "liberal," "rigid," or "prejudiced," because their sentences appear to be so. To infer judicial attitudes indirectly from judicial conduct and not from specially designed questionnaires can lead to circularity in reasoning. It is arguable that one should not, by observing sentencing behaviour, impute an attitude and then employ that attitude to explain the behaviour, but this is precisely what most of these studies appear to do.

This type of analysis suffers from three additional problems. It is possible that information other than that known to the researcher from official records affected the decision of the court, it is *probable* that the researcher would take into account some information that was never placed before the court or, if made available, was not considered, and it is *certain* that the researcher and the court would differ to some degree in the weights attached to information actually considered.

It is not difficult to demonstrate that there appears to be lack of uniformity in sentencing practice in Canada. In a country as large and as diversified as Canada there is bound to be some variation. Provincial and regional differences in the crime problem and the resources available to meet it are likely to have an impact. Table 1 shows the distribution of sentences by provinces in indictable cases.[28] The figures denote the use of particular forms of sentences as a percentage of a total number of offenders sentenced in the province.

TABLE 1

Range in sentencing practice by province, 1964

Type of sentence	Highest percentage	Lowest percentage	Average percentage
Suspended sentence with probation	28.7	11.9	18.9
Suspended sentence without probation	20.5	7.6	11.6
Fine	31.1	20.5	24.1
Institution	53.5	32.5	45.7

TABLE 2

Range in sentencing practice by judicial district, Ontario 1964

Type of sentence	Highest percentage	Lowest percentage	Average percentage
Suspended sentence with probation	43.0	0	24.0
Suspended sentence without probation	34.0	0 (two districts)	7.0
Fine	39.0	2.0	24.0
Gaol	60.0	4.0	24.0
Reformatory	37.0	1.0	12.0
Penitentiary	23.0	0 (two districts)	6.0

In units as large as provinces, individual differences between courts tend to cancel out, giving an impression of more uniformity than actually exists. A more accurate assessment of the situation can be made from an examination of differences in practice among individual courts within provinces.

Table 2 shows variations in sentencing practice between courts situated in thirty-seven judicial districts in Ontario during the year 1964.[29] The figures denote the use of particular forms of sentence as a percentage of the total number of offenders sentenced for indictable offences in the judicial district.

It would appear from this table that courts in Ontario vary immensely in sentencing practice. In the course of one year, one court used probation in nearly half the cases coming before it, while another never used this form of disposition. Similarly, the use of suspended sentence without probation ranged from 0 to 34 per cent, fines from 2 to 39 per cent, short-term gaol sentences from 4 to 60 per cent, reformatory sentences from 1 to 37 per cent and long-term penitentiary sentences from 0 to 23 per cent. These differences appear to be too large to be explained solely in terms of differences in the types of cases appearing before courts in different areas. But this is something that can, and will, be tested empirically. Apparent inconsistency, therefore, becomes the first "fact" about sentencing in Ontario that this study attempts to explain.

Why are there inconsistencies in sentencing practice among Ontario magistrates? Are they simply due to variations in the cases coming before different courts? Are they due to differences in the social contexts in which the courts are situated? Are they due to the personal characteristics of the magistrates concerned? It is in response to these questions that this enquiry began.

NOTES TO CHAPTER 1

1 The Challenge of Crime in a Free Society - A Report by the President's Commission on Law Enforcement and the Administration of Justice (Washington, 1967), 141.

2 The two most authoritative statements in Canada concerning the aims of sentencing are to be found in: The Report of the Royal Commission to Investigate the Penal System (Ottawa, 1938), hereafter cited as Archambault Report, and, The Report of a Committee Appointed to Inquire into the Principles and Procedures Followed in the Remission Service (Ottawa, 1956), hereafter cited as Fauteux Report. Both these reports emphasized the "corrective" aspect of sentencing. See Archambault Report, 8-9, and Fauteux Report, 5-7. More recently, the then Minister of Justice, the Hon. Guy Favreau, stated: "I believe that the leading principle of correctional reform must be the protection of society through the rehabilitation of delinquents." G. Favreau, "An Address delivered to la Societé Canadienne de Criminologie" (Montreal, November 1964), unpublished.

3 For a thorough discussion of the efficacy of general deterrence see J. Andenaes, "General Prevention - Illusion or Reality," Journal of Criminal Law, Criminology and Police Science, 43 (1952), 176.

4   The most visible expression of this doctrine is in the passing of habitual criminal legislation in most countries. In Canada, this finds expression in sections 660 and 661 of the Criminal Code which provide for indeterminate sentences of preventive detention for habitual criminals and dangerous sexual offenders respectively. See generally A. W. Mewett, "Habitual Criminal Legislation Under the Criminal Code," *Canadian Bar Review* 39, (1961) 43-58.

5   James Fitzjames Stephen, the man who drafted the abortive English code which eventually formed the basis of the Canadian Criminal Code insisted that the criminal law should operate to "give distinct scope" to moral indignation and hatred of the criminal. J. Stephen, *History of the Criminal Law*, vol. 2 (London, 1883), 81.

6   For a review of the principles of sentencing as enunciated by the Courts of Appeal in Canada see J. Decore, "Criminal Sentencing: The Role of the Canadian Courts of Appeal and the Concept of Uniformity," *The Criminal Law Quarterly*, 6 (1964), 324-80. For an interesting comparison with the Court of Appeal in England see D. Thomas, "Theories of Punishment in the Court of Criminal Appeal," *Modern Law Review*, 27 (1964), 546-67.

7   This generalization appears in almost every review of recent research. See, for example, R. Hood, "Research into the Effectiveness of Punishments and Treatments," a paper read to the 2nd European Conference of Directors of Criminological Research Institutes, Strasbourg, 26-28 November 1964 (Strasbourg, 1965); N. Walker, *Crime and Punishment in Britain* (Edinburgh, 1965), 257; L.T. Wilkins, "The Effectiveness of Punishment," *Report of Criminological Scientific Council* (Strasbourg, 1967), 9-104.

8   The problem is one of balancing concern for community protection with individual liberty. It can be shown that adherence to the concepts of treatment and deterrence is likely to lead to both inconsistency and rather more severe sentencing practice. Barbara Wootton, for example, who is one of the most outspoken advocates for a social control policy in sentencing, admits that such a policy should not be equated with leniency. B. Wootton, *Crime and the Criminal Law* (London, 1963), 88-9. The challenge to the rehabilitative ideal has come from many quarters. David Matza, a sociologist, argues that the concept of individualization and treatment leads to both rampant inconsistency and injustice. See D. Matza, *Delinquency and Drift* (New York, 1964), 114-5. See also the classic essay by Francis Allen, "Criminal Justice, Legal Values and the Rehabilitative Ideal," in F. Allen, ed., *The Borderland of Criminal Justice* (Chicago, 1964), 26-7. More recently, Norval Morris raised the civil liberties issue and suggested a way out of the dilemma. He argues that "power should not be taken over a criminal's life in excess of that which would be taken if reform was not an objective." See N. Morris, "Impediments to Penal Reform," *University of Chicago Law Review*, 33 (1966), 627-56. There is empirical evidence that the adoption of the rehabilitative ideal leads to rather more punitive sentencing practices. See, for example, the evidence that Sol Rubin cites in *The Law of Criminal Correction* (St. Paul, Minn., 1963), 444-5, 685; see also *The Challenge of Crime in a Free Society*, 160, and the fascinating study by Stanton Wheeler of the attitudes and court practices of juvenile court judges in Boston, in which he found that judges who identified with a treatment doctrine tended to commit children to institutions more frequently than those primarily concerned with punishment, S. Wheeler, E. Banouch, M. Cramer and I. Zola, "Agents of Delinquency Control: A Comparative Analysis," in S. Wheeler, ed., *Controlling Delinquents, (New York, 1966), 31-60f.* Perhaps the best recent analysis of the issues is contained in H. L. Packer, *The Limits of the Criminal Sanction* (Stanford, 1969).

9   Many people have commented on this phenomenon. See, for example, W. Middendorff, *The Effectiveness of Punishment* (South Hackinsock, NJ, 1957), 28-38.

10   *The Challenge of Crime in a Free Society*, 145.

11 The President's Commission on Law Enforcement, *Task Force Report: The Courts*, (Washington, 1967), 23.

12 J. Hall, and G. O. W. Mueller, *Cases and Readings on Criminal Law and Procedure*, 2nd ed. (Indianapolis, 1965),33.

13 R.G. Hood, *Sentencing in Magistrates' Courts* (London, 1962).

14 For reviews of these studies see, for example, E. Green, *Judicial Attitudes in Sentencing* (London, 1961), 8-20; H. Mannheim, "Sentencing Revisited," in M. Wolfgang, ed., *Crime and Culture* (New York, 1968), 349-74 and especially at 368-73; Middendorff, *The Effectiveness of Punishment*, 28-38.

15 T. Sellin, "Race Prejudice in the Administration of Justice," *American Journal of Sociology*, 41 (September 1935), 212-17.

16 M. McGuire and A. Holtzoff, "The Problems of Sentencing in the Criminal Law," *Boston University Law Review*, 413 (1940), 426-33.

17 F. Gaudet, "The Sentencing Behavior of the Judge," in V. Brandom and S. Katash, eds., *Encyclopedia of Criminology* (New York, 1949), 449-61.

18 Green, *Judicial Attitudes in Sentencing*, 100.

19 *Ibid.*, 101-2.

20 Using the tests of significance (rather than measures of association) that Green employed, it was possible to obtain these results with only 10 to 15 per cent of the total variation being accounted for.

21 Hood, *Sentencing in Magistrates' Courts*, 119-20.

22 *Ibid.*

23 *Ibid.*, 76.

24 *Ibid.*

25 S. Shoham, "The Procedure and Sentencing Powers of the Criminal Courts in Israel," in *Crime and Social Deviation* (Chicago, 1966), 166-89.

26 *Ibid.*, 187.

27 S. Jaffary, *The Sentencing of Adults in Canada* (Toronto, 1963).

28 Dominion Bureau of Statistics, *Statistics of Criminal and Other Offences*, (Ottawa, 1964).

29 *Ibid.*

2

The Theoretical Basis to the Study

The General Scheme

This is a study of the sentencing behaviour of magistrates. It is concerned with *what* decisions different magistrates make, *how* they make them, and *why*.

The research described did not begin with a theory of judicial behaviour, but rather with a set of questions and several explicit assumptions about where their answers might be found. Guided by these questions and assumptions the study was initiated with an attempt to gain familiarity with magistrates, their world, and their way of making decisions. The first objective was to penetrate beneath the formal justification for sentencing, as expressed in reported cases, in order to understand the "inside story" or "meaning" of sentencing as magistrates themselves experience it in their everyday world.

The research started with about three months of informal discussion with a number of magistrates, supplemented by observations of their conduct on the bench. Out of this experience a partially structured interview schedule was designed. It covered areas which appeared to be significantly associated with the practical and theoretical issues in sentencing as they affect magistrates in their daily work. For a period of approximately six months this writer conducted confidential interviews with most of the full time magistrates in the province of Ontario, some seventy-one in all. Co-operation from magistrates was excellent, not one refusing to participate in a long, sometimes exacting and potentially damaging personal interview. These interviews took the form of conversations and their purpose was to reveal the backgrounds, definitions, intentions, and motivations of magistrates, in addition to their methods of making decisions in individual cases.

Based on knowledge derived from the interviews and the findings of previous research, two more specifically focused instruments were designed and implemented. One was a self-administered questionnaire probing certain dimensions of the attitudes that magistrates appear to hold towards crime, punishment, and related issues, and the other was a decision-making guide that was used by each magistrate in a sample of cases appearing before them in the course of their work. The purpose of this latter document was to reveal the mental processes involved in reaching sentencing decisions. In addition, certain data were collected from police officers, probation officers, and other sources concerning some 2400 criminal cases dealt with by magistrates in the sample over a period of eighteen months.

Questions and Assumptions Underlying the Design.

The Level of Analysis

The first problem faced in designing this study concerned the level of analysis to be used. Initially there appeared to be three choices: first, sentencing could have been studied at the *legal-institutional* level at which legislation and case law concerning sentencing would have been analysed with the traditional analytical tools of legal logic. The purpose of a study of this kind would have been to reveal inconsistencies or anomalies in what the law or lawyers have said about sentencing, or to identify certain weaknesses in the formal legal structure.

Secondly, sentencing could have been studied at the *sociological* level at which the norms, values, and constraints attached to the role of magistrate within the legal framework would be described and the relationships of this role to the roles of other people who participate in the decision-process analysed. A study of this kind would have described the social environment in which sentencing takes place, and determined the degree to which the behaviour of magistrates is influenced by contextual or structural factors.

Finally, sentencing could have been studies at the *psychological* level, at which the sentencing behaviour of magistrates would have been looked at in terms of the way in which they function psychologically. The purpose of such a study could have been to determine the relationship of judicial behaviour to such general factors as personality, emotional maturity, or attitudes, or it might have focused more specifically on such areas as the relationship of perception, learning, memory, or intelligence to the way in which decisions are made.

While useful research could be conducted within each of these levels, it seemed more productive to analyse sentencing at all three. The three approaches are complementary and are so inter-dependent as to make interpretation of data collected at one level difficult without data collected at another. For example, the beliefs and attitudes of a magistrate (a psychological problem) may be difficult to understand without knowledge of his loyalties and group affiliations (a sociological problem) and some of these loyalties and group affiliations in turn may arise largely out of the legal structure in which he operates (a legal-institutional problem).

While it would appear that judicial decision-making provides a convenient meeting ground where the relevant disciplines can be used to support one another to provide a more complete picture of sentencing than could be achieved from any one discipline alone, the real problem is knowing how to use concepts, materials, and methods, derived from a variety of academic disciplines, towards the development of an *integrated* theoretical framework.[1] Any study should have a measure of unity and logical consistency. A mere mixing of theories, concepts, and methods does not constitute inter-disciplinary research. It is not achieved by con-ducting several independent studies within one research project - this type of research is more appropriately called multi-disciplinary. Nor does it necessarily come about by putting together a research team consisting of people drawn from different theoretical backgrounds. How then is it to be achieved?

A possible answer to this question was found by turning to the phenomenon itself. Interaction between the personality and the environment of a magistrate takes place at the point of decision when the magistrate, through his own selective, cognitive, processes defines his "effective" environment, or what Lewin would call his "life space."[2] The way in which magistrates define their world and their relationship to it is likely to reveal both a great deal of their personalities and many of the significant influences in their environments. In a very practical way it became essential to understand how each magistrate defines each case appearing before him, *his* way of doing things, *his* stand on issues and problems commonly met in the court-room, his relationship to others, and his purposes in sentencing.

The decision not to begin with a theory of judicial behaviour, but rather with an effort to gain familiarity with magistrates, helped the researcher to identify some of the significant variables which are involved in the decision-process. It also guarded against the danger of over-simplification — the danger of attributing sentencing to a single cause or variable. More importantly, by looking at sentencing through "the eyes of magistrates," it was possible to transform all legal, sociological, and psychological data into one form. This facilitated the integration of data, theory, and method. Moreover, this was a natural transformation as it occurred in the minds of magistrates and was not a matter of reducing data to one form after it had been collected. This helped make all the data congruent and thus went some way to overcoming one of the major obstacles to interdisciplinary research.[3]

The Units of Analysis

The second problem to be overcome was that of determining the kind and amount of data which should be collected. Having assumed that legal, sociological, and psychological factors are involved in sentencing only raises the difficulty of selecting those variables from each of these areas that are likely to be most relevant. It is well known that in the social sciences researchers from each discipline usually proceed by abstracting a few variables from the larger field in which they commonly operate. They ascribe importance to them and ignore the others.[4]

If for no other reason than to simplify the problem for the purposes of analysis, or the need to economize on time or effort, it is inevitable that some restrictions are placed on the kind of data collected. In this process of selection, some distortion and misrepresentation of the phenomena are bound to occur. Distortion arises because the "facts" are taken out of the social context from which they derive their meaning and are dealt with as so-called "independent" variables.[5] The resulting hypotheses, models, or theories based on the data collected become abstractions and constitute a "way of looking" at the phenomenon rather than a replication of the phenomenon itself.[6] In this study, it was assumed that there were three main classes of variables that ought to be considered, consisting of variables related to the cases dealt with, the legal and social environments in which sentencing takes place, and the personalities and backgrounds of the magistrates concerned. The next section will describe the considerations which led to the selection of specific variables within each main class.

The Legal and Factual Make-up of the Cases

An examination of the cases dealt with by magistrates will reveal that there are many factors related to the offence, the offender, and the surrounding circumstances which may affect the selection of a penalty.

As already mentioned, it is unlikely that official records will provide an adequate source of information as the crucial problem is to identify the precise factors actually considered by magistrates in the process of judgement.

It was decided to deal with this problem by examining the facts of the cases as perceived and understood by magistrates themselves. For a period of eighteen months magistrates completed "sentencing study sheets" with regard to seven indictable offences. The instrument was completed at the time of the determination of sentence and was designed to reveal the mental processes involved. Magistrates were required to rate the seriousness of offences, indicate how they perceived offenders, identify and place in order of importance various features of cases considered to be of overriding importance, and to give reasons for the sentences imposed. These facts revealed from sentencing study sheets constituted the "effective information set" or "information-space" of the magistrates concerned. The design of the study sheet is described in Chapter 16 and a copy is reproduced in Technical Appendix 9.

Legal Constraints on Behaviour

The law, contained in legislation and in reported cases, defines the scope of legally permissible sentencing alternatives. However, legislation sets down only the maximum penalties which may be imposed and in Canada, as in most other countries, these maximum penalties are very high.[7] Moreover, there is a wide variety of maximum penalties provided for offences which do not appear to be inherently different from one another. The gradation of maximum penalties has not been derived systematically in accordance with a logically consistent scheme of values. Rather, the Criminal Code is an historical product reflecting the social values of various times in which it was amended. While the Criminal Code may provide some guidance to the courts in assessing the severity of various types of offences, the statutory scale of offences is indefinite, wanting in both precision and logical coherence. It is, therefore, at best an inadequate guide.

Some control over sentencing is exercised by the appeal courts. In written judgements they have laid down the "principles" to be applied in assessing a penalty, and the doctrine of *stare decisis* requires the lower courts to take these principles into account in cases before them.[8] The difficulty faced by the lower courts arises from the fact that the standards laid down by the appeal courts are often imprecise and contradictory, and tend to be unstable in the sense that they change over relatively short periods of time. It is not difficult to find cases in which appeal courts in different provinces appear to contradict one another and, in some instances, themselves.[9] These considerations lead one to conclude that magistrates are likely to vary in their interpretations of what the law demands of them in sentencing. Accordingly, it was considered important to know how each magistrate defines the scope of discretion given to him by statute and the principles of sentencing as laid down by the appeal courts. In other words, it was considered necessary to know the amount of discretion or "room for manoeuvre" each magistrate believes the law provides.

Social Constraints on Judicial Behaviour

Apart from legal constraints, there are likely to be certain restraining influences in the social environments of magistrates. For the most part, the social environment provided by other people in their immediate work situations is likely to be especially significant. It can be expected that the views and practices of other magistrates, public opinion in the community in which the court is situated, and the views of people directly connected with the decision-process, such as those of the crown attorney, probation officer, police officer, and defence counsel are likely to have an influence.

Previous research has indicated that behaviour is altered in the direction of conformity to group standards, particularly the standards of people who are important or significant to the individual concerned. These people have been variously called opinion leaders, taste makers, or innovators, but in this study the sociological term "significant others" will be used.[10] It was considered essential to know the answers to these questions: Who are the significant others in the social world of magistrates? What do magistrates believe that these people expect of them in sentencing? To what degree do magistrates feel obliged to conform to these expectations?

The magistrate's definition of his relationship to others in his immediate environment and his conscious awareness of their influence in sentencing, constitutes the "social-space" in which he operates and it was felt necessary to devote a portion of the study to probing its dimensions.

Situational Constraints on Judicial Behaviour

Certain situational factors in the environment of magistrates are likely to have an influence on their sentencing behaviour. The pattern of crime in the community, the adequacies of treatment and other resources to deal with it, the work-load of the magistrate, and a host of other factors may influence a court directly or indirectly. But before they are likely to have a direct influence, the magistrate must both be aware of them and define them as being important. For example, a rising crime rate is likely to be a significant factor in sentencing only if it is perceived as rising and is considered to be important enough to justify a departure from normal sentencing practice. Not all the features of the external environment will be significant. Through his own selective cognitive processes the magistrate defines for himself his "effective environment" or what may be called his "definition of the situation."[11]

In summary, the significant influences in the environment of a magistrate are likely to be revealed by understanding how he defines that environment for himself. His definition of the facts of the case (his information-space), his definition of the law (his effective room for manoeuvre), his definition of his relationship to significant others (his social-space), and his definition of the significant aspects of the external situation, constitute his "life-space."

Personality Factors in Sentencing

Having assumed that judicial behaviour occurs in interaction of the magistrate with his environment, and having specified how we intend to identify the significant aspects of that environment, we are still left to consider what aspects of a magistrate's personality, being, or self, are likely to be involved in the process of selecting a penalty.

Some would argue that it is not important to study the psychological processes involved in how judges or magistrates respond to crime and criminals in their official sentencing capacities. A psychological interpretation of the decision-process may appear to some to be inconsistent with the traditional legal view of a society governed by laws and not men. It seems strange that society, on the one hand, is prepared to view criminal behaviour as an expression of personal and social forces operating within and upon individual offenders, while on the other hand it tends to resist the view that these same factors may influence the behaviour of police officers, judges, correctional workers, and others who deal with offenders in official and unofficial ways.

Students of the judicial process have always maintained that there is a relationship between the personality of an individual judge and the decisions he makes in exercising discretion given to him by the law.[12] Indeed, it would now be considered naive to assume that judges and magistrates can be expected to process information impartially and apply mechanically the appropriate legal principles to sentencing problems. Few sentencing judges themselves would claim that sentencing is a completely rational and mechanical process. The comment often made by judges that "sentencing is an art, not a science" reflects both the nature of the phenomenon and the difficulty experienced by the commentator in giving an adequate description of it. But our interpretation of the actual relationship of personality factors to decision-processes in sentencing is for the most part a body of impressions, partial truths, myths, and speculations. As Joel B. Grossman points out:

> While scholars and social scientists have long since disabused themselves of the aesthetically pleasing but inaccurate view of the appellate judge's task as primarily mechanical and syllogistic, they are still seeking answers to the elusive question: To what extent is a judge a creature or a captive of personal values and attitudes developed during his pre-judicial experiences?[13]

In coming to grips with this question, the study was faced with two main streams of thinking with respect to the psychology of human behaviour. The first tradition postulates an irrational model of man: specifically, it holds that man has very little power of reason and reflection, a weak capacity to discriminate, the most primitive self-insight, and a very short memory. Whatever mental capacity an individual does possess is easily overwhelmed by emotional forces of which he may be unaware. This line of thinking is greatly influenced by psychoanalytic thought, and psychoanalytic interpretations of the judicial process appear in the literature from time to time.[14]

The second approach evokes a rational model of man. It

assumes that man has a mind, that he seeks understanding, that he attempts consistently to make sense of the world about him, that he possesses discriminative and reasoning powers that will assert themselves over time, and that he is capable of self-criticism and insight.[15] Each school can point to evidence with which to support its assumptions, and can make fairly damaging criticisms of its opponent.

Our dilemma was whether to view magistrates as significant, rational persons who seek meaning and purpose in their behaviour on the bench, or to regard them as "things" whose behaviour is a result of basic biological instincts and psychological drives or needs over which they have very little control and are largely unaware. As R.D. Laing, the well-known phenomenological psychiatrist, points out in his book, *The Divided Self:*

> Man's being can be seen from different points of view and one or other aspect can be made the focus of study. In particular, man can be seen as a person or a thing. Now, even the same thing, seen from different points of view, gives rise to two entirely different descriptions, and the descriptions give rise to two entirely different theories, and the theories result in two entirely different sets of action. The initial way we see a thing determines all our subsequent dealings with it.[16]

Prior knowledge of magistrates supplemented by further observation of their behaviour on the bench and informal discussions with them concerning that behaviour, led to the conclusion that a great deal of sentencing behaviour, much of which may appear to be irrational to the outside observer, could be explained without having to invoke psychoanalytical or biological assumptions.

In previous studies, students of sentencing have been restricted to an examination of sentencing as revealed in the official records, particularly police records, and reasons for judgement handed down by the court. The frequently replicated finding is that observed variation in sentencing behaviour cannot be wholly or even largely explained by either observed variation in the types of cases dealt with, or the official reasons for judgement given.[17] It is then often suggested that sentencing is an irrational process.

But a sentence which may appear irrational to the outside observer may be perfectly rational to the sentencing judge or magistrate. This is not to deny the influence of unconscious motivation, drives, needs, and other basic psychological processes about which a sentencing magistrate may be totally unaware. However, these factors are likely to find expression in consciously held definitions, perceptions, attitudes, and beliefs. It was felt that in this study it would be more productive to deal with larger psychological units such as opinions or beliefs, which are within the conscious awareness of the magistrates themselves, and certain constructs such as attitudes which are inferred from deliberated responses to questionnaires.

Another consideration entered into the decision. Since the research was attempting to consider the social situations in which sentencing takes place and the interaction of those situations with the personalities of magistrates, it seemed to be more appropriate to incorporate only those psychological mechanisms which relate directly to the way in which magistrates experience their environment. We were not seeking a personality theory of magistrates as men but rather a theory of men as practising magistrates. This meant seeking a psychological framework which could be fitted into a more general study of the social processes involved in sentencing. The search was for psychological mechanisms which represented a compromise between inner forces of individual magistrates and their definitions of the external world to which they relate.

The concept of "attitude" seemed to meet those requirements as it provided the key to understanding how a magistrate defines "self" in relation to the persons, problems and ideas he confronts in his daily work.

Attitudes were defined as: "A set of evaluative categories relevant to the judicial role which the individual magistrate has adopted (or learned) during his past experience with persons, problems or ideas in his social world. These evaluations consist both of beliefs about and feelings towards the object of the attitude, which may be a particular crime, a particular type of offender, or an idea of a problem commonly associated with cases coming before the courts."[18] Several attitude scales were developed, tested, and administered to magistrates. Attempts were then made to predict sentencing behaviour from the attitude scores derived.

The Sample

The sample consisted of two components: magistrates and cases. The sample of magistrates comprised seventy-one full-time magistrates in the province of Ontario. In 1965, there were eighty-three full-time magistrates in the province. All who dealt annually with at least seven hundred Criminal Code cases were asked to participate.[19] Of the seventy-eight magistrates meeting this requirement, none refused. Later two declined for age and health reasons, one died prior to the commencement of the project, and four withdrew during the project when special circumstances made it impossible for them to continue as fully as they would have liked. The response of the remainder was excellent.

Choosing a sample of cases was more difficult. It was not possible, nor necessarily desirable, to collect detailed information on all cases. It was necessary to select offences which occurred relatively frequently so that a sufficient number of each type would be dealt with by each magistrate. It was also desirable to choose cases which represented different kinds of decision problems faced by magistrates in sentencing, and varied along certain theoretically important dimensions. In the end it was decided to collect detailed information with respect to seven indictable offences. They were: breaking and entering, fraud, taking a motor vehicle without consent, robbery, assault occasioning bodily harm, indecent assault on a female, and dangerous driving. An additional sample of cases was selected for less detailed study, consisting of all indictable cases dealt with by Ontario magistrates during the years 1966 and 1967.

The Data-Base to the Study

Information about Cases

The great variation possible in the legal and factual make-up of the cases coming before the courts made it necessary to collect as much information as possible concerning the nature and severity of each crime and about the criminal records and social histories of the offenders concerned.

Information about the seven offences mentioned above was obtained from an "offence description card," designed for use by police officers in every case for which a magistrate completed a sentencing study sheet. Police officers recorded certain information about the offences, so that the severity of each offence could be rated on the scale developed by Sellin and Wolfgang as reported in their pioneering work, The Measurement of Delinquency.[20] In addition, they recorded the steps taken in the criminal proceedings, the ages, occupations, marital status, and criminal records of the offenders, and certain information about the victims and the offenders' relationships to their victims.

Further information about the offenders concerned was received from probation officers who completed a standardized social history, called an "offender assessment guide." Most of the information required by this document is of a type that appears frequently in pre-sentence reports. Much of it requires replies to questions of fact, but parts of it require probation officers to interpret information and make etiological and treatment-relevant distinctions. A personality classification, that could be used by probation officers whether or not they had had social work training, was developed.

These two documents provided the main classificatory variables concerning the substantive facts of the cases. While it is not possible to be absolutely certain that in each case all relevant information was collected, data were obtained on all variables concerning criminal cases that previous research has shown to be associated with the sentencing decisions of the courts, supplemented by other information that it was felt might affect the selection of a penalty. In a total sample of some 2500 cases, approximately one hundred individual pieces of information on each case were collected. These data served the purpose of providing statistical control over different fact patterns in the individual cases coming before the courts. This permitted an examination of how magistrates respond to roughly similar types of cases.

Information about Contextual Situations

Of equal theoretical interest were features of sentencing problems faced by magistrates that were independent of the substantive facts concerning the cases. Of particular interest was the situational context in which sentencing takes place.

Magistrates' courts in Canada are established for particular judicial districts. In Ontario, these districts coincide with political divisions known as counties. There are some fifty-three counties in Ontario and there are very wide variations in the ecological, demographic, and economic characteristics.

For the most part magistrates in Ontario are long-term residents of the communities in which their courts are situated.[21] To the extent that social and cultural forces do influence judicial attitudes and conduct, they are likely to have a greater impact on magistrates than on judges of higher courts who are usually not as closely tied to community life. It was therefore deemed advisable to collect as much information as possible on the social and economic characteristics of each judicial district in order to examine the relationship of these characteristics to the attitudes and conduct of magistrates in the particular communities. Fortunately, the Census Divisions used by the Dominion Bureau of Statistics coincide with judicial districts.[22] For each judicial district in Ontario information was compiled relating to each of the following variables: density, urbanization, nativity, age distribution, ethnic distribution, religious distribution, occupational distribution, mobility and growth, crime rate, work-load of magistrates. These contextual variables were used to develop a situational classification for the purpose of comparing and evaluating patterns of sentencing decisions made in different contexts throughout the province.

Information about Magistrates

The main sources of information about magistrates were a personal interview and an attitude questionnaire. The design of the attitude questionnaire is described in some detail in Chapter 7.

Designing an interview schedule was something of a problem. On the one hand, it was necessary to have an accurate record of conversations between this writer and magistrates. This called for the standardization of interviewing procedures. It was also necessary to record and tabulate the answers in such a way that they could be coded for computer analysis. On the other hand, it was considered unwise to structure the interview too much, as this might have prevented magistrates from answering questions in their own way, and restricted the topics for discussion only to those determined in advance.

It was felt that a taperecorder would be too threatening for some magistrates and for this reason it was decided to rely on an interview guide with a built-in recording schedule. The first version of this instrument consisted of a number of broad headings with a list of possible questions under each heading. Pilot interviews led to certain changes and additions. Slowly the number of main topics for discussion, the number of questions needed for each topic, and the number of response categories required were determined. As far as it was possible, questions were formulated in words familiar to and habitually used by magistrates. An "other" category was always provided at the end of each question and space was left for recording any further comments or qualifications made by magistrates, as well as observations made by the interviewer about the way in which the answers were given.

Because these interviews were intended to probe many highly personal and emotionally charged areas, it was considered unwise to rely on single questions. Several questions dealing with various aspects of each sensitive topic were dispersed throughout the interview. No fixed sequence of questions was determined, which left the interviewer free to determine the sequence on the basis of the readiness of a magistrate to take up a topic. Some of the questions were pre-coded, and the answers to them could be scored objectively or semi-objectively, while some were completely open-ended and required a verbatim recording of replies. The content of the questions asked will be evident from the analyses which are to follow.

The seventy-one magistrates were interviewed during the spring and summer of 1966. Each interview took place in the local community where the magistrate lived and worked. Most of them took place in the magistrate's office immediately after court was adjourned for the afternoon. The purpose of this procedure was to interview magistrates in familiar surroundings closely associated in both time and space to their working environments. Usually the interviewer would observe in the court during the morning, have lunch with the magistrate, and conduct the interview in the afternoon. The average length of the interview was approximately three hours, but they ranged from one-and-a-half hours to almost five hours.

Identical questions were put to magistrates, but the sequence of questions depended upon the interviewer's judgement of the level of anxiety generated. For the most part the interviews unfolded naturally. Each topic was introduced by a broad, open-ended question and further questions were asked only if the answers were ambiguous, incomplete, or off the point. The interview began with neutral questions and as the atmosphere became more relaxed the conversation was steered to more controversial and feeling-laden areas. The interviewer tried to avoid expressing his own views, while at the same time showing interest in and sympathy for magistrates' efforts to express their feelings.

Three interviews were recorded independently by an additional person who sat unobtrusively some distance away from the magistrate and the interviewer. Comparisons of the answers recorded by the interviewer and this additional person showed that only 4 out of 195 answers given by these three magistrates were recorded differently. This gave an inter-rater reliabilily coefficient of approximately 0.98, which is well in excess of the minimum required for research of this kind.[23]

Scheme of Analysis

The analysis presented in this study can be conveniently divided into four parts. The next three chapters are descriptive and are intended to serve the function of introducing the reader to magistrates and to analyses which are to follow. The topics covered in these chapters include the jurisdiction and sentencing powers of magistrates, the method of their appointment to the bench, their social backgrounds, and the similarities and differences among them in penal philosophy.

Following this come four chapters dealing with the attitudes magistrates hold to crime, punishment, and related issues. An entire chapter is devoted to the meaning of judicial attitudes, followed by chapters describing the construction of attitude scales, the content and structure of attitudes held by different population groups, and the relationship of judicial attitudes to sentencing behaviour.

The next section consists of three chapters dealing with the social and legal constraints impinging upon the discretion of the court in sentencing. The analyses described will show how magistrates define the operative constraints arising out of the law and the social system. It will be demonstrated that these constraints are significantly associated with the behaviour of magistrates on the bench.

The fourth section consists of six chapters describing the way in which magistrates search for, interpret, and use information in the process of coming to decisions. It will be shown that magistrates tend to develop distinct "styles" of information-use, characterized by the type and amount of information they seek, the way in which they interpret information once received, and their mechanisms for organizing and integrating information in the process of judgement. The end result is the development of a number of "sentencing profiles" for particular groups of magistrates.

Finally, different parts of the study are drawn together and a tentative model of judicial behaviour is put forward. This ends the analysis. In the last chapter an attempt is made to formulate certain penological and criminological conclusions arising out of the findings. Several proposals will be put forward concerning changes that might usefully be considered towards the improvement of sentencing.

A Final Word about the Statistical Methods Employed

Until recently a student of the judicial process could roam freely through the literature and only an occasional statistic would mar an otherwise serene landscape of rhetoric. He now faces a very different situation. Opening any recent book he may find himself confronted with chi squares, t-tests, and even regression equations and factor analysis. These disconcerting experiences inhibit adventure beyond the safe confines of law books, and they also tend to encourage a form of sectarianism where virtue is made out of ignorance and any researcher who uses any but the most elementary research tools is seen as an invader who threatens to subvert theory to the interests of a strange and irrelevant methodological gamesmanship.

Nothing could be further from the truth. Measurement is an adjunct to theory and subservient to it. The fundamental issues in research are conceptual and theoretical rather than methodological. A sophisticated methodology cannot cure a badly conceived project, although the use of statistics sometimes gives the appearance of certainty where none exists. Once the subsidiary role of methodology in research is recognized, there would be little need for the opponents of empirical methods to legitimize their understandable lack of expertise in this area by attacking those who use the available tools of analysis. This process would be made easier if some self-defined methodologists would be rather more modest in the claims made for their techniques, and at least make some concession to their readers by explaining their methods in ordinary language.

Sentencing is a complex phenomenon. There are many variables operating, and this calls for methods designed to handle them. Multi-variant procedures in statistics open new areas of enquiry that were closed to researchers only a few years ago. Not to use them for fear of offending those not familiar with them is both wasteful and self-defeating. There is nothing particularly magical or unfathomable about most statistical methods, provided the reader has the interest and is given enough supporting information to understand, if not the techniques, at least the rationales underlying them. In any event, much of the analyses used in this study were based on simple methods. Whenever simple methods would do, they were used. When the issues became more complex, methods were used that were considered appropriate to the problem.

Every effort was made to make the research methods used in this study comprehensible to the average reader who may have little experience in statistics. It was assumed that the reader will have at least passing acquaintance with descriptive statistics: means, medians, percentages, and so on.[24] As far as the more complicated methods are concerned, an attempt has been made to satisfy both the uninitiated and the expert, by explaining the logic of the more complex methods in ordinary non-mathematical language in the body of the chapters, and by placing most of the complicated formulae and calculations in the appendices. Several chapters have technical appendices which contain the bulk of the statistical work used to support the conclusions drawn. Only those tables and figures which were considered to be good examples of the main patterns which emerged were included in the body of each chapter. As far as it was reasonable to do so, the findings were presented in a non-technical form. There is, of course, a danger in this practice. Out of the mass of data collected, which was analysed in many different ways, it is possible to select only those findings which support the arguments one may wish to make. For this reason, it was decided to make the whole of the statistical material available, allowing the reader to judge for himself whether the conclusions drawn are supported by the evidence. Because of the enormous bulk of the statistical work done, it was decided not to include it here, but rather in a separate companion volume.[25]

NOTES TO CHAPTER 2

1   The problems involved in interdisciplinary research have been discussed by many writers. For a summary see R. Tyler, "Trends in Interdisciplinary Research," in D. Ray, ed., *Trends in Social Science* (New York, 1961), 136-51. For references to criminological research see F. Ferracuti and M. Wolfgang, *The Subculture of Violence* (London, 1967), 1-94; and H. Mannheim, *Comparative Criminology*, vol. 1 (London, 1965), 17-8.

2   K. Lewin, *Principles of Topological Psychology* (New York, 1936).

3   The problem of "reductionism" has been discussed by many social scientists. For a recent discussion see M. Sherif, "Theoretical Analysis of the Individual- Group Relationship in a Social Situation," in G. Direnzo, ed., *Concepts, Theory and Explanation in the Behavioral Sciences* (New York, 1966), 47-74.

4   In this connection see G. Direnzo, "Conceptual Definition in the Behavioral Sciences," *ibid.*, 6-18.

5   Direnzo, *ibid.*, 7

6   Sherif, "Theoretical Analysis," 50.

7   The following maximum penalties are provided by the Canadian Criminal Code for the offences listed below. *Offences punishable by life imprisonment* include: some forms of treason (s.47); failure to disperse on the reading of the riot act (s. 69); piracy (s.75); breach of duty explosives (s.78); causing injury with intent to procure a conviction (s.113); rape (s.136); statutory rape (s.137); criminal negligence (s.142); non-capital murder (s.206); manslaughter (s.207); killing an unborn child (s.209); attempted murder (s.210); accessory to murder (s.211); overcoming resistance with intent (s.218); interfering with transportation with intent (s.220); failure to guard dangerous places (s.228); kidnapping (s.233); procuring miscarriage (s.237); robbery (s.289); stopping mails with intent (s.290); breaking and entering (s.292); destruction of property endangering life (s.372). *The following offences are punishable by fourteen years imprisonment:* some forms of treason (s.47d); alarming Her Majesty (s.49); assisting the enemy to leave Canada (s.50); intimidating Parliament (s.51); inciting mutiny (s.53); sedition (s.60);

piratical acts (s.76); breach of duty re explosives (s.77); causing injury with intent (s.79); bribery of officials (s.100); bribery of officers (s.101); perjury (s.112); false statements (s.114); giving contradictory evidence (s.116); fabricating evidence (s.117); incest (s.142); buggery (s.147); procuring defilement (s.155); counselling suicide (s.212); causing bodily harm with intent (s.216); administering noxious things (s.217); breach of criminal trust (s.282); refusing to deliver property (s.283); extortion (s.291); breaking and entering (s.295); possession of housebreaking tools (s.295); forgery (s.310); uttering a forged document (s.311); possession of counterfeiting equipment (s.312); unlawfully drawing a document (s.317); obtaining by means of a forged document (s.318); using counterfeit stamp (s.319); selling defective stores (s.361); wilful destruction of public property (s.372); arson (s.374); making counterfeit money (s.392); possession of counterfeit money (s.393); uttering counterfeit money (s.395); clipping coins (s.398); making counterfeiting tools (s.401); conveying counterfeiting tools (s.402); conspiracy to murder (s.408a); conspiracy to bring false accusation (s.408b). Source: A. Mewett, ed., *Martin's Annual Criminal Code*, 1965 (Toronto, 1965).

8 For a discussion of how *stare decisis* works see R. Cross, *Precedent in English Law*, 2nd ed. (Oxford, 1968); see also B. Cardozo, *The Nature of the Judicial Process* (New Haven, 1921), 142-68; and J. Stone, *Legal System and Legal Reasoning* (London, 1964).

9 For an excellent review of disparity between the provincial courts of appeal In Canada see J. Decore, "Criminal Sentencing: The Role of the Court of Appeal and the Concept of Uniformity," *The Criminal Law Quarterly*, 6 (1964), 324-80.

10 The "symbolic interaction" school in sociology employs this term frequently, See H. Blumer, "Society as Symbolic Interaction," in A. Rose, ed., *Human Behaviour and Social Processes* (Boston, 1962); G. Mead, *Mind, Self, Society* (Chicago, 1934); C. Cooley, "The Roots of Social Knowledge," *American Journal of Sociology, 32* (July 1926), 59-79; M. Polanyi, *Personal Knowledge* (Chicago, 1958).

11 A well-known concept; see, for example, A. Kuhn, *The Study of Society - A Unified Approach* (New York, 1963); A. Rose, *Human Behavior and Social Processes - an Interactionist Approach* (Chicago, 1962); D. Krech and R. Crutchfield, *The Individual in Society* (New York, 1962).

12 For a good critical review of writings in this area see J. Grossman, "Social Backgrounds and Judicial Decision-Making," *Harvard Law Review, 69* (1966), 1551-64.

13 *Ibid.*, 1554.

14 The best-known writings in this area include: P. Roche, *The Criminal Mind* (New York, 1958), 64-195; F. Alexander and H. Staub, *The Criminal, The Judge and the Public* (Chicago, 1956), 209-23; C. Winick, I. Gerver, and A. Blumberg, "The Psychology of Judges," in H. Toch, ed., *Legal and Criminal Psychology* (New York, 1961), 136; Cardozo, *The Nature of the Judicial Process*, 142-78.

15 For an elaboration of the two schools of thought see M. Smith, J. Bruner and R. White, *Opinions and Personality* (New York, 1956), 7-28.

16 R. Laing, *The Divided Self* (London, 1959), 22; see also E. Tolman, *Purposive Behavior in Animals and Man* (New York, 1932).

17 For a good review of early research in this field see E. Green, *Judicial Attitudes in Sentencing* (London, 1961), 8-20. For a more recent review see H. Mannheim, "Sentencing Revisited," in M. Wolfgang, ed., *Crime and Culture* (New York, 1968), 349-74.

18 This is a shortened version of the definition given in full in Chapter 6 of this book.

19 Criminal Code offences include all those indictable and summary conviction offences under federal legislation which are defined in the Criminal Code of

Canada. We will see in the next chapter that they amount to less than fifteen per cent of all offences against penal law. They are, however, the more serious offences.

20 T. Sellin and M. Wolfgang, *The Measurement of Delinquency* (New York, 1964).

21 See Chapter 4.

22 The data used were based on the 1961 Census. Dominion Bureau of Statistics, *Census of Canada - 1961* (Ottawa, 1964).

23 For a discussion of rater reliability see L. Cronbach, *Essentials of Psychological Testing* (New York, 1966), 126-42; and J. Guilford, *Psychometric Methods* (New York, 1954), 279-81. The texts found particularly helpful in designing our interview guide and conducting the interviews included A. Anastasi, *Psychological Testing* (New York, 1963); Guilford, *Psychometric Methods;* H. Hyman *et al., Interviewing in Social Research* (Chicago, 1954); A. Oppenheim, *Questionnaire Design and Attitude Measurement* (London, 1966); S. Payne, *The Art of Asking Questions* (Princeton, 1951); and C. Sellitz, M. Jahoda, M. Deutsch, and S. Cook, *Research Methods in Social Relations* (New York, 1959).

24 A good introductory text is J. Spence, *et al., Elementary Statistics,* 2nd ed. (New York, 1968).

25 Sets of supporting statistical material are available from the Centre of Criminology, University of Toronto, Toronto 5, Canada, or from the author.

3

Jurisdiction, Appointment, and Tenure

The Constitutional Basis for the Magistrates' Courts

The administration of criminal justice in Canada is governed by the distribution of legislative and judicial powers under the proisions of the British North America Act.[1] Section 91 (27) of this Act assigns to the National Parliament of Canada exclusive powers to make laws in relation to criminal law and procedure, and assigns to the provincial legislatures exclusive power to create, organize, and maintain provincial courts, and to govern the administration of justice in the provinces. But the actual division of power is rather more complicated.

Under section 96 of the BNA Act, the Federal Government appoints and pays, not only the judges of the national courts such as the Supreme Court of Canada, the Exchequer Court, and the Admiralty Court, but also the superior court judges of the provinces. Magistrates, justices of the peace, and other inferior court judges are appointed under provincial legislation.[2] No judicial officer in Canada is elected.

At the same time, section 92 (15) of the Act gives the provincial legislators power to create offences and impose penalties for contravention of provincial statutes. Some of this power is delegated by the provinces to municipalities. This means that while the Federal Parliament created the Criminal Code, a great deal of penal law is to be found in provincial statutes and municipal by-laws. In fact, little more than six per cent of convictions for con-travention of penal statutes are concerned with indictable and summary offences under national legislation. Criminal offences consist, in the main, of violation of municipal parking regulations (57.3 per cent), provincial offences (22.3 per cent) and violations of other provincial statutes (6.2 per cent).[3]

Jurisdiction of Magistrates

The first Criminal Code in Canada was enacted by Parliament in 1892.[4] It was based largely on Sir James Stephen's English Draft Code which was not adopted in the United Kingdom. Minor changes have been made from time to time, but the bulk of provi-sions relating to the definition of offences and punishments available to the courts are those in the original Code.

An offence under the criminal law of Canada is either an indict-able offence or an offence punishable on summary conviction. Originally, these two categories of offence could be distinguished in terms of the procedure by which cases would be tried. Indict-able offences were usually more serious, and originally a jury trial was provided at the option of the accused. However, over the years, some of the less serious indictable offences came to be reserved for the exclusive jurisdiction of the magistrates' courts. These now include certain thefts, false pretences, and some assaults.[5] In Canada, a magistrates' court, or its equivalent, is the only court that can deal with offences punishable under sum-mary conviction. This category includes all provincial and muni-cipal offences, as well as summary offences under federal legisla-tion, and amount to some ninety-eight per cent of all cases dealt with in the criminal courts. The indictable offences over which magistrates have absolute jurisdiction amount to fifty-four per cent of the indictable cases dealt with by all the courts in Canada.[6]

With the consent of the accused, the magistrate may deal with most of the remaining indictable offences. The vast majority of the accused, when given a choice, elect trial in magistrates' courts.[7] Another fifty per cent of indictable cases come into magistrates' courts in this way. The total intake of these courts thus includes all summary offences and ninety-four per cent of in-dictable offences. This is a broader jurisdiction than that given to any lower court of criminal jurisdiction in Europe, the Common-wealth, or the United States.[8]

There is an interesting contrast between the ways in which magistrates' courts have evolved in Canada and the United Kingdom. Over the years, the tendency in the United Kingdom has been to restrict the breadth of jurisdiction and the powers of magistrates' courts to less serious offences and less severe penalties, whilst in Canada the tendency has been to give more power to these courts.[9] The contrast is all the more striking by reason of the fact that in England, a magistrates' court consists of three members aided by a legally-trained clerk, while in Canada the court consists of one magistrate, possibly without legal qualifications, and in all cases without the benefit of legal advice from a clerk.[10] In outlying districts, where the prosecution of offences is often handled by police officers, many cases are dealt with without one legally-qualified court officer being present.

The breadth of a Canadian magistrate's jurisdiction becomes particularly significant when viewed in relation to the enormous discretionary power in sentencing given to him by the Criminal Code. Depending on the maximum penalty provided by the Code for a particular offence, a magistrate sitting alone may: sentence to life imprisonment, commit to preventative detention, impose whipping, order forfeiture, or fine in any amount.[11] In short, he may impose any penalty except death. No lower court judge sitting alone in any other country is given this power.[12]

Types of Sentence Available to Magistrates

General Powers

The punishments authorized under the criminal law depend upon the nature of the offence, and include fine, forfeiture, suspended sentence with or without probation, imprisonment, whipping, and death.[13]

In some cases, the law prescribes different degrees or kinds of punishment for an offence. For example, the Code provides that anyone who commits robbery is guilty of an indictable offence and is liable to imprisonment and to be whipped.[14] In such circumstances, the kind and degree of punishment to be imposed are at the discretion of the court which convicts the accused. The court may sentence the offender to any authorized terms of imprisonment, up to and including life. It may impose a fine in addition to imprisonment, and whipping in addition to either. If no previous conviction against the offender is proved, the court may suspend the passing of sentence, pending his good behaviour. At the discretion of the court, a recognizance of suspended sentence may include a condition that the offender report to a probation officer.

Imprisonment

There are three types of institutional sentence available to magistrates: common gaol, reformatory, and penitentiary. The length of sentence imposed, and the act under which it is imposed, to some extent determine the type of institution to which the offender will be sent. A sentence of imprisonment of two years or more is served in a federal penitentiary. A sentence of under two years is spent at one of the provincial gaols or reformatories. If the sentence is a "definite" sentence of under two years, i.e., a sentence fixed solely by the court, the offender is committed to one of the provincial gaols. If it is relatively short (e.g., six months or less) the offender is likely to serve the sentence in a county gaol. There are virtually no training or treatment facilities available in the latter institutions.[15] Reformatory sentences are provided in the Prisons and Reformatories Act.[16] This statute enables courts in Ontario to sentence a person to a definite term of up to two years less one day, and an additional indeterminate term not exceeding two years less one day. In this type of sentence, the offender serves the definite term and is then automatically considered for parole by the Ontario Board of Parole. If it is granted he will serve all, or any part that the Board sees fit, of the indeterminate portion within the community, under parole supervision. Definite indeterminant sentences are generally considered to be "training" sentences. They provide the flexibility deemed necessary by institutional personnel to gear the length of imprisonment to their judgement of the offender's progress, and they provide for follow-up supervision.

In Ontario, a large variety of different kinds of reformatories have been established. A system of classification and allocation exists, and unless the offender is serving a very short term of imprisonment, he is usually considered for placement in the institution considered to be best suited to his needs.

The Ontario Board of Parole can make decisions only with respect to the indeterminate portion of definite-indefinite sentences. A National Parole Board is authorized to grant parole with respect to definite sentences. In theory, this board can release any offender, except one serving a commuted term of life imprisonment for murder, on the day he is committed to an institution. In practice, however, the National Parole Board rarely interferes with sentences of less than six months, and usually will not consider an offender for parole until he has served at least one-third of his sentence.[17]

Special provisions are available for female offenders sentenced in Ontario. Under the provisions of the Prisons and Reformatories Act, Ontario courts are authorized to sentence females to completely indefinite sentences of up to two years less one day.[18] These sentences are served in the provincial reformatory for women. Females serving indefinite sentences may be released at any time at the discretion of the Ontario Board of Parole.

Occasionally, a magistrate will recommend, on the warrant of commitment, that an offender serve his sentence in a particular institution. More frequently, magistrates will recommend that he receive treatment or training of a particular type. While these recommendations are taken into account by institutional officials, the ultimate authority rests with the responsible minister and his staff.

Fines

The Criminal Code rarely provides for a fine as a specific punishment for an indictable offence. It does however, provide that courts may fine instead of imposing imprisonment if the maximum penalty prescribed by the Code is for five years or less, and it may fine in addition to imprisonment if the maximum penalty provided is more than five years.[19] There is no limit to the amount that a court may order a person to pay by way of fine upon conviction for an indictable offence. For summary conviction of offences under the Code, the maximum fine is five hundred dollars.[20] For both indictable and summary conviction cases, the Code authorizes a convicting court to direct that a fine shall be paid forthwith, or that it shall be paid at such time and on such terms as the court may fix.[21]

Canadian courts do not use fines as frequently as do courts in the United Kingdom. In Canada they are used in approximately 28 per cent of cases involving persons aged seventeen or over, convicted of indictable crimes.[22] In contrast, courts in the United Kingdom, which have a similar classification of offences, use fines in approximately 57 per cent of indictable cases involving persons within the same age-group.[23]

Forfeiture

Courts are authorized to forfeit articles that are considered to be dangerous or contrary to the public interest if held in private ownership.[24] Money seized is usually deposited with the Provincial Treasurer. Goods may be either destroyed or sold at public auction, and the proceeds deposited in the Provincial Treasury.

Suspended Sentence

At common law the criminal courts had power to add to a sentence of imprisonment a requirement that the offender enter into a recognizance, with or without sureties, to keep the peace and be of good behaviour for a fixed period of time.[25] In default of entering into such a recognizance or giving of securities, the offender was liable to imprisonment for a further year. This power found statutory expression in the 1892 Code.[26] A similar power was provided with respect to summary conviction offences under the first Canadian Criminal Code, except that the recognizance of suspended sentence could be given in lieu of, rather than in addition to, any other sentence.[27] The aim of these provisions was to provide some degree of supervision of the offender subsequent to his release from prison. However, the attempt was not very successful. Apart from forfeiture of the amount of the bond for failure to keep the peace, there was no way to enforce the recognizance.

In the original Code there was power to grant suspended sentence under section 971, but this power was limited to first offenders, and to offenders not punishable with more than two years imprisonment. In 1900 an amendment extended the application of suspended sentence to offences punishable by more than two years of imprisonment, provided that crown counsel consented to such a disposition.[28] In 1936, the provisions were made applicable to summary conviction offences, and in 1955 the requirement of consent from crown counsel was eliminated.[29] The court was not bound to order suspended sentence, but might do so at its discretion, having regard to the "youth, character and antecedents of the offender, the trivial nature of the offence, and extenuating circumstances."[30]

In contrast to the recognizance to keep the peace, suspended sentence had more teeth. Under section 638 (4), failure to live up to the conditions of suspended sentence exposed the offender to a fresh appearance before the court, and sentence on the original charge. Conditions imposed under a suspended sentence were limited to the payment of costs, no provision being made originally for supervision or probation. In 1966, Canadian adult courts used suspended sentence in approximately 12 per cent of indictable cases. The figure is much lower in Ontario, where the courts restrict this measure to less than 7 per cent of indictable cases.[31]

Probation

Probation found its way into Canadian Law through the back

door. By a 1921 amendment to the Criminal Code, the courts were given discretion to append a condition to the then existing recognizance of suspended sentence, requiring an offender to report to an officer designated by the court.[32] To this day, probation is tied to this ancient form of recognizance, and is subject to very severe restrictions on its use. As a result, probation is limited to first offenders and in certain circumstances to second offenders. Failure to live up to the conditions of suspended sentence exposes the offender to the risk of being sentenced again for the original offence.[33] There is no specific penalty in Canadian law for breach of probation.

Legislation is pending which will give probation independent legal status, widen the scope of its application, and provide for specific penalties for its breach. These changes are long overdue. The *Archambault Report* in 1938 and the *Fauteux Report* in 1956, together with numerous briefs and reports by professional bodies, including judges and magistrates, have recommended that the restrictions on probation be removed.[34] There are no restrictions on the use of probation in the United Kingdom, except for murder, where a mandatory term of life imprisonment must be imposed.[35] Restrictions of several kinds exist in several states of the United States, and in some European countries, but none appear to be as severe as those in Canadian law. As a result, probation is used by adult courts in Canada in only eighteen per cent of indictable cases. This contrasts with about twenty per cent in the United Kingdom, which also has provision for conditional and unconditional discharge, and over fifty per cent in comparable cases dealt with by the United States federal courts.[36]

Restrictions on the use of probation and an apparent unwillingness to use fines appear to be reflected in the high rate of imprisonment in Canada. About forty-four per cent of all adult offenders convicted of indictable offences are sentenced to imprisonment in this country.[37] The figure is somewhat less in Ontario, where the courts imprison approximately thirty-nine per cent. In contrast, only about twenty-one per cent of persons aged seventeen and over are imprisoned for indictable offences in the United Kingdom.[38] In fact, it appears that Canada has one of the highest rates of imprisonment in the world, as Table 3 indicates. In this table comparisons are made of the rate of committal to penal institutions of persons sixteen years of age or over, in various countries for which comparative statistics are available.[39]

There are many factors which may explain the relatively high rate of imprisonment in Canada. First of all, the law itself is

TABLE 3

Comparative imprisonment rates per 100,000* per year

Norway	44
UK	59
Sweden	63
Denmark	75
Finland	153
USA	200
Canada	240

* Persons in general population age sixteen or over.

rather punitive. The Canadian Criminal Code was drafted in the nineteenth century when deterrence and retribution were the predominant goals of the criminal justice system. Because of legislative inactivity since that time the present criminal law and sentencing practice continue to reflect these themes. Sentencing laws in Canada are characterized by high maximum penalties (there are fifty-six offences within the jurisdiction of a magistrate that are punishable with maximum penalties of twenty years imprisonment or more), restrictions on the use of probation, no provision for conditional or unconditional discharge, and a failure to provide fines as a specific punishment for certain less serious offences. The absence of alternative methods for dealing with social problems such as alcoholism and drug addiction, except through the criminal justice system, tends to swell the prison population. Lack of community resources, particularly probation services in many provinces, force the courts to use institutional sentences more often than they would desire. It may also be that Canadians, compared to Scandinavians and others, are rather more intolerant of social deviance, and this may be reflected in the policies and practices of the courts in dealing with criminal offenders.

However, the trend in Canada is away from a heavy reliance on institutional measures. From Figure 1 it can be seen that the use of institutional sentences has decreased steadily during the past five years, whilst fines have correspondingly increased. There is a slight increase in the use of probation, but the trend is not statistically significant. It appears that fines are taking the place of short-term institutional sentences. This is evidenced by the fact that over the past five years, the average length of institutional sentence for indictable cases has increased from a mean of 0.83 years in 1960 to 1.17 years in 1966.[40]

Per cent use

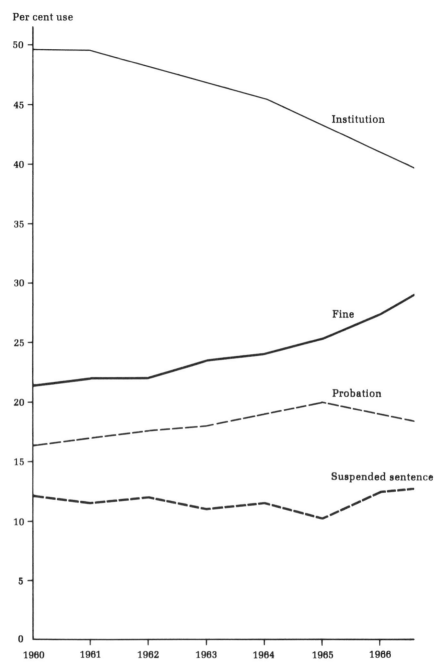

Figure 1 Trends in Canadian sentencing practice, 1960-7 (indictable cases only).
Source: Dominion Bureau of Statistics.

Methods of Appeal from Magistrates' Decisions

A distinction must be made between appeals from convictions for summary offences, and for indictable offences. Summary offences, whether federal or provincial, may be considered together. Except for certain provincial liquor offences, the method of appeal is largely the same in both cases. Under the provincial Summary Conviction Act, the federal procedure has been substantially adopted.[41]

Two methods of appeal are available from conviction for a summary offence: (i) an appeal by way of a stated case through a judge of the Supreme Court on a question of jurisdiction or law; and (ii) an appeal to a county or district court judge on any question of law or fact. When an appeal is by way of stated case, the court is confined to the matter set out in the case stated, and the appellant is thereafter precluded from appealing to a county or district court judge. On appeal to a district or county court judge, a trial *de novo* is held, except in cases under the Liquor Control Act and the Liquor Licensing Act.[42] A trial *de novo* is a completely new and independent trial in every respect, unless by consent the parties agree to abide by the record of the evidence at the original trial before the magistrate or justice of the peace. The parties may produce whatever evidence they wish from whatever witnesses they may wish to call, whether or not these witnesses were called at the original trial.

Whether an applicant proceeds by way of a stated case before a Supreme Court judge or by way of trial *de novo* before a county or district court judge, a further appeal lies in each case to the Court of Appeal, with leave of the Court of Appeal, on any ground that involves a question of law alone.[43] And in each case, a further appeal lies from the Court of Appeal to the Supreme Court of Canada, with leave of the Supreme Court of Canada, on any question of law or jurisdiction relating to a conviction or acquittal which has been determined by the Court of Appeal. No appeal lies to the Supreme Court of Canada on a question of sentence.

For indictable cases, an appeal lies directly to the Court of Appeal in the province. Unlike summary conviction appeals, the appeal is on the record, but the Court of Appeal has power "where it considers it in the interests of justice," to consider further evidence.[44] In contrast to summary conviction appeals, the right of appeal of the Crown in indictable cases is more circumscribed than that of the accused. The latter has an absolute right of appeal from conviction on any ground of appeal that involves a question of law alone, and with leave of the Court of Appeal he may appeal from a conviction on any other ground, as well as his sentence.[45] On the other hand, the Crown may only appeal from acquittal on the sole ground of an error in law. Like the accused, the Crown may appeal a sentence with leave of the Court of Appeal, or a judge thereof.

The courts of appeal of different provinces have established different policies for determining the degree to which they will interfere with a sentence imposed by a magistrate.[46] The Court of Appeal in Ontario has interpreted its power of review rather liberally, and will alter a sentence even if the court below did not "err in principle." In effect, the Court of Appeal imposes the sentence that it feels should have been imposed in the first instance.

The fact that no appeal to the Supreme Court of Canada is available on matters of sentence, has led to noticeable lack of uniformity in sentencing practices and principles among the various provincial courts of appeal in the country.[47]

Appointment and Tenure of Magistrates in Ontario

Until November 1968, magistrates were appointed under the terms of the Magistrates' Act by the Lieutenant-Governor in Council.[48] They held office "during pleasure," and could be removed for "misbehaviour," or for "inability to perform," after a judicial enquiry by a Supreme Court judge.[49] During the past twenty years, only two magistrates tendered their resignations to the Attorney-General before the removal orders were issued.[50] There were a number of instances brought to this writer's attention where resignations had been offered in circumstances suggesting encouragement by the Attorney-General, but the details were never made public.

Magistrates were normally appointed in the first instance as deputy-magistrates.[51] A deputy-magistrate enjoyed the powers of a full magistrate, the only distinction being one of salary. Salaries were not fixed by statute. The amount of salary and promotion from deputy to full magistrate were matters left to the discretion of the Attorney-General.[52]

Magistrates normally retired upon reaching the age of seventy.[53] However, they could be re-appointed on an annual basis until the age of seventy-five. Every magistrate was appointed as a magistrate in and for the Province of Ontario. While they were usually assigned to a particular judicial district (usually a county) they were authorized to deal with any case coming before a magistrates' court in the province.

Some magistrates held court in various places within their judicial district. One magistrate appointed for a northern Ontario district regularly sat in fourteen different places and travelled over 12,000 miles per year in his official capacity. However, most magistrates held court in one place, usually the county seat. In the larger areas, several magistrates were appointed for a particular judicial district. In Toronto alone, some seventeen magistrates hold court regularly.

All Canadian magistrates' courts, or their equivalent, consist of one magistrate sitting alone. Federal legislation is silent as to minimum educational qualifications for magistrates, and only in three provinces have the provincial legislators seen fit to make legal qualifications a requirement for appointment to the bench.[54]

Changes Introduced in 1968

One of the dangers involved in a long-term study of the courts is the possibility of fundamental changes occurring in the law affecting the jurisdiction or administration of them while the study is still in progress. Magistrates' courts in Ontario were legislated out of existence shortly after the data for this study were collected. This is not the disaster it may appear to be, for as we shall see, none of the changes affected the jurisdiction or sentencing powers of the individuals involved.

Over the years, magistrates' courts have been under considerable and mounting criticism, not all of it informed. Members of the press and the provincial legislature, lawyers, academics, and individual members of the public have levelled many criticisms at this bench, the most important of them centring around four essential points: the lack of professional qualifications on the part of some magistrates; the political nature of appointments; the low status given to the courts, reflected particularly in inadequate salaries and poor courtroom facilities; and an inadequate system for dealing with complaints about the conduct of magistrates. Despite certain changes that were made to improve the status of magistrates' courts, the criticisms continued, culminating in the *Report* of the Royal Commission Enquiry into Civil Rights (the *McRuer Report*).[55] This report stated: "magistrates' courts are probably the most important and most neglected courts in Ontario." A number of recommendations were made, the most important being that all magistrates should be legally qualified, that all should receive the same salary, that the office of deputy-magistrate should be abolished. that salaries of magistrates should be equivalent to that of county court judges, and that a Judicial Council should be constituted to advise the Attorney-General on new appointments to the bench and to receive complaints about the conduct of magistrates.

The main recommendations of the *McRuer Report* were accepted by the Ontario Provincial Government, and in November 1968, a "Provincial Courts and Judges Act," replaced the Magistrates' Act.[56] Magistrates' courts were abolished and a Provincial Court with a "Criminal," and a "Family," division was substituted. There were three changes of some substance in the new Act. For the first time in Ontario, minimum professional qualifications for new appointments to the bench were set down in legislation.[57] The Act provides that newly appointed Provincial Court judges shall not exercise the power of a magistrate under those provisions of the Criminal Code dealing with indictable offences, unless they are either a member of the Bar of five years standing, or, if not legally qualified, a Provincial Court judge for at least five years. Magistrates appointed before the Act came into force became judges of the Provincial Court, regardless of professional qualifications.

The second change was the creation of a Judicial Council consisting of the Chief Justice of the High Court, both Chief Justices of the Provincial Court (Criminal and Family Divisions), the Treasurer of the Law Society of Upper Canada, and two persons appointed by the Attorney-General.[58] The functions of this Council are to consider and make recommendations with respect to proposed appointments of Provincial Court judges, and to review complaints with respect to alleged misbehaviour or neglect of duty on the part of judges. This Council exercises administrative and advisory powers only. Removal of a judge remains, as in the Magistrates' Act, the prerogative of the Lieutenant-Governor in Council (the Provincial cabinet), and this can only be done after a full judicial enquiry by a judge of the Supreme Court of the province.[59] Certain provisions were made for the appointment of a Chief Judge in each division, and senior judges in large urban areas.

It is too early to determine the impact of these changes on the quality of performance by judges. However, it can be expected that the provisions go at least some way toward improving the status of this court, and indicate that proper recognition is being given to its importance. It was not within the competence of the Provincial Legislature to change either the jurisdiction or the powers of the magistrates' court. As far as day-to-day work is concerned, the new Provincial Court is the magistrates' court under a new title.

Because the data for this project were collected before the changes were made, the judicial officers in this study will be referred to as magistrates, and the discussion of the law affecting jurisdiction, tenure and appointment, will be that derived from the Magistrates Act and other statutes in existence in 1967.

NOTES TO CHAPTER 3

1 British North America Act, *Stats. of England*, 1867, C.3.
2 Ontario magistrates were appointed under the Provincial Magistrates Act, *Ontario Stats.*, 1961, ch. 226.
3 Dominion Bureau of Statistics, *Statistics of Criminal and Other Offences, 1966* (Ottawa, 1967).
4 Criminal Code, *Stats. of Canada*, 1892, C. 29.
5 With respect to theft and false pretences, if the value of the property concerned is under $50 then the magistrate has absolute jurisdiction. With respect to assault, the offences within the absolute jurisdiction of a magistrate, provided by the Criminal Code, include: obstructing a police officer (s. 110); common assault (s. 231); and assaulting a peace officer (s. 232 (2) (a)). See A.W. Mewett, ed., *Martin's Criminal Code* (Toronto, 1965).
6 *Statistics of Criminal and Other Offences, 1966.*
7 *Ibid.*
8 For a description of the jurisdiction of English magistrates see R.M. Jackson, *The Machinery of Justice in England*, 5th ed. (Cambridge, 1967), 178-98.
9 For a comment on these developments in England see *ibid*. In contrast, see S. Ryan, "The Adult Court,", in W.McGrath, ed., *Crime and its Treatment in Canada* (Toronto, 1965), 136-208. It should be stated, however, that in both countries the number of offences triable summarily by consent is steadily being increased.
10 Jackson, *The Machinery of Justice*, 179.
11 The maximum penalty usually depends on the offence, see Mewett, ed., *Martin's Criminal Code*, ss. 5(1)(b),620,621; but if no penalty is provided the maximum is five years for an indictable offence (s. 633), and six months for summary offences (s. 694).
12 This conclusion was based on a search of the Criminal Codes from all Western European countries, the US, Russia, and all other countries for which formal statements of the criminal law are available.
13 Mewett, ed., *Martin's Criminal Code.*
14 *Ibid.*, s. 288.
15 A number of attempts to relieve this situation have been made, culminating in 1968 in the transfer of all responsibility for the administration of these institutions from the county to the province. The plan is to provide for regional classification and detention centres. See Department of Correctional Services, *The Ontario Plan in Corrections* (Toronto, 1968).
16 Prisons and Reformatories Act, *Rev. Stats. of Canada*, 1957, C. 217.
17 This is a matter of policy not law. See G. Street, *Canada's Parole System* (Ottawa, 1966); F. Miller, "Parole," in McGrath, ed., *Crime and its Treatment in Canada*, 326-65; and *Parole Regulations*, P.C. 1960 - 681 (S.O.R/60 - 216), s. 2.
18 Prisons and Reformatories Act, s. 57.
19 Mewett, ed., *Martin's Criminal Code*, s. 622.
20 *Ibid.*, s. 694.
21 *Ibid.*, ss. 622, 694.
22 DBS, *Statistics of Criminal and Other Offences, 1966.*
23 *Criminal Statistics - England and Wales, 1966* (London, 1967).
24 Mewett, ed., *Martin's Criminal Code*, ss. 88,96,171,179 (5), 405,623.

25 G. Williams, "Suspended Sentence at Common Law," Public Law (1963), 441-55.
26 Stats. of Canada, 1892, s. 958.
27 Ibid., s. 959 (1).
28 Ibid., 1900, C.46, s. 2.
29 Ibid., 1955, C.51, s. 638.
30 Ibid., s. 638.
31 DBS, Statistics of Criminal and Other Offences.
32 Criminal Code Amendment Act, Stats. of Canada, 1921, C. 25, s. 19.
33 Ibid., s. 19.
34 Report of the Royal Commission to Investigate the Penal System (Ottawa, 1938); Report of a Committee Appointed to Inquire into the Principles and Procedures Followed in the Remission Service (Ottawa, 1956); see also "Proposals for the Development of Probation in Canada," Canadian Journal of Corrections, 9 (1967), 152-68; The Report of the Sentencing Committee of the Ontario Magistrates' Association (1961, 1962), mimeo; and E. Kenrick, "The Role of the Adult Court in Corrections," Canadian Journal of Corrections, 10 (1968), 151-78.
35 The Sentence of the Court (London, 1964), 3; and Criminal Justice Act, Stats. of England, 1948, s. 3.
36 DBS, Statistics of Criminal and other Offences, 1966; Criminal Statistics - England and Wales, 1966; National Conference on Law Observance and Enforcement, "Report on Probation and Parole," Wickersham Commission Report (Washington, 1963); see also B. Meeker, "Probation as a Sentence," Canadian Journal of Corrections, 9 (1967), 281-305, and especially at 291.
37 DBS, Statistics of Criminal and Other Offences, 1966.
38 Criminal Statistics in England and Wales, 1966.
39 N. Christie, paper read to the Research Symposium at the National Institute of Mental Health, Washington, DC (1963); L. Wilkins, Social Deviance (London, 1964), 83; DBS, Statistics of Criminal and Other Offences, 1966; Dominion Bureau of Statistics, Census of Canada (Ottawa, 1964).
40 DBS, Statistics of Criminal and other Offences, 1966.
41 Rev. Stats. of Ont., 1960, C. 387, s. 3, as amended by Ont. 1964, C. 113, s. 1.
42 Ibid., s. 41; Mewett, ed., Martin's Criminal Code, s. 720 (a) (b), s. 743 (1).
43 Supreme Court Act, Rev. Stats. of Can., 1952, C. 259, s. 41 (1)(3).
44 Mewett, ed., Martin's Criminal Code, s. 583 (a), (b).
45 Ibid., s. 584.
46 For a good review of the differences among courts of appeal see J. Decore, "Criminal Sentencing: The Role of the Canadian Courts of Appeal and the Concept of Uniformity," The Criminal Law Quarterly, 6 (1964), 324-80.
47 Ibid.
48 Magistrates' Act, Rev. Stats. of Ont., 1960, C. 226.
49 Ibid., s.3.
50 Inquiry re Magistrate J. Bannon and Magistrate George W. Gardhouse (Toronto, 1968).
51 Magistrates' Act, s. 3.
52 The salaries of full-time magistrates were fixed by Order of Council on 13 October 1966, as follows.

Position	Annual salary rate ($)	
	Minimum	Maximum
Chief Magistrate for Ontario	-	18,000
Magistrate being a member of the Law Society of Upper Canada	14,000	17,000

	Minimum	Maximum
Magistrate not being a member of the Law Society of Upper Canada	13,000	15,000
Deputy-magistrate, being a member of the Law Society of Upper Canada	10,500	12,000
Deputy-magistrate, not being a member of the Law Society of Upper Canada	9,500	11,000

53 Magistrates Act, s. 24.
54 These are Nova Scotia, British Columbia, and Ontario.
55 Royal Commission Enquiry into Civil Rights, *Report No. 1*, vol. 2 (Toronto, 1968). See also M.L. Friedland, "Magistrates Courts; Functioning and Facilities." *The Criminal Law Quarterly, II*, (1) (Nov. 68), 52-75.
56 Provincial Courts and Judges Act, *Stats. of Ont.*, 1968. C. 103.
57 *Ibid.,*s. 9 (2).
58 *Ibid.*, s. 7.
59 *Ibid.*, s. 4.

4

Background Characteristics of Magistrates

Introduction

Over a total life span, individuals change their attitudes, values, behaviour, and self-concepts as they assume new roles and undergo new experiences. New roles and experiences vary, however, in the extent to which they affect or induce change in the individual depending on the demands of the role, the degree to which it is compatible with past roles and experiences, and the strength of the personalities concerned. Magistrates are appointed to the bench when they are well into middle age. They have had a significant background of life experience prior to appointment. One might expect that this experience will largely determine the attitudes, expectations, and frames of reference that they bring with them to the bench. On the other hand, it may be argued that the judicial role is sufficiently powerful to restrain any tendency to allow past experience to influence their behaviour once appointed. Magistrates are bound by law, their oath of office, and the traditions and values of their profession, to insulate their private biases from their public behaviour. It may also be expected that the longer magistrates are on the bench, the less important past experience will be. In any event, the role of past experience in present behaviour is a question that can, and in this study will, be tested empirically.

Previous Research

There are numerous studies which have demonstrated relationships between the social backgrounds and past experience of judges and their conduct on the bench. It has been shown that there are relationships between political affiliation[1], social class background[2], age[3], religion[4], and ethnic background[5], and judicial behaviour. At the same time, many criticisms have been made of attempts to *explain* judicial behaviour in terms of these characteristics.[6]

Critics made the point that attempts to abstract a single item or variable from the background of a judge in isolation of all the other variables bearing on his behaviour, lead to an overly simplistic view of the sources and motivations of judicial behaviour.[7] It has been pointed out that even if all relevant background characteristics are taken into consideration, research of this kind faces the problems of demonstrating how the past influences the present.[8] Scholars have also questioned the assumption, made for the purposes of analysis, that judicial behaviour can be viewed in terms of a simple stimulus-response model.[9] It is argued that analyses which assume that the facts of the cases (the stimulus) and the decision of the court (the response) are perceived and understood equally by all judges give a false picture of the judicial process. Finally, these studies have been criticized on methodological grounds.[10] Nearly all of them were studies of courts consisting of several judges. Regardless of the level or type of court being studied, unanimous decisions were eliminated. This meant that the largest group of cases were excluded from analysis, and undue emphasis was placed on differences among judges.

Joel B. Grossman summarizes these criticisms particularly well:[11]

There is no doubt that preliminary attempts to isolate particular background variables have initially and necessarily overlooked the essentially cumulative and often random nature of human experience, as well as slighting the impact of institutional influences on the judicial mind. That judges are (or were) republicans or catholics or corporate law professors may tell everything about some judges. More likely, it would tell only part of the story ... Some categorisation is inherent in all scholarship, but the demands of quantitive analysis in this regard may sometimes seem to be fulfilled at too great a cost.

Knowledge of social background characteristics of magistrates alone offers no key to understanding how they will behave on the bench. But such knowledge will, at least, shed some light on the selection method for appointment, and together with other data, may provide some insight into the judicial process. In this study, social characteristics of magistrates are presented only as a background to further analyses which are to follow. The material presented was derived from interviews with magistrates, during which they related their life histories.

The Social Class Background of Magistrates

One of the myths that many Canadians like to perpetuate is that their society has no classes. It is a comfortable myth, as it presents an image of a society that provides equal opportunity for all its members to achieve the economic and social rewards coming from success in academic, business, or professional life. This being the case, the myth holds that able people from humble origins can, primarily through education, reach the pinnacles of success and power in whatever field of activity they choose. One would expect, therefore, that the composition of the "power elite," including the judiciary, particularly at the magistrates' level, would reflect the basic structure of society.

But as John Porter demonstrated in his explosive book, The Vertical Mosaic, "social images are one thing and social realities another."[12] Porter destroyed effectively the myth of equality by showing that a great deal of the social, political, and economic power in Canada, particularly in eastern Canada, is represented by a surprisingly small minority of Canadian families possessing certain attributes, and that these families tend to pass on the advantages of their class position to their children, by providing advantageous educational and social environments, as well as the goals and values that make for success in competitive society.[13] In fact, Canada has an identifiable class-structure and this class-structure is reflected in the composition of the magistrates' bench in Ontario.[14]

In Table 4, the occupations of magistrates' fathers are listed and ranked in order of frequency. The largest category consists of businessmen of various kinds. In actual fact, most of these owned and operated retail stores and should, therefore, be classed as small businessmen. The professional category, some twenty in all, consists of thirteen lawyers, three judges, and only four from professions not associated with the law. If one groups the three police officers with the judges and lawyers, it indicates that nearly one in three magistrates had fathers whose occupations were associated with the law in some way.

TABLE 4

Occupations of magistrates' fathers

Category	Number	Per cent
Businessmen	19	26.8
Lawyers	13	18.3
Skilled wage-earners	13	18.3
Civil servants	8	11.3
Farmers	4	5.6
Other professionals	4	5.6
Police officers	3	4.2
Judges	3	4.2
Clergymen	2	2.8
Unskilled wage-earners	1	1.4
Total	70	100.0

TABLE 5

Per cent distribution of labour force by occupations:
magistrates' fathers compared to total male labour force, 1931

Occupational category	Magistrates' fathers	Total labour force*
Professional	26.9	3.7
Business	26.8	6.9
Skilled or semi-skilled wage-earner	22.5	23.3
Clerical	11.3	10.5
Farmer	5.6	19.7
Unskilled wage-earner	1.4	35.9
Total	100.0	100.0

*Source: H.D. Woods and Sylvia Ostry, *Labour Policy and Labour Economics in Canada* (Toronto, 1962), table 35.

The social class backgrounds of magistrates become significant when one compares them with the distribution of occupational groups in the total labour force during 1930, when most magistrates were still living at home. As can be seen from Table 5, the skilled wage-earners category is a large one (sixteen, or twenty-three per cent). This is roughly representative of the proportion in this category in the total male labour force. What is interesting is the gross over-representation of both businessmen and professionals among the fathers of magistrates, and at the same time the gross under-representation of farmers and un-skilled earners. More than half the magistrates come from business or professional families, while not many more than one in ten of the general population are drawn from these occupational groups. At the same time, more than one in three of the male labour force were in the unskilled wage-earner category, while only one magistrate had a father in this group.

These data compare with those in previous studies which have shown that a social class factor distinguished those who achieve high judicial office from the general population.[15] It is interesting that this factor appears to hold in Canada, even at the magistrates' level.

These findings may disturb those who value an open, democratic, society which emphasizes equality of opportunity, and representation of all social groups in the agencies of governmental control. However, career choice is a complicated matter, and it must be pointed out that working-class children who reach university do not choose the legal profession as frequently as do their middle-class counterparts.[16]

Of greater import is the possible impact of middle-class upbringing on the eventual behaviour of magistrates on the bench. As many sociologists have pointed out, social class is more than an economic category.[17] People experience class membership in terms of beliefs and values that are associated with it. People are linked together in social groups by ideas. Social class is one such group, and its strength depends on the degree to which its members accept its collective sentiments and values as their own. And, of course, in a pluralistic society, such as Canada's, ideas, values, and sentiments compete with one another.

By convention we are taught that the court, particularly the magistrates' court, represents the community.[18] The standards against which behaviour is judged are supposed to be the standards of the average "reasonable man."[19] But how is a magistrate to learn about the standards of this hypothetical "average man," when his past experience and, as we shall see, his current life activities, were and are restricted to social intercourse with a small segment of society? Is it not more likely that a magistrate will reflect the standards he learned in his pre-judicial experience, reinforced by the standards of those with whom he is currently in frequent contact, namely, middle-class standards? Whether or not this is as it should be, it is a question worth exploring, and later some answers will be given.

The Pattern of Upward Mobility in Magistrates' Families

It appears that magistrates come from families that are quickly ascending the social class ladder. In Table 6, the occupational distribution of brothers and brothers-in-law of magistrates is compared to that of the total male labour force in 1951. It can be seen from this table that over-representation in the professional category becomes even more pronounced in the magistrates' generation. Over one-half of the brothers and brothers-in-law of magistrates are professional people, compared to slightly more than one-twentieth of the total labour force. Together with the business category, over three-quarters of family contemporaries of magistrates are in the top fifteen per cent of the labour force. Not one of these family members is in the unskilled wage-earner category, and only fourteen per cent are in the skilled wage-earner category, compared to twenty-four per cent and thirty-four per cent in these respective categories in the general population.

The pattern of upward mobility holds for all occupational categories. If the father was a farmer or unskilled wage-earner, the sons become skilled wage-earners or businessmen; if the father was a skilled wage-earner, the sons become businessmen or professionals, and if the father was a businessman, the sons become professionals. Only in three cases did sons fail to achieve a higher class standing than their fathers. While upward mobility has been a feature of Canadian society since the war, the rate of mobility is much more accelerated among magistrates' families than in the general population.

TABLE 6

Per cent distribution of labour force by occupations:
siblings of magistrates compared with total male labour force, 1951

Occupational category	Siblings of magistrates	Total labour force*
Professional	54.7	5.5
Business	19.8	10.3
Skilled and semi-skilled wage-earner	13.9	34.4
Clerical	4.6	11.5
Farmer	6.9	13.5
Unskilled wage-earner	—	23.7
Total	100.0	100.0

* Source: Woods and Ostry, *Labour Policy and Labour Economics.*

These findings suggest that magistrates come from families that were relatively sucessful, at least in economic terms. This is probably a good thing, as it suggests that magistrates are likely to be capable, confident people. But it also suggests that the parents of magistrates probably encouraged ambition, hard work, delayed gratification in the expectation of long-term rewards, and held all the other values that make for success in business and professional life. Whether these values exist among magistrates, and whether the adoption of them influences the way in which magistrates deal with those who have failed in life, are questions that will be explored later.

Age, Birthplace, Religion, Education, and Marital Status

The demographic characteristics of magistrates are presented in Table 7. Comparisons are made with all adult males in Ontario, and a number of interesting facts emerge, all of which support the conclusion, among others, that magistrates represent a relatively small segment of the population.

Age

Magistrates range in age from thirty-four to seventy-one, with a mean age of fifty-five. Leaving aside those persons under thirty who would normally not be considered for judicial appointment, magistrates as a group are still older than the rest of the adult population. Of males over thirty in the general population, about two-thirds (67.7 per cent) are forty or more, compared to over ninety-seven per cent of magistrates.

Despite the fact that there are no age qualifications set down in legislation with respect to the appointment of magistrates, only five magistrates in the sample were appointed before they reached forty, probably reflecting the general view that maturity and experience are essential attributes for magistrates. Comparisons with similar jurisdictions are not possible, due to the unavailability of data. The impression is that magistrates as a group are considerably younger than judges of superior, district, and county courts in Canada, and possibly somewhat younger than English magistrates.[20] Later in this book it will be shown that the age of a magistrate is closely associated with certain attitudes and beliefs that he holds.

Birthplace

Nearly all magistrates (sixty-five out of seventy-one) were born in Canada. Of the remainder, four were born in the United

Kingdom and two in the United States. It is interesting to note that while the "other European" category comprises over twelve per cent of the Ontario male population, this group is not represented on the magistrates' bench. This probably does not reflect bias against immigrants on the part of the Attorney-General in appointing magistrates, but rather the simple fact that most foreign-born do not have the professional qualifications to become lawyers.

TABLE 7

Demographic characteristics of magistrates compared to general population statistics

	Per cent magistrates	Per cent all males in Ontario*
Age		
30-39	2.8	32.3
40-49	25.3	26.6
50-59	39.4	20.0
60-69	28.2	13.4
70-79	4.2	7.7
Birthplace		
Canada	91.6	77.9
United Kingdom	5.6	8.0
United States	2.8	1.1
Other European	-	12.6
Other	-	0.4
Religion		
Roman Catholic	16.9	30.6
Anglican	26.8	17.6
United Church	29.6	25.9
Presbyterian	12.7	7.8
Other protestants	5.6	9.1
Jewish	2.8	1.8
Other	1.4	Unknown
Education		
None	-	1.2
Elementary	-	46.0
Secondary	32.4	44.8
Some university	14.1	3.1
Degree	49.3	4.9
Marital status		
Single	1.4	50.5
Married	96.8	47.0
Divorced	1.4	4.4
Separated	Unknown	Unknown

Source: *Dominion Bureau of Statistics, Census 1961.*
*These percentages were calculated only on the population of adult males aged 30-70.

Religion

John Porter has shown that the elite in each area of the Canadian social system is dominated by men of Anglo-Saxon heritage, with Anglican, United, and, to a lesser extent, Presbyterian, backgrounds.[21] This appears to hold true in the legal setting (and as we shall see, since judicial appointments are political appointments, also in the political setting). Roman Catholics and "other protestants," are greatly under-represented among magistrates, while the Anglican, United, and Presbyterian churches are all over-represented. Roman Catholics comprise over thirty per cent of the general population, but only twelve per cent of magistrates are Catholics. The majority of Catholic magistrates (nine out of twelve) are appointed for judicial districts where the Catholic population exceeds fifty per cent of the total.

Jewish magistrates appear to be over-represented, but the percentage figure is unreliable due to the small number (two). One must also remember that in Ontario, Jewish men are greatly over-represented in the legal profession from which most judicial appointments are made. Exact figures are not available, but it is estimated that about one in five lawyers in Ontario is Jewish. This suggests that Jews are under-represented among magistrates as far as their numbers in the profession would warrant.

These findings cannot be explained in terms of a religious bias in appointments to the bench. Religion is closely associated with ethnic affiliation, education and, more importantly, social class. They do, however, show that magistrates do not represent the religious distribution in the province. Later we shall show the differences in attitudes held by magistrates of different religious affiliations.

Education

Legal training is not a prerequisite to appointment to the magistrates' bench.[22] However, fifty-six out of seventy-one magistrates now on the bench, or approximately seventy per cent, are lawyers. Of the lawyers, thirty-five (seventy per cent) took a liberal arts BA prior to entering law school. The rest either took the required two years at university, and then completed the three years' law school course leading to an LL B, or, as in the case of some of the older magistrates, entered law school direct from high school to complete the then offered five-year LL B programme.

For nearly all legally-trained magistrates (fifty out of fifty-six) the law school of choice seems to have been Osgoode Hall, until recently a school administered by the Law Society of Upper Canada, and not affiliated with a University. For many years, this school had the reputation of providing a more solid practical training than some of the newer, more academically-oriented schools in the province.

Of the fifteen "lay" magistrates, nine were previously employed as justices of the peace or clerks of the court, and one was a police chief. These ten so-called "lay" magistrates probably came to the bench with more technical knowledge of the rules of procedure and practice in the criminal courts than many lawyers.

The policy of appointing lay magistrates has been the subject of considerable criticism from many people in and out of the profession.[23] In general it is felt that despite the technical competence certain lay magistrates might pick up, and conceding that a number of them have admirable personal qualities, legal training is essential for a person to discharge properly the larger judicial role inherent in the resolution of both legal and social issues arising out of the cases.[24] Moreover, it is felt that the standing of the magistrates' court among lawyers and the public at large suffers because it does not require that only professionally qualified people can be considered for appointment to the bench.

Marital Status

Marital stability is a striking feature of magistrates as a group. All but six were married, and of the remainder, five were widowers, and only one was in each of the divorced and single categories. Single and divorced magistrates are greatly under-represented as compared with the general population.

Table 8 demonstrates that over the years there have been marked fluctuations in the proportions of legally- and non-legally-trained persons appointed. There are three discernible time periods which mark changes in the proportion of legally-trained persons appointed to the magistrates' bench. During the pre-war and war period, about four out of five new appointments were lawyers. In the immediate post-war period, only about half were legally-trained, while in the 1960s the balance again shifted in the direction of more lawyers, with about three out of four appointments coming from this group. The interesting fact is that these trends closely follow broad economic trends in the province, and more particularly, the changing size in the gap between an average lawyer's income and a magistrate's salary.[25] To many lawyers in private practice during the thirties, and to some of the legally-trained veterans returning from overseas, the steady income of a magistrate's salary looked attractive. In the fifties, lawyers' salaries in Ontario rose sharply, while the salaries of magistrates made only modest gains. In this period, legally-trained persons did not come forward. In the 1960s, not only did magistrates' salaries make a remarkable recovery, nearly doubling in the space of five years, but also considerable effort was made to improve the office and court room facilities, working conditions, and status of the court.[26]

Prior Work Experience

Legally-Trained Magistrates

Of the fifty-six legally-trained magistrates, forty-nine (or eighty-seven per cent) acted primarily as defence counsel prior to appointment, while eight (thirteen per cent) were full-time crown attorneys for most of their previous legal experience. All legally-trained magistrates had at least ten years' experience at the Bar prior to appointment.

TABLE 8

Appointment of legally-trained and non-legally-trained
magistrates over a thirty-two years time span.

Year of appointment	Lay magistrates	Legally-trained magistrates
1936-40	6	19
1941-5	9	24
1946-50	10	10
1951-55	14	15
1956-60	3	9
1961-5	5	12
1966-8	2	11
Total	49	100

Source: Inspector of Legal Office, Province of Ontario, *Report* (Toronto, 1936-68).

It does not appear that magistrates were selected from those lawyers whose practice was devoted largely, or even substantially, to criminal law matters. Only eight out of the forty-six magistrates with some experience as defence counsel devoted twenty per cent or more of their practice to this type of work. Like most lawyers in Ontario, these magistrates earned the greatest part of their income from the civil side of a law practice. Table 9 shows the proportions of the practices of legally-trained magistrates that were devoted to criminal court work.

Legally-trained magistrates appear to represent the Bar as a whole, rather than that minority of lawyers who can properly be called "criminal lawyers." Until recently, criminal lawyers did not enjoy much status in the profession, although there were a few outstanding exceptions. The recent introduction of legal aid has made it financially possible for a young lawyer to earn a livelihood primarily from criminal court work.[27] At the same time, renewed interest in the administration of criminal justice, on the part of both the professional Bar and the public in general, has made a career as a criminal lawyer more prestigious.

Magistrates Without Legal Training

Of the fifteen magistrates without legal training, nine were previously justices of the peace, clerks of the court, or both; four were in private business; one was a school teacher; and one was a chief of police. In the larger urban areas, all the lay magistrates appointed had some prior court experience. Later we shall explore the similarities and differences in attitudes, beliefs, and sentencing behaviour between legally- and non-legally-trained magistrates.

Military Service

About half the magistrates had military experience. Twenty ended their military career as commissioned officers, nine as non-commissioned officers, and five as regulars. Once again a pattern of success is evident.

Occupational Stability

Prior to appointment, the majority of magistrates did not change jobs frequently, forty-three holding only one or two previous jobs,

TABLE 9

Proportion of practice devoted to criminal court work among magistrates with some experience as defence counsel

Proportion of practice (per cent)	Number	Per cent
0	1	2.2
1-9	27	58.7
10-19	10	21.7
20-29	3	6.6
30-39	1	2.2
40-49	3	6.6
50-59	1	2.2
Total	46	100.0

and only eleven holding four or more. Bearing in mind that most magistrates were at least forty when appointed, these facts assume some significance. The picture of stability in family, economic, and, as we shall see, community life is further enhanced.

Community Ties

Years of Residence in Local Community

Nearly all magistrates are home town people, who have spent the greater part of their life in the local community where they now work. This fact is clearly evident from Tables 10 and 11.

For most magistrates, the only time spent away from their home community was that spent at school or in military service. The relative lack of geographic mobility of magistrates in Ontario compared with the general population is quite striking. Almost forty per cent of the total adult population was born outside the census division where they now live, compared to less than five per cent of magistrates.

Formal Links to the Community

Most magistrates are very active in the life of their community. Fifty-eight magistrates (nearly eighty per cent), are active members of service clubs, such as Rotary, Elks, or Kinsmen. Twenty (twenty-eight per cent) are also members of the Masonic Order. About one-third hold office in public service or charitable organizations, such as the Community Chest, and of this group, more than half are members of more than one. Two out of every three are active participants in purely social or recreational clubs, and seven out of ten are actively involved in their church.

As far as professional organizations are concerned, over half the magistrates are members of local police commissions. In rural and small town areas the figure is much higher (nearly eighty per cent), as magistrates in some of the larger cities are not normally considered for this position. One in four hold office in local Bar associations. Nearly half (forty-four per cent), sit as judges of the Family and Juvenile Court. Only fifteen magistrates (twenty-one per cent) do not have formal links to the community through club or organizational ties, but of these twelve attended church regularly.

What is the significance of all this? It appears that, on the whole, magistrates are gregarious, out-going people who are often called upon by the community to give leadership or otherwise play a part in the life of the community. In doing so, they are likely to engage in social intercourse with a highly select group of persons. For the

TABLE 10

Years of residence in local community

Years	Number of magistrates	Per cent
1-9	1	1.4
10-19	8	11.3
20-29	13	18.3
30-39	7	9.9
40-49	16	22.5
50-59	17	23.9
60-69	9	12.7
Total	71	100.0

TABLE 11

Proportion of adult life in local community

Proportion	Number of magistrates	Per cent
One-quarter or less	2	2.8
More than quarter, less than half	7	9.8
More than half, less than three-quarters	9	12.7
Three-quarters and more	53	74.7
Total	71	100.0

most part, the organizations mentioned above are made up of professional and business people with perhaps a sprinkling of skilled wage-earners. It is these people who form the reference groups for magistrates, and the main source of information concerning the views and attitudes of the community. Because of this, one would expect that to the extent that the social and cultural milieux of a magistrate are important in the formation or change of attitudes and beliefs, middle-class values are likely to be encouraged and reinforced. Later we will see if this is so.

Political Affiliation

Appointments to the bench in Canada are "political," in the sense that most appointments are made from supporters of the party in power.[28] At the magistrates' level, appointments are made by the Attorney-General for the province. While appointments to the magistrates' bench of known supporters of opposition parties are not unknown, it is unusual for such an appointment to be made unless a suitably qualified party supporter does not come forward.

This does not mean that prior to appointment most magistrates were actively engaged in politics. Out of seventy-one magistrates, six had been candidates for election, and another seventeen held executive positions in local party organizations. Of the remainder, thirty-five were known to be nominal party members, and seven had no known political affiliation. Three were known as supporters of an opposition party. On appointment, all magistrates dropped visible links to party organizations, but it was noticed in the course of this project that at least five were still active behind the scenes.

Since the Progressive Conservative Party has been in power in Ontario for more than twenty-five years, most magistrates are, or were, Conservative Party supporters. This does not mean, however, that most magistrates are overtly small "c" conservative in outlook or temperament. The Progressive Conservative Party in Ontario occupies a broad band of "right of centre" political thinking, and, if success at the polls is any guide, it enjoys support from many sections of the electorate. It is not inconsistent to be a Conservative in Ontario and at the same time support some social welfare legislation. However, it is no doubt true that most magistrates, like their fellow conservatives, would not go as far in this direction as supporters of the two main opposition parties, the Liberals and New Democrats.

Length of Experience as a Magistrate

One would expect judicial experience to be a powerful factor, not only in shaping a magistrate's behaviour, but also in determining his conception of himself. The judicial role is a highly specialized one, based on tradition and circumscribed by law. Norms deeply rooted in law and in the professional role of the magistrate do more than define appropriate and inappropriate judicial behaviour. They affect the nature of his relationships with other persons and determine the values and sentiments that he can properly express in dealing with them.

The judicial role is highly visible, and it is acted out in the court room with rituals and ceremonies which tend to create social distance between the magistrate and others he comes into contact with. This social distance serves the function of isolating him from influences which may alter or conflict with his concept of self as he sees it in relation to his role. The wearing of robes, the elevated position of the magistrate in the court room and all the other ceremonies of deference shown, help define and enhance his position in relation to all the other members of the court. Off the bench, the high degree of formality which characterizes relationships tends to be somewhat eased, but all the parties are likely to be aware of the pre-eminent position of the magistrate.

On appointment, the magistrate must learn quickly the specific and expected pattern of behaviour appropriate to the judicial role. Whatever his background of experience, immediately on appointment he must give the appearance of impartiality, caution, wisdom, certainty, and dignity. In other words, he must appear to be comfortable in his new role, and never show signs of conflict with it. Enormous pressure is thus placed on him to alter any dissonant attitudes, feelings, or beliefs in the direction of conformity to role expectations. Simply stated, judicial experience serves to socialize magistrates into accepting the norms of judicial office.

To the extent that a magistrate internalizes these norms they become part of his self-image. He tends to see the world from a particular point of view, and may find it difficult to behave, and in time even to think, in ways inconsistent with that viewpoint.

For all these reasons, it was felt that judicial experience is likely to be an important variable in the shaping of judicial attitudes, self-concepts and behaviour. Later in this book we will examine the relationship of length of experience to these factors. First, let us look in Table 12 at the varying lengths of experience that magistrates have.

TABLE 12

Length of experience on the bench

Years	Number of magistrates	Per cent
1- 5	19	27.1
6-10	19	27.1
11-15	16	22.9
16 and more	16	22.9
Total	70	100.0

Magistrates range in length of judicial experience from one year to thirty-six years, with a mean of approximately fourteen years. For research purposes, the wide spread in judicial experience is useful, as it allows one to examine the similarities and differences in judicial attitudes and behaviour among magistrates of varying lengths of experience.

The study now turns to an examination of the beliefs and attitudes held by magistrates with respect to a host of issues bearing on sentencing. We will then return to social characteristics, this time exploring similarities and differences in attitudes and beliefs among magistrates with different backgrounds.

NOTES TO CHAPTER 4

1   S. Ulmer, "The Political Party Variable in the Michigan Supreme Court," *Journal of Public Law*, 11 (1962), 352; S. Nagel, "Political Party Affiliation and Judges' Decisions," *American Political Science Review*, 55 (1961), 843; U. Torgenson, "The Role of the Supreme Court in the Norwegian Political System," in G. Schubert, ed., *Judicial Decision Making* (Chicago, 1963), 221-4; and P. Russell, *Bilingualism and Biculturalism in the Supreme Court of Canada* (Final Report to the Royal Commission on Bilingualism and Biculturalism, Division II) (Ottawa, 1969).

2   S. Ulmer, "Public Office in the Social Backgrounds of Supreme Court Justices," *American Journal of Economic Sociology*, 57 (1962), 57; and Schmidhauser, "Stare Decisis, Dissent and the Backgrounds of Justices of the Supreme Court," *University of Toronto Law Journal*, 14 (1962), 194.

3   Ulmer, "*Political Party Variable*"; Ulmer, "Social Backgrounds of Supreme Court Justices"; Schmidhauser, "Backgrounds of Justices of the Supreme Court."

4   S. Nagel, "Ethnic Affiliations and Judicial Propensities," *Journal of Politics*, 24, 92; Schmidhauser, "Backgrounds of Justices of the Supreme Court"; Schmidhauser, "The Justices of the Supreme Court: A Collective Portrait," *Midwestern Journal of Political Science*, 3 (1959), 1.

5   Nagel, "Ethnic Affiliations and Judicial Propensities; Schmidhauser, "Backgrounds of Justices of the Supreme Court," "Justices of the Supreme Court."

6   For an excellent critical summary of recent research see J. Grossman, "Social Backgrounds and Judicial Decision-Making," *Harvard Law Review*, 79 (1966), 1551-64.

7   See, for example, L. Fuller, "An Afterword: Science and the Judicial Process," *Ibid.*, 1604-28.

8   Grossman, "*Social Backgrounds and Judicial Decision-Making*," 1554.

9   *Ibid.*, 1557.

10   *Ibid.*, 1555. Grossman quotes an unpublished Ph D thesis by D. Bowen in which the combined predictive power of all background characteristics explained less than 30 per cent of the variation in decision behaviour of the courts, and no single variable explained more than 16 per cent.

11   Grossman, "*Social Backgrounds and Judicial Decision-Making*," 1551.

12   J. Porter, *The Vertical Mosaic* (Toronto, 1965), 3.

13   *Ibid.*, especially chaps. 1-8, 12, 13, and 17.

14   *Ibid*, especially conclusions.

15   Grossman, "*Social Backgrounds and Judicial Decision-Making*," 1554.

16   Porter, *The Vertical Mosaic*, chap. 6.

17   See, for example, L. Schumpeter, *Imperialism and Social Classes* (New York, 1955), 105; L. Reissman, *Classes in American Society* (Glencoe, 1959); and R. Bendix and S. Lipset, *Class, Status and Power* (Glencoe, 1953).

18   See, for example, B. Cardozo, *The Nature of the Judicial Process* (New Haven, 1921); and P. Devlin, *The Enforcement of Morals* (Oxford, 1965), 15.

19   Devlin, *ibid.*, 15.

20 Comparisons with English magistrates were based on information kindly supplied by Dr Roger Hood of Cambridge, who has collected data in this regard; for Canada see Russell, *Bilingualism and Biculturalism.*
21 Porter, *The Vertical Mosaic,* chap. 6.
22 See Chapter 3.
23 See, for example, *Royal Commission Enquiry into Civil Rights, Report No. 1,* vol. 2 (Toronto, 1968), 539.
24 For a contrary view by a lay magistrate see A. Falzetta, "The Appointment of Magistrates," *Canadian Journal of Corrections,* 9 (1967), 137-46.
25 Magistrates' salaries more than doubled during the years 1961-8 after remaining at a relatively low figure (maximum $12,000) for nearly ten years previously.
26 See *Royal Commission Enquiry into Civil Rights,* 538; and Chapter 3 of this study.
27 A government-sponsored legal aid scheme came into existence in 1966 with the passing of The Ontario Legal Aid Act, *Stats. of Ontario,* 1966, C. 80.
28 *Royal Commission Enquiry into Civil Rights,* 539.

5

Penal Philosophy: Similarities and Differences Among Magistrates

Problems in penal philosophy have exercised the minds of legal philosophers, members of royal commissions, academics, and essay writers of all sorts. Most of the writing in this area is about what "ought to be" the purposes of sentencing, and most of the arguments revolve around the merits of the classical doctrines of retribution, deterrence, reformation, and incapacitation.[1] These arguments are rarely supported by empirical evidence, either as to the way in which these doctrines find expression in the sentencing behaviour of the courts, or as to the relative merits of them, in terms of the more general and agreed purpose of the penal system, i.e. the protection of society.

Discussions on what ought to be the purposes of sentencing are often interesting exercises in logic, and they are sometimes helpful in clarifying differences in opinion about the main directions in which the penal system as a whole should be moving. But as an abstract question, penal philosophy has very little meaning to a busy magistrate. He does not have the time for, nor does he necessarily see the relevance of, abstract doctrine. At the same time he must establish in his daily work some general guide-lines which serve to direct him in the proper exercise of discretion. These guidelines may be more or less articulated, specific, or general in application, strong or weak, and shared to a greater or lesser extent by his colleagues. None-the-less, they serve as guideposts, or rules of thumb in the application of punishment. This study is concerned with how general philosophical principles become translated into the specific, concrete and, inevitably, more limited rules used in individual cases. In short, it is concerned with the "practical" penal philosophies of magistrates.

In concrete terms, penal philosophy is studied as a strategy for making decisions. It is seen as a frame of reference around which decisions are made, and consists of all the rules of thumb, priorities, and assumptions that are consciously applied in dealing with cases. A magistrate may employ many strategies depending upon the nature and circumstances of the problem that he is facing. This being the case, it is useful to think of penal philosophy as a composite consisting of a number of decision-making rules.

Magistrates were asked several questions relating to each of the following areas:

1 How much importance does the magistrate attach to the classical purposes in sentencing?
2 How effective does the magistrate believe different kinds of sentences are in achieving these objectives?
3 What criteria are used in deciding among sentencing alternatives?
4 What are the magistrate's views as to the causes of crime?
5 How much informational support does he have for his penal philosophy?
6 In what kinds of situations does he find it difficult to achieve his objectives in sentencing?

Answers to these questions were based on self-reports of penal philosophy, i.e. what magistrates believed their decision-making rules were. This approach is vulnerable to the criticism that the answers are likely to be altered in the direction of social acceptability. On the other hand, it is important to know what magistrates believe acceptable answers to be, and if conformity to group norms is important, their actual behaviour on the bench may reflect their "idealized" selves rather than their "real" selves. In any event, many questions put to magistrates did not have obvious socially acceptable answers and, moreover, the data collected made it possible to compare the actual decision-behaviour of magistrates to their images of that behaviour.

The Classical Doctrines

Nearly all magistrates (sixty-five out of seventy-one) believe that it is their role to prevent crime through sentencing. They differ widely, however, in the way in which they aim to achieve this purpose. Magistrates were asked to rate each of the classical purposes of sentencing on five-point scales ranging from "very important" to "no importance." Each doctrine was defined in simple terms, habitually used, and familiar to magistrates. No attempt was made to subdivide these doctrines further into the more narrowly defined categories drawn by some penal philosophers, as it was our judgement that this would impose a degree of sophistication in the application of penal philosophy that would be unwarranted for many magistrates. We were determined to stay within the "framework of meaning" of the magistrates concerned and this made it necessary to avoid forcing them to distort their penal philosophies to fit the formulations of academic writers.[2] The definitions were given as follows:

Reformation. The attempt to change the offender through treatment or corrective measures, so that when given the chance he will refrain from committing crime.

General deterrence. The attempt to impose a penalty on the offender before the court sufficiently severe that potential offenders among the general public will refrain from committing crime through the fear of punishment.

Individual deterrence. The attempt to impose a penalty on the offender before the court, sufficiently severe that he will refrain from committing further crime through fear of punishment.

Punishment. The attempt to impose a just punishment on the offender, in the sense of being in proportion to the severity of the crime and his culpability, whether or not such a penalty is likely to prevent further crime in him, or others.

Incapacitation. The attempt to protect society for a period of time by removing the offender from the community into prison.

The responses of magistrates are indicated in Table 13.

Magistrates as a group tend to rate reformation highest, followed by general deterrence, individual deterrence, incapacitation, and punishment, in that order. Few magistrates would completely rule out any of the classical purposes in sentencing, but it is evident that they vary widely in the relative merits given to each. Marked inconsistency in the principles of sentencing is thus revealed.

TABLE 13

Importance given to the classical purposes in sentencing

	Very important	Quite important	Some importance	Little importance	No importance
Reformation	39	7	16	6	-
General deterrence	26	4	10	27	1
Individual deterrence	16	8	11	22	3
Incapacitation	9	8	21	28	2
Punishment	7	3	8	36	14

It is interesting that the answers are bi-modally distributed with respect to the deterrence doctrines. It seems that magistrates tend to take up extreme positions on these doctrines, rating them as either being "very important," or being of "little importance." This can be explained by the fact that magistrates must find, in the application of punishment, that the deterrent doctrines are sometimes in contradiction to the others (particularly reformation) forcing them to resolve the issue in the direction of one of them at the expense of the others.

It is significant that a sizeable minority of magistrates (eighteen out of seventy-one) consider punishment, in the retributive sense, to be at least of "some importance." It seems that Lord Asquith's statement "retribution is so discredited a doctrine that to attack it is to flog a dead horse," is somewhat optimistic, at least as far as Ontario magistrates are concerned.[3]

While reformation is generally ranked high, it must be remembered that it is the one purpose that is likely to stand in opposition to the others. The other purposes: deterrence, punishment, and incapacitation, all involve the deliberate sacrifice of the offender for the sake of community protection, or in the interests of "justice." Intercorrelations among the weights given to each doctrine bear this out, as can be seen from Table 14.

TABLE 14

Correlations between weights given to different penal philosophy doctrines

	General deterrence	Individual deterrence	Punishment	Incapacitation
Reformation	-0.545	-0.366	-0.250	-0.234
Incapacitation	0.257	0.352	0.437	-
Punishment	0.234	0.250	-	-
Individual deterrence	0.300	-	-	-

Reformation is negatively correlated with all other doctrines. Retribution, individual and general deterrence, and incapacitation are positively correlated with each other. The correlations are statistically significant (at 0.01 or better) but fairly low, indicating that while it is not always inconsistent for a magistrate to believe in reformation and, at the same time, give some weight to the other purposes, it is likely that he would rate these other purposes lower. The fact that the inter-correlations of all purposes but reformation are positive indicates that it may be difficult for some magistrates to discriminate among them. Those who have argued that deterrence and community protection are only disguised forms of retribution will find some empirical support for their views in these findings.

Deriving Penal Philosophy Scores

The appeal courts in Canada have instructed magistrates to give consideration to each of the main purposes in sentencing and to attempt a "wise blending of them."[4] If magistrates did this, the data presented above would suggest that the likely result would be that reformation would be out-weighed by the combined impact of the other purposes. But the courts do not weight these purposes equally, and in individual cases some ordering of priorities among purposes must be made. Depending on the case, one or more of them will be given a predominant position to the possible sacrifice of others. This is why it is misleading to rely solely on the rated importance of each doctrine. This became apparent during the interviews when some magistrates indicated that while they attached the greatest importance to reformation, a reformative sentence was not feasible in many cases. Similarly, some magistrates stated that there was always a punitive element in their sentences, albeit a minor one. This being the case, it was decided to ask magistrates to indicate the frequency in which each of these purposes is likely to be a predominant factor, rating them as "usually predominant," "sometimes predominant," and "seldom predominant." Weighted penal philosophy scores were then calculated by multiplying the frequency of application times the rated importance.

The resulting scores are probably a more accurate reflection of the importance of each doctrine in the magistrate's penal philosophy, and form the basic units for much of the analyses which are to follow in this chapter.

TABLE 15

Penal philosophy scores
(Rated importance times frequency of application)

	Mean weighted score	Standard deviation
Reformation	8.91	3.39
General deterrence	7.71	5.11
Individual deterrence	6.48	3.78
Incapacitation	5.13	2.95
Punishment	4.14	3.70

Beliefs as to the Effectiveness of Different Kinds of Penal Measures

The analysis now turns to an examination of how magistrates seek to achieve their objectives through the selection of penal measures deemed effective. Magistrates were asked to rate the effectiveness of imprisonment, parole, probation, and fines as measures designed to reduce or prevent crime. They were also asked to indicate the mechanism through which these measures prevent crimes, i.e. through treatment, control, deterrence, etc. The results are indicated in Table 16.

TABLE 16

Magistrates' assessments of the effectiveness of different penal measures

	Yes	No
Probation is effective as		
1 Treatment	34	37
2 Control	32	39
3 Treatment or control	45	26
Fines are effective as		
1 A deterrent to the offender	44	27
2 A deterrent to others	15	56
3 A punishment	14	57
4 At least one of 1, 2, or 3	55	16
Institutions are effective as		
1 A deterrent to the offender	42	29
2 A deterrent to others	36	35
3 A punishment	15	56
4 A treatment	30	41
5 At least one of 1, 2, 3, or 4	61	10
Parole is effective as		
1 Treatment	30	41
2 Control	19	52
3 Treatment or control	37	34

Magistrates differ widely in their views as to the effectiveness of different kinds of penal measures. About two out of three believe that probation is effective in preventing crime, but among these there are considerable differences as to whether this is achieved through supervision and control, or through treatment (i.e. counselling and support). A slightly higher proportion think that fines are an effective deterrent to the offender, while only about one in four feels that fines are either a deterrent to others or an appropriate punishment. Magistrates are considerably more confident about the efficacy of institutional measures, particularly as a deterrent to the offender. A significant group (thirty out of seventy-one) also feel that institutions are effective in treating offenders, and most magistrates (sixty-one out of seventy-one) feel that institutions are effective on at least one count. While this area of magistrates' beliefs is marked by inconsistency, it can be concluded that the majority of magistrates believe in the efficacy of the penal measures they apply.

A similar poll among those who have attempted to evaluate penal measures systematically would likely yield a different result. The depressing finding that has emerged from study after study is that, as far as it can be determined, no one penal measure designed to prevent crime in individual offenders through reformation or deterrence is any more effective than any other.[5]

But criminologists do not have to live with the results of their research. Magistrates are placed in the difficult position of having to make decisions without any empirical evidence as to their effectiveness.

At the same time they are under enormous psychological pressure to believe in the efficacy of the penal measures they apply. This pressure is particularly great with respect to measures that involve the deprivation of personal liberty or other forms of unpleasantness to the offender. In this connection it is interesting that the number of magistrates believing in the effectiveness of different penal measures rises proportionately to the severity of the measures concerned. Serious doubts about the efficacy of penal measures would be debilitating to magistrates, as they must make decisions quickly and, more importantly, they must give the appearance of certainty to them. The law and the norms and values associated with it, demand above all else that judicial decisions be certain in their application, uniform, and consistent. Sentencing is too demanding a task for "doubting Thomases."

In the absence of systematic evidence as to the efficacy of different kinds of correctional measures, magistrates must decide on the basis of their personal experience whether particular penal measures work. Each magistrate was asked if he could recall events from his own experience which led him to conclude that his sentences were having an impact on the crime rate in the community. About two out of three magistrates indicated that they could, and nearly all the events related to the "stamping-out" of a juvenile crime wave by means of imposing severe deterrent penalties. Most of these so-called crime waves concerned rowdyism and assaultive behaviour in or near public places of entertainment, such as beaches or dance-halls. There is no reason to doubt that the amount of juvenile crime associated with these activities tended to abate after a while. Criminologists have known for some time that crime follows certain seasonal and other patterns, and so far as it can be determined, these patterns are independent of the penal measures applied.[6] However, judges and magistrates are continually reinforced in their view that it is the penal measure that is responsible. As crime increases, magistrates tend to increase penalties proportionately, and when crime decreases (perhaps due to other factors) they naturally believe that the problem has been brought under control, and start to reduce penalties. After a while the crime rate is likely to increase once again, and magistrates are bound to feel that this is because they have become too lenient. The pattern repeats itself. Personal experience can be a very misleading guide in these matters. These findings underline the need for providing the courts with more systematic evidence as to the results of their decisions.

The analysis now turns to the relationship of penal philosophy to the degree of confidence magistrates have in different penal measures. For each measure, magistrates were split into two groups depending on whether they saw the measure as effective or ineffective. Comparisons were then made of the penal philosophy scores of each group.Where differences appeared they were tested for statistical significance by means of the t-test.[7] The choice of the t-test was made because it is a well-known and widely-used measure for determining the statistical significance of differences in the mean scores of two groups, and because more is known about the sampling distribution of t than other techniques that could have been used. The results are presented in non-technical form in Table 17 and presented in full in Technical Appendix 1. In Table 17 the words "high" and "low" indicate the direction of statistically significant differences in penal philosophy scores of magistrates believing in the effectiveness of the measures concerned.

TABLE 17

Relationship of penal philosophy to confidence
in different kinds of penal measures

| Penal measures seen as effective | Scores on penal philosophy scales | | | | |
	Reformation	General deterrence	Individual deterrence	Incapac- itation	Punishment
Probation	High*	Low	Low	n.s.	Low
Fines	Low	High	High	n.s.	n.s.
Institution	High	n.s.	n.s.	n.s.	n.s.
Parole	High	n.s.	High	n.s.	Low

* All values are statistically significant at at least 0.01.

Magistrates who believe in the effectiveness of probation have relatively high reformation scores and relatively low general deterrence, individual deterrence, and punishment scores. Magistrates believing in the effectiveness of fines have relatively low reformation scores and relatively high general and individual deterrence scores. Magistrates believing in the effectiveness of institutional measures have relatively high reformation scores, while those believing in the effectiveness of parole have high scores on both the reformation and individual deterrence scales and low scores on the punishment scale. The most important fact which emerges from Table 17 is that belief in reformation is associated with belief in the efficacy of most penal measures, including institutional measures. What is the explanation for this?

A magistrate who believes in reformation is caught in a classical dissonance situation. He has a concept of self as a treatment-oriented magistrate. As we shall see, he also sees offenders as needing treatment. But he is faced with a prison system that many people claim to be basically harsh and punitive, and the constraints of the situation demand that he send at least some offenders to prison. He could change his image of offenders, seeing them as "evil" people deserving punishment, but then he would have to change his concept of self to that of a punitive magistrate. The easiest way out of the dilemma is to see prisons as therapeutic institutions. If prisons could be seen as hospitals, then the magistrate has resolved all discrepant beliefs.

A large body of research has accumulated suggesting that individuals tend to arrange the elements of their cognitive system in such a way as to minimize inconsistency.[8] Consistency is maintained through interpreting the world selectively in ways consistent with subjective ends. Later it will be shown that the need for consistency is particularly great for judges and magistrates, and that selective interpretation of information is a major feature of judicial thought. At this stage, all that can be said is that belief in reformation is associated with the view that imprisonment is good for offenders.

Use of Presumptions

Interviews revealed that most magistrates were guided in choosing among various sentencing alternatives by a number of self-imposed guidelines and rules of thumb. These normally came into play as presumptions for and against probation, or for or against imprisonment for offences of different kinds. Presumptions tend to simplify the decision-process. They save the magistrate from the time-consuming task of having to figure out *de novo* how to deal with the case before him. The number and kind of presumptions used characterizes the "style" of decision-making of the magistrate concerned.

In answer to the general question: "In selecting among various sentencing alternatives available to you, are there any general rules that you use?," forty-nine magistrates (seventy per cent) indicated that they operated on the basis of general presumptions and listed what they were. Later, in dealing with specific sentencing problems featured in the interview, it was discovered that every magistrate had at least a few presumptions operating in specific situations.

In answer to the question: "What situations will make a presumption in favour of imprisonment operative?," forty-five magistrates (sixty-four per cent) stated that they would presume in favour of imprisonment for all crimes of violence, while twenty-four magistrates (thirty-four per cent) would do so for all sex offences, fifteen magistrates (twenty-two per cent) for all crimes involving the abuse of trust, and a similar number for any crime against property where the value of goods stolen, damaged, or destroyed, was reasonably high.

Twenty-six magistrates (thirty-seven per cent) would automatically presume in favour of imprisonment if the offender has a previous criminal record, while twenty (twenty-eight per cent) would not presume in favour of imprisonment unless they were convinced that there was no reasonable prospect of the offender staying out of further trouble with the law in the community.

The answers to these questions reveal that for most magistrates, the primary factor which operates in favour of imprisonment is the nature and seriousness of the offence. Presumptions become operative only if the magistrate considers the offence to be particularly serious, and since differences exist among magistrates concerning the seriousness of similar offences, variation in sentencing practice is bound to occur.

Turning to presumptions in favour of probation, it is clear that magistrates differ widely in the extent to which they are willing to use this measure. Almost half consciously apply some restrictions on its use. In some instances, the restrictions are very severe, limiting the measures to young, first offenders convicted of minor offences.

Another revealing set of answers related to the criteria used in deciding between probation and a fine in cases where imprisonment was considered unwarranted. Once again there are marked differences among magistrates. Two out of three would use fines when a deterrent penalty to the offender was deemed necessary,

while one in four fined, in lieu of probation, if they felt that a retributive punishment was warranted. A small number of magistrates would use fines in lieu of probation for older offenders or
for offenders convicted of less serious offences. In contrast, about
half would use probation whenever they felt the offender needed
help. The differences among magistrates reveal a split between
those who have confidence in probation as a correctional
measure and those who are more concerned to punish crime for
deterrent or retributive purposes.

The results of the interviews concerning the use of presumptions
are summarized in Table 18.

TABLE 18

Factors which make presumptions operative

	Number of magistrates	
	Yes	No
In favour of prison		
1 Type of offence		
All crimes of violence	45	26
All sex offences	24	47
All abuse of trust	15	56
All serious crimes against property	15	56
2 Criminal record	26	45
3 Likelihood of reconviction	20	51
In favour of probation		
1 For all who may benefit from probation	38	33
2 For first offenders only	12	59
3 For young offenders only	4	67
4 For young, first offenders only	12	59
5 For young, first offenders convicted of		
minor crimes	5	66
In favour of fine in lieu of probation		
1 Fines used when a deterrent penalty to		
offender is deemed necessary	44	27
2 Fines used when a retributive punishment is		
deemed necessary	17	54
3 Fines used for older offenders	13	58
4 Fines used for less serious offences	8	63
5 Probation used when offender needs help	38	33

The Resolution of Conflict

Certain insights can be gained from knowledge of the rules magistrates employ in resolving conflict, when it arises, between the
needs of the offender and community protection. The question was

put to magistrates in the following way and the distribution of answers is listed below.

Question. If, in a case before you of a fairly serious crime, such as indecent assault on a young person, you were convinced that the only chance of rehabilitation was to allow the offender to remain in the community where he can get psychiatric treatment, but at the same time felt that the chance of the offender becoming rehabilitated and not committing further crime was only about fifty per cent, would you be willing to take that risk?

Answers. Would always take that risk: 14; would probably take the risk: 33; would probably not take the risk: 13; would never take the risk: 11; total: 71.

The distribution of answers to the above questions shows how far apart magistrates are in the rules they apply in resolving conflict between the offender and the community. About two out of three magistrates believe that they would probably resolve such a conflict in favour of the offender, but almost one-third would do the opposite. Further evidence of inconsistency in the principles applied in sentencing is thus revealed.

Relationship of Penal Philosophy to the Use of Presumptions

It was learned that differences in the decision-making rules applied by magistrates are closely associated with differences in their objectives in sentencing as revealed by their penal philosophy scores. With respect to each decision-making rule studied, magistrates were divided into two groups depending on whether they used a presumption or not. The penal philosophy scores of the two groups were compared. t-tests were calculated to see if the use of a particular presumption was associated with statistically significant differences in penal philosophy. The results are summarized in non-technical form in Table 19 and are presented in full in Technical Appendix 1.

In Table 19 the words "high" and "low" indicate the direction of the difference in penal philosophy scores among those who use the particular presumption. If brackets are placed around these words, it indicates statistical significance at 0.05. Otherwise the level of significance is 0.01.

The results of the analysis indicate that the use of presumptions is closely associated with the penal philosophy scores of magistrates. Those who use presumptions in favour of imprisonment for specific offences are likely to have relatively low reformation and relatively high general deterrence and retribution scores. Those who would restrict imprisonment to cases of high risk are likely to have relatively high reformation and relatively low deterrence scores.

TABLE 19

Relationship of penal philosophy to the number and kinds of presumptions used in decision-making

Type of presumption	Reformation	General deterrence	Individual deterrence	Punishment	Incapacitation
In favour of prison	Low	-	-	-	-
For crimes of violence	Low	(High)*	-	High	-
For sex offences	Low	High	-	High	-
For abuse of trust	Low	High	-		
For all serious offences	High	High	(High)	(High)	-
For recidivists Only when community treatment impossible	High	Low	-	-	-
In favour of probation					
For all who can benefit	High	(Low)	(Low)	Low	(Low)
For young offenders only	Low	-	-	-	High
For first offenders only	Low	High	-	-	Low
For young first offenders only	Low	-	-	High	Low
In favour of fine (in lieu of probation)					
For less serious offences	Low	-	High	High	(High)
For older offenders	(Low)	-	(High)	High	-
Resolution of conflict					
For offender	High	Low	(Low)	Low	-
For community	Low	High	(High)	High	-

* Significant at 0.05; otherwise the values are significant at 0.01

Penal philosophy also distinguishes those who would restrict probation to certain classes of offenders. The most restrictive policy is associated with high retribution scores, an intermediate policy with high general deterrence and incapacitation scores, and a liberal policy with high reformation scores. Similarly, those who use fines in lieu of probation for minor offences and for older offenders are likely to have relatively low reformation scores and relatively high scores on all other scales. The resolution of conflict when it is perceived between the offender's needs and community protection follows the same pattern.

Throughout, we see decision-making rules organized around the conflict between belief in reformation and belief in all or any of the other doctrines. The pattern is highly consistent. At face value, it suggests that magistrates have taken up positions on each of the classical doctrines and have resolved all inconsistent elements, albeit in different ways. Because these data are based on self-reports of magistrates, one is tempted to dismiss the findings as "after the fact" rationalizations. However, we shall soon enough see that the actual decision-behaviour of magistrates closely follows the pattern now emerging. It seems that justice is a very personal thing.

Views as to the Causes of Crime

In the course of his work, each magistrate probably deals with more offenders than most other officials associated with the criminal justice system. Each magistrate is supported by several police officers, crown attornies, defence counsel, probation officers, and correctional workers. He observes many offenders in the dock, and he reads many reports prepared by others on their backgrounds and circumstances. It would be interesting to know the impact of this experience on the views magistrates form concerning the causes of crime.

Magistrates were asked: "In the course of your experience you have had occasion to observe many offenders and read many reports about them. What general conclusions have you come to concerning the causes of crime? Magistrates were permitted to give up to three answers; their responses are listed in Table 20.

Most magistrates believe that the causes of crime are to be found in the quality of family life, although there are differences among them as to whether this is due to lack of discipline or to lack of proper care and affection. The second group of factors picked related to questions of morality, disrespect for authority, and the "easy life" that young people now lead. As a group, magistrates seem to prefer individual and familial, rather than socio-economic explanations.

There are some interesting relationships between the weights given to individual causes and the penal philosophies of the magistrates concerned. Magistrates were divided into three equal groups, consisting of those with high, moderate, and low scores on the reformation scale. The results are listed in Table 21.

TABLE 20

Magistrates' views as to the causes of crime

	Mentioned	Not mentioned
Lack of discipline in the home	52	19
Unloving parents	38	33
General decline of moral standards in society	27	44
Too much money given to young people	21	50
Decrease in respect for authority generally	19	52
Poverty	19	52
Alcoholism	17	54
Miscellaneous socio-economic factors	15	56
Lack of religious education	12	59
Lack of intelligence	11	60
Bad companions	8	63
Don't know	6	65

TABLE 21

Ranked positions of magistrates' views as to the causes of crime for magistrates with high, moderate and low reformation scores

High reformation scores (N = 23)	Middle group (N = 24)	Low reformation scores (N = 23)
Lack of parental discipline	Lack of parental discipline	Lack of parental discipline
Unloving parents	Unloving parents	Alcoholism
Affluence	Low moral standards	Intelligence
Poverty	Lack of respect for authority	Lack of respect for authority
Miscellaneous socio-economic factors	Affluence	Lack of religious training
Alcoholism	Intelligence	Poverty
Intelligence	Miscellaneous socio-economic factors	Unloving parents
Low moral standards	Lack of religious training	Low moral standards
Lack of respect for authority	Bad companions	Bad companions
Lack of religious training	Poverty	Affluence
Bad companions	Alcoholism	Miscellaneous socio-economic factors

All groups ranked "lack of parental discipline" highest, but after that different patterns emerged. "Unloving parents" was ranked highly (second) for both the high and middle groups, but given a relatively low position (seventh) for the low group. The rank positions of socio-economic factors seem to be positively associated with belief in reformation. These factors are frequently mentioned by magistrates with high reformation scores, sometimes mentioned by those with moderate scores, and seldom mentioned by those with low scores. Magistrates with low reformation scores tend to personalize the causes of crime around such simplistic notions as lack of intelligence and alcoholism.

The average number of causes mentioned by magistrates in each group is also interesting. Magistrates with relatively high reformation scores mentioned an average of 3.2 factors associated with the causes of crime, those in the middle group mentioned an average of 2.7, and those in the low group mentioned an average of 1.6. Correlational analysis yields a positive correlation of 0.473 (significant at 0.001) between belief in reformation and the number of factors believed associated with the causes of crime.

Taken together these data suggest that belief in reformation is associated with a more complex view as to the etiology of crime. This does not mean, however, that reformation-oriented magistrates have a greater *capacity* for complex thought. Their philosophy *requires* more subtlety and more informational support than any of the other policies. At this stage of the analysis,all that can be said is that reformation-oriented magistrates appear to some extent to be living up to that requirement.

Degree of Mental Illness Perceived

Probably the most revealing set of answers were those made to the following question.

Question. What proportion of offenders appearing in magistrates' courts appear to you to be mentally ill, although not necessarily legally insane or certifiable?

Answers. Most offenders: 10; a significant minority: 26; none or very few: 31; don't know: 4; total: 71.

Mental illness is a vague concept and it is difficult to obtain a clear and accepted definition, even among the experts. None the less, a belief on the part of some magistrates that a significant proportion of offenders are mentally ill may have important implications as to the way they deal with them by way of sentence. Mental illness tends to be exculpatory, i.e., a denial of full responsibility for the crime, and an indication that treatment rather than punishment is needed. It would be difficult for a magistrate to believe in reformation and at the same time believe that most offenders do not need treatment. Let us see whether this is so.

Comparisons were made of the penal philosophy scores of magistrates who differed in the degrees of mental illness they perceived. The positive relationship of belief in reformation to the proportion of offenders seen as mentally ill is very strong. In contrast, the amount of mental illness seen is negatively associated with belief in general deterrence, retribution, and incapacitation. Interestingly, it is not inconsistent for some magistrates to believe in individual deterrence and at the same time feel that many offenders are in some way mentally ill. This can be done by equating criminality with illness, and punishment with treatment.

What we are witnessing in these findings, summarized in Tables 22 and 23, is a belief structure in terms of the causes of crime that supports the penal philosophies of the magistrates concerned. Magistrates appear to interpret selectively the causes of crime and the amount of pathology exhibited by offenders in ways which maximize concordance with their personal objectives in sentencing.

TABLE 22

Proportion of offenders believed mentally ill

	Most	Many	None or few	Total
High reformation scores	8	9	5	22
Middle group	2	14	7	23
Low reformation scores	-	3	19	22
Total	10	26	31	67

TABLE 23

Correlation between penal philosophy and proportions of offenders believed to be mentally ill

	Correlation coefficient	Level of significance
Reformation	0.418	0.01
General deterrence	0.307	0.01
Individual deterrence	0.318	0.01
Punishment	0.301	0.01
Incapacitation	0.314	0.01

Informational support

The work-load of an average magistrate is such that there is little time left in a normal day for general reading, attending lectures and seminars, visiting institutions, or any of the other activities that he may wish to do in order to keep up with developments in his field. If a magistrate does any reading beyond the law reports, it indicates that he attaches high priority to enlarging his knowledge in that area. It also provides a clue to his penal philosophy. Different penal philosophies demand different amounts of informational support. "Forward looking" magistrates who attempt to control future behaviour through reformation and deterrence would feel the need to expand their knowledge of crime and treatment. On the other hand, magistrates who are satisfied to punish past behaviour would not feel the need for such knowledge.

Magistrates were asked to list the journals dealing with crime, apart from the law journals, that they read regularly or frequently. They were also asked to name any major criminological work with which they were familiar. The results are presented in Table 24.

TABLE 24

Number of books and journals dealing with crime and delinquency read by magistrates

	Number	Per cent
Books read		
None	50	70.4
One	5	7.0
Two	8	11.3
Three or more	8	11.3
Journals read frequently		
Ontario Magistrates' Quarterly	63	88.7
The Criminal Law Quarterly	49	69.0
Canadian Journal of Corrections	34	47.8
Federal Probation	12	16.9
British Journal of Criminology	5	7.0
Crime and Delinquency	5	7.0
Journal of Criminal Law, Criminology and Police Science	5	7.0
Others	3	4.2

Two out of three magistrates have not seen fit to do any significant reading in the field of crime and delinquency. Most magistrates read the *Ontario Magistrates' Quarterly* and *The Criminal Law Quarterly,* but these journals cannot be said to be important sources of criminological knowledge. Even among magistrates who attach great weight to reformation, many have not read any of the standard works or journals in the field.

Magistrates were assigned to categories according to the degree of reading claimed. They were given a "familiar" rating if they claimed to have read at least one book and are continuing to read at least two journals (apart from the *Ontario Magistrates' Quarterly* and *The Criminal Law Quarterly*). They received a "some knowledge" rating if they could name any book and could claim to read at least one journal regularly. The rest were given a "no knowledge" score. Comparisons were made between magistrates with high, moderate, and low reformation scores. The results, shown in Table 25, indicated that there was a general tendency for belief in reformation to be associated with a more active search for information, but a surprising number of self-defined reformation-oriented magistrates did virtually no reading in this field.

TABLE 25

Relationship of familiarity with criminological literature to belief in reformation

	Familiar	Some knowledge	No knowledge	Total
High reformation scores	6	11	7	24
Middle group	2	7	15	24
Low reformation scores	1	2	20	23
Total	9	20	42	71

Chi square = 13.588; significant at 0.01.

The reading habits of magistrates were closely associated with their scores on the remaining penal philosophy scales. Thus, the amount of reading done was negatively associated with belief in deterrent doctrines, punishment, and incapacitation. All correlations were significant at at least 0.01. It appears from this that a penal philosophy which stresses reformation demands a great deal more from magistrates than belief in any of the other doctrines.

Reformation-oriented magistrates seek to enlarge their knowledge in other ways. They visit more penal institutions and mental health clinics than do magistrates with high scores on any of the other scales. In addition, they are more active in the seminars and other activities of the Ontario Magistrates' Association. The statistical material supporting these findings is to be found in Technical Appendix 1.

The picture which emerges from this section is one of considerable variation in the amount of knowledge that magistrates seek concerning the treatment of offenders. This variation is closely associated with the penal philosophies of the magistrates concerned. Magistrates who are "forward looking" in their penal philosophy tend to be more active in their search for information. They are concerned about the results of their decisions and they seek to enlarge their knowledge about both the causes of crime and the effectiveness of different forms of correctional methods to deal with it.

Sentencing Decisions that are Most Difficult to Make

In applying his penal philosophy in individual cases, a magistrate sometimes comes across situations which make it difficult for him to achieve his objectives. A magistrate who believes in reformation may find it difficult to effect this purpose with the older, recidivist offender or with offenders convicted of serious crimes. In dealing with these offenders, he may have to act in ways inconsistent with his image of himself as a person who selects the appropriate treatment for all offenders depending upon their needs. Similarly, a magistrate who believes in retribution may experience difficulty in imposing a severe penalty on a pathetic, young offender, or on a breadwinner who has committed a crime clearly due to circumstances beyond his control. The type of case with which a magistrate experiences difficulty is some indication of the extent to which his penal philosophy is applied. The identification of "difficult cases," therefore, provides indications of the boundaries of magistrates' penal philosophies.

Magistrates were asked to indicate the type of case causing the greatest difficulty in sentencing. The answers are listed in Table 26.

Sex offences present difficulty to more magistrates than does any other class of offence. These are often fairly serious crimes in terms of the maximum penalty provided by the Code, but at the same time are usually fairly minor in terms of the actual harm incurred by the victim. The majority of sex offences dealt with by magistrates are marginal indecent assaults on females.[9] Moreover, the offender is usually before the court for the first time, shows remorse, and is willing to receive psychiatric treatment. More often than not, a psychiatric report will recommend treatment as an outpatient at the local mental health clinic. On the other hand, public opinion is often aroused, and the magistrate feels he must do something visible to protect the community from this type of crime. What we have is a classic case of conflict between the competing purposes in sentencing.

TABLE 26

Type of cases causing the greatest difficulty to magistrates in sentencing

Type of case,	Number	Per cent
Sex offenders	20	28.1
Young recidivists	15	21.1
Breadwinners	13	18.3
No difficult cases	13	18.3
First offenders	10	14.0
White-collar offenders	10	14.0
Every case if difficult	10	14.0
Crimes of violence	6	8.4
Young offenders	5	7.0
Young first offenders	5	7.0
Older recidivists	4	5.6

The young recidivist also presents a difficult problem. He has been given a chance and has failed. He is too young to be considered a hardened criminal. To commit him to an institution where he would meet older and more confirmed criminals is likely to be harmful. While it is open for the magistrate to sentence this type of offender to imprisonment, he cannot do so without feeling that perhaps another chance in the community might be warranted.

The *Report of the Departmental Committee on the Business of the Criminal Courts* (the *Streatfeild Report*), stated that sentences which were designed to control future events through reformation and deterrence were more difficult to make than sentences designed to punish past behaviour.[10] To test this statement, comparisons were made of the degree of difficulty experienced in sentencing by magistrates with different penal philosophies. The results indicated that magistrates who experience difficulty in sentencing sex offenders have high reformation scores, those experiencing difficulty in sentencing young recidivists have high individual deterrence scores, and those who find sentencing a relatively easy task, compared to the trial of guilt, tend to have high general deterrence, incapacitation and retribution scores. In each case the difference is statistically significant at 0.01 or better. The results are summarized in nontechnical form in Table 27, and are presented in full in Technical Appendix 1.

TABLE 27

Relationship of penal philosophy to kinds of sentencing
decisions with which magistrates experience difficulty

Type of case causing difficulty	Reforma- tion	General deterrence	Individual deterrence	Punish- ment	Incapaci- tation
First offender	Low	-	-	High	-
Young recidivist	-	-	(High)*	-	-
Sex offender	High	-	-	-	-
Sentencing is simple (compared to trial of guilt)	Low	High	(High)	High	High

*Significant at 0.05, otherwise significant at 0.01.

Partial confirmation for the *Streatfeild Report* can be found in Table 27. It is true that magistrates who usually sentence with reformation as their primary objective find sentencing more difficult than the trial of guilt, while the opposite is true of magistrates with high scores on the other scales. But magistrates seeking to control future events through deterrence also find sentencing to be relatively easy. This may mean either that the deterrent doctrine is nothing more than an acceptable substitute for retribution, or that magistrates believing in deterrence feel that it is not difficult to estimate the impact of their sentences on potential offenders.

It is interesting that magistrates experiencing difficulty with sentencing first offenders have relatively low reformation and relatively high punishment scores. The first offender poses no difficulty to the reformation-oriented magistrate. He is fined or placed on probation. Magistrates concerned with retributive punishment are likely to feel somewhat uneasy about imposing a severe penalty on him. In contrast, the reformation-oriented magistrates find it difficult to sentence the sex offender. The emotion aroused by sex offences and the public's demand for punishment of this type of crime constrain magistrates from selecting sentences which are directed primarily towards the offender's rehabilitation.

A simple fact emerges from this section. Magistrates prefer to deal with cases which fit clearly into the categories of sentence that they use habitually. Punitive magistrates find it easier to deal with recidivist offenders convicted of serious offences. Non-punitive magistrates find it easier to deal with first offenders who need treatment.

Summary and Conclusion

In this chapter penal philosophy was studied as a ·strategy for making decisions. The strategy consists of all the rules of thumb, presumptions, and priorities that are brought to bear on sentencing problems. The data presented lead to a number of unavoidable conclusions.

First, enormous variation exists among magistrates in the way in which they go about making sentencing decisions. This variation is noticeable in every aspect of penal philosophy studied. Magistrates differ widely in their purposes, their views as to the effectiveness of different kinds of sentence, the criteria applied in deciding between different kinds of sentences, the ways in which conflict between the offender's needs and community protection is resolved, the amount of informational support they have for their views, and the kinds of situations in which they experience difficulty in sentencing.

Secondly, it appears that differences among magistrates are not random, but follow certain patterns depending primarily upon the purposes the magistrates have in mind. While there are wide variations in penal philosophies between magistrates, it also appears that most individual magistrates have a fairly consistent and coherent set of beliefs bearing on their personal penal philosophy. Magistrates appear to be inconsistent with each other but consistent within themselves.

Third, the basic conflict around which differences among magistrates appear to be organized seems to be a clash between those who are concerned to treat the offender and those who are concerned to punish him for deterrent or retributive purposes. While the majority of magistrates have images of themselves as being oriented towards the offender and his treatment, the actual decision-making rules applied would appear to be more closely associated with the offence and community protection. It was interesting to note a shift in emphasis from the offender to the offence as the question became more specific and more closely related to actual practice. Throughout, the data indicated the relative simplicity of the purposes, conceptions, and beliefs of magistrates who espouse a deterrent or retributive penal philosophy. Reformation-oriented magistrates, on the other hand, appear to be much more involved in the sentencing process and find it a more complex and demanding task.

Fourth, most magistrates sentence without a great deal of background knowledge about the treatment of offenders. Few do any significant reading in this field, and only a minority visit institutions.

The differences among magistrates in the strategies applied in sentencing were greater than this writer would have expected, bearing in mind that most Ontario magistrates come from roughly similar backgrounds, operate within the same legal framework, and interact with each other in a variety of ways. At this early stage data were emerging which showed that magistrates interpret selectively their worlds in ways consistent with their subjective ends. This feature of judicial decision-making in sentencing will be confirmed over and over again in subsequent chapters. If there was a tendency for magistrates to give socially acceptable answers to the questions asked, either they differed remarkably in their views as to what those answers should be, or the tendency was not strong enough to obscure their true beliefs. Some confidence in the results can be had because penal philosophy was approached from many different angles with remarkably consistent results. But despite the degree of consistency in the data, one must be cautious about findings based on self-reports. The disturbing nature of many of them make it all the more necessary to look at the actual decision-behaviour of magistrates on the bench.

Perhaps the most striking feature of the picture that emerged from this chapter is the apparent rationality of the answers given. Once we know the social purposes of a magistrate, the whole of his penal philosophy unfolds as a logical extension of it. But it is well known that apparently rational opinions can stem from irrational motivations. One cannot help but wonder if the differences among magistrates reflect differences in deeper levels of personality, particularly differences in the more deepseated attitudes and feelings they hold towards crime. The next few chapters deal with the attitudes of magistrates towards crime, social deviance, and related matters. We will then return for a closer look at the decision-process in sentencing, this time focusing on the actual behaviour of magistrates on the bench.

NOTES TO CHAPTER 5

1 Some of the most important writing has been footnoted in Chapter 1. See especially ns. 2-12. See also L. Radzinowicz, *Ideology and Crime* (London, 1966).

2 In particular, no distinction was made between reformation which produces change through suffering (which comes close to individual deterrence) and reformation which produces change through supportive help willingly taken by the subject. Similarly, no distinction was made between retribution as a positive reason for punishing beyond what would be required for other purposes and retribution as a limit on the amount of punishment that could be imposed for deterrent or reformative purposes. For an excellent description on these various theories see N. Walker, *The Aims of the Penal System* (Edinburgh, 1966); and for a discussion of the merits of each doctrine see H.L. Packer, *The Limits of the Criminal Sanction* (Stanford, 1969).

3 L. J. Asquith, "Problems of Punishment," *The Listener*, 43 (11 May 1950), 821.

4 See, for example, *Reg. v. Willaert* (1953), 105 C.C.C. 172; *Reg. v. Inaniev* (1950), 127 C.C.C. 40; *Reg. v. Jones* (1956), 115 C.C.C. 277; and *Reg. v. Switslifhoff* (1950), 1 W.W.R. 913.

5 See Chapter 1, n.7; see also N. Morris and G. Hawkins, *The Honest Politician's Guide to Crime Control* (Chicago, 1970).

6 See, for example, the classical works of A. Guerry, *Statistique Morale de l'Angleterre et de la France* (Tours, 1866); and M.Quetelet, *Statistique Morale de l'influence du libre arbitre de l'homme sur les faits sociaux* (Brussels, 1847).

7 An easy to follow description of the *t*-test is to be found in S. Diamond, *Information and Error* (New York, 1959), 101-17.

8 A good review of the literature together with several new contributions is contained in S. Feldman, ed., *Cognitive Consistency: Motivational Antecedents and Behavioral Consequents* (New York, 1966).

9 For empirical support see H. Mohr, *et al.*, *Exhibitionism and Pedophilia* (Toronto, 1964).

10 *Report of the Inter-Departmental Committee on the Business of the Criminal Courts* (The *Streatfeild Report*) (London, 1961), 76-7.

6

The Meaning of Judicial Attitudes

What is an Attitude?

More than thirty years ago, Gordon Allport stated: "... attitude is probably the most distinctive and indispensable concept in social psychology."[1] Since then, the concept has, if anything, grown in importance and is employed frequently not only in psychology, but in nearly all the behavioural sciences, particularly sociology, political science and, more recently, law. Probably no other term appears so frequently in social science literature. The reason for the importance of the concept is obvious. It provides the link between the individual and his social environment - between the inner state of man and the world to which he must adjust.

In everyday use, the term is employed as a convenient form of shorthand to summarize what we observe about an individual's behaviour towards another person, a class of persons, or even an idea or an event. When we say that one person has an attitude towards another, we usually mean that the net effect of his behaviour toward that person indicates that he has either positive or negative feelings about him, as the case may be.

In social science literature, "attitude" has many definitions. Lewis has identified more than twenty in common use, and points out that no one definition is greatly superior for all purposes, or there would not be so many alternatives.[2] A review of the literature will show that common to the majority of definitions is the notion that an attitude is "a learned disposition to respond to a social object or a class of objects, in a consistently favourable or unfavourable way."[3]

Defined in this way, attitudes can be distinguished from other forms of psychological mechanisms such as drives or needs, by reason of their two essential features. First, attitudes are not innate. They are *learned* through interaction with persons and groups with which the individual identifies. The common thread that runs through most definitions is that they are a form of mental organization built up through many experiences.[4] Secondly, while attitudes are inferred from consistent behaviour expressed in the words and actions of individuals, not all behaviour reflects an attitude. The distinguishing feature is that attitudinal behaviour is directed towards a *social object*, i.e., an object of some significance to the social group to which the individual belongs.

Considered in this way the study of attitudes cannot be strictly psychological. Attitudes should be studied in relation to the social milieu in which they are expressed, current patterns of acceptability and rejection in the group, and the norms and standards of behaviour with which the individual identifies. From a sociological viewpoint, attitudes are "the concrete representation, in the individual, of cultural norms."[5] Ever since Thomas and Znaniecki's classic study, *The Polish Peasant*, attitudes have had an important and permanent place in sociological writing.[6]

Different kinds of behaviour have been used to assess attitudes, but the most common are the verbal or written responses to specially designed questionnaires. Thus an attitude score, like an intelligence score, is "what the test measures," and is only valid to the extent that the test measures reliably what it purports to measure.

An attitude was conceived by Allport, and by many of those who followed him, as a simple concept, characterized by bi-polarity in the direction of feeling towards an object.[7] It is this positive or negative feeling (usually called "affect") aroused in the individual, that is the essence of an attitude conceived in this way. Most attitude scales so far developed are based on this conception, and are designed to obtain a numerical score for the individual tested, so that his attitude can be placed on a particular point on a continuum, ranging from strongly positive to strongly negative.

Allport admitted that his definition of attitude was over simplified, as two people can be equally hostile towards a particular person, but hold quite different views as to his characteristics, and, in addition, differ as to the action they would be prepared to take towards him. All the same, the view that social attitudes and social behaviour were intimately linked prevailed until the advent of empirical research which finally laid this simplistic notion to rest.

In an influential article, Leonard Doob challenged the view that there was a necessary connection between attitudes and behaviour.[8] He saw attitudes partly as a disposition to respond emotionally to an object. But just as one had to learn how to respond to an object emotionally, one had to learn what overt behavioural response to make. Since two people holding the same feeling to an object could learn to make different responses to it, it was necessary to view attitudes as having *two* components, an affective component and a *conative*, or "action-tendency" component. Chein's critique resulted in the addition of yet another component.[9] He criticized both Allport's and Doob's definitions on many grounds, the most important being that they both tended to ignore the *cognitive* or "belief" component of attitudes. Chein pointed out that attitudes are closely linked to the selective manner in which individuals perceive events related to them, the scales of judgement they apply to these events, and the residue of remembered information (the essence of an attitude), that they bring to bear on new events. Chein would prefer to call attitudes: "dispositions to evaluate certain objects and situations in certain ways."[10] According to Chein, when a person's attitude is engaged in an issue, his social judgement is no longer neutral; he is attracted or repelled, for or against, favourable or unfavourable. In other words, he does not make an impartial discrimination, but an *evaluation* of the problem.

It is the evaluative nature of attitudes that is given the greatest emphasis by most contemporary theorists in the field. In an important book published recently, Fishbein defined attitudes as "a set of evaluative categories that the individual has formed (or learned) during his interaction with persons and objects in his social world."[11] He goes on to say, "when faced with persons, objects or events relevant to his attitude, the individual uses these categories for classifying specific items as acceptable/unacceptable, good/bad, truthful/erroneous, or in other appropriate evaluative terms."[12]

This is a particularly useful definition. The word "evaluative" suggests both a belief about an object (cognition), and an emotional response to it (affect). More importantly, the definition focuses on the functions that attitudes serve for individuals. In particular, it concentrates on the way in which attitudes enable an individual to give meaning to the ambiguities of the world around him. Holding an attitude enables an individual to categorize and interpret problems, and the individual is thus saved from the time-consuming and sometimes painful process of working out *de novo* how he should respond to them. Attitudes are thus seen as a set of filters through which information is selectively experienced. Perceived in this way, attitudes are likely to be relevant to the decision-process, and as such, provide a way of looking at sentencing.

Most modern texts dealing with attitudes define them as having all three components: an *affective* component, consisting of the positive and negative feelings and emotions aroused in the individual by the attitude object; a *cognitive* component, consisting of beliefs about the characteristics, qualities or attributes of the object, and a *conative* component, consisting of verbal expressions of intention to act towards the object in particular ways, or expressions of preference for certain forms of collective action, for or against the object.[13]

Conceived in this way, an attitude towards corporal punishment, for example, would include not only the individual's expression of positive or negative feelings towards this form of punishment, but also his ideas as to its effects, his stated willingness to use it personally in specific situations, and his views as to the desirability of its use by the school, the courts, and other public agencies.

As a theoretical statement this concept would seem to have a number of advantages over a simple uni-dimensional concept, and it would be reasonable to expect that such a formulation would lead to better understanding and prediction of behaviour. This, however, has not been the experience of the past fifty years of attitude research. What research evidence exists indicates that if there is a relationship between attitudes and overt behaviour, it is the behaviour which influences attitudes and not vice versa. Brehem, for example, presents research evidence showing that when an individual is forced to behave in ways inconsistent with his private feelings, the result is usually a shift in his feelings towards conformity with his behaviour.[14]

The inability of investigators to produce any consistent evidence of how attitudes may influence overt behaviour poses one of the great dilemmas of the behavioural sciences. Responses to the attitude-behaviour discrepancy have been varied, but in the main they fall into two rough categories - that of the theory builders, and that of the methodologists.

The response of the methodologists has been to blame our inability to demonstrate a relationship between attitudes and behaviour on the measuring instruments, and they have concentrated more on the technical and statistical problems of scale construction than on the theoretical problems of what is being measured. The contribution of Thurstone, Likert, Torgenson, Guttman, Edwards, and others to the development of precise, reliable, and standardized procedures for measuring attitudes cannot be overestimated.[15] At the same time, it must be noted that these methodological advances seem to have been achieved at the expense of over-simplification in theoretical treatment. Methodologists have almost invariably constructed scales that yield a single score representing the affective component and no other. This is understandable, as multi-dimensional concepts created by the theorists are often impossible to operationalize for the purposes of scale construction.

The most typical response by the theory builders to the attitude-behaviour dilemma has been to expand the definitions of attitudes still further. In a recent study, Smith, Bruner, and White mention seven dimensions along which attitudes may vary: differentiation, salience, time perspective, informational support, object value, orientation, and policy stand.[16] The difficulty with these formulations is that while a large number of interesting theoretical distinctions are made, procedures for measurement are not provided. The result is a gap between those concerned primarily with the measurement of attitudes and those concerned primarily with the associated theoretical problems.

Another response to the attitude-behaviour discrepancy is to assume that there are different classes of attitudes: for example, "verbal attitudes" and "action attitudes."[17] Another has been to equate attitudes with behaviour, using attitude as a descriptive term summarizing observed consistencies in behaviour. This has been the most common use of the term with respect to judicial attitudes. The best known writings in this field, including Green's study of sentencing, *Judicial Attitudes in Sentencing*, and Schubert's *The Judicial Mind*, all impute mental states in judges from observed behavioural consistencies.[18]

What seems to be a potentially more fruitful approach is the one adopted by Cook and Sellitz, Fishbein, and others.[19] These writers hold that overt behaviour is a function of many variables, of which attitude is only one. Behaviour is seen as a possible consequence of an attitude but not part of an attitude.

Cook and Sellitz identify two classes of variable, other than attitudes, which should be considered in predicting behaviour. They are *other characteristics of the individual,* including his attitudes to other objects present in the situation, his motivational state, and his expressive style, and *other characteristics of the situation* including normative prescriptions as to appropriate behaviour, the expectations of others, and the possible consequences to the individual if he behaves in various ways.[20]

In this study, attitudes are used to predict judicial behaviour. As we shall see, these efforts are to some extent successful. But attitudes and behaviour are not studied in isolation from other variables. In particular, the relationship of judicial attitudes to behaviour is studied in the context of the social constraints perceived by magistrates, which limit or influence otherwise the degree to which attitudes of magistrates find expression in their behaviour. In addition, the attitude-behaviour relationship is studied in the context of the decision-making process in sentencing, incorporating into the analysis an examination of the characteristic ways in which different magistrates use information in coming to decisions, i.e. their "styles" of decision-making. It will be demonstrated that behavioural prediction is significantly improved by including both of these classes of variables.

A Definition of Judicial Attitudes

Definitions are matters of convenience. All the same, they provide a framework around which research can be built. The view was taken in this study that an operational definition of judicial attitudes would be more useful if it stated not only what judicial attitudes are, but also said something about how they originate, and specified the functions they serve for magistrates in sentencing.

The Origin of Judicial Attitudes

The assumption made is that prior to appointment a magistrate forms certain opinions and beliefs concerning the world and his relationship to it. He takes certain stands on family, social, religious, economic, and political issues. He develops certain premises and enduring expectations about the way the world operates, and adopts certain standards that define appropriate and inappropriate behaviour in that world. In doing so, he is exposed to the concepts of crime, punishment, right, wrong, good, bad and other evaluations of the behaviour of others. In accepting or rejecting these concepts he develops certain broad predispositions that serve as potentials for specific judicial attitudes that he will form later.

On appointment to the bench he accepts a specific social role and is exposed to many powerful social norms related to that role. These norms define appropriate and inappropriate behaviour related to the judicial office, and serve two functions as far as group membership is concerned. One is a selective function concerning initial entry and continuing membership in the group, and the other is a socializing function leading to ideological conformity within the group. One would expect magistrates to be selected from a group of persons who would fit the role most comfortably in terms of their own personalities, attitudes, and beliefs.

When he begins to function as a magistrate, the individual is involved in a further socialization process, in which persons around him direct their efforts, both intentionally and unintentionally, toward the task of shaping him to conform to a particular social mould. At the same time, he may feel that some of these pressures are particularly chafing to the integrity of his own individuality, and he may resist the pressures.

In this study magistrates are not viewed as passive agents, absorbing sponge-like the influences in their social environments. They are seen as active agents in the development of beliefs, feelings, values, and standards which define their relationship to their judicial role. In some way a magistrate must fashion for himself an accommodation between individuality and social conformity, between self and the demands of playing a particular social role. The result is seen as a development of a relatively stable and enduring set of judicial attitudes.

An Operational Definition of Judicial Attitudes

In this study, judicial attitudes are defined as follows.

Judicial attitudes in sentencing are a set of evaluative categories, relevant to the judicial role, which the individual magistrate has adopted (or learned) during his past experience with persons, problems, or ideas in his social world. For the individual magistrate, holding an attitude relevant to a given sentencing problem serves the purpose of enabling him to classify the crime, or ideas and events, associated with it as calpable-exculpable, praiseworthy, truthful-erroneous, or in other evaluative terms. The evaluations consist of beliefs about and feelings towards the issues involved, as well as dispositions to respond to them in positive or negative ways.

Before an attitude can be expressed towards a tangible problem in the case before him, a magistrate is engaged in a process of judgement in which the crime, offender, idea, or problem is placed in a framework and assigned to a category. The category belongs to a psychological scale of judgement which the individual magistrate has formed previously for that class of item. It is this scale of judgement which forms the basis of his attitude. Attitudes are thus conceived as information-processing structures, and as such would appear to be relevant to the decision-process in sentencing.

NOTES TO CHAPTER 6

1 G. Allport, "Attitudes," in C. Murchison, ed., *A Handbook of Social Psychology* (Worcester, Mass., 1935), 798.
2 E. Lewis, "Attitudes: Their Nature and Development," *Journal of Genetic Psychology* 21(1939), 367-99.
3 See, for example, Allport, "Attitudes," 180; H. Fishbein, "Attitude and the Prediction of Behaviour," in H. Fishbein, ed., *Readings in Attitude Theory and Measurement* (New York, 1967), 377-483; D. Krech and R. Crutchfield, *Social Psychology* (New York 1948), 152; T. Newcomb, *A Dictionary of the Social Sciences* (London, 1964), 174; and M. Sherif, "Introduction," in C. W. Sherif and M. Sherif, eds., *Attitude, Ego-involvement and Change* (New York, 1967), 1-5.
4 As long ago as 1937 Newcomb stressed the social learning element in the formation of attitudes. See C. Murphy, L. Murphy, and T. Newcomb, *Experimental Social Psychology* (New York, 1937), 1045-6. See also M. Sherif, "Group Influences upon the Formation of Attitudes," in T. Newcomb, ed., *Readings in Social Psychology,* 3rd ed. (New York, 1958), 219-32; E. Hartley, "Attitude Research and the Jingle Fallacy," in *Attitude, Ego-involvement and Change,* 92-5; and M. Fishbein, "Attitude and the Prediction of Behaviour," 49-50.
5 L. Thurstone, "Theory of Attitude Measurement," *Psychological Review,* 36 (1929), 222.
6 W. Thomas and F. Znaniecki, *The Polish Peasant in Europe and America* (New York, 1927).
7 Allport, "Attitudes," 810; see also M. Rosenberg and C. Hovland, "Cognitive, Affective and Behavioral Components of Attitudes," in C. Hovland and M. Rosenberg, eds., *Attitude Organization and Change* (New Haven and London, 1960), 1-15; D. Krech and R. Crutchfield, *Theory and Problems of Social Psychology* (New York, 1948), 5 and 223; and M. Smith, J. Bruner, and R. White, *Opinions and Personality* (New York, 1956), 33.
8 L. Doob, "The Behavior of Attitudes," *Psychological Review* 54 (1947), 135-56.
9 I. Chein, "Behavior Theory and the Behavior of Attitudes," *ibid.,*55 (1948),
10 *Ibid.,* 178.
11 M. Fishbein, "Attitude and the Prediction of Behavior," 388-400.
12 *Ibid.,* 392.
13 See, for example, T. Newcomb, *A Dictionary of the Social Sciences;* M. Fishbein, "Attitude and the Prediction of Behavior"; and M. Sherif, "Introduction."
14 For a review of the attitude-behaviour dilemma, see J. Brehem, "A Dissonance

Analysis of Attitude-Discrepant Behavior," in *Attitude Organization and Change*, 164-97; see also M. DeFleur and F. Westie, "Verbal Attitudes and Overt Acts," *American Sociological Review*, 23 (1958), 667-73; L. Warner, "Verbal Attitudes and Overt Behavior," *Social Forces*, 46 (1967), 106-7; H. Gerard, "Deviation, Conformity and Commitment," in I. D. Steiner and M. Fishbein, eds., *Current Studies in Social Psychology* (New York, 1965), 263-77; and Fishbein, "Attitude and the Prediction of Behavior," 477-92. For one of the few apparently successful attempts to predict behavior from attitude scales see L. Wilkins, *Prediction of the Demand for Campaign Stars and Medals* (London, 1948).

15 L. Thurstone and E. Chave, *The Measurement of Attitudes* (Chicago, 1929); R. Likert, "A Technique for the Measurement of Attitudes," *Archives of Psychology*, 140 (1932); W. Torgenson, *Theory and Methods of Scaling* (New York, 1958); L. Guttman, "The Basis for Scalogram Analysis," in S. Stouffer, ed., *Measurement and Prediction* (Princeton, 1950); and A. Edwards, *Techniques of Attitude Scale Construction* (New York, 1947).

16 Smith, Bruner, and White, *Opinions and Personality*, 33-47.

17 For a discussion of this dichotomy see S. Cook and C. Sellitz, "A Multiple Indicator Approach to Attitude Measurement," *Psychological Bulletin*, 62 (1964), 36-55.

18 E. Green, *Judicial Attitudes in Sentencing* (London, 1961), G. Schubert, *The Judicial Mind* (Chicago, 1965).

19 Cook and Sellitz, *"Attitude Measurement,"* 37-8.

20 *Ibid.*, 38.

7

The Measurement of Judicial Attitudes

A Phenomenological Approach to Scale Construction

Having defined judicial attitudes in sentencing as a set of evaluative categories used by magistrates in assessing crime and determining the appropriate judicial response to it, we now turn to the problem of developing an instrument to measure them. Of all the methods for measuring attitudes, by far the most widely used is the so-called "attitude scale."[1] Attitude scales differ in content, method of construction, scoring, and basis for interpretation, but in the most commonly used methods, their objective is identical, i.e., to assign an individual to a numerical position on a continuum - a number which will indicate, for example, the degree of favourableness or unfavourableness to a particular issue.

A fundamental distinction should be made between scales which are *logically* (theoretically) derived, and those which are *empirically* (phenomenologically) derived. In the former the researcher makes *a priori* theoretical assumptions about the existence of certain attitudes held by the subjects of his investigation. He then proceeds to construct items or questions which appear to him to be psychologically related to the attitude domains postulated by his theory. In doing so, the investigator imposes his own categories, definitions, and meanings on the subjects of his research, by defining in *advance* what attitude domains he wishes to measure, and then selecting an established instrument purporting to measure these domains, or creating a new instrument consisting of items which appear to be psychologically related to the attitudes suggested by his theory.

The degree of success of this approach depends mainly on two assumptions: one, that subjects whose attitudes the researcher wishes to measure do, in fact, hold attitudes related to the measuring instrument used; and two, that the attitudes being measured relate to an issue of some importance to the individual concerned, and are, therefore, likely to find expression in a broad band of thinking about, responding to, and acting towards the object of the attitude.

This approach is appropriate when a researcher is fairly certain of the attitudes of his subjects. Guided by findings of previous research in the same or similar areas, or from personal knowledge of his subjects, he may feel confident that the attitude items used relate to an area of fairly central concern to the subjects in his sample.

The main limitation in this approach lies in the fact that there is no way of testing these assumptions before administering the instrument. Neither the instrument itself, nor the theory underlying it, offers any guidance as to which attitude domains are central to the concerns of the subjects involved. Nor will the investigator get any help from the instrument of his theory in interpreting the results. In these matters, he must be guided inevitably by what prior knowledge he has of his subjects. As a result of such knowledge, he may feel justified in using an established instrument developed in another context, or in creating a new instrument based on certain assumptions which he is prepared to make. But he must accept the fact that these approaches are to some extent artificial in that they are not derived naturally out of the phenomena which he is studying, but rather are forced upon the subjects by the nature of the theoretical assumptions made.

Scales which are empirically or phenomenologically derived are particularly suited to situations in which the investigator feels that the nature of the attitudes held by his subjects are not sufficiently well known to use a logically derived scale, or instrument developed in another context. The phenomenological prospective in attitude research seeks to determine, "without regard to conventional attitudinal categories, exactly what there is for the person, what structures, with what properties and related in what ways."[2]

In this study, the possibility of using an established instrument was explored. Eysenck's Liberalism-Conservatism Scale, Ador-no's Authoritarianism Scale, Gough's Rigidity Scale, Rokeach's Dogmatism Scale, and a number of other instruments were considered.[3] The savings of time, thought, and money in using an established instrument were obvious and tempting. More importantly, the use of a validated instrument for which there are a host of reported studies of previous applications with diverse groups in different regions and cultures, would permit a comparison of the responses of magistrates in Ontario with those found in other studies, and thus provide more freedom to interpret the findings, and greater confidence in the results. Unfortunately, it was not possible to find a validated instrument that met the crucial requirement of dealing directly with what prior knowledge of magistrates led one to conclude were the everyday concerns of magistrates in Ontario in their role of sentencing offenders.

Political liberalism, right-wing authoritarianism, dogmatism and rigidity may be indirectly relevant to the thought processes of magistrates in sentencing, but most of these variables do not seem to deal with the pervasive socio-legal norms which define the judicial role, and are likely to influence the conduct of magistrates on the bench.

Another factor affected the decision not to use an established instrument. Magistrates involved in the planning of the study felt that some magistrates in Ontario would be reluctant to use instruments that did not give the appearance of being germane to the stated purposes of the research.

It was decided to construct an instrument specifically tailored for our purposes. The instrument was to consist of a number of scales, each containing a number of opinion statements with which magistrates would be asked to agree or disagree. By choosing statements to which magistrates had been previously exposed, worded in familiar language, and directly relevant to the judicial task of evaluating and responding to criminal conduct, the objections raised to some of the other instruments were overcome. Moreover, using items which were the magistrates' own, which were meaningful to them, and for which they were likely to have worked out appropriate responses, was thought to give a more valid picture of the salient attitudes held.

A phenomenological approach seems to avoid some of the pitfalls of traditional methods of scale construction. In particular, it assists the researcher to place himself within the "framework of meaning" of his subjects.

This is not to say that there are no difficulties or limitations with the technique. In the first place, two assumptions are still made. The procedure assumes that the subjects concerned do have attitudes and that they are relatively stable and measurable. There are also special problems of measurement. In particular, the technique usually requires careful pilot work. Since scales derived from this procedure are new, there are additional requirements for demonstrating their reliability and validity. In the end, the procedure requires a great deal more work. It is not put forward as a superior method for all purposes. In this research it was deemed a better method for mapping the evaluative categories employed by magistrates in assessing crime and imposing punishment.

Selecting Attitude Statements

A phenomenological approach demands that statements used to construct scales be in their natural form, common to the experience of the subject concerned. Ideally, the items should be selected from the evaluative statements actually used by the individuals involved, or from those that have been made by well-known persons in their environment.

This approach differs in some respects from traditional methods of scale construction. It is usually considered desirable to avoid the use of statements to which individuals are likely to link socially acceptable responses in their reference groups. It is said that in such circumstances, responses are not likely to be "true" responses but rather altered in the direction of conformity to group norms. It is, therefore, common to create items for which there are no socially acceptable responses.

The position taken in this study is that the very essence of a social attitude is the individual's placement of self in relation to group standards. Instead of viewing the process of conformity to normative standards as a problem, this study attempts to focus on how magistrates define their own attitudes in relation to those of their reference groups. To do otherwise would mean restricting the area of enquiry to topics of little contemporary significance in sentencing, or to frame questions in obscure language, and thereby confuse magistrates as to the true meaning of the questions concerned. In any event, the attempt to isolate magistrates from their reference groups in responding to a questionnaire is likely to fail. In every situation that could be imagined, it was difficult to see how it would be possible to isolate magistrates from the presence (at least symbolically) of the researcher, and more importantly, that of other people who are significant to them.

Despite paying lip service to the dangers of "response set" arising out of the fact that there are socially desirable and undesirable responses to most attitude items, investigators using attitude scales usually produce questionnaires consisting of items that are very clearly linked to socially approved responses. The F-Scale in the California Personality Inventory and Eysenck's Liberalism-Conservatism Scale, to give but two examples, exude social desirability.[4]

The selection of statements to be considered for inclusion in scales was made in the light of several criteria.

1 The items should require an evaluation and not just a statement of factor belief.
2 The items should relate to a topic about which magistrates have more or less crystallized views.
3 The topic should be one of continuing contemporary interest in sentencing, about which there has been considerable discussion among magistrates, so that magistrates will be aware of the stands of others.
4 The area should be a controversial one, in which there is substantial division of opinion.
5 The items should not encourage easy acquiescence but should require some thought on the part of magistrates before answering them.
6 Items should be interesting and related to issues of some social significance in and for themselves.
7 There should be a sufficient number of items dealing with each subject, so that the whole range of positions on each issue is covered.

The main source from which items were collected were reported cases in which magistrates themselves stated the sentencing principles followed in dealing with cases. Articles written by magistrates and reports of magistrates' study groups were other important sources. The decisions of appeal courts, the writings of legal scholars and the published reports of speeches related to crime and punishment made by judges, magistrates and others, were sources from which further items were collected. A few items were selected from established instruments. The F-Scale in the California Scale contains a few dealing directly with crime and punishment, and it was decided to include these.

In all, some two hundred evaluative statements dealing with crime, punishment, and related issues were collected. These two hundred statements formed an "item pool," out of which the original scales were constructed.

Editing Attitude Statements

As a first step, each item was examined as to wording. Items that were obviously ambiguous or too complex, in the sense of containing more than one thought, were excluded on inspection. Also rejected were items which were redundant, in the sense of clearly duplicating the thought of another item which was expressed in clearer language. As a result of a preliminary inspection, it was possible to reject approximately forty items.

The next step was to ensure that each item selected would mean the same thing to different people, and that they were as free as possible from being occupationally or vocationally linked, in the sense of requiring specialized factual knowledge on the part of respondents.

An instrument containing one-hundred-and-sixty items was administered to a group of middle-class persons occupying one multiple housing development in a suburb of Toronto. They were asked to query any item they did not understand. As a result of this procedure, a few additional items were discarded and changes were made in the wording of others. The results of these preliminary steps was the selection of an item pool consisting of one-hundred-and-forty-three statements.

Initial Assignment to Scales and the Development of Quasi-Scales

There are a number of methods for developing scales from an item pool. The purpose of each is the same, i.e., to assign to each scale the smallest number of items which can represent the whole range of positions taken with respect to the issue posed.

It was decided to develop two sets of attitude scales, one derived from Item Analysis and another from Factor Analysis.[5] In neither procedure is it necessary to determine *in advance* which items go together to form scales. Even if the manifest content of an item does not appear to relate directly to the object in question, it can, by virtue of the statistical techniques employed, be shown to belong to a group of items and thus be included in the final scale.

Scales derived from item-analysis are often called Likert scales, but a distinction must be made between Likert methods of scoring (described above) and Likert methods of scale construction (described immediately below).

The first step in constructing Likert scales is to sort the individual items into rough categories in terms of similarity of content. The next step is to carry out an "item analysis," to decide which are the best statements for each scale. This is usually done by calculating correlation coefficients for each item with the total score on the scale, and retaining those items with the highest correlations. In the Likert method there is no necessity for an item to have very clear relationship to the attitude being measured, as it can, by virtue of its correlation with the total score, be shown to belong with the others.

Method of Scoring

It was decided to use the method of scoring associated with the name Likert.[6] In the Likert procedure, subjects indicate different levels of agreement or disagreement (usually five) with each statement ranging from "strongly agree" to "strongly disagree." These five positions are given in simple weights of five, four, three, two, and one for scoring purposes. Items that are reversed, i.e. worded in a negative direction, receive reverse scoring. The direction of scoring is indicated by the name of the scale; thus a high score on a "punishment" scale indicates agreement with pro-punishment items, and disagreement with anti-punishment items. A total score is calculated for each individual representing his position on the scale.

The questionnaire used contained the following instuctions.

Instructions. This questionnaire is designed to obtain your confidential opinions on various issues related to the sentencing of offenders. They were collected from statements made by judges and magistrates in Canada, the United States, and England, and from other sources. They cover many different and opposing points of view and were chosen in such a way that most people are likely to agree with some and disagree with others. There is no best answer to these questions, except that of *your* completely frank personal opinion. Please record your completely confidential opinion regarding each statement, using the following system of marking: ++ if you strongly agree with the statement: + if you agree on the whole but not strongly; 0 if you cannot decide for or against, or if you think the question is worded in such a way that you cannot give an answer; - if you disagree on the whole but not strongly; -- if you strongly disagree.

Please work as quickly as you can, giving your initial impression of the statement listed.

While the procedure has certain disadvantages, it is more reliable than most other methods, and because of its simplicity it has become one of the most popular methods of scale construction.

The most serious criticism levelled against this type of scale is its lack of reproducibility (in the statistical sense).[7] This means that the same score may be obtained in many different ways. For example, the score of a given individual who falls in the middle point of the scoring range can be achieved in two quite different ways; by taking a neutral position on most or all of the items, or by taking a strongly favourable position on some items and a strongly unfavourable position on others. If this latter response is common, it suggests that the scale is measuring two different things, and this should be revealed by item-analysis. On the other hand, an individual may receive a neutral score because the object of the attitude has no meaning for him. The "phenomeno-logical" approach to the initial selection of items for possible in-clusion in scales should guard against this problem.

As a first step in the construction of Likert scales, each of the one-hundred-and-forty-three statements was examined as to con-tent. This writer, his research assistant, and two outside experts in attitude research placed each item into one of several piles ac-cording to the "face" or manifest content of the item. Each pile was to consist of items that were roughly associated with the same concept or idea. Instructions were given not to be overly rigorous in the assignment to piles as item-analysis would later determine whether the item properly belongs in that group.

Where there was disagreement concerning the placement of a particular item, the criterion used for the resolution of the prob-lem was to include the item if two out of four judges believed it belonged in a particular category. On this basis, it was possible to assign all but seven items to specific categories.

By examining the content of items in each category, it was pos-sible to label the four main groups tentatively as "punishment" (forty-five items), "treatment orientation" (thirty-six items), "be-lief in deterrence" (twenty-six items), and "tolerance of deviance" (nineteen items). In addition, there was a miscellaneous or un-classified group (seventeen items). The result of this preliminary sorting was the creation of a set of "quasi-scales" which would be subjected to item analysis, tests of reliability, and tests of valid-ity in an effort to develop true scales.

Item-Analysis

Item-analysis is a term used to describe a number of different techniques for examining the relationship of the score given to an individual item to the scores given to the rest of the items on the scale to which the item belongs.[8] For example, if an individual gave a higher than average score to a particular item, he should also have a higher than average over-all score on the scale to which that item belongs. If the scores given to a particular item bear no relationship to the scores given to remaining items on the scale, then the particular item can be said to be "bad," and should be rejected. Item analysis not only reduces scales to manageable size, but also improves their internal consistency.

The five quasi-scales went through a number of item-analysis procedures, each one presenting more difficult demands on these scales than the previous one.

Pilot No. 1

The first item-analysis procedure used was the least rigorous and the least demanding. At this stage, the "known groups" method of item-analysis was used. Items (i.e., statements) were shuffled in random order and placed in a questionnaire.

The next step was the selection of two populations of people who were thought to be far apart in their attitudes to crime and punishment, so that it would be possible to determine which of the items distinguished the two groups. A population of twenty social work students and twenty-five middle-ranking police officers in Metropolitan Toronto was selected. It could be expected that police officers, as compared to social work students, should score items in a pro-punishment, pro-deterrence, anti-treatment, and anti-tolerance direction. The questionnaire was administered and the responses to each item were examined. A record was kept of the number of "errors" in responses to each item. An "error" was defined as a response to an item that was contrary to expectation, i.e., in the opposite direction expected, by reason of the fact that the individual was either a social worker or a police officer. Items were rejected if twenty-five per cent or more of the responses were contrary to expectation.

Only ten items failed to meet the criterion. On examination, it seemed that these items were badly worded, in the sense of being unclear as to meaning, and they were, therefore, dropped.

The responses to the largest quasi-scale, the punishment scale, are reproduced in Figure 2. It can be seen that social work students and police officers occupy opposite positions with respect to the punishment of crime, only one social work student (the most punitive), and one police officer (the least punitive), coming close in their scale scores.

The responses to the deterrence and tolerance of deviance

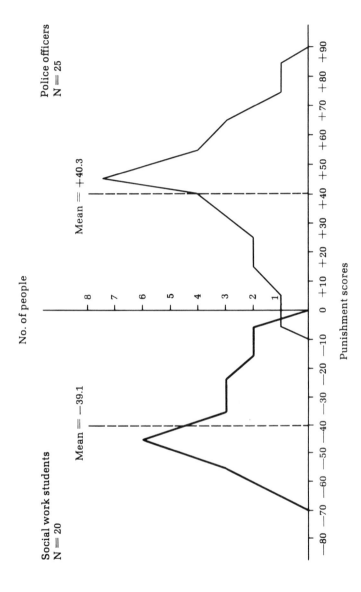

Figure 2 Distribution of punishment scores of social work students and police officers

scales followed a similar pattern. The differences in the mean scores for the two population groups on each of these scales were significant at greater than 0.001.

It was difficult to get a consistent pattern of responses to items assigned to the treatment scale. On examination of responses to these items, it was apparent that the scale, in its original form, tended to measure several different things. The scale was divided into a series of sub-scales, and a further examination was made of the pattern of response. This time a better level of internal consistency was achieved, although some of the minor scales seemed to be comprised of too few items to form true scales. The sub-scales were tentatively labelled "corporal punishment," "capital punishment," "confidence in probation," "confidence in correctional institutions," "alcoholism," and "attitude towards science." There was still a residual group of items (twenty-three) which seemed to deal more generally with the concept of treatment and for the time being it was labelled, "treatment-orientation."

At this stage all that could be safely stated was that it appeared that the analyses were on the right track. The main scales seemed to measure something which clearly distinguished between these two population groups. However, since it could be expected that these groups held diametrically opposing attitudes to the issues posed, it was not possible to draw very firm conclusions about the sensitivity of the instrument to measure subtle differences among people. Further tests on different population groups were to follow.

One significant fact did emerge at this stage. Some police officers appeared to have attitudes that were so extreme in the pro-punishment direction that it was almost impossible to gauge their attitudes accurately. Even to the most extreme statements, such as, "It is right and proper that criminals should be hated," some police officers responded with, "strongly agree."

This suggests a number of things. First, even in a society which discourages expressions of extreme punitivism, some police officers are willing to reveal their own extreme positions. Second, a punishment scale derived from statements made by judges and magistrates may not provide an opportunity for individuals occupying more extreme positions with respect to the punishment of crime to express the extent of their feelings. Finally, even though the numbers within each of the two population groups were small, it appeared that the distribution of the responses were roughly normal with a slight skew in each case towards the mid-range of the scale. Further testing of larger samples in different population groups tended to confirm these early impressions.

Pilot No. 2

The next step was to determine whether the scales would distinguish among people whose attitudes were much closer than the two population groups already tested. As part of a course in research methods given by the Department of Sociology at the University of Toronto, a class of third-year sociology students undertook a project to test the hypothesis: "There are no statistically significant differences in the attitudes to crime and punishment held by students at the University of Toronto enrolled in Arts and Engineering Courses." A stratified random sample was obtained of first-year sociology and philosophy students, fourth-year students in subjects emanating from sociology and philosophy (i.e. anthropology, sociology, psychology, political science, economics), first-year engineering students, and fourth-year engineering students. The total sample of two hundred represented about seventeen per cent of the student population from which it was drawn.

An instrument consisting of items drawn from the punishment and tolerance scales was administered to these students. In Table 28 the mean scores of students by year and faculty are presented.

Positive scores are in the non-punitive direction of the punishment scale and in the pro-tolerance direction on the tolerance scale. Differences in the mean scores of the two groups were tested for statistical significance by use of the *t*-test. The results indicate that arts students are considerably less punitive than engineering students. This holds true for both first- and fourth-year classes (the *t*-values were significant in both instances at better than 0.001).

At the same time, arts students were somewhat more tolerant than their counterparts in engineering (but the *t*-values were significant at only 0.05). It also appears that fourth-year arts students are less punitive and more tolerant than their colleagues in the first year (*t*-values significant at 0.05), while no statistically significant differences in attitudes appeared to exist between first- and fourth-year engineers. In fact, fourth-year engineers have slightly lower tolerance scores than those in the first year (although the differences were not large enough to be statistically significant). These results are in accordance with the findings published in *Anti-Democratic Attitudes in American Schools.* A number of studies were reported in which scales measuring "authoritarianism" and "prejudice," followed a low-high continuum among students on various US campuses, from social science through theoretical-natural science and applied science to military, physical education, and finally to engineering.

While these findings were encouraging, in the sense of providing some early evidence of validity, the main interest at this stage was to use the responses of students for the purposes of further item-analysis.

TABLE 28

Anti-punishment and tolerance scores of students by faculty and year

Course	Number	Mean	Standard deviation
Anti-punishment			
First-year soc. and phil.	46	8.11	13.48
Fourth-year soc. and phil.	25	14.56	15.12
First-year engineering	78	2.44	12.07
Fourth-year engineering	50	5.00	13.52
Tolerance			
First-year soc. and phil.	46	12.13	8.55
Fourth-year soc. and phil.	25	15.31	7.38
First-year engineering	78	10.15	8.74
Fourth-year engineering	50	9.62	8.03

A more rigorous item-analysis procedure was used at this stage. For each scale, in turn, students were ranked from high to low depending upon this score. The top one-quarter and the bottom one-quarter were selected as criterion groups, providing fifty cases in each group. The responses of the two criterion groups to each item were examined and counts were made of the number of "non-conforming" responses to each item. A response was non-conforming for an individual in the high group if that response was lower than the mean score for the total population. The reverse was true for the low group.

As a result, eleven items from the punishment scale and eight items from the tolerance scale were rejected. The instrument now consisted of one-hundred-and-thirty-four items divided into four main scales and four subsidiary scales.

Pilot No. 3

The procedure outlined immediately above was repeated on an-other sample of persons, this time consisting of twenty-five police officers, twenty-five law students, twenty-three probation officers, and twenty-five social work students. This time, all four main scales were subjected to item-analysis. As a result, twelve items from the treatment scale, seven from the deterrence scale, four from the tolerance scale, and four from the punishment scale were rejected. It was decided to abandon the scientific-method sub-scale as it had too few items for meaningful analysis.

A new instrument was drawn consisting of one-hundred-and-seven items divided into four main scales and four sub-scales. The items for each scale are listed in Technical Appendix 2.

The Main Study

The procedures used so far were rather crude. They were designed to sort out a few obviously offending items from a large group of items assigned to each scale. They also served the purpose of providing some assurance that the scales that were beginning to emerge had validity in the sense of being able to distinguish among different populations of people. The next stage was to process the remaining items through a more rigorous item-analysis procedure.

A new sample was drawn, consisting of one-hundred-and-six-teen probation officers divided into two groups (those with degrees and those without), one-hundred-and-three police officers, seventy-three magistrates, fifty law students, and fifty-nine social work students.

The one-hundred-and-seven item questionnaire was administered to these groups. When the questionnaires were returned and the scores tabulated and placed on computer cards, a series of item-analysis procedures were adopted. In this procedure, a score was obtained for each item together with a score for the sum of the remaining items on the scale to which the particular item belonged. These two scores were correlated. A high "item-total" correlation indicates that responses to the item are in accordance with the responses to the remaining items on the scale. Items on each scale were ranked in order of the size of the correlation coefficients from highest to lowest. Items with the lowest correlations were dropped.

A rule of thumb was used discarding items; namely, at any one time, no more than one in ten items on a scale could be discarded. This means that on a thirty-item scale, it was possible to discard up to three items at a time. This procedure was repeated until the size of each scale was reduced to approximately twenty items. A lower limit of twelve items was set for the major scales.

To guard against reducing scales to the extent that they no longer had validity, analyses were done at the end of each item-analysis procedure to determine the ability of the scale to discriminate among the different groups tested. The reliability of the instrument was also tested at the end of each procedure. The results of these analyses are discussed in the next section.

As a result of these procedures, ten items were dropped from the punishment scale, six from the treatment scale, seven from the tolerance scale, and one from the deterrence scale. The subscales were left intact, as any further reduction in numbers would not have been possible because of the small number of items.

This ended the item-analysis procedures. An original item pool of approximately two hundred was reduced to sixty-three items, each one assigned to one of four main scales. These scales are reproduced in Technical Appendix 2.

Reliability of Likert Scales

The reliability of a test usually refers to its internal consistency.[10] A test is internally consistent if the scores derived from it can be repeatedly obtained from the same or from a similar population of respondents. Reliability is a minimum requirement of a test and it is the one most frequently reported.

Variation obtained in the scores obtained from a test may be the result of two factors - "true variance" and "error variance." True variance represents real differences in response to a test on the part of the subjects tested. Error variance is due to fallibility in the test itself. All tests are subject to some error. Error may occur because of lack of clarity in the wording of the questions, differences in motivation, fatigue and boredom on the part of respondents, and inaccuracies in the recording and coding of responses.

Various formulae have been derived to measure the extent of error, i.e. the reliability of a test. Since it is usually not practical to repeat a test on the same population, most of these formulae are based on deriving two sets of scores from the same test for the purpose of testing the correlation of the test "with itself." This is usually done by splitting the questionnaire into two equivalent halves, and comparing the results.

At the end of each item-analysis procedure, each Likert scale was randomly divided into two halves (in the case of scales consisting of an odd number of items, into approximate halves). The reliability formula applied was the one based on analysis of variance approach developed by Hoyt.[11] This is usually considered to be the safest formula to use as it can be shown that it tends, if anything, to underestimate the true reliability of a test.

No hard and fast rules exist as to the minimum reliability required of a test. It is generally accepted, however, that tests used for research purposes should have reliability coefficients of 0.5 or better (although in some cases, coefficients may be as low as 0.3 without invalidating the test). Tests used for diagnostic work on individuals about whom decisions will be made should have reliability coefficients approaching 0.9.[12] The reliability coefficients of the main Likert scales are presented in Table 29. Since the item-analysis procedures used drastically reduced the number of items in each scale, it was decided to check for reliability after each item-analysis procedure. The scales are labelled Likert 1, Likert 2, and Likert 3, indicating their stage of development.

TABLE 29

Split-half reliability tests on Likert scales (using Hoyt's formula: $2\left[1 - \frac{(Sa^2 + Sb^2)}{St^2}\right]$

Scales	Likert 1	Likert 2	Likert 3
Deterrence	0.839	0.870	0.868
Punishment	0.940	0.940	0.937
Treatment	0.908	0.905	0.906
Tolerance	0.807	0.779	0.803

In their finished form, the major Likert scales have reliability coefficients (calculated by the most conservative formula) well in excess of the minimum requirements for research purposes, and in most instances approach the requirements of tests used for individual diagnostic work. It is interesting to note that there did not appear to be a significant drop in the reliability of these scales as they were reduced in size through item-analysis. This suggests that item-analysis tended to reject not only items unrelated to the other items on the scale, but also items which were, of themselves, unreliable.

Validity of Likert Scales

The term, "validity" has been used to mean a number of different things, but it most commonly refers to whether the test actually measures "what it purports to measure."[13] Reliability is necessary for validity but does not guarantee it. A test may yield consistent results in similar situations, and yet leave the investigator in doubt as to what those results mean.

Often the investigator is satisfied with face validity, i.e., validity based on the fact that the test "looks" valid. The Likert scales developed in this study seem valid, in the sense that each consists of items all of which appear to measure the same aspect of the attitude concerned. But many writers have demonstrated that one can have little confidence in face validity.[14]

There is no direct way to validate a test. Evidence of validity can only be obtained by demonstrating the relationship of a test with an outside criterion. As J. P. Guilford states, "the key to successful validation is a good criterion measure."[15] Criteria that are often used include: correlations with more established tests, the capacity of the test to discriminate among different population groups, and, best of all, the capacity of the test to predict actual behaviour. It is the latter two criteria that were used in this study.

We have already seen that the Likert scales discriminated between social work students and police officers, and among students by faculty and year. We will now look at the ability of these scales to discriminate among a more diverse group of people.

Five criterion groups were selected for whom data were already available. They consisted of seventy-three magistrates, one-hundred-and-three police officers, one-hundred-and-sixteen probation officers, fifty-nine social work students, and fifty law students. For each scale the mean and the standard deviation for each criterion group were calculated. Considerable variation in means scores were revealed. Tests of significance (in this case the F-test) were calculated to see whether the observed differences in mean scores could have occurred by chance. On a total population of 401 people, divided into five groups, an F-value of 4.32 is needed to indicate significance at 0.001.

In Table 30 the mean and standard deviations for each criterion group, together with the value of F, are presented. Similar data with respect to the sub-scales and earlier versions of the major scales are presented in Technical Appendix 2.

In all cases, F-values vastly exceed that required to indicate significance at 0.001. For the major scales, the actual values range from a low of 59.8 for the deterrence scale, to a high of 136.8 for the treatment scale. Even the sub-scales discriminate among these groups to a high degree. F-values range from a low of 12.6 for the confidence in correctional institutions sub-scale, to a high of 81.9 for the confidence in probation sub-scale. With values as high as these, any discussion about which of the scales discriminates best becomes meaningless.

TABLE 30

Likert scales: means, standard deviations and F-ratios for criterion groups

| | | | | | Social | |
| | | Police | Magis- | Probation Law | work | |
Scale		officers	trates	officers	students students	F-ratio
Deterrence	Mean	37.99	36.28	28.55	28.50	24.59	
	S.D.	6.39	6.26	7.28	6.99	4.79	59.83
Corporal	Mean	17.42	13.64	12.11	10.06	8.49	
punishment	S.D.	2.24	3.62	3.84	4.03	2.94	82.65
Capital	Mean	13.40	11.87	8.64	8.74	6.39	
punishment	S.D.	1.97	2.53	3.82	3.95	2.92	64.50
Punishment	Mean	94.18	77.51	63.65	63.18	56.14	
	S.D.	15.57	13.69	14.17	15.69	12.43	94.74
Treatment	Mean	52.56	64.54	74.67	71.40	81.56	
	S.D.	10.09	8.94	7.93	9.70	6.09	136.82
Confidence in	Mean	9.91	9.53	8.74	8.04	8.00	
correctional	S.D.	2.10	2.10	1.98	2.20	2.02	12.63
institutions							
Tolerance	Mean	27.94	32.34	36.12	39.86	40.34	
	S.D.	5.77	5.36	5.57	6.15	4.97	67.78
Confidence in	Mean	12.64	17.75	20.21	16.98	20.07	
probation	S.D.	3.97	3.46	3.11	3.11	2.54	81.95

Population groups

The substantive content of the findings are of some interest. On each scale, police officers and social work students are at opposite ends of the continuum. Moreover, these two groups are clearly separated from the rest of the groups studied. On each scale, the mean scores for magistrates are closer to those of police officers than to those of any other group. This does not mean that

most magistrates are "policeminded." Mean scores tend to obscure individual differences. Some magistrates appear to be more
punitive than some police officers, while at the same time others
appear less punitive than some probation officers.

It is also interesting to note that probation officers, who are
ostensibly in the business of treatment, do not appear to have significantly higher treatment scores or significantly lower punishment scores than, for example, law students. (The significance of
the differences in the mean scores for these two groups in each
case was not significant at 0.05.) Law students appear to have
higher tolerance of deviance and tolerance of alcohol scores than
probation officers (the differences are significant at 0.01). At the
same time probation officers seem to have higher corporal punishment scores than law students (the difference is significant at
0.05). This suggests that a "punitive syndrome," consisting of high
deterrence, punishment, and corporal punishment scores, and
low treatment and tolerance scores, is to some extent evident in
all persons who deal with offenders in the administration of
criminal justice, even in a treatment role. Probation officers must
make some accommodation to the goals of the penal system as a
whole. They appear less punitive in their attitudes than police officers and magistrates, but only to a degree. This may be due
more to their age differences (being approximately 4 and 7 years
younger on average than police officers and magistrates respectively), than to their different occupational role and background.

Weaknesses in Likert Scales

A disturbing possibility becomes apparent at this stage. In
developing scales through Likert procedures, it was assumed that
they measure different things. While one would not expect that
the scales would be entirely independent of one another, there
was little reason to believe that they would be equivalent forms
of the same test. However, the striking similarity in the way in
which the mean scores for each criterion group are ordered from
police officers at one end, through to social work students at the
other, indicates the possibility of high intercorrelations among
the scales. In order to explore this possibility, scores on each
scale were correlated with scores on the others. The results are
presented in Table 31.

Correlations between the main scales range from a low of 0.632
between treatment and tolerance, to a high of -0.847 between
treatment and punishment. This means that between one-third

and two-thirds of the variance in scores on these scales is "common variance." The common variance is so large that it indicates that the main Likert scales are not independent of one another, but rather are different ways of representing one underlying attitude.

TABLE 31

Intercorrelations between Likert scales

	Deterrence	Tolerance	Treatment
Punishment	0.798	-0.748	-0.847
Treatment	-0.712	0.632	
Tolerance	-0.666		

A fundamental weakness in Likert scales is thus revealed. The procedure provides no criteria for knowing whether the items originally assigned to various scales are truly independent of one another. While it appears that through item-analysis it was possible to develop reliable and valid scales, at least in terms of agreed criteria, at the same time it seems that instead of having four different scales, we end up with one scale in four broadly equivalent forms.

It may be that there is only one underlying dimension to the attitudes people have to crime and punishment. On the other hand, it is not possible to determine whether this is so on the basis of the analysis used so far. This is a situation which calls for factor analysis, and the next section will deal with the development of scales derived from factor analysis, showing that there are, in fact, a number of "independent" dimensions to the attitudes to crime and punishment which people hold.

The Development of Scales through Factor Analysis

The internal consistency methods of item-analysis provide some safeguard against the inclusion of unrelated items in a Likert scale, but a superior technique for ensuring uni-dimensionality is through the use of factor analysis. This is a statistical technique which frees the researcher from making assumptions about which items "hang together" to form scales. It permits the development of scales strictly out of the responses to the data.

Factor analysis is based on correlating the responses to all items with each other, and then extracting one or more "factors" the items, or at least most of them, have in common.[16] The use of factor analysis can show that a seemingly unified attitude dimension developed through a Likert procedure in fact "breaks up" into several independent dimensions. Eysenck has shown, for example, that political orientation does not consist of a left-wing-right-wing dimension, but rather of two independent dimensions.[17]

Factor analysis is widely used in psychological testing, and while it has its critics, it is generally considered advantageous to use this technique in new areas where the content and structure of attitudes are relatively unknown.[18] It can show, for example, that attitudes and opinions on a wide variety of issues that appear to be divergent have a common attitude structure.

One way to describe factor analysis in non-mathematical terms is to picture the responses to an attitude questionnaire as being scattered in some defined space, such as a balloon. If the balloon is pencil-shaped, it can be said that one main dimension (its length), and perhaps one smaller dimension (its width), describe its main structure. Factor analysis would draw hypothetical lines through the centre of these main dimensions and would calculate the relative importance of each. But the balloon may be perfectly round. In such a case, no factor would be extracted, and it would be said that there is no one dimension underlying the responses to the questionnaire. If the balloon should happen to be a "mickey-mouse" shaped balloon, the factor structure would be more complex, and it would be described in a number of different dimensions. The importance of a dimension (its length in the analogy given) is usually expressed in terms of the proportion of the variance in the responses to the data "accounted for" by that dimension. There are no hard and fast rules concerning the amount of variation that must be explained before a factor can be considered "significant," but it is commonly accepted that it would be dangerous to interpret factors which account for much less than five per cent of the total variance in responses to the original items.

Factor analysis is a way of getting an over-view of a large number of correlation coefficients, to see if the common variance which they express, which has been measured only in terms of variables taken two-by-two, can be described in broader terms. The analysis starts with a correlation matrix in which each variable is correlated against every other variable. It extracts the number of dimensions (factors) which underlie the relationship between the variables. By calculating the correlation of an item with the factor (i.e. the "item loading"), it is possible to select a scale consisting of items with the highest loadings on a particular factor. If the analysis extracts, for example, three basic dimensions underlying the responses to an attitude questionnaire, it would be possible to develop three separate attitude scales, consisting of a dozen or more items with the highest factor loadings on each dimension. The statistical technique ensures that these dimensions are independent of one another.

There are a number of factor analysis methods, each of which has certain advantages and disadvantages, and it is a matter of judgement concerning which is the most appropriate to use in a particular situation. The methods of Hotelling and Kelly are considered to be rigorous mathematically and can be used objectively in the sense of requiring relatively few assumptions concerning the nature of the data.[19] This technique is sometimes called Principal Component Analysis or Principal Factor Analysis.[20]

Construction of Factor Scales

One of the limitations to factorally derived scales is that they tend to be unstable, i.e., the scales derived tend to differ depending on the population from which they were drawn. To guard against this, it was decided to construct scales out of the responses to the questionnaire of all population groups tested, i.e. police officers, probation officers, magistrates, social work students, and law students. While scales derived from a diverse group of people are likely to have less predictive value, in the sense of predicting magistrates' behaviour, they are more likely to represent widely-held attitudes to crime and punishment.

It was also decided to factor analyse the pool of one-hundred-and-seven items, including items that were rejected by some of the later item-analysis procedures used in the development of Likert scales. This was done because these item-analysis procedures may have excluded a category of items that, of themselves, formed an independent dimension to the attitudinal structure of the population groups tested.

Extraction of Principal Factors

The statistical program extracted the main factor, i.e., the factor which expressed more variance than any other, first . It then extracted a second factor (controlling for the first), which accounted for as much as possible of the outstanding variance (i.e., the remaining unexplained variance). The procedure was repeated until no additional factor could be extracted. The computer was given a "stop" instruction which automatically terminated the extraction of factors when less than five per cent of the remaining unexplained variance was "mopped up" by a further factor.

Five factors were thus extracted. The first factor accounted for forty-two per cent of the total variance. In other words, almost half of the variation in the responses to the attitude questionnaire could be explained in terms of one factor. The program went on to extract four further factors, but between them these factors accounted for less than seventeen per cent of the remaining variance. They must be considered to be minor factors. In all, nearly sixty per cent of the total variance could be explained in terms of five factors. Table 32 contains the exact amount of variation explained by each factor.

It appears that attitudes to crime and punishment among the groups tested are structured around a principal dimension (component), with four smaller dimensions running in other directions. What we seem to have is a structure approximating a somewhat irregularly shaped, but pencil-like, balloon.

Calculation of Factor Loadings

The next stage was the calculation of correlations of individual items with the factors extracted. These correlations are expressed in terms of "loadings." A high loading indicates that the item is closely associated with the factor. In terms of the analogy used, these items can be pictured as being placed close to either end of the dimension or line drawn through the data in the balloon. By examining the item with high loadings, it is possible to interpret the factor.

Interpreting factors is always something of a problem. It often happens that a particular item has a high loading on more than one factor. It may also happen that two factors look alike, although the statistical technique ensures their independence. In the end, it is a matter of judgement, based on the over-all impression given by loading as on all the items, which determines the label given to a particular factor.

In Table 32, loadings of the twelve "best" items are presented in order of the magnitude of their loadings on Factor 1. Technical Appendix 2 contains the loadings of the remaining items on this factor, together with the loadings of items on each of the other four factors.

TABLE 32

Factor analysis - unrotated factor loadings: factor 1

Item	Loading
Capital punishment should be retained for certain types of murder	1.070
Capital punishment is a deterrent to murder	1.066
Crimes such as indecent assault on children should be punished severely	1.061
For certain crimes, corporal punishment should be imposed	1.016
Prisons should be places of punishment	1.024
Capital punishment should be abolished completely	-1.007
The most important single consideration in determining the sentence to impose should be the nature and gravity of the offence	0.991
The strap should be used more often with young offenders	0.974
The failure to punish crime amounts to giving a licence to commit it	0.945
Crime creates an imbalance in the social order that can only be put right by an appropriate punishment	0.933
Criminals are being mollycoddled by the correctional agencies	0.928
Criminals should be punished for their crimes whether or not the punishment benefits the criminal	0.877

The first unrotated factor was not difficult to interpret. Clearly it measures the degree to which an individual wishes to see offenders punished severely. The high loadings on the corporal and capital punishment items, together with high loadings on items related to a desire that prisons should be places of punishment rather than of treatment, are fairly clear indications of what this factor represents.

The other factors were not so easy to interpret. While there were noticeable differences in the items with high loadings on different factors, it was apparent that many items had high loadings on more than one. It was difficult to find items with high loadings on Factors 3, 4, or 5 that did not have high loadings on Factor 1 as well. This is not surprising in view of the fact that Factor 1 accounted for over seventy per cent of the explained variance. The problem of making psychologically meaningful distinctions between factors is a common one and it is usually handled by means of rotation.

Rotation of Factors

Rotation is a way of moving the main axes (dimensions) through the data so that individual items will be located closer to one of the dimensions and further from others. In terms of the analogy used, rotation can be likened to walking around and over and under the balloon, in order to select new viewpoints which will show the configuration of individual items with special clarity.

A number of different rotation techniques are available. In this study one of the "orthogonal" types was used.[21] In this type of rotation the axes (dimensions) remain at right angles to each other. This preserves the independence of each factor from the others.

It should also be stated that rotation does not increase the total amount of variance explained by the factors. All it does is redistribute the relative proportions of variance explained by each. In this way certain minor factors extracted in the original analysis can assume greater significance. The main purpose, however, is to display the configuration of scores in a way which provides the most meaningful perspective over the whole domain.

TABLE 33

Variance accounted for by principle component factors

	Factors					
	1	2	3	4	5	Total
Unrotated factors						
Per cent total variance	42.259	5.447	4.686	3.730	2.881	59.004
Per cent explained variance	7.62	9.23	7.94	6.32	4.88	100.000
Rotated factors						
Per cent total variance	19.934	12.23	15.984	6.297	4.576	59.004
Per cent explained variance	33.78	20.69	27.08	10.67	7.75	100.000

The proportion of variance explained by the rotated factors is presented in Table 33. Rotation succeeded in distributing the amount of explained variance more equally among the factors. More importantly, it led to a clearer resolution of the problem of interpretation. Each factor was represented by a number of distinctive items with high factor loadings on one scale only. It was now possible to make psychologically meaningful distinctions among the scales derived.

Labelling of Factors

In Tables 34 to 39, each factor is represented by the fifteen best items (i.e., items with the highest factor loadings on them).

Factor 1 is labelled "justice." It seems to relate to the concept of "just deserts." The items are offence-oriented rather than offender-oriented. There is no indication that these items are related to hatred of offenders, or desire for vengeance, but rather to a concern that crime be punished in proportion to its severity. The concept of justice is very closely associated with the notion of fairness. A magistrate concerned with justice would not only ensure that the punishment is severe enough, bearing in mind the seriousness of the offence, but also that it must not exceed the limit that is appropriate to the offence.

Factor 2 is labelled "punishment corrects." This factor is associated with the notion that offenders deserve and need punishment, in order to prevent them from committing further crime. It represents a desire to stop crime at almost any cost to the offender including in some instances capital punishment. Thus, items with high loadings include: belief in capital and corporal punishment, confidence in correctional institutions and a general belief that one can and should stop offenders from committing crime through the threat or application of punishment. The factor appears to measure something close to the doctrine of individual deterrence. It appears distinguishable from the first factor in the sense that, in this case, punishment is directed to the offender rather than to the offence.

Factor 3 is labelled "intolerance." A large number of items not relating specifically to crime but rather to other forms of social deviance have high loadings on this factor. Concepts of "evil," "morality," and "sin," are found among items with high factor loadings.

Factor 4 is labelled "social defence." Most of the items appear to be related to the concept of general deterrence. Items with high loadings on this factor are associated with the general view that crime poses a threat to the social order and that potential offenders should be intimidated from committing crime by the threat of punishment. A number of items express the view that sentencing should express society's "revulsion" to, and "denunciation" of crime. It is distinguishable from factors 1 and 2 in that punishment is directed primarily to potential offenders in the community at large.

Factor 5 is labelled "modernism." Items with high negative loadings deal with such concepts as the use of alcohol, the need for self-discipline, the value of hard work, concern about the lowering of moral standards, and antagonism to social welfare measures. It appears that this factor measures differences among individuals in the degree to which they identify with what is commonly known as "new-world" puritanism. People holding these values tend to look upon failure through alcoholism, crime, or any other cause as being "sinful." At the opposite end of the continuum are the values associated with the modern welfare state. These include concern to help those less fortunate than oneself, and a recognition that personal failure in life is not necessarily an indication of laziness or other defect of character. The scale is labelled in the positive form, i.e., modernism.

Rotation succeeded in providing five interpretable factors. We have yet to see whether scales derived from this procedure are reliable (consistent) and whether they are valid in the sense of predicting a criterion.

The final stage of factor analysis involved calculation of "factor scores" for each individual. This score is an estimate of the correlation between an individual's response to the questionnaire, and a factor.[22] The size of the correlation derived is an indication of the importance of the factor to the individual concerned. Each person's attitudes are thus represented by the five factor scores. These factor scores form the basis for analysis which are to follow.

TABLE 34

Factor analysis - rotated factor loadings: factor 1, justice

Item	Loading
In sentencing, the duty of the court should be to punish; the reformation of offenders belongs to the correctional agencies	0.921
Most of those who advocate reformative treatment of criminals do not attach sufficient weight to the seriousness of the crimes they commit	0.831
Criminals are being mollycoddled by the correctional agencies	0.815
Probation should only be given to first offenders	0.815
Prisons should be places of punishment	0.790
The frequent use of probation is wrong because it has the effect of minimizing the gravity of the offence committed	0.768
The sentence imposed on the offender should be based on what he has done and not on what sort of person he is, or what he may do in the future	0.768
The most important single consideration in determining the sentence to impose should be the nature and the gravity of the offence	0.758
Criminals should be punished for their crimes whether or not the punishment benefits the criminal	0.699
The failure to punish crime amounts to giving a licence to commit it	0.697
The court should not give priority to the reformation of the offender	0.697
The use of alcohol usually leads to the lowering of moral standards	0.663
Many social workers defeat the interest of justice by trying to help the criminal	0.652
The strap should be used more often with young offenders	0.643
Criminals should be punished for their crime in order to require them to repay their debt to society	0.640

TABLE 35

Factor analysis - rotated factor loadings: factor 2, punishment corrects

Item	Loading
Capital punishment should be abolished completely	-0.890
Corporal punishment should have no place in modern penal practice	-0.821
Capital punishment should be retained for certain types of murder	0.815
Crimes such as indecent assault on children are the result of mental illness; offenders who commit these crimes belong in hospitals not prisons	-0.783
Most criminals are sick people who need treatment	-0.766
Capital punishment is a deterrent to murder	0.752
For certain crimes, corporal punishment should be imposed	0.750
Most criminal acts are the result of forces largely beyond the control of the offender	-0.682
Crimes such as indecent assault on children should be punished severely	0.649
Most offenders suffer from defects and weaknesses that cannot be overcome without help	-0.613
The vast majority of inmates of penal institutions would pose no real threat to society if released under the ordinary supervision of a probation officer	-0.574
It is important to sentence each offender on the basis of his individual needs and not on the basis of the crime he has committed	-0.527
Prisons are more likely to confirm an offender in crime than to rehabilitate him	-0.508
Our present treatment of criminals is too harsh	-0.498
The strap should be used more often with young offenders	0.491

TABLE 36

Factor analysis - rotated factor loadings: factor 3, intolerance

Item	Loading
Obedience and respect for authority are the most important virtues children should learn	0.883
The punishment awarded by the court should always be in proportion to the nature and gravity of the offence	0.679
Men and women should be permitted to find out if they are sexually suited before marriage	-0.676
Crimes are sins with legal definitions	0.666
No weakness or difficulty can hold a person back if he has enough will-power	0.654
Crimes such as indecent assault on children should be punished severely	0.609
Crime creates an imbalance in the social order that can only be put right by an appropriate punishment	0.608
The most important single consideration in determining the sentence to impose should be the nature and gravity of the offence	0.605
In sentencing, there should always be a balance between the sentence imposed and the moral wrong committed by the offender	0.602
In sentencing, the courts should try to uphold the moral standards of decent people	0.593
In order that society function properly, the majority must set standards of behaviour for all	0.593
Capital punishment should be retained for certain types of murder	0.592
For certain crimes, corporal punishment should be imposed	0.592
Crimes such as incest endanger the very bases of society	0.583
A nation which tolerates wide variations in standards of behaviour among its members cannot exist for very long	0.574

TABLE 37

Factor analysis - rotated factor loadings: factor 4, social defence

Item	Loading
Neither the treatment nor the application of penalties is a deterrent to potential offenders	-0.740
Most people are deterred by the threat of heavy penalties	0.651
The majority of potential offenders are deterred by the threat of punishment	0.629
The main objective in the sentencing of offenders should be to deter potential offenders from committing a crime	0.581
Sentences imposed in criminal courts should reflect the revulsion felt by the majority of citizens to crime	0.551
Crimes against the person such as robbery should be punished in a manner which satisfies the feelings of the community	0.536
Capital punishment is a deterrent to murder	0.529
Society should be willing to avenge crime	0.495
The failure to punish crime amounts to giving a licence to commit	0.469
Probation should be reserved for those who are not likely to offend again	0.460
The sentence of the court should always express an emphatic denunciation by the community of the crime	0.434
It is Christian and praiseworthy that society should be willing to avenge crime	0.423
Life in prisons should be made an unpleasant experience	0.384
The sentence imposed by the court is a significant force in sharpening the public's sense of right and wrong	0.384
Crime creates an imbalance in the social order that can only be put right by an appropriate punishment	0.377

TABLE 38

Factor analysis - rotated factor loadings: factor 5, modernism

Item	Loading
The use of alcohol usually leads to the lowering of moral standards	-0.604
For certain crimes, corporal punishment should be imposed	-0.530
Corporal punishment should have no place in modern penal practice	0.499
Capital punishment should be abolished completely	0.485
Capital punishment should be retained for certain types of murder	-0.480
The strap should be used more often with young offenders	-0.468
Social drinking is likely to lead to alcoholism	-0.431
The certainty of discovery is a more significant element in deterring crime than the severity of the penalty that might be imposed	0.398
Most adult offenders should be required to perform hard physical labour	-0.390
Most criminals deliberately choose to prey upon society	-0.327
On the whole, welfare measures such as unemployment insurance and social assistance contribute to social problems including crime	-0.327
The moral standards of some national groups are considerably lower than that expected of most Canadians	-0.324
Standards of morality in Canadian society are declining	-0.320
Most of those who advocate reformative treatment of criminals do not attach sufficient weight to the seriousness of the crimes they commit	-0.313

Reliability of Factorally Derived Scales

Using the same formula that was used for calculating the reliability of the Likert scales, reliability coefficients were calculated for the five factor scales. The results are indicated in Table 39.

Each of the factor scales have reliability coefficients well in excess of the minimum required for research purposes. The coefficients are not quite as high as those derived from Likert procedures, but since the factorally derived scales are easier to interpret and are independent of one another, they would seem to be superior to Likert scales.

TABLE 39

Split-half reliability tests on factor scales using Hoyt's formula

Scale	Reliability
Justice	0.832
Punishment corrects	0.771
Intolerance	0.619
Social defence	0.901
Modernism	0.611

Validity of Factor Scales

The next step is to determine the validity of factorally derived scales. The first test of validity utilized the "known-groups" method used in respect to the Likert scales. For each scale the mean and standard deviation for each criterion group was determined. F-tests were then calculated to see whether the observed differences in mean scores were statistically significant. The results are presented in Table 40.

TABLE 40

Factor scales: means, standard deviations, and F-ratios for criterion groups

Scale		Population groups					
		Police officers	Magis-trates	Probation officers	Law students	Social work students	F-Ratio
Justice	Mean	70.68	50.20	39.67	43.92	36.08	
	S.D.	13.51	10.95	10.94	10.90	9.08	132.600
Punishment	Mean	59.39	53.22	41.41	39.68	31.64	
corrects	S.D.	7.73	7.33	10.57	9.69	7.20	124.690
Intolerance	Mean	79.17	68.24	58.29	51.02	48.22	
	S.D.	10.58	9.23	12.43	12.34	9.38	105.350
Social	Mean	61.84	55.39	43.05	44.88	38.20	
defence	S.D.	12.33	11.11	11.72	11.69	9.09	60.135
Modernism	Mean	31.56	40.29	46.13	48.50	55.17	
	S.D.	5.66	6.34	9.07	9.06	6.97	110.470

As in the case of the Likert scales, the factorally derived scales distinguish clearly among the population groups tested. In each case, the F-value is vastly in excess of that required to be significant at 0.001. On the basis of these findings it is not possible to determine which of the two scale construction techniques is more valid. The determination of this issue will have to wait for the comparisons that will be made of the ability of scales derived from each of the procedures used to predict judicial behaviour. This will come in the next chapter. For the present, it can be said that both Likert and factor analytic methods produce scales which are reliable and valid. Reliability coefficients are somewhat higher for Likert scales, but the scales derived through factoral procedures appear easier to interpret.

In the next chapter we will take a closer look at the content and structure of attitudes to crime and punishment as revealed through factor analysis.

NOTES TO CHAPTER 7

1 For a simple introduction to scaling techniques see A. Oppenheim, *Questionnaire Design and Attitude Measurement* (London, 1966), 120-59. For more advanced reading see W. Torgenson, *Theory and Method of Scaling* (New York, 1958).
2 R. Macleod, "The Logical Approach to Social Psychology," *Psychological Review*, 54, 193-210.
3 H. Eysenck, *The Psychology of Politics* (London, 1954); T. Adorno, Else Frenkel-Brunswick, D. Levinson, and R. Sanford, *The Authoritarian Personality* (New York, 1950); H. Gough and N. Sanford, *Rigidity as a Psychological Variable*, unpublished; and H. Rokeach, *The Open and Closed Mind* (New York, 1960).
4 See (for the F-scale) Adorno et al., *The Authoritarian Personality* and (for the liberalism-conservatism scale) Eysenck, *The Psychology of Politics*.
5 The factor analysis method used is also called "Principle Component Analysis"; its rationale and references will be supplied later.
6 R. Likert, "A Technique for the Measurement of Attitudes," *Archives of Psychology*, 40 (1932).
7 For a discussion of this problem and a possible solution see L. Guttman and E. Suchman, "Intensity and a Zero Point for Attitude Analysis," *American Sociological Review*, 12 (1947), 57-67.
8 A simple description is contained in Oppenheim, *Questionnaire Design*, 133-42; for a more complete discussion see B. Green, "Attitude Measurement," in Lindsey, ed., *Handbook of Social Psychology* (New York), 335-69.
9 H. Remmers, *Anti-Democratic Attitudes in American Schools* (Chicago, 1963). See also A. Rhodes, "Authoritarianism and Fundamentalism of Rural and Urban High School Students," *Journal of Educational Sociology*, 34 (1960), 97-105.
10 See P. Guilford, *Psychometric Methods* (New York, 1958); and L. Cronbach, *Essentials of Psychological Testing* (New York, 1960), chaps. 4 and 5.
11 Hoyt's Formula can be found in Cronbach, *Essentials of Psychological Testing*, 126-42.
12 Guilford, *Psychometic Methods*, 417.
13 Cronbach, *Essentials of Psychological Testing*, chap.5.

14 For example see Guilford, *Psychometric Methods*, 438.

15 *Ibid.*, 279.

16 For a full description of Factor Analysis see H. Harman, *Modern Factor Analysis* (Chicago, 1960).

17 Eysenck, *The Psychology of Politics*, chap. 5.

18 A good discussion of when to use factor analysis is in Guilford, *Psychometric Methods*, 510-4.

19 For a comparison of different methods see Harman, *Modern Factor Analysis*, chap. 14.

20 The statistical analysis was contained in a complex computer programme "package" called "Data Text," developed at the Department of Social Relations, Harvard University, 1966.

21 The method known as "Varimax" was used. These rotations were designed to be a mathematical approximation of simple structure as proposed by Thurstone in *Multiple Factor Analysis*. The procedures are described in Harman, *Modern Factor Analysis*, chap. 14.

22 These factor scores were calculated by a method equivalent to the "Direct Solution" matrix inversion procedures outlined in Harman, *Modern Factor Analysis*, 337-8.

8

The Content and Structure of Attitudes to Crime and Punishment

Factor analysis scales revealed a number of interesting things about how attitudes to crime and punishment are structured in the minds of different population groups. Unlike the pattern derived from Likert procedures, the population groups tested did not order themselves in the same way on each scale. This can be seen from Table 41 which contains the mean factor scores of each group.

TABLE 41

Principal component analysis, means of rotated factor scores

Groups	Justice	Punishment corrects	Intolerance	Social defence	Modernism
Magistrates	-0.344	0.618	0.145	0.485	-0.194
Law students	0.141	-0.247	-0.965	0.373	0.183
Social work students	-0.377	-0.851	-0.469	0.316	0.741
Police officers	1.028	0.439	0.569	-0.187	-0.156
Probation officers with degrees	-0.527	-0.287	-0.135	-0.200	-0.012
Probation officers without degrees	-0.528	-0.182	0.233	-0.350	-0.401

On the justice scale, police officers, as one might expect, have a very high mean score (1.208). Interestingly enough, law students · are next at 0.141. Then comes a big drop to magistrates at -0.344, social work students at -0.377 and, finally, probation officers at -0.528.

The concept of justice is an important one to law students. In its abstract and idealized form, it means that every case is dealt with consistently and fairly. Magistrates, on the other hand, have come to know that abstract justice cannot always be achieved when personal circumstances of individual offenders and the demands of the other purposes in sentencing interfere. It is difficult to explain why probation officers tend to score so low on this scale. Perhaps it relates to the fact that they are inclined to ignore the offence in dealing with individual offenders, and are entirely person-oriented.

On the punishment corrects scale, magistrates score the highest (0.618). Police officers come second at 0.439. There is a rather substantial drop to probation officers without degrees at -0.182, law students at -0.247 and probation officers with degrees at -0.287. Social work students have by far the lowest mean score at -0.851.

These findings are most revealing. More than any other group, magistrates believe that "punishment is good for offenders." This notion makes it possible for them to resolve the contradictory demands made on them in sentencing, as once accepted, it leads them to believe that they can punish and treat offenders at the same time. We see in this scale, the closest division of opinion between magistrates and police officers on the one hand, and students and probation officers on the other.

The intolerance scale is anchored at either end by police officers (0.569) and law students (-0.965). The gap between these two groups is enormous. Next to police officers come probation officers without degrees (0.233), probation officers with degrees (-0.135) and social work students (-0.469).

The fact that law students appear to be significantly more tolerant than social work students is of some interest. It suggests that law students are not particularly bothered by crime and social deviance. On the other hand, social workers seem to be more concerned. Unlike police officers, social work students do not wish to punish crime, and unlike magistrates, they do not feel that punishment helps the offender. Social workers want to "treat" offenders.

Magistrates tend to score highest on the social defence scale (0.485). This is what one would expect in view of the fact that the protection of society is a value that is given a great deal of verbal support by the courts. It is somewhat surprising to see the relatively low mean score for police officers on this scale. Despite the fact that police officers are charged with the responsibility of preventing and controlling crime, it seems that their underlying attitudes relate to more deeply-seated feelings of "justice" and intolerance of deviance. Law students have a fairly high mean score on this scale. This probably reflects the view that the courts should be instruments of social control. Social work students seem to reflect this view as well.

As indicated by the mean scores on the modernism scale, probation officers without degrees appear to uphold the traditional values of hard work and self-discipline. Next to them come magistrates. It is social work students who appear to identify with a more "modern" outlook with respect to crime and social deviance. They occupy a mean position on the scale, well above any of the other groups. Police officers and law students occupy middle positions.

It is easier to interpret the attitudes of these groups in terms of their relationship to each other than by simply looking at each attitude score independently. In Figures 3 to 7, the relationships of pairs of attitude scores for each group are plotted in two-dimensional space.

In Figure 3, the mean scores for each criterion group on the concern for justice and punishment corrects scales are plotted against each other. On these two dimensions police officers and magistrates are isolated from the other criterion groups. We see the extreme position of police officers on the justice scale. While magistrates have relatively low justice scores, they occupy an extreme position on the punishment corrects scale.

In Figure 4, mean scores on the justice scale are plotted against mean scores on the intolerance scale. Once again police officers are isolated from the other criterion groups in both an intolerant and pro-justice direction. This time, law students also appear to be some distance away from the other groups, occupying an extremely tolerant position with respect to crime. Magistrates, probation officers, and social work students cluster fairly closely together.

In Figure 5, which plots intolerance against punishment corrects, we see magistrates and police officers occupying fairly similar positions. These two groups are relatively intolerant and, at the same time, believe that punishment corrects. Occupying diagonally opposite positions are social work students.

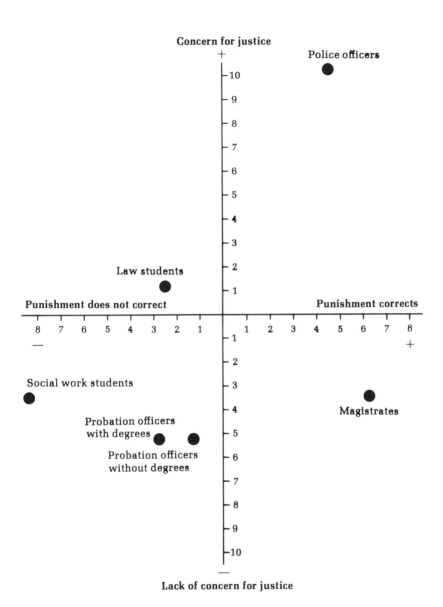

Figure 3 Plotted factor scores for criterion groups: rotated factors 1 and 2

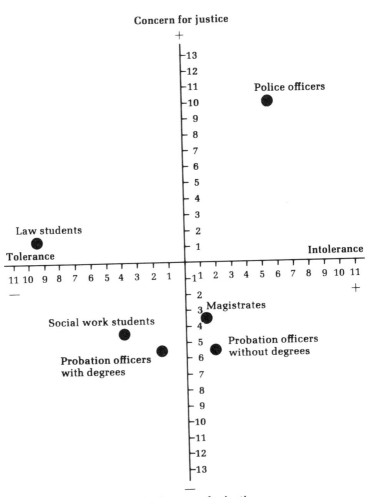

Figure 4 Plotted factor scores for criterion groups: rotated factors 1 and 3

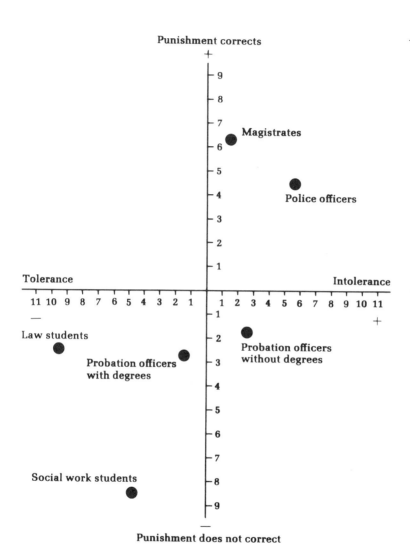

Figure 5 Plotted factor scores for criterion groups: rotated factors 2 and 3

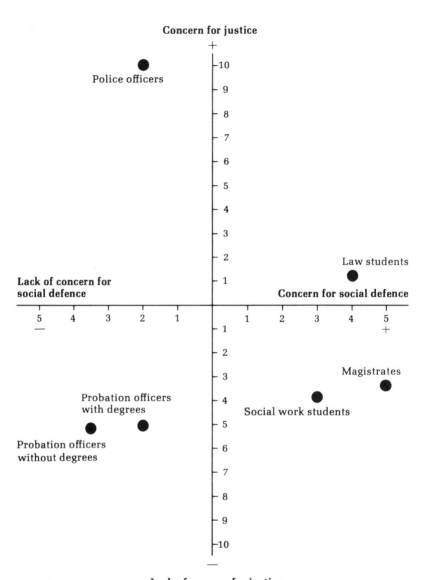

Figure 6 Plotted factor scores for criterion groups: rotated factors 1 and 4

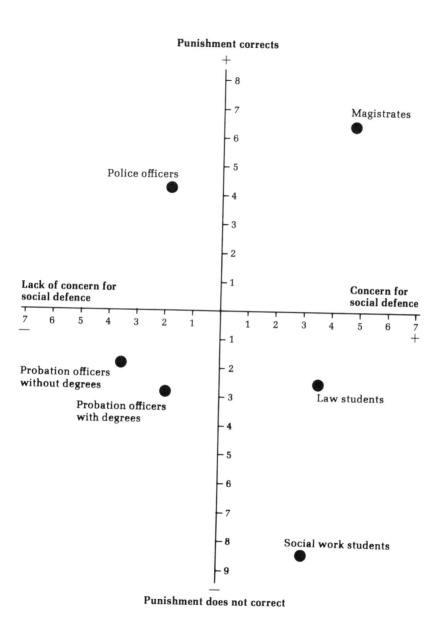

Figure 7 Plotted factor scores for criterion groups: rotated factors 2 and 4

In Figure 6, concern for social defence is plotted against concern for justice. Here we can see that while police officers occupy extreme positions on the justice scale, they do not appear to be particularly concerned about social defence. Law students, social work students, and magistrates cluster together on the concern for social defence side, with law students being more concerned for justice than either magistrates or social work students. Probation officers with and without degrees occupy similar positions in the direction of not being particularly concerned for either justice or social defence.

Perhaps the most interesting relationship of factor scores for magistrates is revealed in Figure 7 which plots punishment corrects against social defence. Here we see magistrates clearly isolated from all the other groups. On both these scales magistrates occupy relatively extreme positions which are diametrically opposite to probation officers with and without degrees. Armed with a philosophy which emphasizes both the protection of the community and the correction of offenders through punishment, magistrates would be able to impose rather severe penalties without any sense of guilt about sacrificing the offender for the good of the community. The way in which the demands of one's occupational role affect one's attitudes is thus revealed. It can also be seen that while law students and social work students are concerned about social defence, they do not appear to feel that punishment is an effective way to achieve this objective. This is particularly true for social work students who occupy an extremely negative position on the punishment corrects scale.

9

The Prediction of
Sentencing Behaviour from
Attitude Scales

Obtaining Measures of Judicial Behaviour

The ultimate test for validity of an attitude measure is its ability to predict significant behaviour. The first step is to obtain a good behavioural criterion. This was not difficult in this case as the sentencing decisions of magistrates are a matter of public record. For the purposes of research, these decisions have additional advantages in being specific, reasonably reliable, and easily quantifiable.

In response to a special request, the Judicial Section of the Dominion Bureau of Statistics provided a complete breakdown of the sentencing behaviour of Ontario magistrates during the years 1966 and 1967. These data included the frequencies with which sentences of different kinds were given by individual magistrates for each Criminal Code offence.

The data were organized in a number of different ways. First, the frequencies with which each magistrate used suspended sentence, probation, fines and institutions in all indictable cases (grouped together) were determined. Second, the frequency with which each magistrate used specific types of institutional sentence was obtained, i.e. gaol, reformatory or penitentiary. Third, the mean length of institutional sentence given (in months) was calculated for each magistrate. Finally, the proportions of each magistrate's sentences falling within specific categories were determined in terms of percentages. The data were then analysed in terms of specific offences, and similar statistics to those men - tioned above were obtained for each magistrate.

Because some magistrates did not deal with a sufficient number of cases for meaningful analysis with respect to some of the less frequently occurring offences, it was sometimes necessary to group offences within a category, such as "crimes against the person with violence," or "offences against property without violence." For offences such as theft, breaking and entering, assault, and causing a disturbance, it was possible to use the specific offence.

In all, valid data were obtained with respect to sixty-seven measures of sentencing behaviour. These measures became the dependent variables, i.e., the variables that were to be predicted from the attitude scores of magistrates. If the attitude measures used are valid and significantly associated with the sentencing behaviour of magistrates, they should be able to predict not only what type of sentence will be imposed, but also its length or amount.

Prediction Equations

Likert Scales

When we speak of forecasting one score from another we usually speak of regression, and in a sense, prediction. A regression equation expresses the rate of change in one variable (the dependent variable) as a proportion of the change taking place in one or more other variables (the independent variables).[1]

The procedure can best be demonstrated non-mathematically. For example, we may wish to predict the proportion of suspended sentences given in indictable cases with reference only to the punishment scores of magistrates on Likert scales. A graph could be drawn with two main axes - one representing punishment scores of magistrates and the other representing the proportion of sentences falling within the suspended sentence category. For each magistrate we have a set of two scores, a punishment score and a sentencing score. If one made a mark on the graph where each pair of scores was located, the result would be a "scatter" diagram which would provide a rough visual check on the possible existence of a relationship between the attitude score and the behavioural measure.

Figure 8 is a scatter diagram representing this relationship. It can

Punishment scores

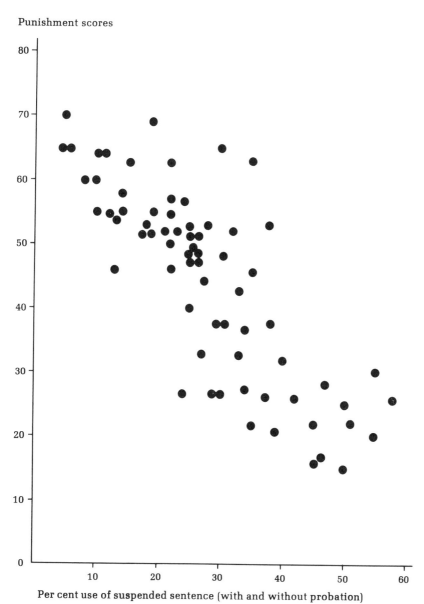

Per cent use of suspended sentence (with and without probation)

Figure 8 Scatter diagram showing relationship of punishment scores to the use of suspended sentence in indictable cases

be seen that there is a tendency for magistrates with low punishment scores to use suspended sentences more frequently. The relationship is by no means perfect, otherwise all the dots would be on a completely straight line. However, the relationship is a strong one. The correlation coefficient (r) which expresses this relationship is, in this case, 0.432. In mathematical terms, the proportion of common variance between the two sets of variables is r^2, or 18.6 per cent.

Correlations were calculated between each behavioural measure and each of the five Likert scales. In Table 42 correlations between the Likert scales and the sentencing behaviour of magistrates in all indictable cases (combined) are presented. Technical Appendix 3 contains correlations for specific offences.

The attitudes of magistrates as represented by Likert scale scores appear to be moderately associated with their sentencing behaviour. While there were a number of significant correlations between attitudes and behaviour, in many instances no statistically significant relationship appeared. In fact, less than half the behavioural measures used were associated with the attitudes of magistrates as represented by the Likert scales, and in no case was the size of the correlation coefficient achieved greater than 0.5.

The deterrence scale appears to be the best predictor of judicial behaviour in sentencing. Magistrates with high deterrence scores tend to favour institutional sentences as opposed to other forms of sentence, and they tend to use penitentiary and moderate-term reformatory sentences as opposed to short-term sentences in the common gaol.

The next best scale, in terms of prediction, appears to be the treatment scale which is positively associated with the frequent use of suspended sentence without probation, and negatively associated with the use of fines and short term gaol sentences. Magistrates with high treatment scores tend to use reformatory sentences when institutional sentences are used, and penitentiary sentences infrequently. Moreover, magistrates with high treatment scores tend to use shorter gaol sentences when this form of disposition is applied.

The punishment scale predicts only a few categories of sentence. Magistrates with high punishment scores tend to use suspended sentence without probation less frequently, and at the same time use penitentiary sentences more frequently. Moreover, there appears to be a tendency for magistrates with high punishment scores to favour penitentiary sentences as opposed to other

TABLE 42

Correlation between Likert scores and sentencing behaviour: all indictable cases

Sentencing behaviour	Attitudes				
	Deterrence	Punishment	Treatment	Tolerance	Probation
Suspended sentence with probation	-	-	-	-	0.284
Suspended sentence without probation	-	-0.310*	0.499*	-	-
Fine	-	-	-0.319*	-	-
Institutions	-	-	-	0.251	-
Gaol, less than 6 months	-0.398*	-	-	-	-
Gaol, more than 6 less than 24 months	-0.251	-	-0.235	-	-
Total gaol	-0.402*	-	-	-	-
Reformatory, less than 12 months	0.362*	-	-	-	-
Reformatory, more than 12 less than 24 months	-	-	-	-0.249	0.278
Total reformatory	0.268	-	-	-	-
Total penitentiary	-	0.344*	-0.248	0.247	-0.300
Gaol, less than 6 months as a proportion of all institutions	-0.404*	-	-	-	-
Gaol, less than 12 months as a proportion of all institutions	-	-	-0.258	-	-
All gaol as a proportion of all institutions	-0.382*	-	-	-	-
Reformatory, less than 12 months as a proportion of all institutions	0.329*	-	-	-	-
Reformatory, more than 12 less than 24 months as a proportion of all institutions	-	-	0.304*	-0.336*	0.428*
All reformatory as a proportion of all institutions	0.282	-	0.316*	-	0.235
Penitentiary as a proportion of all institutions	-	0.388*	-0.269	-	-
Average gaol sentence (in months)	-	-	-0.338*	-	-0.260
Average reformatory sentence (in months)	-	-	-	-	-
Average penitentiary sentence (in months)	0.432*	-	-	-	-
Average all institutions (in months)	0.392*	0.320*	-	-	-

*Significant at 0.01; otherwise significant at 0.05.

forms of institutional sentence. Finally, as one would expect, magistrates with relatively higher punishment scores tend to give longer terms of imprisonment.

The tolerance and probation scores are correlated with a few behavioural measures, but the number of significant correlations do not greatly exceed that which could be expected by chance.

Factorally Derived Scales

Factorally derived scales are somewhat better at predicting the behaviour of magistrates than Likert scales. Within broad categories of crime the two categories of scale seemed roughly equivalent in their abilities to predict. But when one considered individual offences factorally derived scales were clearly superior. With the identical behavioural variables used in predicting from Likert scales, correlational analysis indicated that at least one factor score was significantly associated with the sentencing behaviour of magistrates in nearly all the sixty-seven categories studied. At the same time it appears that the relationship between attitudes and behaviour of magistrates is a complex one. Different patterns of relationship appeared depending on the type of offence considered (Tables 43 and 44).

The justice scale is significantly associated with most of the behavioural measures used. Dealing with indictable cases in general, concern for justice is associated with: the less frequent use of probation, more frequent use of fines and institutions, longer sentences to institutions, and a preference for penitentiary and gaol sentences as opposed to reformatory sentences. In general terms, it appears that high justice scores are associated with a relatively stern sentencing policy.

On the other hand, different patterns emerge when one considers specific offences. For offences of a severe nature, such as offences against property with violence and offences against the person, concern for justice is positively associated with the frequent use of institutional sentences. In contrast, with respect to minor offences, such as theft, others against property without violence, and non-indictable offences generally, concern for justice is associated with a low rate of imprisonment. It appears that concern for justice not only demands that crime be punished but also ensures that the punishment given is only as severe as the offence itself warrants. The *limiting* nature of the justice doctrine is thus revealed.

High punishment corrects scores are associated with the greater use of reformatory institutional sentences, and the avoid-

TABLE 43

Correlations between factor scores and sentencing behaviour: all indictable cases

Sentencing behaviour (Proportions within each category)	Justice	Punishment corrects	Intolerance	Social defence	Modernism
Suspended sentence with probation	-0.283	-	-	-	-
Suspended sentence without probation	-0.402*	-	-	-	-
Suspended sentence (combined)	-0.439*	-	-	-	-
Fine	0.347*	-	-	-	0.234
Institutions	-	-	-	-	-
Gaol, less than 6 months	-	-0.259	-	-	-
Gaol, more than 6, less than 24 months	0.353*	-	-0.255	-	-
Total gaol	0.332*	-	-	-	-
Reformatory, less than 12 months	-0.383*	0.311*	0.251	-	-
Reformatory, more than 12, less than 24 months	-0.265	0.334*	-	-0.317*	-
Total reformatory	-0.413*	0.394*	-	-	-
Total penitentiary	0.310*	-0.298	-	0.281	-
Gaol, less than 6 months as a proportion of all institutions	0.265	-0.304*	-	-	-
Gaol, more than 6, less than 24 months as a proportion of all institutions	0.397*	-	-0.262	-	-
All gaol as a proportion of all institutions	0.400*	-	-	-	-
Reformatory, less than 12 months as a proportion of all institutions	-	-	-	-	-
Reformatory, more than 12, less than 24 months as a proportion of all institutions	-0.397*	0.271	0.247	-	-
All reformatory as a proportion of all institutions	-0.519*	0.326*	0.245	-	-
Penitentiary as a proportion of all institutions	0.352*	-0.356*	-	0.399*	-
Average gaol sentence (months)	0.402*	-	-	-	-
Average reformatory sentence (months)	-	-	-	-	-
Average penitentiary sentence (months)	-0.439*	-	-	-	-

*Significant at 0.01; otherwise significant at 0.05.

TABLE 44

Correlations between factor scores and sentencing behaviour: specific offences

Sentencing behaviour (proportions within each category)	Attitude scores				
	Justice	Punishment corrects	Intol-erance	Social defence	Modernism
Theft					
Suspended sentence with probation	-0.269	0.362*	-	-	-
Suspended sentence without probation	-0.269	-	-	-	-
Suspended sentence (combined)	-0.440*	0.312*	-	-	-
				-	
Fine	0.397*	-	-		0.285
Other offences against property without violence					
Suspended sentence with probation	0.265	-	-	0.295	-
Suspended sentence without probation	-0.342*	0.257	-	-	0.268
Suspended sentence (combined)	-	-	-	0.258	0.294
Fine	0.451*	-0.401*	-0.418*	0.262*	-
Institution	-0.275	-	-	-0.358*	-0.269
Total against property without violence					
Suspended sentence with probation	-	0.264	-	-	-
Suspended sentence without probation	-0.277	-	-	-	-
Suspended sentence (combined)	-0.288	0.246	-	-	-
Fine	0.386*	-	-	-	0.267
Institution	-	-	-	-	-0.361*
Total against property with violence					
Suspended sentence with probation	-	-	-	-	-
Suspended sentence without probation	0.498	–	0.372*	-0.267	-0.370*
Suspended sentence (combined)	-0.260	-	-	-	-0.339*
Fine	-	-	-0.334*	-	-
Institution	0.243	-	-	-	0.357*

TABLE 44 continued

Correlations between factor scores and sentencing behaviour: specific offences

Sentencing behaviour (proportions within each category)	Attitude scores				
	Justice	Punishment corrects	Intolerance	Social defence	Modernism
Total against person					
Suspended sentence with probation	-	-	-	-	-0.343*
Suspended sentence without probation	-0.449*	-	-	-	-
Suspended sentence (combined)	-0.429*	-	-	-	-0.327*
Fine	0.406*	-0.412*	0.240	-0.326*	0.441*
Institution	-	0.385*	-	0.261	-
Breaking and entering					
Suspended sentence with probation	-	-	-	-	-
Suspended sentence without probation	-0.453*	-	0.306*	-	-0.306*
Suspended sentence (combined)	-	-	-	-	-0.289*
Fine	-	-	-0.282	-0.239	-0.318*
Institution	-	-	-	-	-
Non-indictable common assault					
Suspended sentence with probation	-0.247	-	-	-	-0.343*
Suspended sentence without probation	-	-	-	-	-
Suspended sentence (combined)	-	-	-	-	-
Fine	-	-	-	-	-
Institution	-	-	-	-	-0.269
Causing a disturbance					
Suspended sentence with probation	-	-	-	-	-0.326*
Suspended sentence without probation	-0.398*	-	-	-	-
Suspended sentence (combined)	-0.435*	-	-	-	-
Fine	0.578*	-	-0.361*	-	0.255
Institution	-0.416*	-	0.422*	-	-

TABLE 44 continued

Correlations between factor scores and sentencing behaviour:
specific offences

Sentencing behaviour (proportions within each category)	Attitude scores				
	Justice	Punishment corrects	Intol- erance	Social defence	Modernism
Total non-indictable					
Suspended sentence with probation	-	-0.268	-	-	-0.427*
Suspended sentence without probation	-	-	-	-	-
Suspended sentence (combined)	-0.246	-	-	-	-
Fine	0.245	-	-0.243	-	-
Institution	-	-	-	-	-

*Significant at 0.01; otherwise significant at 0.05.

ance of gaol sentences and penitentiary sentences. There appears to be a relationship between the view that punishment is "good for offenders," and the selection of institutional sentences that will provide education, training, self-discipline, and work.

Turning to specific offences, punishment corrects scores are significantly associated with sentencing behaviour of magistrates in different ways depending on the nature of the offence. For example, magistrates with high punishment corrects scores tend to favour the use of probation and suspended sentence for offences such as theft and others against property without violence, while avoiding the use of these measures for minor, non-indictable offences. It appears that magistrates who believe that "punishment corrects" apply corrective punishment only in cases where the offence itself suggests that corrective punishment is likely to be needed. Of greater significance is the apparent relationship between high punishment corrects scores and the length of institutional sentences given. Magistrates with high scores on this scale tend not only to use reformatory type institutional sentences more often but also tend to give longer sentences to these institutions. It appears that these magistrates have accepted the views of prison officials and others that relatively lengthy reformatory sentences are necessary for offenders to complete trade training and other programmes available in these institutions.

A belief that punishment corrects can serve to justify sentences that would otherwise be considered excessively punitive. Many sentences given by magistrates with high scores on this scale would likely be considered unfair by magistrates with high scores on the justice scale. Moreover, the validity of sentences based on this notion rests on the assumption that penal measures are effective ways of rehabilitating or treating offenders. While the research evidence is negative in this regard, magistrates are not provided with it, and all the propaganda directed to them serves to strengthen the belief that long sentences are necessary if rehabilitation is to take place.[2] It will be remembered that magistrates, more than any other population group studied, identify with this doctrine. Belief in it helps to reconcile punitive and rehabilitative aims in sentencing. Magistrates identifying with this view can feel that institutional sentences do some good both for society and for individual offenders.

Concern for social defence appears to be associated with the use of long-term imprisonment. Magistrates with high scores on this scale appear in general to prefer penitentiary sentences as opposed to reformatory or gaol sentences. When one looks at specific offences, it can be seen that magistrates with high social defence scores use suspended sentence, fines, and institutions more frequently than probation for minor offences against property. On the other hand, fines are used less often for serious offences against property and for offences against a person. For these types of cases institutional sentences are preferred. It appears that the social defence scale measures the degree to which magistrates are willing to sacrifice deliberately the interests of the offender for the sake of community protection. In contrast to magistrates with high punishment corrects scores, those with high scores on the social defence scale do not use imprisonment as a treatment, but rather as a deterrent to others.

High modernism scores are associated with the greater use of fines and the use of longer terms of reformatory sentences. This is what one would predict in view of the fact that these two types of sentences are generally considered "progressive." The modernism dimension is also closely associated with the decisions magistrates make with respect to specific offences. High modernism scores are associated with a tendency to use institutions rather than suspended sentences with respect to offences against property with violence, particularly breaking and entering. High scores are also associated with a tendency to use fines rather than suspended sentence or probation for less serious offences against the person. On the other hand, with respect to offences such as theft, high modernism scores are associated with a tendency to use suspended sentence or fines rather than institutions. With respect to non-indictable offences of a minor nature, high scores are associated with a tendency to use fines instead of probation or suspended sentence. This scale seems to measure differences among magistrates with respect to the degree to which they identify with a "progressive" sentencing policy. This is a policy which encourages the use of fines for minor offences, the use of reformatory-type sentences of substantial length when institutional sentences are used, and the restriction of probation to cases where it is likely to be effective.

Some of the relationships between the intolerance scale and sentencing behaviour are surprising. Magistrates with high scores on this scale seem to use suspended sentence more frequently for serious offences, such as breaking and entering, and institutional sentences more frequently for minor offences, such as causing a disturbance. Why this should be so is difficult to explain. It is possible that magistrates with high intolerance scores do not distinguish between offences of greater or lesser severity to the same extent as those with low scores on this scale. It should be pointed out, however, that this scale has the fewest number of significant correlations with judicial behaviour. The possibility of chance variation in these circumstances makes one cautious about "over-interpreting" the data.

None of the scales was very good at predicting the proportion of probation dispositions. It was discovered later that the information provided to the Dominion Bureau of Statistics with respect to the number of people placed on probation was unreliable. This information is provided by clerks of the court. Sometimes these persons failed to distinguish between suspended sentence without probation and suspended sentence with probation. This is why a dependent variable called "suspended sentence (combined)" was included in the analysis. Once this was done, many more relationships became statistically significant.

It must also be pointed out that the behavioural measures are not independent of one another. In dealing with proportions of sentences falling within a category, the high proportion in one category would necessarily result in a lower proportion in some of the others. Thus, a high proportion of gaol sentences results in a lower proportion of either reformatory or penitentiary sentences or both. One therefore expects significant correlations between attitudes and behaviour to cluster together, as indeed happens.

A number of implications arise out of these findings. First of all, it appears that factorally derived scales are better at predicting behaviour than Likert scales. Secondly, it appears that the justice and punishment corrects dimensions are closely associated with general patterns of behaviour regardless of the specific type of offence considered. Third, modernism, social defence, and intolerance are associated to varying degrees with the behaviour of magistrates depending on the specific offence. Fourth, these findings suggest that the relationship of attitudes to judicial behaviour is a complex one. While there is a general tendency for the justice and punishment corrects dimensions to be associated with judicial behaviour over a wide range of situations, many different patterns of relationships show up on examination of individual offences.

It is interesting to note an apparent relationship between "punitive" behaviour and "modern" thinking.[3] One cannot describe either the attitudes or the behaviour of magistrates in terms of a simple punitive/non-punitive dimension. In fact, concern for justice, a doctrine considered old-fashioned and out of date by some, appears to have a number of *redeeming* features. In contrast to magistrates with high scores on the modernism and punishment corrects scales, magistrates with high justice scores appear to impose upon themselves certain restrictions on the degree to which they will interfere in the life and liberty of the subject solely by reason of the fact that an individual has committed an offence. In practical terms, a person who has committed a fairly minor offence should consider himself fortunate to come before a magistrate concerned with "justice" rather than one interested in either his correction through punishment or in being "modern."

From the point of scale construction, the most heartening aspect of these findings is that it is possible to develop reliable and valid scales through factor analysis. Scales derived through these procedures can predict not only the frequency with which magistrates tend to use particular types of sentences, but also the amount or lengths of such sentences.

Multiple Regression Analysis

So far we have looked at the relationship between individual factor scores and sentencing behaviour. This is somewhat artificial because each magistrate has positions on all scales. It would seem more profitable to look at the relationship of combinations of attitudes to judicial behaviour rather than individual correlations. This calls for a multiple regression approach.

Multiple regression is simply an elaboration of the correlational analysis described above. Unlike simple correlation, multiple regression seeks to express the amount of change in the dependent variable (in this case the sentencing behaviour of magistrates) in terms of several independent variables (in this case the five factor scores).

In this study a step-wise multiple regression program was employed.[4] At the first step, the computer calculates the correlation between the behavioural characteristic and the "best" predictor of that characteristic, i.e., the one factor score most closely associated with it. At step two, the program seems to explain the remaining unexplained variance (which now becomes the dependent variable) in terms of the best of the remaining factor scores. At each step the computer calculates the weights that are to be attached to each of the dependent variables. The procedure is repeated until the size of the correlation coefficient can no longer be significantly increased by the addition of another variable. This procedure often demonstrates that variables which are not significantly correlated to start with become so once the impact of other variables has been accounted for. Thus, it will be shown that while social defence scores are not individually correlated with the use of gaol sentences, they do become so once scores on the justice scale have been taken into account.

In order to avoid capitalizing on chance variation in the data, the computer was instructed not to include a variable in the analysis unless the degree to which it adds significantly to the predictive power of the equation was at 0.01 or better. However, once in an equation, a factor score could remain unless its contribution to the predictive power of the total equation did not fall below 0.05. In other words, the computer was instructed to make it difficult for a factor score to get in a regression equation, but once in it could stay as long as it made some contribution to the power of the equation.

The computer program used provided a print-out indicating the size of the correlation coefficient at each step, the weights attached to each factor score (re-calculated at each step), and the amount of variance that remained to be explained.

This procedure yielded correlation coefficients that were considerably higher than those obtained from simple correlational analysis. For the sixty-seven regression equations calculated the size of the correlations between clusters of attitude scores and behavioural characteristics ranged from a low of 0.3 to a high of 0.67, with a mean correlation of 0.45. Once again, the lowest

correlations were in respect to predictions of the use of probation and suspended sentence without probation. As mentioned
earlier, the probable reason for this is the unreliability of the data
with respect to these two types of sentence.

It would be too cumbersome to present all the regression equations in the body of this chapter. They are presented in full in
Technical Appendix 3. What is presented in Table 45 are
summaries of the regression equations for main categories of sentence for all indictable offences (taken together) and for theft, the
most commonly occurring single offence.

In this table, the regression equations are translated into a non-
mathematical form. Each step in the equation is represented by
the factor score included at that step. The factor scores are written in a positive or negative form depending on whether the regression equation added or subtracted them. The size of the correlation coefficient at each step is presented on the right hand
column of the table.

It can be seen from the table that the relationship of attitudes to
sentencing behaviour is a fairly complex one. In most instances,
several attitude scores are associated with the behavioural criteria used. Moreover, they are associated with judicial behaviour in
a theoretically meaningful way.

The frequent use of suspended sentence without probation in
indictable cases is associated with a lack of concern for abstract
justice, tolerance of deviance, the view that punishment does not
correct the offender, and modernism in outlook. Taken together
these attitudes represent a liberal, non-punitive sentencing philosophy.

The use of ordinary gaol terms in indictable cases is associated
with belief in justice, and a lack of concern for social defence.
This is as one would expect, as short term imprisonment does not
provide protection to society or treatment for the offender, but
can only serve the purpose of punishing crime in the interest of
justice.

The relationship of attitudes to the use of reformatory sentence
is particularly interesting. Magistrates who use reformatory sentences in a large number of cases have a tendency not be be concerned with justice, but at the same time to feel that punishment
is a corrective to the offender, and to be rather traditional in outlook and intolerant. The use of long terms of imprisonment in the
penitentiary appears to be related simply to concern for justice
and concern for social defence. We see in this table that attitudes
are related not only to the frequency with which institutional sen-

TABLE 45

Stepwise regression of attitude scores against sentencing behaviour: all indictable cases and cases of theft

Step	Independent variables (attitude scores)	r
	Proportion of suspended sentences without probation in indictable cases	
1	Not concerned for justice	0.402
2	Tolerant	0.448
3	Does not feel punishment corrects	0.489
4	Modern in outlook	0.516
	Proportion of probation dispositions in indictable cases	
1	Not concerned for justice	0.283
2	Feels punishment corrects	0.371
	Proportion of fines in indictable cases	
1	Concerned for justice	0.413
2	Concerned for social defence	0.432
3	Modern in outlook	0.463
	Proportion of common gaol sentences in indictable cases	
1	Concerned for justice	0.332
2	Lacks concern for social defence	0.380
	Proportion of penitentiary sentences in indictable cases	
1	Concern for justice	0.310
2	Concern for social defence	0.402
	Proportion of reformatory sentences in indictable cases	
1	Not concerned for justice	0.427
2	Feels punishment corrects	0.499
3	Traditional	0.560
4	Intolerant	0.640
	Proportion of suspended sentences without probation for theft	
1	Lacks concern for justice	0.269
2	Does not feel punishment corrects	0.310
3	Concerned for social defence	0.394
4	Tolerant of deviance	0.432
	Proportion of probation dispositions for theft	
1	Feels punishment corrects	0.342
2	Concerned for justice	0.376
	Proportion of fines for theft	
1	Concerned for justice	0.397
2	Concerned for social defence	0.442
	Proportion of institution for theft	
1	Traditional	0.372
2	Intolerant	0.449
3	Feels punishment corrects	0.489
4	Concerned for social defence	0.566

tences are used, but also to the types of institutional sentence selected.

When we examine the relationship of attitudes to sentencing behaviour in cases of theft, a fairly similar pattern emerges. The main difference in the attitude-behaviour relationship between theft and all institutional sentences combined appears to be a tendency for magistrates who frequently use institutional sentences for theft to be traditional in outlook and rather intolerant in their attitudes to social deviance. Once again, this is as one would expect. Theft is not often a particularly serious offence. A tolerant magistrate or a magistrate who identifies with modern doctrines would not be likely to use imprisonment for cases of this kind.

Summary and Conclusion

In this chapter the relationship between judicial attitudes and judicial behaviour was demonstrated. It was shown that factorally derived scales are better predictors of judicial behaviour than scales derived through Likert procedures. The justice and the punishment corrects scales were more closely associated with the larger number of sentences than were the other scales. However, when specific offences were considered all the scales were associated with behaviour of magistrates with respect to most of the offences considered.

Simple correlational analysis revealed statistically significant relationships between attitudes and behaviour in nearly all cases considered (sixty-seven in all), but not all attitude scales were statistically associated with every type of sentence.

With the use of multiple regression methods, it was possible to demonstrate that the sentencing behaviour of magistrates (for every offence studied) was significantly associated with the attitudes of the magistrates concerned. Over sixty-seven different measures of behaviour were used, and in each case the statistical relationship between attitudes and behaviour was strong enough to exclude the possibility of the relationship arising solely due to chance to less than one in a thousand. Moreover, it was shown that the relationship between judicial attitudes and judicial behaviour is not a simple one that can be described purely in terms of a simple punitive, non-punitive dimension. Many different combinations of attitude scores were associated with the behaviour of magistrates in specific situations. Depending on the type of case, severe sentences may be associated with the view that "punishment corrects," or they may be associated with "intolerance" of deviant behaviour, or with concern for "social defence" or even with identification with "modern" ideals. In fact, concern for "justice," which is normally associated with punitiveness, can very often be shown to be associated with more moderate and less severe sentencing behaviour.

The fact that variation in sentencing behaviour is associated with the variation in the attitude of individual magistrates to the degree demonstrated, indicates that the judicial process is not as uniform and impartial as many people would hope it to be. This may disturb those who value the concepts of impartial justice and equality before the law. However, before one can draw firm conclusions concerning the degree to which the attitudes of magistrates affect their behaviour, further analyses in two areas are needed.

It is well known to researchers that a statistically significant correlation does not indicate a causative relationship. Without further data, it is impossible to determine whether the attitudes of magistrates cause them to behave in the way they do or whether the behaviour of magistrates on the bench is determined by other factors, which also cause them to develop the attitudes they have. For example, some magistrates may be responding, both in their sentencing behaviour and in their attitudes, to public opinion in the community in which they are situated. There may also be situations in which magistrates cannot use probation frequently, as probation officers and supporting community services are not fully available in their local communities. These questions will be explored in the next three chapters.

There is another set of factors which must be taken into account in interpreting the findings described in this chapter. The behavioural variables used in this chapter were the proportion of sentences of different kinds for specific offences. The offences were described strictly in terms of their legal definitions. It is well known that many different factual combinations can arise within a specific legal-category. Thus, a robbery may include such disparate combinations of factors as a dispute over a bottle of wine between two alcoholics and an armed robbery of a bank.

It may be that magistrates who sentence more severely in respect of a particular offence have had to deal with more serious crimes within that category. While this is possible, the data presented here suggest that it is not very likely. The fact that relationships between attitudes and behaviour followed a consistent pattern over a large number of different offences, some of which are likely to be rather uniform in their character, suggests that there are relationships between the attitudes and behaviour of magistrates irrespective of specific factual combinations of cases coming before the courts.

NOTES TO CHAPTER 9

1   An easy to follow description of regression analysis is to be found in S. Diamond, *Information and Error* (New York, 1959), 171-2 and 193-5.
2   For references see Chapter 1, n. 15.

3　These findings are in accordance with those reported by S. Wheeler, *et al.*, "Agents of Delinquency Control," in S. Wheeler, ed., *Controlling Delinquents* (New York, 1966), 31-60.

4　The statistical program was contained in the computer package called "Trec: A Stepwise Multiple Regression Programme with Transformation Package" (Dept. of Political Economy, University of Toronto; assembled 1966).

10

Legal Constraints on Sentencing

Sentencing takes place within a legal and social framework, which imposes certain constraints on the discretion of the court. The extent to which attitudes of magistrates find expression in their behaviour is likely to depend not only on the strength of these attitudes, but also on how magistrates define the operative constraints and the degree to which they feel obliged to conform to them. This chapter explores the ways in which magistrates define the law as it affects sentencing. The next chapter deals with constraints arising out of the social world of magistrates, and following this is a chapter dealing with how socio-legal constraints affect sentencing behaviour.

Legislative Constraints

As we have already seen, the formal law as expressed in the Criminal Code and related statutes provide enormous discretionary power to Canadian magistrates. Apart from the requirement of not exceeding the very high maximum penalties provided by the Code, the only areas in which legislative restrictions are imposed relate to the use of probation and the provision for minimum penalties with respect to two relatively minor offences.[1] It was decided to seek information from magistrates concerning the degree to which they feel satisfied with existing law, and more particularly, the degree to which they feel bound by its prescriptions.

Magistrates were asked to indicate the legislative changes affecting sentencing that they would like to see enacted. Their answers are presented in Table 46.

TABLE 46

Recommended changes in the law as it affects sentencing

Change recommended	Number	Per cent
Removal of restrictions on the use of probation	38	53.5
Removal of all minimum penalties	21	29.6
Provisions for unconditional discharge	20	28.2
Make suspended sentence enforceable	17	23.9
Provide minimum penalties for certain offences	6	8.5
Abolish short-term imprisonment	5	7.0
Make pre-sentence reports mandatory	4	5.6
Abolish statutory remission	4	5.6
Reduce maximum penalties for certain offences	3	4.2
Other	1	1.4
No change needed	14	19.7

The majority of magistrates (fifty-seven out of seventy-one), would like to see changes made in the law with regard to sentencing. It is interesting that most magistrates recommended changes that would increase their power to use community-based sentences as opposed to institutional sentences. It would appear that magistrates find the existing restrictions in Canadian law to be punitive in nature. It is also interesting that few magistrates would like to see the discretionary power given to them decreased in any way. Not one recommended the introduction of guidelines in the law concerning the selection of sentence.

The most significant restriction in the Criminal Code affecting the selection of sentence arises out of the provisions of section 638 of the Code, dealing with probation. This section specifies that no person may be placed on probation if he has a previous conviction for a similar offence within five years, or two previous convictions for any indictable offence. Some magistrates have found a number of rather ingenious ways of avoiding these requirements.

The most frequently used device is one in which the magistrate instructs the crown attorney not to prove previous convictions in cases where probation is a possibility. While magistrates have no authority to instruct the Crown in these matters, an informal agreement is often worked out.

The second, and somewhat more dubious device, is one in which the magistrate refuses to convict in cases where probation is not legally possible. The offender is placed on "informal" probation for a specified period of time (usually one year), and the magistrate receives a report from the probation officer at the end of that time. If the probationer lives up to the conditions imposed, the magistrate acquits him of the charge.

Probation officers have objected to this type of "probation." They feel that there is no legal basis for supervision and no authority for them to return the offender to court for violation. Despite the fact that the chief probation officer has publicly denounced this type of disposition, and has instructed probation officers not to accept cases coming to them in this way, in a number of areas the practice persists.[2]

Magistrates were asked to indicate the degree to which they conform to the requirements of section 638 of the Criminal Code. The answers are presented in Table 47. Nearly two out of three magistrates are willing on occasion to avoid the requirements of the Criminal Code dealing with selection for probation. Nearly one in five admit that they completely ignore the law in this regard. These findings are an indication of the degree to which some magistrates are willing to bend the law in the interests of achieving what they believe to be a just and reasonable result in the circumstances.

TABLE 47

Conformity to the law regarding selection for probation

Degree of conformity	Number	Per cent
Always conforms to s.638	25	35.3
Sometimes conforms to s.638	31	43.6
Ignores s.638	15	21.1
Total	71	100.0

It is particularly interesting that avoidance of the law is in the direction of being more favourable to the offender than the relevant legislation would require. The restrictions with respect to selection for probation have been the subject of considerable criticism over the years by most professional groups dealing with crime, including the Ontario Magistrates' Association.[3] Legislation has recently been passed removing restrictions.[4] What we are witnessing in these findings is the way in which the informal processes of the administration of criminal justice keep abreast of popular thinking well in advance of legislative change. It is unfortunate, however, that current practice with respect to the selection for probation is not uniform.

Since only some magistrates indicated willingness to evade the law, it would be interesting to know if they are distinguishable from their colleagues in any way. First of all let us see if they have different conceptions as to the purpose of probation. Magistrates were divided into two groups depending upon whether or not they stated that they conformed to the requirements of section 638. Each group was then divided into two, depending on whether probation was seen as a form of treatment, or as surveillance, supervision, and control. The result is the two by two Table 48.

TABLE 48

Conformity to the law with respect to probation among magistrates who see probation as a form of treatment and those who see it as supervision and control

| | | Degree of conformity to the law | | | |
		Conforms	Does not conform	Total	Per cent
Perceived purposes of probation	Treatment	9	35	44	68.7
	Supervision and control	15	5	20	31.2
	Total	24	40	64	
	Per cent	37.5	62.5		100.0

Yates chi square = 15.205; significant at 0.001.

Two out of three magistrates who conform to the requirements of the Criminal Code view probation as a method of supervision and control. In contrast, nearly nine out of ten who do not conform to these provisions, view probation as a form of treatment.

So it appears that legal constraints on the use of probation are onerous only to magistrates with a treatment philosophy.

To explore further the relationship of penal philosophy and attitudes to the way in which the law is perceived, correlations were calculated between the degree of conformity to section 638 and the scores of magistrates on the main penal philosophy and attitude scales and certain other factors. These correlations are presented in Table 49.

TABLE 49

Correlations between conformity to section 638 and attitudes and penal philosophy

Variables correlated with conformity to s.638	Correlation	Level of significance
Attitude scores		
Concern for justice	0.251	0.05
Concern for social defence	0.388	0.01
Penal philosophy		
General deterrence	0.444	0.01
Individual deterrence	0.235	0.05
Reformation	-0.587	0.01
Punishment	0.323	0.01
Incapacitation	0.383	0.01
Knowledge		
Knowledge of literature: psychological	-0.387	0.01
Knowledge of literature: sociological	-0.319	0.01
Knowledge of correctional institutions	-0.400	0.01
Proportion of offenders believed mentally ill	-0.354	0.01
Decision-making rules		
Rated importance of information for sentencing: criminal record	0.334	0.01
Rated importance of information for sentencing: background of offender	-0.334	0.01
Confidence in correctional institutions	0.431	0.01
Causes of crime: no. of factors chosen	-0.254	0.05
Other social constraints		
Objectivity of press reports	-0.382	0.01
Concern about public opinion	0.335	0.01
Accepts recommendation from probation officer	-0.257	0.05

Answers to the question on conformity to the law with respect to probation are closely associated with answers to many other questions in the interview as well as scores derived from the attitude questionnaire. As far as attitudes are concerned, conformity to the restrictions with regard to probation is positively correlated with high justice and social defence scores. As far as penal philosophy is concerned, conformity to the law is positively associated with belief in individual and general deterrence as well as retribution and incapacitation, while being negatively associated with belief in reformation.

Magistrates who conform to these requirements appear to have less knowledge about the causes of crime and give less weight to both psychology and sociology as significant sources of information. As one would expect, conformity to section 638 is associated with giving greater weight to the criminal record and less weight to the background of the offender. Magistrates who conform to the law also appear to be more concerned about public opinion and at the same time feel that press reports about the magistrates' court lack objectivity.

These data reveal a consistent pattern of beliefs bearing on sentencing. The way in which a magistrate defines his relationship to the law and the degree to which he is willing to conform to its dictates depends on whether his personal penal philosophy and attitudes coincide with its prescriptions. It appears that the law is not always an important constraining influence in the behaviour of magistrates, at least in this area of sentencing. While this particular section of the Code is in general disrepute, further evidence was forthcoming confirming that "punitiveness" in attitudes and beliefs is associated with satisfaction with existing law.

Magistrates were asked whether they were satisfied with other areas of the law as it affects sentencing. Comparisons were made of the penal philosophy and attitude scores of the two groups. The results are presented in Table 50.

Magistrates attaching great weight to justice and deterrence are likely to be satisfied with existing law. In contrast, magistrates more concerned about reformation are likely to be dissatisfied. We also see that magistrates who feel that a greater proportion of offenders are mentally ill are not likely to be satisfied with the law affecting sentencing. This is what one would expect in view of the fact that Canadian law affecting sentencing was drafted at a time when retribution and deterrence were the predominant theses. Since that time, reformation has assumed great-

TABLE 50

Relationships of penal philosophy and attitudes
to satisfaction with existing law

Variable		Group 1 Satisfied	Group 2 Not satisfied	t-value	Level of significance
Attitude score	Mean	0.278	-0.573	3.487	0.001
Justice	S.D.	0.919	0.814		
	N	15	54		
Penal philosophy	Mean	7.333	9.370	-2.095	0.040
score	S.D.	3.697	3.229		
Reformation	N	15	54		
Penal philosophy score	Mean	8.357	5.904	2.218	0.030
Individual	S.D.	2.763	3.872		
deterrence	N	15	54		
Proportion of	Mean	2.333	2.780	-2.010	0.049
offenders believed	S.D.	0.724	0.764		
mentally ill	N	15	54		

er significance in the penal philosophy of the courts, while the legislation has remained relatively unchanged.

Perhaps the most significant findings relate to the degree to which different magistrates felt that the law should widen or reduce the discretion given to them. Seven magistrates felt that the discretionary power of the courts should be reduced, forty-five were satisfied with the existing power given, nineteen felt that discretionary powers should be widened. Comparisons were made of attitudes and penal philosophies of those who wanted discretion reduced and those who wanted it increased. The results are presented in Table 51.

Magistrates who want their discretionary power in sentencing increased are distinguishable from those who want it reduced by having significantly higher reformation and significantly lower individual deterrence scores on the attitude scales. They also believe that a greater proportion of offenders are mentally ill, their knowledge of the literature related to the causes of crime tends to be greater, and they use more information in sentencing. It is evident that treatment-oriented magistrates feel the need for maximum discretion, while punishment-oriented magistrates would like the law to be more restrictive.

As it is, Canadian law gives enormous discretionary power in sentencing to magistrates. Only seven would like to see this pow-

TABLE 51

Relationship of attitudes and penal philosophy to
amount of discretion needed in sentencing

Variable		Discretion should be reduced	Discretion should be increased	t-value	Level of significance
Social defence	Mean	1.174	0.025	2.144	0.042
	S.D.	1.314	1.176		
	N	7	19		
Individual deterrence	Mean	9.714	4.000	4.085	0.000
	S.D.	3.861	2.784		
	N	7	19		
Reformation	Mean	6.143	10.316	-3.311	0.003
	S.D.	2.734	2.888		
	N	7	19		
Proportion of offenders believed mentally ill	Mean	2.286	3.000	-2.43	0.024
	S.D.	0.488	0.707		
	N	7	19		
Knowledge of literature on causes of crime	Mean	1.000	1.737	-2.624	0.015
	S.D.	0.000	0.733		
	N	7	19		
No. of items of information used in sentencing	Mean	1.000	2.000	-3.575	0.002
	S.D.	0.000	0.730		
	N	7	19		

er reduced. While freedom from legislative constraints is something most decision-makers are likely to want, the proper scope of discretionary power is a question that cannot be left solely to the opinions of judges or magistrates, as important as these opinions may be. The determination of this issue is something the legislature should decide as a matter of policy, and it will properly consider not only the views of judges and magistrates but also their behaviour on the bench. To the extent that this study provides any empirical evidence that may be helpful in this regard, it is to be found in the data presented in subsequent chapters which describe how magistrates perform under conditions of almost total freedom from legislative constraint.

The Decisions of the Appeal Courts

We have seen that the formal law laid down in legislation provides minimal control over the exercise of discretion in sentencing. When the law attempts to direct magistrates in their sentencing behaviour, many magistrates find ways of avoiding its requirements. A naïve view of the judicial process would lead one to believe that the appeal courts would exercise control in areas where legislative guidance is lacking. But a closer examination of the situation reveals that there are a number of factors which militate against effective control by the appeal courts.

In the first place, less than one per cent of magistrates' decisions in indictable cases are appealed.[5] Secondly, only about one quarter of these appeals are successful.[6] Third, the appeal courts are not always specific in their reasons for varying sentence, and because of this magistrates are left in some doubt as to the thinking of the appeal court judges. Fourth, even if principles of sentencing are articulated, there are often rapid shifts in the emphasis on the part of the appeal courts with respect to the proper considerations that should be applied in sentencing. The kinds of decisions made and the reasons for judgement given tend to differ depending upon the particular composition of the court dealing with the case. Fifth, many magistrates feel that they have little to learn from appeal court judges. These magistrates point out that they have much more experience in sentencing than judges of the higher courts. It is also true that most magistrates do more reading, attend more conferences, and participate more actively in workshops and seminars about sentencing than many appeal court judges. Finally, some magistrates feel that they can do as they please in sentencing, without fear of interference by the court of appeal, as long as their reasons for judgement are stated in a satisfactory way.

The Ontario Court of Appeal has usually taken a liberal attitude as to its powers of review on appeal.[7] Unlike appeal courts in some of the other provinces, the Ontario Court of Appeal has usually (but not consistently) taken the view that it is open to them to substitute the proper sentence that in their judgement ought to have been given, even if the magistrate did not err significantly.[8] As a result, a large number of minor modifications in sentence have been made. For example, the Ontario Court of Appeal sometimes substitutes a sentence of six months definite and twelve months indeterminate for an original sentence of nine months definite and nine months indeterminate. This type of "tinkering" with magistrates' sentences without a clear rationale for it, has led many magistrates to become confused as to the principles followed by the Court of Appeal. For all these reasons, it appears that the Ontario Court of Appeal does not exercise effective control over sentencing in magistrates' courts. Let us see whether this is so.

Magistrates were asked to indicate the degree to which they find the decisions of the Appeal Court in Ontario helpful to them in laying down principles of sentencing which ought to be applied. The results are indicated in Table 52.

Less than half the magistrates find the decisions of the Court of Appeal helpful to them in sentencing. In fact, ten magistrates feel that the Court of Appeal plays a disruptive role through constant

TABLE 52

Magistrates' views as to the amount of guidance in sentencing received from the Ontario Court of Appeal

	Number	Per cent
Of considerable help	9	12.7
Of some help	24	33.8
Of little or no help	26	36.6
Of hindrance	10	14.1
N.A.	2	2.8
Total	71	100.0

shifts in the policies it adopts. These findings indicate that a great deal must be done to bring magistrates and appeal court judges closer together in sentencing philosophy.

To explore this possibility magistrates were asked to suggest ways in which the role of the Ontario Court of Appeal could be strengthened. Their suggestions are summarized in Table 53.

The suggestions given show the confusion on the part of many magistrates as to the principles and policies followed by the Ontario Court of Appeal in sentencing. While it is understandable that some magistrates would like to see the Court of Appeal show greater respect for the views of magistrates, it is not likely that many appeal court judges would care to admit that magistrates have authority in these matters.

It is difficult to test the degree to which magistrates actually conform to decisions of the appeal courts, as most reported appeal judgements are not specific enough in their directions to the lower courts to set up a genuine experiment. It was possible, however, to determine the degree to which magistrates conform to one specific rule laid down by appeal courts; namely, that it is improper for magistrates to consider the possibility of parole in determining the appropriate length of institutional sentence to impose.[9]

Magistrates were asked to indicate whether they adjusted their sentences in the light of the possibility of parole being granted. Two out of three admitted that they sometimes increased the

TABLE 53

Suggestions for improving the role of the Ontario Court of Appeal in sentencing

Suggestions made	Number	Per cent
By giving more specific reasons for judgement	35	49.3
By being more consistent in principles followed	27	38.0
By giving greater weight to the views of magistrates	12	16.9
By holding joint conferences with magistrates	11	15.5
Don't know	18	25.4

length of sentence imposed. The reasons given were interesting.

Of the forty-two magistrates admitting to this practice, twenty-one (50 per cent) stated that they did so in order to give the institutional personnel ample opportunity to work with the offender, in hopes that he would respond quickly and be considered for early parole, but in the certain knowledge that if he did not respond, he would be kept inside.

Nine magistrates (21 per cent) stated that they often considered parole either when imposing a long sentence directed to the deterrence of potential offenders, or when forced to do so by reasons of aroused public opinion. They would immediately write to the Parole Board requesting that the offender be considered for parole. In this way they felt that they could appear to be punitive without serious consequences to the offender. The difficulty with this policy is that parole is a matter for the complete discretion of the Board, and there is no guarantee that the magistrate's recommendations will be accepted.[10]

Twelve magistrates (29 per cent) admitted that they increased sentences in order to ensure that the offender would not be "back on the streets" in a relatively short time. These magistrates are aware that parole is not normally considered until after the offender has served at least one-third of his sentence.

Two significant facts emerge from these findings. First, the majority of magistrates admit that they deliberately evade the directions of the Ontario Court of Appeal in this matter. Second, different motivations exist among those who do. "Forward-looking" magistrates, i.e. those concerned about the impact of their decisions on the future behaviour of the offender and the public at large, will sometimes increase their sentences (because of the existence of a parole system), in the belief that this will further their reformative or deterrent objectives. "Backward-looking" magistrates, i.e. those concerned solely with punishing past criminal behaviour will do the same, but only to ensure that the offender gets his "just deserts."

Conclusion

The data presented in this chapter lead to the conclusion that the law expressed in legislation and reported cases offers little guidance to magistrates. Moreover, it appears that, to the extent that control is exercised, it is resented by many magistrates, particularly those with a treatment philosophy. Magistrates seem to enjoy the enormous discretionary power given to them and many wish it to be increased still further.

Those magistrates who find the law repressive resort to devices which enable them to achieve their objectives in sentencing, without fear of review. But this is not to say that the law exercises no control over the behaviour of magistrates. Legal training and experience on the bench bring the magistrate into direct contact with certain standards, expectations, values, and sentiments associated with the law and the professional role of the judge. To the extent that a magistrate adopts them, they form part of his personal penal philosophy and attitudes. We have already seen how closely associated penal philosophy and attitudes are to the behaviour of magistrates on the bench. The general conclusion that can be made is that the socializing and educative influences of legal experience are far more important in controlling judicial behaviour than the formal rules laid down by parliament and the appeal courts.

NOTES TO CHAPTER 10

1 These offences are: theft from the mails (Criminal Code, s.298); and a second conviction for driving a motor vehicle whilst impaired (Criminal Code, s.223).
2 For a description of other practices sometimes resorted to in order to avoid the restriction on probation, see St. John Madeley, "Probation," in W.T. McGrath, ed., Crime and its Treatment in Canada (Toronto, 1965), 229-330.
3 See Report of the Sentencing Committee of the Ontario Magistrates' Associa-

tion (1961, 1962), mimeo. See also "Brief of the Canadian Corrections Association on the Development of Probation in Canada," *Canadian Journal of Corrections*, 16 (1968), 151-78.

4 Bill C-195 (An Act to Amend the Criminal Code) repeals ss.637-40.

5 Dominion Bureau of Statistics, *Statistics of Criminal and Other Offences* (Ottawa, 1966).

6 *Ibid.*

7 See J. Decore, "Criminal Sentencing: The Role of the Canadian Courts of Appeal and the Doctrine of Uniformity," *The Criminal Law Quarterly*, 6 (1964), 324-80.

8 *Ibid.*

9 *Reg.* v. *Holden* (1962), 39 Crim. Rep. 228; *Reg.* v. *Roberts* (1963), 1 C.C.C. 27.

10 Parole Act, *Stats. of Canada*, 1958, ch. 38.

11

Social Constraints on Sentencing

Magistrates' courts are highly structured social organizations. Within the court structure exists a network of social roles and personal relationships. The magistrate, the crown attorney, the defence counsel and the probation officer occupy positions to which are attached a number of obligations and privileges closely defined by law or convention or both. While each of these officers commands an area of specialized confidence and responsibility, particularly with regard to the trial of the issue of guilt, at the sentencing stage they are all involved in the decision-process to varying degrees. The formality which characterizes working relationships tends to disappear once the issue of guilt is determined. Less formal social relationships develop permitting the nature of face-to-face personal relationships between the individuals concerned to influence the outcome of sentencing decisions.

While in many instances, the magistrate maintains his dominant position by keeping a certain social distance between himself and other persons involved, this is not always the case. Sometimes the probation officer exerts a great influence, and indeed, interviews with magistrates revealed a number of instances in which the probation officer actually made the sentencing decisions. In other instances, it is the views of the crown attorney that appear to dominate. Sometimes a confident and personable defence counsel can exert an enormous influence on the sentencing decisions made in regard to his clients.

Public opinion also plays a role in the thinking of magistrates. As we have already learned, magistrates identify closely with their communities. It is equally true that the community shows great interest in the court. Crime often evokes strong emotional feelings on the part of the public. The trial and sentence of offenders is performed in public and the decisions of the court are subject to press comment. In smaller communities particularly, the local press devotes a great deal of its news coverage to the magistrates' court. Sensational criminal trials often receive extravagant attention in the mass media.

At the same time, magistrates will often direct their sentences primarily to the general public. The control of crime through general deterrence can only be successful when the sentence and the reasons for it are spelled out for all to hear. In a sense, therefore, the relationship between the court and the community is reciprocal.

Perhaps the greatest social influence in the environment of magistrates is their relationship with each other. Magistrates interact in a variety of ways. Some share offices, others meet regularly through committee and other work, and still others belong to the same social organizations. Reciprocal relationships which result out of this interaction are likely to produce a tendency towards consensus in outlook.

All in all, magistrates are subjected to enormous conformatory pressures. This is what Nigel Walker meant when he said: "... the sentencer is chiefly conscious of the probation officer looking over one of his shoulders and the appellate court looking over the other."[1]

In this chapter an attempt is made to identify significant social influences in the environments of magistrates. Since the material presented is based on interviews, the data are limited to identifying those social influences that magistrates themselves are aware of.

Two sets of questions were asked with respect to each constraining influence. The first set of questions asked magistrates to indicate what they felt other people expected of them in sentencing. The second set of questions concerned the degree to which magistrates felt obliged to take these expectations into account.

The following areas were explored.

1 The magistrate's knowledge of the views and practices of his

fellow magistrates, and the degree to which he feels constrained to conform to these views and practices in the interest of uniformity.

2 His relationship with other people in his immediate working environment, particularly the probation officer and the crown attorney; his definition of their proper role in sentencing, and the degree to which these people actually participate in decision-making.

3 His definition of his relationship to his employer, i.e. the Department of the Attorney-General; his view of the Department's expectations of him, and the degree to which he feels obliged to conform to these expectations.

4 His estimate of public opinion, and the degree to which public opinion is given weight in sentencing decisions.

Relationships with Fellow Magistrates

There are a number of reasons which suggest that the relationships of magistrates with each other should be a significant force in controlling the way in which they behave on the bench.

A strong feeling of fellowship exists among magistrates. We have seen that many magistrates do not look to the Ontario Court of Appeal for guidance, and as we shall see, most magistrates view the public as being hostile. With some justification, many magistrates feel that they are under-paid, over-worked, and misunderstood. This leads to a closing of ranks and, more significantly, the intensification of personal relationships.

Views and attitudes about sentencing are shared in a variety of ways. Magistrates are of equal status, and influence exists primarily through communication with each other. Reciprocity is the key to the exchanges. Some magistrates have daily conversations about sentencing with their colleagues. Sometimes these conversations are initiated by a magistrate seeking advice. More often they are a more subtle exchange of views among equals. Care is usually exercised by magistrates giving advice to show deference to the person seeking it.

This writer witnessed many of these exchanges. It seemed that often magistrates were not seeking advice, but rather a basis for legitimizing their sentences in the eyes of their colleagues. In sensitive areas of sentencing, such as in the case of sex offenders, magistrates would often seek reinforcement, and this was done by soliciting the opinions of magistrates whose views and practices were close to their own.

Before personal influence can be exercised by one magistrate over another, it can be expected that the following elements should be present: (i) the magistrate seeking advice must have some doubt about the way in which he should sentence; (ii) he must have respect for the views and practices of the magistrate giving advice; (iii) the differences in opinion between the two magistrates must not be so great as to make a consensus impossible; and (iv) the magistrate giving advice must be willing to state it in terms which show sufficient deference to his colleague.

But first let us look at the degree to which individual magistrates feel there is consensus among magistrates as a group as to

TABLE 54

Degree of consensus among magistrates

Question	Answer		
	Type of answer	Number	Per cent
To what extent do magistrates in Ontario share a common sentencing philosophy	A large measure of uniformity	28	39.5
	Some measure of uniformity	15	21.2
	A complete lack of uniformity	18	25.4
	Don't know	10	14.0
Total		71	100.0

the proper principles of sentencing (Table 54).

Less than half the magistrates feel that there is uniformity among magistrates in sentencing. This being the case, only a minority would feel obliged to follow group norms in the interest of uniformity. The rest must work out for themselves, possibly in collaboration with those magistrates for whom they have great respect, the proper principles upon which sentencing should be based.

Magistrates were then asked to state what they believed were the principles followed by most other magistrates. They were asked to indicate the relative merits attached to deterrence, reformation, and punishment by their colleagues. The results are presented in Table 55.

TABLE 55

Magistrates' views as to the sentencing philosophy of their colleagues

Ordering of priorities among purposes	Number	Per cent
First: deterrence Second: reformation Third: punishment	10	14.09
First: deterrence Second: punishment Third: reformation	3	4.26
First: reformation Second: deterrence Third: punishment	16	22.54
First: reformation Second: punishment Third: deterrence	1	1.41
First: punishment Second: deterrence Third: reformation	2	2.82
First: punishment Second: reformation Third: deterrence	4	5.63
All three equal	13	18.31
Don't know	22	30.99

Nearly one in three magistrates could not indicate the relative merits attached by their colleagues to the classical purposes in sentencing. Among those who felt that there was a rough ordering of priorities by magistrates as a whole, there was considerable division of opinion. Sixteen magistrates felt that reformation was the main principle followed by Ontario magistrates, while ten thought deterrence was given the greatest weight. A significant minority (six) felt that punishment was the main theme underlying sentencing in Ontario. Obviously, there is substantial lack of agreement among magistrates as to the principles of sentencing followed by their colleagues. This leaves it open for magistrates to interpret the norms of the profession in ways compatible with their personal views.

To explore this possibility, correlations were calculated between magistrates' personal penal philosophy scores and their images of the penal philosophy of others. The results are presented in Table 56.

TABLE 56

Correlations between own penal philosophy and images of the penal philosophies of others

	Images of penal philosophy of others		
Own penal philosophy	Punishment	Reformation	Deterrence
General deterrence:	-0.266	-0.340	0.463
Reformation:	-0.260	0.379	–
Punishment:	0.300	–	–

Magistrates differ widely in their personal penal philosophies. They also differ widely in their images of the penal philosophies of others. However, personal penal philosophy and the image of the penal philosophy of others are highly correlated. Most magistrates over-estimate the size of the group agreeing with them in sentencing. This militates against any effective change in sentencing as it allows magistrates to feel, regardless of their personal philosophy, that they are in the mainstream of thinking with respect to sentencing.

There appear to be two possible explanations for this. First, magistrates may develop their personal penal philosophies out of their images of the penal philosophies of others. Ever since the writing of William James, social psychologists have stressed the social origins of the images people form of themselves.[2]

An alternative explanation is one that would stress the selective way individuals perceive the expectations of others. The data are consistent with the view that magistrates interpret selectively the norms of sentencing in ways compatible with their subjective ends. While both factors are likely to play a role, it is the latter explanation that appears to be more consistent with the data as a whole. There does not appear to be a consensus among magistrates as to sentencing. The vagueness of formulation of the principles in sentencing and the contradictions among the many statements made, allow individual magistrates to select those principles and purposes which are more consistent with their own views.

Not all magistrates view themselves to be in line with majority thinking in sentencing. A significant minority (twenty-six) view their own sentencing principles and practices as deviating from those of the majority. Most of these magistrates (twenty out of twenty-six) believe that most other magistrates are too favourable to the offender. As one would expect, these magistrates tend to have higher general deterrence and individual deterrence scores on the penal philosophy scales, and higher social defence but lower punishment corrects scores on the attitude scales. These findings are summarized in Table 57, together with other data tending to show that the "deviant" magistrate is generally one who views himself as being more punitive than his colleagues. This suggests that the operative norms in the social world of magistrates (at least those derived from interaction among magistrates) are ones which stress reformation and treatment above deterrence and punishment.

TABLE 57

Relationship of penal philosophy, attitudes, and beliefs to images of sentencing behaviour of others

		Sentences of other magistrates are too favourable to offenders			
Variable		Yes	No	t-value	Level of significance
Penal philosophy					
General deterrence	Mean	10.000	6.776	2.463	0.016
	S.D.	5.487	4.696		
	N	20	49		
Individual deterrence	Mean	8.895	5.521	3.576	0.001
	S.D.	4.280	3.122		
	N	19	48		
Reformation	Mean	6.950	9.740	-3.328	0.001
	S.D.	2.417	3.416		
	N	20	50		
Attitudes					
Punishment corrects	Mean	0.985	0.509	2.507	0.043
	S.D.	0.757	0.916		
	N	20	50		
Social defence	Mean	0.925	0.288	2.320	0.023
	S.D.	1.203	0.964		
	N	20	50		
Beliefs					
Proportion of offenders believed mentally ill	Mean	2.211	2.851	-3.275	0.002
	S.D.	0.713	0.722		
	N	19	47		
Knowledge of literature on causes of crime	Mean	1.050	1.540	-3.304	0.002
	S.D.	0.224	0.646		
	N	20	50		
Rated importance of information regarding background of offender	Mean	1.300	1.804	-2.687	0.009
	S.D.	0.470	0.778		
	N	20	46		

We now turn to an examination of the degree to which magistrates feel obliged to conform to the views and practices of others. Magistrates were asked the following question (Table 58).

TABLE 58
Conformity to other magistrates

Question	Answer	Number	Percent
To what extent do you feel it necessary to take into account either the opinions or the practices (or both) of other magistrates in Ontario?	I attempt some uniformity in principle only	48	67.6
	I attempt uniformity in practice as well as principle	11	15.5
	I attempt uniformity in sentence only in regard to minor offences	8	11.2
	I do not consider either the principles or practices of other magistrates	4	5.6
Total		71	100.0

The majority of magistrates would like to achieve uniformity in principles only. This is so despite the fact that few magistrates were able to state what these principles are. The fact that four magistrates believed that they could safely ignore the views and practices of other magistrates is somewhat surprising in view of the great stress placed on uniformity by nearly all persons writing in this field. In contrast, eleven magistrates attempted to use a tariff system in which the sentences imposed would be determined by the "going rate" for specific sentences.

There were no statistically significant differences in either attitudes or penal philosophy among magistrates differing with respect to the doctrine of uniformity. The explanation for this may lie in the fact that "uniformity" is such a prestige-laden concept that, regardless of personal views, at least lip service must be given to it.

The analysis now turns to the degree to which personal influence is exercised by individual magistrates over others. Magistrates were asked to state the frequency with which they discuss sentencing problems with others, directly or by telephone. They were then asked to name the three magistrates whose views on sentencing they most respected.

Fifteen magistrates indicated that they have daily conversations with one or more colleagues about sentencing. Twenty-one stated that they usually had occasion to discuss sentencing with another magistrate at least once a month or more often. Of the remainder, fourteen indicated that they contacted other magistrates about sentencing problems less frequently than once a month, and twenty-one stated that they discussed sentencing with other magistrates only on rare occasions, and never to seek advice.

It is significant that almost half the magistrates in Ontario do not communicate with each other about sentencing more frequently than once a month. In some cases this is caused by the geographic isolation of certain magistrates while in others it seems to reflect self-imposed social isolation. This fact assumes some importance because the magistrates' court in Canada is one of the few courts of criminal jurisdiction that is comprised of a single judicial officer. With no requirements making pre-sentence reports mandatory and enormous discretionary power given in sentencing one might expect that nearly all magistrates would feel obliged to consult with others about sentencing at frequent intervals. This is probably not a matter that should be left solely to the discretion of the court. If "two heads are better than one" in sentencing, it should perhaps be set out in legislation. The matter will be pursued at greater length in the final chapter.

There are some interesting differences between magistrates selected as commanding the greatest respect and those not so selected. Magistrates enjoying respect among their colleagues tend to be older, to be legally trained, to come from professional backgrounds, and most significantly, they tend to be less concerned with justice and more tolerant of deviant behaviour. The statistical work supporting these findings is to be found in Technical Appendix 4.

Difference in social background characteristics are not surprising as they relate to the prestige which is attached to social class and education among the public in general. It is significant, however, to learn that the leading magistrates in Ontario, at least in the eyes of their colleagues, are not representative of magistrates as a whole in terms of sentencing attitude. Further confirmation can be obtained from Table 59, which indicates that magistrates elected to leading positions in the Magistrates' Association tend to be non-punitive and treatment-oriented. Once again we see the emergence of non-punitive constraints within the social world of magistrates.

TABLE 59

Relationship of the degree of participation in the Magistrates' Association to attitudes and penal philosophies of magistrates

Number of years on the Executive correlated with:	Correlation	Level of significance
Attitudes		
Intolerance	-0.330	0.01
Modernism	0.424	0.01
Penal philosophy		
Reformation	0.279	0.05
Punishment	-0.263	0.05
Knowledge		
Favours sociological explanation of crime	0.255	0.05
Relationships to others		
Satisfaction with probation officers	0.350	0.01
Accepts recommendations from probation officers	0.425	0.01
Frequency of discussion with other magistrates	0.590	0.01

Relationships with Probation Officers

In Ontario, probation officers are appointed under the terms of the Probation Act.[3] They are designated as officers of the court and are required to prepare pre-sentence reports for magistrates and judges when requested to do so. Usually, probation officers are appointed to a particular court and over a period of time many develop personal relationships with the magistrates concerned.

The *Archambault Report* of 1938 strongly recommended the use of the pre-sentence report, stating that these investigations were "essential to the proper operation of the administration of justice."[4] The *Fauteux Report* of 1956 reaffirmed the value of the pre-sentence report and strongly recommended its use.[5] The Ontario Magistrates' Association has on a number of occasions emphasized the importance of the probation officer's role in sentencing.[6] It would appear, then, that the probation officer's value in sentencing is supported by legislation, by policy-making bodies, and most importantly, by the courts.

The majority of magistrates (fifty-one out of seventy-one), expressed general satisfaction with individual probation officers with whom they have had experience. Twelve indicated that they were satisfied with some probation officers only, and only four indicated negative feelings towards all.

At the same time, a large number of magistrates (thirty-three) indicated that probation officers tended to have a number of shortcomings. The kinds of shortcomings indicated (Table 60) are interesting as they provide certain insights into the way in which magistrates define their relationship to the correctional ideals that probation officers represent.

TABLE 60

Magistrates' views as to shortcomings probation officers tend to have

Shortcomings mentioned	Number	Per cent
Unrealistic in estimating chance for reformation	16	14.5
Lacks objectivity in dealing with offenders	13	11.8
Insufficient training and experience	11	10.0
Gives irrelevant information to the court	8	7.3
Usurps magistrates' function in sentencing	6	5.5
Deliberately distorts in favour of the offender	5	4.5
Easily manipulated by offenders	5	4.5
Too lenient in supervision	4	3.6
Other	8	7.3
No shortcomings	38	34.6

It is evident that over half the magistrates feel that probation officers tend to be "biased" in favour of the offender. Most of these (twenty-nine out of thirty-eight) feel that probation of-ficers are honestly but unrealistically optimistic about the chances of reformation. A smaller number (five) feel that proba-tion officers deliberately distort their pre-sentence reports in order to present a favourable picture of the offender.

The degree of confidence that the magistrate has in the proba-tion officer will affect the degree to which he is allowed to partici-pate in sentencing. Magistrates were asked to indicate the extent to which they would like probation officers to make recommenda-tions or suggestions as to sentence. They split into three groups with respect to this question. Twenty-four stated that they would welcome specific recommendations in all cases, twenty-six indicated that they would accept advice with regard to the offender's prospect for probation only, and twenty indicated that they would not welcome, nor accept, recommendations or advice in any case. Of this latter group, however, more than half (twelve) would accept a pre-sentence report in certain circumstances provided that the probation officer did not attempt to influence directly or indirectly the decision of the court.

Of the twenty-four magistrates who welcomed recommendations from probation officers in all cases, a small number (six) appeared to be willing to abandon their sentencing role entirely. In three cases it was discovered that the probation officer was asked to make specific suggestions as to the sentence that should be imposed. Despite the fact that all probation officers have been instructed by the Chief Probation Officer not to usurp the magistrates' role in sentencing in this way, it was discovered that in two cases it was the probation officer who actually made the decisions.[7] In both cases the probation officer felt embarrassed by his role and only discharged it reluctantly. In one case, the magistrate was ill, and found sentencing to be an especially stressful task. In the other, the probation officer enjoyed enormous respect from the magistrate who, while recognizing that the court was the final arbitrator, never had occasion to overrule a suggestion from him.

There are some interesting relationships between the attitudes and penal philosophies of magistrates and the degree to which the probation officer is allowed to participate in the decision-process (Table 61). Magistrates who give the probation officer a greater role in sentencing tend to have higher reformation scores, greater knowledge of psychological literature, and are likely to have made a greater number of visits to correctional institutions. In addition, these magistrates are more likely to rate information about the offender's background higher and the criminal record lower. They are also more likely to have served a number of years on the executive of the Ontario Magistrates' Association, to be legally trained, and apart from legal training, they are more likely to have had some university experience.

Taken together, the findings indicate that the degree to which the probation officer is permitted to participate in sentencing depends on the penal philosophy and attitudes of the magistrate, the kind of information that he feels is necessary in sentencing, the self-confidence he has as a lawyer and a magistrate, and the strengths of the personalities concerned.

TABLE 61

Relationships of penal philosophies and attitudes of magistrates to the degree to which probation officers are permitted to participate in sentencing

Sentencing recommendations correlated with:	Correlation	Level of significance
Attitudes		
Punishment corrects	0.264	0.05
Intolerance	-0.304	0.01
Social defence	-0.395	0.01
Penal philosophy		
Reformation	0.312	0.01
Knowledge		
Knowledge of psychological literature	0.353	0.01
Number of visits to correctional institutions	0.271	0.05
Information-seeking strategies		
Rates offender's background higher	0.371	0.01
Rates criminal record higher	-0.234	0.05

Relationships with Crown Attorneys

In Canada, the role of a crown attorney in sentencing is not clear. Unlike the practice in England, it is not usual for the Canadian Crown Attorney to speak to sentence in open court unless specifically requested to do so. But different practices exist in different courts. Some crown attorneys take a broad view of their role in sentencing, and frequently make statements concerning aggravating or mitigating circumstances. Some will try to present as fair and balanced a picture of the offence and the offender as the circumstances will justify. Others appear to define their role as being advocates for the community, the police, and the state, and will frequently impress upon the court the need for a severe penalty.

There are two areas in which crown attorneys perform a specialized role in sentencing. Under the provisions of the Criminal Code, a second conviction for impaired driving automatically results in a prison term.[8] However, before this penalty can be applied the Crown must notify the accused that it intends to prove the previous conviction. The magistrate has no control over this procedure and must impose at least the minimum penalty when it is used. Similarly, the Criminal Code provides for committal to preventive detention of persons found to be "dangerous sexual offenders."[9] Once again the discretion in initiating these procedures is the sole responsibility of the Crown (in this case, with the consent of the Attorney-General), and once the court has found the offender to be a dangerous sexual offender, in terms of the definition in the Code, it must commit to preventive detention. Secondly, the crown attorney can influence sentencing through the informal bargaining process which takes place prior to and during the trial. While bargains between defence counsel and crown attorney are usually concerned with the reduction of charges in exchange for pleas of guilty, sometimes the bargain includes the type of sentence that will be asked for. At times, the magistrate is involved in this process. If he is to allow the bargaining process to proceed he must give consent to the compromise reached. However, magistrates are rarely involved in direct negotiations over these matters. It is much more usual for them to be informed by the crown attorney that the offender will plead guilty to a particular charge provided that the Crown will not press for a sentence in excess of an agreed amount.

Bargaining has never been fully recognized as a legitimate practice in Canada, at least not to the same extent as in some American jurisdictions.[10] There is by no means a uniform set of rules governing this process, and the way it functions depends primarily on the kinds of relationships that have grown up between magistrates, crown attorneys, and defence counsel in particular parts of the province.

Magistrates were asked to indicate the degree to which the crown attorney speaks to sentence in open court in their area. The answers are indicated in Table 62.

TABLE 62

Frequency in which crown attorneys speak to sentence in magistrates' courts

Frequency	Number	Per cent
In most cases	25	35.2
In some cases	32	45.1
In few cases	13	18.3
N.A.	1	1.4
Total	71	100.0

Table 62 indicates that about one in three magistrates regularly receive sentencing recommendations from crown attorneys. A slightly larger number (45 per cent) sometimes receive submissions, but in most of these cases the submission is made only on request from the magistrate. Thirteen magistrates (18 per cent) never receive verbal submission from crown attorneys concerning sentence.

The impact of the crown attorney in sentencing will depend not only on the frequency in which he makes submissions, but also, and more importantly, on the degree to which the magistrate feels that the crown attorney's views should be considered. Magistrates were asked to indicate how helpful the crown attorney's views as to sentence were in determining the appropriate disposition to make (Table 63).

TABLE 63

Magistrates' views as to the value of crown attorneys' submissions

Value indicated	Number	Per cent
Very helpful	35	49.3
Sometimes helpful	29	40.9
Seldom helpful	7	9.8
Total	71	100.0

Nearly all magistrates feel that the crown attorney's views as to sentence are helpful to them in determining the appropriate disposition to impose. There is a tendency, however, for magistrates who rate the crown attorney's views higher to be more offence-oriented in their penal philosophy ($r = 0.311$; significant at 0.01). In general terms, however, it appears that the relationship between crown attorney and magistrate depends more on the personalities involved than on the penal philosophy or attitudes of the magistrate concerned.

Relationships with the Department of the Attorney-General

The independence of the judiciary from political control is one of the safeguards of freedom in a democratic society. While it is rare that direct political interference is exercised over Canadian magistrates, a number of factors militate against complete independence of the courts, particularly at the lower level.

We have seen that appointments to the bench in Canada are "political" in the sense of selections being made from supporters of the party in power. Magistrates in Ontario are appointed by the Provincial Cabinet on recommendation from the Attorney-General. In theory, once appointed, a magistrate should be completely free from any interference by the Attorney-General or his agents. However, a number of factors make complete independence difficult to achieve.

First of all, magistrates' salaries are not fixed but are rather a matter to be determined by the Attorney-General. Similarly, promotion from deputy- to full magistrate is at the complete discretion of the Attorney-General. Moreover, since the Attorney-General is responsible for the proper administration of justice in the province, he is understandably concerned that magistrates' courts operate fairly and efficiently.

On many occasions, attorneys-general in the province have made it clear that they cannot, and will not, interfere directly in the judicial process.[11] On the other hand, a large number of people appointed to the magistrates' bench are not legally qualified, and they need, and seek, advice. For many years, the Deputy-Attorney-General and the Inspector of Legal Offices as well as other officials in the Department, made themselves available to magistrates wishing to be advised on legal and administrative problems arising out of their work. This was an unsatisfactory arrangement as it was liable to the criticism that political control would thus appear to be exercised over the judiciary.

The first attempt to solve this problem was the appointment of a Chief Magistrate in 1963. Among other things, his role was to act as a buffer between magistrates and the Department, but a number of magistrates still preferred to have direct access to the Attorney-General and his Deputy.

On more than one occasion the Attorney-General has publicly, albeit gently, reprimanded magistrates for conduct which he considered to be inconsistent with the best interests of the administration of justice in the province.[12] It is generally known that certain magistrates have been privately reprimanded by officials in the Department concerning their conduct. When this did not succeed, the Attorney-General has sometimes refused to recommend an increment in salary for the offending magistrate. On occasion, magistrates have not been promoted from deputy- to full magistrate. In a number of more subtle ways, certain magistrates have become aware of the attitude of the Department to their work. Leave to attend conferences, holiday leave, the assignment of work-loads, and other matters within the control of the Department were handled in such a way that certain magistrates became aware that their standing with the Attorney-General was good or bad, as the case may be.

While the motives of the Attorney-General and other officials in his department were laudable, the situation was not satisfactory. Most magistrates and many members of the professional Bar were aware that some of them were in disfavour with the Attorney-General. This not only made it difficult for the magistrates concerned to perform their duties adequately, but also led to the suspicion that direct political interference was being exercised.

To some extent the problems inherent in this situation have been relieved by the appointment of a Judicial Council under the terms of the new Provincial Court Judges Act.[13] It is too early to see whether the problem will be completely resolved through this mechanism. In any event, recognition has been given to it, and it is likely that the Attorney-General would be all too pleased to be relieved of the responsibility of dealing with complaints about magistrates' behaviour.

Magistrates were asked to indicate whether any member of a government department (municipal, provincial, or federal) had in any way attempted to interfere in their work. Fifty-five magistrates (77 per cent) indicated that on no occasion had there been any direct approach made to them concerning what they should do in a particular case. However, ten indicated that attempts had been made on one occasion, and five that this had occurred on more than one.

Magistrates were then asked to indicate whether they felt their freedom from the possibility of political interference was as great as that enjoyed by judges of the higher courts. Only twenty-eight magistrates indicated that magistrates were as free from influence as higher court judges. Twelve indicated that the "possibility" of influence exists at the magistrates' level, but that such control is rarely exercised. A distressingly large number of magistrates (26 or 38 per cent) indicated that political control was frequently being exercised by the Department of the Attorney-General.

The thirty-eight who indicated that control can be exercised over the judicial work of magistrates by the Department of the Attorney-General were asked to indicate the mechanisms through which such control is actually imposed.

Table 64 indicates that a significant minority of magistrates feel that certain sanctions are likely to be imposed by the Attorney-General in the event of misbehaviour on their part. Deputy magistrates in particular feel under some pressure to conform. The fact that over half of the magistrates feel that their salary depends in part on their standing with the Attorney-General should be of some concern to those who value the complete independence of the judiciary from government control.

TABLE 64

Magistrates' views as to the mechanisms of control over their work by the Department of the Attorney-General

Mechanism of control	Number	Per cent
Control of salary	36	50.7
By intervention of Inspector of Legal Offices	35	49.3
By withholding promotion from deputy-to full magistrate	25	35.2
Through publicly reprimanding magistrates	13	18.3
Intervention by the Chief Magistrate on behalf of the Attorney-General	12	16.9

Relationship to the Public at Large

Before a magistrate is likely to be influenced by the feelings of the community, it is likely that five factors should exist; (i) the magistrate should feel that the public, or at least a significant proportion of it, is interested in what happens in magistrates' courts; (ii) he should be aware of (or at least have an image of) what the public thinks; (iii) he should define that opinion as significant and a proper consideration in sentencing; (iv) he should feel that the public would like the court to change its practice in some ways, and (v) the difference between the magistrate's definition of the expectations of the public, and his privately-held views as to the proper course of action, must not be so large that reconciliation between the two becomes impossible.

Magistrates were asked to indicate the degree of interest shown by the local community in the magistrates' courts. Forty-two magistrates (59 per cent) indicated that the community as a whole showed great interest in their work. Twenty-four (34 per cent) stated that the community showed interest in magistrates' courts only on those occasions when unusual press publicity was given, and only three felt that the community as a whole was dis-interested.

Similar findings emerged from questions concerning the amount of newspaper publicity given to sentences pronounced in magistrates' courts. Forty-four magistrates (62 per cent) indicat-ed that complete coverage was given. Fourteen (20 per cent) stat-ed that reporting was uneven, and only eight (11 per cent) indicat-ed that very little of what happened in magistrates' courts was re-ported in the press. Less than half of the magistrates felt that press reports were truthful and objective. Sixteen indicated that the press tended to "overly dramatize" the cases appearing in court, and ten stated that the press "deliberately distorted" the news from court to increase circulation, and another seventeen felt that the press frequently made innocent errors.

To complete this section of the interview, magistrates were ask-ed to indicate the degree to which they were concerned about their image in the community as represented by the press. Nearly all magistrates (sixty-four out of seventy-two) expressed con-cern about this area. Only six magistrates indicated that they were not particularly interested with the way in which the court was represented to the public by the mass media.

Taken together these data indicate that the first condition for influence by public opinion has been met. Most magistrates feel that the decisions they make in court are closely watched by the press and the public at large. Many of them feel that the press presents an inaccurate image of the court to the public and nearly all are concerned about the effect of publicity on the way in which the public views the court.

In order to determine the image magistrates have of what public opinion demands of them in sentencing, the question in Table 65 was asked.

As can be seen, magistrates who have formed images of public opinion, feel that the public is punitive and would like the court to be somewhat sterner with offenders. These findings suggest that to the extent that public opinion plays a role in sentencing, it is likely to influence judicial behaviour in the direction of being more severe. To explore this area more fully, magistrates were asked to indicate what they felt the majority of people in their local community thought of probation. Twenty-nine magistrates (41 per cent) felt that the majority of people saw probation as "getting off" or unwarranted "leniency." Only eleven (15 per cent) indicated that most people saw probation as a method of supervi-sion or treatment of the offender. The remaining magistrates, twenty-two (31 per cent) felt that either the public was divided about probation or had no discernible views concerning it.

TABLE 65

Perception of public opinion

Question	Answer	Number	Per cent
On the whole, are people in this community in favour of a sterner or more lenient approach to sentencing offenders than is presently practised?	Sterner	37	52.0
	More lenient	4	5.6
	Depends on type of case	9	12.7
	Community divided	7	9.9
	Community supports existing practice	5	7.0
	Don't know	9	12.7
Total		71	100.0

It appears that the second condition for influence to exist is satisfied. Most magistrates have an image of what public opinion demands of them in sentencing.

Before public opinion can play a role in sentencing, the magistrate must define it as a proper element to consider. Magistrates were asked to indicate the degree to which they take the views of a community into account in considering the appropriate sentence to impose. Forty-five (63 per cent) admitted that public opinion was an important consideration in sentencing. Of this group, however, thirty-one indicated that they were only "guided" by public opinion and not "controlled" by it. Twenty-two magistrates (31 per cent) stated that they never considered public opinion, and three indicated that they seldom did so.

Another question in the same area asked magistrates to indicate the degree to which they agreed with the statement that the court is the "conscience of the community." With respect to this question magistrates split nearly in half, thirty-four magistrates agreeing with the statement, and thirty-seven disagreeing with it, at least in part.

These data indicate that, at least for some magistrates, the fourth condition for influence by public opinion appears to be satisfied. Over half the magistrates define public opinion as an appropriate consideration to take into account in sentencing.

The analysis now turns to the manner in which public opinion plays a role in the conscious processes of selecting a penalty. In answer to the question: "Have you ever felt that the feelings of a community prevented you doing what you would otherwise do?," forty-three magistrates (60 per cent) stated "never," while twenty (28 per cent) indicated that public opinion prevented them from using probation in cases of relative severity. Only three magistrates (4 per cent) felt that public opinion prevented them from imposing a severe penalty. These data give further support to the conclusion that public opinion plays, if anything, a punitive role in sentencing.

There were a number of interesting relationships between the attitudes and penal philosophies of magistrates and the way in which they define the constraints imposed upon them by the public at large. Magistrates with higher reformation scores are more likely to define the press as being "objective," express little concern about the kind of publicity they get from the mass media, feel that citizens' attitudes towards the court are favourable, and do not feel that they represent public opinion on the bench. At the same time, magistrates with high deterrence scores feel that the press lacks objectivity, are concerned about the image of the court presented by the mass media, feel that the attitude of the average citizen towards the court is negative, and feel that they represent public opinion on the bench. Similarly, magistrates concerned for justice feel that the community shows little interest in what happens in court, feel that the press lacks objectivity in reporting events from the court, define the attitude of the average citizen to the court as essentially negative, and feel that they represent public opinion on the bench. Magistrates concerned for social defence tend to believe that the press lacks objectivity in reporting events from the court, express concern about the image of the court represented by the mass media and feel that they represent the average citizen on the bench.

A seeming contradiction exists in these data. Magistrates with punitive attitudes and beliefs tend to feel that public opinion and the press are hostile towards them. This is so despite the fact that public opinion is defined as demanding more severe penalties. At the same time, magistrates identifying with a reformative philosophy appear to define public opinion and the press as being supportive, while at the same time being not particularly concerned about their image in the community.

The explanation for these findings may be that either treatment-oriented magistrates have greater confidence in themselves, or it may be that these magistrates do, in fact, live in communities that are more supportive of a rehabilitative policy. In any event, it does appear that magistrates who are relatively punitive in their outlook appear to define the outside world as hostile. It will be remembered that those magistrates who defined themselves as "outsiders" in terms of disagreement with sentencing policies of other magistrates also tended to be more punitive. It was also found that magistrates elected to executive positions in the Ontario Magistrates' Association tended to have higher reformation and lower retribution and deterrence scores. Similarly, magistrates selected as commanding the greatest respect in terms of their views in sentencing, were relatively non-punitive in outlook. In this connection it will also be remembered that relationships between probation officers and magistrates were characterized by good relationships between non-punitive magistrates and probation officers and bad relationships between punitive magistrates and probation officers. Significantly, punitive magistrates did not appear to have better relationships with crown attorneys than did non-punitive magistrates. And as we have just seen, despite the fact that the majority of magistrates feel that public opinion is punitive, negative feelings towards the public tend to be expressed more often by punitive magistrates.

These data suggest the existence of a set of beliefs related to self-confidence and a willingness to accept suggestions from others on the part of non-punitive magistrates. The data support the conclusion that punitive magistrates tend to be rather more socially isolated and take a decidedly more aggressive and negative stand to the world in general.

It appears that the fifth, and final, condition for influence by public opinion is satisfied. Magistrates tend to define the constraints imposed by public opinion in ways which minimize inconsistency with their private beliefs.

Conclusion

The operative constraints in the social world of magistrates are both punitive and non-punitive in nature. The degree to which these constraints actually influence sentencing seems to depend on how magistrates define them. Non-punitive magistrates tend to view the social influences in their environment as being supportive of a non-punitive sentencing policy. The reverse is true for punitive magistrates, and this held true for each area examined. It appears that magistrates define selectively their social world in ways that maximize concordance with their private beliefs. The only qualification to the general pattern which emerged is that punitive magistrates appear to be somewhat more socially isolated and are more likely to deny the influence of others in their sentencing behaviour. The next chapter will explore the degree to which social and legal constraints in the environment of magistrates influence their sentencing behaviour.

NOTES TO CHAPTER 11

1 N. Walker, *Crime and Punishment in Britain* (Edinburgh, 1966), 213.
2 W. James, *Principles of Psychology* (New York, 1890). Social influences in the formation of self-concepts have been reported in many studies. See, for example, P. Lazardfeld, B. Berelson and H.Gaudet, *The People's Choice* (New York, 1944); and B. Raven, "Social Influence on Opinions and the Communication of Related Control," *Journal of Abnormal and Social Psychology*, 58 (1959), 119-29.
3 The Probation Act, *Rev. Stats. of Ontario*, 1960, C.308.
4 *The Report of the Royal Commission to Investigate the Penal System (Archambault Report)* (Ottawa, 1938), 98.
5 *The Report of the Committee Appointed to Inquire into the Principles and Procedures Followed in the Remission Service (Fauteux Report)* (Ottawa, 1956), 26.
6 *Reports of the Sentencing Committee of the Ontario Magistrates' Association* (1961-1966), mimeo; and especially 1962.
7 In this connection see G. McFarlane, "Theory and Development of Pre-Sentence Reports in Ontario," *Canadian Journal of Corrections*, 7(1965), 201-24 and especially at 217.
8 A. W. Mewett, ed., *Martin's Criminal Code* (Toronto, 1965), s.223 (b).
9 *Ibid.*, s. 661(3).
10 For a comparison with the US situation see D. Newman, *Conviction: the Determination of Guilt or Innocence without Trial* (Boston, 1966); see also, *The Challenge of Crime in a Free Society - A report by the President's Commission on Law Enforcement and the Administration of Justice* (Washington,1967), 134-6.
11 The only direct attempt to influence magistrates in their judicial discretion to come to this writer's attention concerned some remarks made to magistrates at their annual meeting at Niagara Falls in 1962 by the then Attorney-General of Ontario, Mr Cass. Much more typical are the statements made by Mr A.A. Wishart QC, Attorney-General, in the Provincial Legislature: "There have been no occasions upon which instructions have been given to Magistrate Langdon or to any other magistrate ..." Extracted from *Debates in the Ontario Legislature, Provincial Hansard* (31 January 1967), 84.
12 For example, when questions were raised in the Legislature about requests made for pre-trial reports by a particular magistrate, the Attorney-General replied: "The magistrate has, on occasion, asked for reports which were not required or authorized. It was, therefore, necessary for the director of probation services to suggest to our learned magistrate that further consideration be given by him to the types of cases where reports would be requested." *Ibid.*, 84.
13 The Provincial Courts Act, *Stats. of Ontario*, 1968, c.104, s.7. See Chapter 3.

12

The Impact of Socio-Legal Constraints on Sentencing

In the preceding two chapters it was assumed that the degree to which the attitudes of magistrates find expression in their behaviour will depend, in part, on the degree to which they feel obliged to conform to socio-legal constraints impinging on their discretion. This chapter describes research which tests this assumption. The analysis presented begins with simple correlations between preceived constraints and sentencing behaviour. It then combines attitudes and perceived constraints into a series of multiple regression equations which predict sentencing behaviour from both classes of variables.

The Creation of Perceived Constraint Variables

A number of variables were created from magistrates' responses to questions asked in the interview related to their assessments of the law as it affects sentencing, and their perceptions of what other people expect of them. Brief descriptions of each of these variables follow:

Variable 1: Conformity to the law. This variable was created out of responses to questions concerning conformity to section 638 of the Criminal Code dealing with eligibility for probation, and with the Ontario Court of Appeal decisions which state that it is improper for magistrates to consider the possibility of parole in determining the appropriate length of sentence. A simple conformity score was calculated representing the sum of the scores given to both these questions.

Variable 2: Conformity to other magistrates. This variable represents the degree to which magistrates feel obliged to conform to other magistrates in the interest of uniformity in sentencing.

Variable 3: Attitude to the sentencing practice of other magistrates. This variable consists of the assessments magistrates make of their fellow magistrates' sentencing philosophies and practices. It was derived from answers to the questions concerning whether other magistrates are "too punitive," "too lenient," or "neither too lenient nor too punitive."

Variable 4: Perceived accordance with other magistrates. This variable measures the degree to which magistrates feel that their own sentencing behaviour is in accordance with that of their colleagues. Each magistrate was given a score representing the degree to which they feel their personal sentencing practice is in line with that of the majority of magistrates in the province.

Variable 5: Satisfaction with probation officers. This variable simply measures the amount of confidence magistrates have in the probation officer. The variable was created out of the answers to several questions in the interview, during which magistrates were asked to indicate their satisfaction with probation officers and the confidence they had in their reports.

Variable 6: Attitude to the crown attorney. This variable is similar to variable 5 except that it relates to the confidence magistrates have in the crown attorney.

Variable 7: The role of public opinion. This variable measures the degree to which magistrates feel that public opinion is an important element to consider in sentencing.

Variable 8: Perception of public opinion. This variable is a measure of magistrates' perceptions of community expectations of them in sentencing. It was created out of responses to questions concerning whether or not the community as a whole would like the court to become more lenient or more severe, as the case may be.

Variables 9-13: Relationships with individual magistrates. It will be recalled that each magistrate was asked to identify up to three other magistrates whose views on sentencing they most respect.[1] Five variables were created consisting of the mean scores on the five attitude scales of the magistrates so selected.

Correlational Analysis

Correlations were calculated between the thirteen perceived constraint scores described above, and the sixty-seven measures of sentencing behaviour described earlier.[2] The analysis revealed that only a few of these correlations were statistically significant. There was a tendency for magistrates who do not conform to the law with respect to sentencing to use suspended sentence and probation more frequently. There was also a tendency for magistrates who are relatively more positive to the crown attorney to use institutional measures more frequently, particularly gaol sentences. Similarly, magistrates who perceive public opinion as demanding a more punitive approach in sentencing are likely to use institutional measures, particularly gaol and penitentiary sentences, more frequently. But out of eight-hundred-and-seventy-one correlations calculated, only fifty-six were statistically significant at 0.05 or better. In a correlation matrix of this size one could expect forty-three to be statistically significant due to chance variation alone.[3] It must be concluded, therefore, that there is no simple relationship between the perceived constraint variables used and sentencing behaviour of magistrates. Let us now see what happens when the analysis incorporates the attitude scores of magistrates.

Regression Analysis

Sixty-seven equations were calculated which regressed the attitude and perceived constraint scores of magistrates against their sentencing behaviour. The computer was instructed to select freely those independent variables which best predict the sentencing behaviour of the magistrate concerned. The results indicated that statistically significant relationships between attitudes and perceived constraints on the one hand, and sentencing behaviour on the other were achieved in nearly all cases, ranging from a low of 0.33 to a high of 0.74, with a mean correlation of approximately 0.6. In regression analysis a significant improvement in the predictive power was achieved through the addition of perceived constraint variables. In sixty-three out of sixty-seven equations the computer selected one or more perceived constraint variables in addition to certain attitudinal variables. It appears from this that the constraints operating in the social world

TABLE 66

Regression of attitudes and perceived constraints against sentencing behaviour

Step	Attitudes	Perceived constraints	r
Suspended sentence (combined) (all indictable cases)			
1	Lacks concern for justice		0.439
2		Negative relationship with Crown	0.535
3		Law seen as flexible	0.597
4	Tolerance of deviance		0.625
Fines (all indictable cases)			
1		Respects magistrate not concerned for justice	0.376
2	Concern for justice		0.516
3	Concern for social defence		0.570
4		Believes own practice different	0.599
Institution (all indictable cases)			
1		Positive relationship with Crown	0.337
2	Traditionalism		0.409
3		Sees other magistrates as too lenient	0.468
4	Concern for social defence		0.492
5		Respects magistrates concerned for justice	0.521
Gaol as a proportion of all institutions (all indictable cases)			
1	Concern for justice		0.400
2		Positive relationship with Crown	0.462
3		Considers community punitive	0.504
4	Lacks concern for social defence		0.525
5		Considers public opinion unimportant	0.549
6	Traditionalism		0.567
7	Does not feel punishment corrects		0.596
8		Respects magistrates who feel that punishment corrects	0.622
Reformatory as a proportion of all institutions (all indictable cases)			
1	Lacks concern for justice		0.519
2		Considers community lenient	0.560
3	Feels punishment corrects		0.586
4		Respects magistrates who do not feel that punishment corrects	0.615
5		Negative relationship with Crown	0.645
6	Traditionalism		0.663
Penitentiary as a proportion of all institutions (all indictable cases)			
1	Concern for social defence		0.399
2	Concern for justice		0.513

of magistrates assume significance, in both a statistical and theoretical sense, only when the attitudes of magistrates have been accounted for. The advantages of multivariate procedures are thus revealed. The importance of perceived constraints in the behaviour of magistrates would not have been revealed from simple correlational analysis. More significantly, it does appear that the operative constraints in the social world of a magistrate as perceived and defined by him, while closely related to his attitudes, do make an independent contribution to his sentencing behaviour.

It is too cumbersome to present all the regression equations calculated in the body of this chapter. They are provided in full in Technical Appendix 5. In Table 66 regression equations are translated into a non-technical form with respect to the behaviour of magistrates for all indictable offences (combined).

It can be seen from these tables that attitudes and perceived constraints combine in a rather interesting way to produce certain consequences in the form of sentencing decisions. Magistrates who use suspended sentence frequently with and without probation in indictable cases are not concerned with abstract justice, are rather tolerant of deviant behaviour, do not have much confidence in the crown attorney's opinions as to sentence, and see the law as flexible and therefore do not conform rigidly to its strict requirements.

Magistrates who use fines frequently in indictable cases are concerned for justice and for social defence. They tend to respect magistrates who are relatively concerned for justice, and to believe that their own sentencing practice is different in a significant degree from that of other magistrates.

Magistrates relying heavily on institutional sentences in indictable cases tend to be traditional in outlook, are concerned for social defence, have positive relationships with the crown attorney, tend to see other magistrates as too lenient, and respect magistrates who are concerned with justice.

The attitudes and perceived constraints of magistrates combine in rather different ways with respect to the selection of particular types of institutional sentence. Thus, magistrates who rely heavily on gaol sentences when institutional sentences are used tend to be concerned with justice and social defence, to be rather traditional in outlook, and do not feel that punishment corrects. At the same time, they tend to have positive relationships with crown attorneys, consider the community to be punitive, do not feel that public opinion is important, and respect magistrates who feel that punishment is a corrective.

In contrast, magistrates who rely heavily on reformatory sentences when institutional sentences are used lack concern with justice, feel that punishment corrects, and are rather traditional in outlook. At the same time, they consider that the community supports a lenient sentencing policy, they respect magis-

TABLE 67

Regression of attitudes and perceived constraints against sentencing behaviour (total against person, all indictable)

Step	Attitudes	Perceived constraints	r
	Suspended sentence with probation		
1	Traditionalism		0.343
2		Respects magistrates concerned for justice	0.409
3	Feels punishment corrects		0.457
	Suspended sentence without probation		
1	Lacks concern for justice		0.449
2		Negative relationship with probation officers	0.494
3	Tolerance		0.532
4	Does not feel that punishment corrects		0.593
5		Respects magistrates not concerned for justice	0.647
6	Modern		0.670
	Fine		
1	Modern		0.441
2	Does not feel that punishment corrects		0.673
3		Respects magistrates who feels that punishment corrects	0.690
4	Intolerant		0.704
5	Concern for justice		0.738
	Institution		
1	Feels punishment corrects		0.385
2		Positive relationship with Crown	0.481
3		Conforms to other magistrates	0.531
4		Respects tolerant magistrates	0.568
5	Traditional		0.598
6	Concern for justice		0.638

TABLE 68

Regression of attitudes and perceived constraints against sentencing behaviour (total against property, all indictable)

Step	Attitudes	Perceived constraints	r
Suspended sentence with probation			
1		Respects magistrates concerned for justice	0.305
2	Feels that punishment corrects		0.470
Suspended sentence without probation			
1	Lacks concern for justice		0.276
2		Negative relationship with probation officers	0.342
3	Does not feel that punishment corrects		0.386
4	Tolerant		0.453
5	Modern		0.501
Fine			
1		Respects magistrates not concerned for justice	0.411
2	Concern for justice		0.572
3		Respects modern magistrates	0.625
4		Believes own practice different	0.648
5	Does not feel that punishment corrects		0.667
Institution			
1	Traditional		0.361
2	Intolerant		0.452
3		Respects traditional magistrates	0.531
4		Positive relationship with Crown	0.573
5		Conforms to other magistrates	0.608

trates who do not feel that punishment corrects, and they have negative relationships with the crown attorney.

Turning to penitentiary sentences, it appears that the motivation for using this type of sentence is related simply to two attitude scores, namely, social defence and concern for justice.

Different patterns emerge with respect to individual offences. While all the material is not presented in this chapter, the general pattern can be seen from an examination of Tables 67 and 68, which show the relationship of attitudes and perceived constraints to sentencing behaviour with respect to two main classes of offence, i.e. offences against the person and offences against property.

One of the more interesting facts to emerge from these tables is the difference in attitudes and beliefs associated with the use of suspended sentence with probation and suspended sentence without probation. The frequent use of probation is associated with the view that punishment corrects, while the frequent use of suspended sentence without probation is associated with the view that punishment does not correct. Moreover, the frequent use of suspended sentence without probation is associated with having negative relationships with probation officers.

It can also be seen that heavy reliance on institutions is also associated with the view that punishment corrects, with positive relationships with crown attorneys, and with conformity to both the law and to other magistrates. Fines are associated with the view that punishment does not correct, with concern for justice, tolerance and with modernism.

Conclusion

The simple fact which emerges from these data is that the attitudes, definitions of constraints, and sentencing behaviour of magistrates are organized in congruence with one another. A punitive sentencing policy is associated both with punitive attitudes and with a belief that the law and the social situation demands a punitive response from the magistrate. A lenient sentencing policy is associated both with lenient attitudes and beliefs that the situation calls for a more lenient policy. While magistrates tend to define the operative constraints in a way which maximizes concordance with their personal attitudes, both classes of variable make an independent contribution to the prediction equations derived. This shows that there is not a complete identity between attitudes and perceived constraints. The degree to which a magistrate will allow his personal attitudes to find expression in his behaviour will depend on how he defines the expectations of the law and of "significant others" in his social environment. This means that whilst the attitudes of magistrates act as filters through which the world is selectively perceived, these filters screen out only partially what is objectional in that world. Certain reality aspects of the social environment do penetrate the consciousness of a judge resulting in a modification of his behaviour on the bench.

One fundamental question remains unanswered. Is sentencing behaviour a consequence of attitudes and beliefs, or are there attitudes and beliefs of magistrates caused by other factors which also cause magistrates to behave in the way they do? An attempt to answer this question will be made in the next chapter. For the present, however, it may be concluded that the sentences magistrates impose are largely consistent with their attitudes and with their beliefs concerning what the law and other people expect of them.

NOTES TO CHAPTER 12

1 See Chapter 11.
2 These were the same data used in predicting from attitudes alone.
3 One in twenty correlations are statistically "significant" at 0.05 due to chance alone. This makes it extremely dangerous to rely on a few correlations extracted from a large matrix. Computer technology provides an opportunity to prove nearly any proposition provided one has enough variables.

13

The Relationship of Social Characteristics to Attitudes and Beliefs

This chapter will describe variations in attitudes and beliefs and in sentencing behaviour, among magistrates with different background characteristics. It will also describe the similarities and differences among magistrates who work in different social settings. The purpose of the analyses is to show the relationship of past experience to present behaviour. Most of the findings will be described in general terms. Statistical work supporting them is included in Technical Appendix 6.

Age

There were no statistically significant relationships between the ages of magistrates and their scores on any of the major attitudes or penal philosophy scales. There were, however, a number of significant relationships between specific beliefs and age.

Older magistrates tend to be somewhat more offence-oriented than offender- oriented. They also appear to be rather more discriminating in assessing offences, considering a larger number of factors to be "essential" to the proper assessment of a criminal act.

There is a slight tendency for them to minimize sociological explanations of crime. They rate lower the value of sociology, they tend to feel that the causes of crime are not to be found in "cultural conflict" among minority groups, and they tend to select fewer factors concerning the causes of crime than do younger magistrates.

The older the magistrate is, the less likely he is to consider it important to discuss sentencing with other magistrates. Older magistrates are *more* likely to feel that their own sentencing practice and principles are in accordance with their fellow magistrates, but at the same time they are *less* likely to feel that they must conform blindly to the practices of other magistrates. They adopt a moderate position with respect to the doctrine of uniformity, feeling that the most that can be hoped for is to achieve some measure of uniformity in the "principles" applied.

As magistrates grow older they appear to be less concerned about political interference in the judicial process. While they are aware of the possibility of interference, they express less concern about it.

The general picture which emerges is one of a relationship between the age of a magistrate and a greater feeling of independence, self-reliance, confidence, and moderation.

Family Background

A professional family background is associated with being treatment-oriented in attitudes and beliefs. Magistrates with professional family backgrounds attach less weight to "justice" and "deterrence" and more weight to "reformation." In considering information, they attach more importance to the background of the offender than to the offence. These magistrates believe that a large proportion of offenders are mentally ill, and they have a more positive attitude to parole and other forms of correctional methods. In contrast, magistrates from working-class backgrounds appear to be rather more "punitive" in their attitudes and beliefs. These findings are in accordance with those reported in a number of studies, which have shown the relationship between class backgrounds and attitudes.[1]

Education

There were no statistically significant relationships between the number of years a magistrate spent at school and his attitudes or beliefs. However, there were a number of significant relationships between the type of educational experience and these factors. Most of these differences showed up between legally-trained and lay magistrates.

Magistrates with legal training have lower justice scores than lay magistrates. They appear to be more subtle in the way in which they assess both crime and criminals, taking more factors into consideration. Legally-trained magistrates have a more positive attitude towards parole, while lay magistrates are likely to feel that parole is an unwarranted interference in their decisions.

It was particularly interesting to note that lay magistrates appear to be more "legalistic" in their approach to sentencing. They tend to conform rigidly to the requirements of the law with respect to selection for probation, restricting this type of disposition to those clearly eligible under section 638 of the Criminal Code. Similarly, they refuse to take the possibility of parole and statutory remission into account in determining the appropriate length of sentence, thus conforming to the appeal court decisions dealing with these matters.[2] It appears that lay magistrates adhere strictly to the formal requirements of the law. In contrast, legally-trained magistrates are likely to interpret the law more flexibly, responding more to what they believe to be its true meaning and spirit.

A factor of personal confidence appears to distinguish lay and legally-trained magistrates. Lay magistrates are less willing to allow others to participate in the decision-process. They feel that neither the probation officer nor the crown attorney have much to contribute to the decision of the court. Similarly, these magistrates are less likely to admit the influence of public opinion to their decisions. They state that they do not discuss sentencing problems with their friends, they express greater concern about the possibility of political interference in their work, and they tend to feel that the press lacks "objectivity" in reporting news from magistrates' courts.

Taken together these data suggest that legal training leads to a more creative and flexible approach to the law, a somewhat more offender-oriented penal philosophy, and a great deal more confidence in self.

Religion

There were a number of significant differences in the attitudes and beliefs of magistrates of different religious denominations. Roman Catholic magistrates have lower "justice" scores than magistrates of other faiths. At the same time, these magistrates have higher "intolerance" scores than others. Among the protestant magistrates, those of the United and Presbyterian churches tend to have high justice and low intolerance scores. Anglican magistrates occupy middle positions on all the attitude scales.

It was also noted that there was considerable variation among protestant magistrates on all the scales. Among the most "punitive" and the most "non-punitive" groups of magistrates there were a number from each of the non-Anglican protestant denominations. It appears that the split within certain protestant churches in Canada between liberal and orthodox wings is reflected in the attitudes of magistrates.

Religion distinguishes between magistrates with respect to a number of specific beliefs. Anglican magistrates appear to be more offence- than offender-oriented. They attach greater importance to the offence than to either the offender's background or his criminal record, and in considering information relevant to each of these areas they tend to use more information concerning the offence and less information concerning the offender's background or the criminal record. Similarly, Anglican magistrates have a more negative attitude towards parole than either Roman Catholics or other protestants.

It is difficult to interpret these findings without becoming involved in theological discussions which are beyond the capacity of this study.

It should be pointed out that religion is closely associated with a number of other variables, particularly ethnic background and social class. The structure of family life is also likely to be different among Roman Catholics and protestant magistrates. To the extent that family background is a determinant of attitudes, religion may be associated only with differences in attitudes rather than with the cause of them. Finally, there is a tendency to appoint Catholic magistrates to judicial districts which have a large Catholic population, and protestant magistrates to judicial districts where the bulk of the population is protestant. We shall see that magistrates tend to reflect, in terms of their attitudes and beliefs, the kinds of communities in which they live. This may mean that the religion of the magistrate is not as important as the religious distribution in the community in which he lives.

Previous Employment Experience

The type of experience magistrates had immediately prior to their appointment is closely associated with the attitudes and beliefs they hold at present. Indeed, previous employment experience is much more closely associated with the attitudes and beliefs of magistrates than are any of the more remote background factors such as age, religion, or family background.

Magistrates who were employed as crown attorneys, clerks of the court, or justices of the peace tend to be offence-oriented in their attitudes and beliefs. Moreover, the number of years spent on the prosecution side of the administration of justice is associated with being rather more extreme in this direction.[3] Thus, the number of years in prosecution-type work is associated with high scores on the justice, social defence, deterrence, and punishment scales, and low scores on the reformation scale. In terms of specific beliefs, the longer the magistrate's experience in prosecution, the more likely he is to feel that fewer offenders are mentally ill, that certain minority groups have greater criminal tendencies than the general population, that information concerning the offence is more important than information concerning the offender, and that recommendations from probation officers as to sentence should not be considered.

Magistrates with prosecution experience also tend to believe that the majority of magistrates in the province emphasize retribution at the expense of reformation. Their knowledge of correctional institutions tends to be lower (they make fewer visits), and they do less reading of the literature concerning the causes and treatment of crime. They are also more likely to conform to the law with respect to selection for probation, and are less likely to discuss sentencing with their friends. They believe the press lacks objectivity in reporting the work of the court, and they deny the influence of public opinion in their decisions. It appears from this that these magistrates tend to have somewhat negative feelings towards "outsiders."

Those legally-trained magistrates who have no previous experience in criminal matters tend to be more offender-oriented than those who had experience as criminal lawyers. Magistrates without lengthy experience in criminal courts have higher reformation and lower punishment scores and they tend to consider information about the offender's background and criminal record to be more important than information concerning the offence. This suggests that while magistrates who acted as defence counsel are more offender-oriented than those who acted primarily for the Crown, the longer an individual spends in either type of work the more likely he is to move towards an offence-oriented position. It appears, therefore, that experience in the criminal courts leads towards some accommodation with the punitive goals of the criminal justice system.

Length of Experience as a Magistrate

In Chapter 4 we saw that magistrates varied in length of experience from six months to thirty-two years, with a mean of fourteen years. It was stated that length of experience should be an important variable in shaping attitudes and beliefs. To some extent this expectation is confirmed.

Length of experience appears to be associated with a more moderate and more coherent penal philosophy. The longer a magistrate is on the bench the more likely he is to believe in deterrence and the less likely he is to believe in either retributive punishment or reformation. On a punitive/non-punitive dimension the doctrine of deterrence appears to lie between retribution and reformation. It would appear, therefore, that judicial experience tends to lead magistrates to take up middle positions with respect to the main doctrines applicable to sentencing. Moderation in outlook is revealed in a number of other ways. Experienced magistrates are more likely to attach "some value" to psychiatry and psychology, and are less likely to rate these disciplines as either being of "no value" or of "very great value." Similarly they are more likely to view the practices and principles of other magistrates as providing a "general guide." In contrast, less experienced magistrates are more likely to attempt complete uniformity in both principles and practices, or to reject the doctrine of uniformity entirely.

Experienced magistrates express greater satisfaction with the conditions under which they work, and appear to have greater confidence in their independence. These magistrates define the attitude of the community to the court as being "positive." They feel their personal image in the community is one of "respect" and they feel that the press is "fair" and "objective." They express less concern about the rise in the crime rate, and they do not feel that political interference in the judicial role is a serious problem. In short, it appears that length of experience is associated with a feeling of confidence and self-reliance among magistrates. It will be noted that these findings are similar to those presented earlier concerning age. Since age and length of experience are highly correlative, it is difficult to know which of the two variables is more important in shaping attitudes and beliefs. It should be pointed out, however, that the pattern is much stronger with respect to length of judicial experience than to age.

Work-Load

The work-load of a magistrate has a direct influence on the way in which he makes decisions. It affects not only the time he has to consider each case, but also the degree to which he is able to devote time and thought to general considerations in sentencing, to attend lectures and seminars, and to read.

Magistrates with heavy work-loads tend to have higher intolerance and social defence scores. They are likely to restrict the use of psychiatric reports to cases where "fitness to stand trial" is the only issue, and they have a more restrictive policy with respect to the use of the pre-sentence report.

The greater the work-load of the magistrate, the more likely he is to have negative attitudes towards both his colleagues and other professional people with whom he comes in contact. Busy magistrates tend to feel that their personal penal philosophy is "different" in a significant way from that of most of their colleagues. They are likely to express negative attitudes towards probation officers and psychiatrists. They feel that public opinion is "unsympathetic," and they deny the role of public opinion in their sentencing decisions.

The work-load of a magistrate is reflected in his sentencing behaviour. Busy magistrates tend to use fines in Criminal Code cases more frequently. They not only use fines frequently in lieu of probation and suspended sentence, but also in lieu of short-term institutional sentences. This is understandable, as for a busy magistrate fines have the advantage of requiring less thought or consideration than either probation or institutional sentences. Fines fit more easily into a tariff system in which the penalty imposed is automatically determined by the nature of the offence. Fines may be justified either as a deterrent, or as a punishment, and they avoid the damaging effects of imprisonment on the offender. This means that, regardless of penal philosophy, magistrates can find adequate justification for heavy reliance on this form of sentence.The relationship of the work-load of magistrates to the use of fines in Criminal Code cases is strikingly demonstrated by Table 69.

Further evidence of the degree to which the work-load of a magistrate affects the way in which he makes decisions in sentencing can be obtained from that part of the interview which explored the rules of thumb and presumptions that magistrates use in sentencing. Busy magistrates tend to have a restrictive policy with respect to the use of probation. They consciously restrict probation to a small number of cases in which the chances of re-conviction are thought to be particularly low. At the same time, these magistrates use a large number of presumptions in sentencing. Significantly, these presumptions are likely to be in favour of imprisonment even in cases of minor offences against property. The automatic use of presumptions tends to simplify the decision-process. It reflects a rigid, yet more expedient, penal philosophy.

Taken together these data indicate that the attitudes and penal philosophies of magistrates, as well as the rules they apply in making decisions, are partially determined by the pressures of work. This may be considered to be an optimistic finding as it suggests that it might be possible to change the attitudes of magistrates provided more favourable working conditions are created.

TABLE 69
Relationship of case load size to the
use of fines in indictable cases $(r = 0.89)$

		Number of cases	
		Above average	Below average
Use of fines	Below average	7	26
	Above average	26	7

Community Characteristics

In their attitudes and beliefs, magistrates appear to reflect the types of communities in which they live. Correlations between certain demographic characteristics of judicial districts and the attitudes of magistrates yielded a large number of significant findings, summarized in Table 70.

Magistrates with high justice scores are likely to live in communities that are characterized by a high degree of urbanization, a high crime rate, and a highly mixed ethnic composition, comprised of many recent immigrants from continental Europe and very few people from the province of Quebec. These communities can be identified as the big cities in the so-called "Golden Horseshoe" of Ontario, namely Toronto, Hamilton, Windsor, and Oshawa.

TABLE 70

Correlation matrix between demographic characteristics of
judicial districts and attitude scores

Characteristics of judicial districts	Attitude scores				
	Justice	Punishment	Intolerance	Social defence	Modernism
Density	0.510*	-	-0.253	0.250	-
Growth	-	0.500*	-0.268	-0.252	-
Distribution					
Age 15-19	-0.365*	-	0.273	-	-
Age 20-24	0.235	-	-	0.498*	-
Age 25-29	0.439*	-	-	0.316*	-
Urbanization					
Rural, total	-0.433*	-	0.295	-	-
Urban, total	0.442*	-	-0.298	-	-
Under 10,000	-	-	0.250	-0.246	-
10,000 to 100,000	-0.323*	-	-	-	-
Over 100,000	0.402*	-	-	-	-
Average income	-	0.234	-	-	-
Ethnic distribution					
British	-	0.345*	-0.234	-	0.243
French	-0.365*	-	0.435*	-	-
Other European	0.487*	-0.251	-0.351	-	-
Languages spoken					
English only	0.337*	-	-0.462*	-	-
French only	-0.332*	-	0.379*	-	-0.305*
English and French	-0.347*	-	0.427*	-	-
Birthplace					
Ontario	-0.489*	-	-	-	-
Quebec	-0.317*	-	0.480*	0.268	-
Religious distribution					
Roman Catholic	-	-	0.346*	-	-
United Church	-	0.230	-	-	-
Anglican	-	0.279	-0.344*	-	-
Other protestant	-	-	-0.287	-	-
Other	0.535*	-	-0.284	0.241	-
Crime Rate	-	-0.347*	0.391*	-	-

* Indicates significance at 0.01

Magistrates who believe that punishment corrects are likely to
come from prosperous, high growth-rate communities with a predominantly British population and a low crime rate. Most of
these are new communities on the periphery of the "Golden Horseshoe."

Magistrates with high intolerance scores tend to come from rural, stable, French-speaking communities with a high crime rate.
Farming and logging are likely to be the main industries. The majority of the population is likely to be of the Roman Catholic faith.

Magistrates who attach great weight to social defence are likely to come from urban, high crime-rate environments. There is a

large number of Italian and French-speaking people in these communities. Moreover, there is a large number of young people in these communities who are "at risk," in the sense of being within the younger age-groups that commit most crime.[4]

Magistrates identifying with the so-called "modern" doctrines tend to come from communities that consist of a large proportion of British and a small proportion of French people. These communities tend to be rather stable in terms of growth-rate, and the crime rate is not particularly high.

A number of important implications arise out of these findings. In the first place, it appears that the attitudes of magistrates do, in fact, reflect the types of community in which they live. This is not altogether surprising, but it does lend further weight to the view that judicial attitudes are not isolated from external influences.

Secondly, the attitudes of magistrates appear to be those that are most appropriate to the problems they face in their local community. Magistrates from urban, high crime-rate areas appear to be more punitive, but this is understandable in view of the situations they face. Whether or not a punitive response to a difficult crime problem is the one that should be made, it is the one which makes it easier for these magistrates to cope with the problems they face in their daily work.

The fact that magistrates from rural French-speaking communities tend to be rather intolerant of crime and social deviance, and yet are less concerned for justice and social defence, is of some significance. If one can assume that these are the views of the community as a whole, it appears likely that to some extent magistrates represent majority thinking in their local communities. Perhaps the most interesting finding is that the view that "punishment corrects" is particularly marked among magistrates from wealthy, high growth-rate communities with a heavy preponderance of people of British origin. These magistrates express a tough-minded but corrections-oriented point of view. The crime rate is low, and the resources of the community are fairly adequate. There is probably less tension in the community due to the fact that ethnic minorities make up such a small proportion of the total population. They can and do believe in the efficacy of penal sanctions.

The one demographic characteristic which distinguishes best among magistrates in terms of their attitudes and beliefs is the degree of urbanization of the community in which they live. The next section will look at this in more detail.

Urban-Rural Differences

Magistrates were divided into two groups of thirty-five each depending upon whether they came from large urban centres or small towns and rural communities. A comparison of the attitudes and beliefs of the two groups yielded statistically significant differences with respect to most of the questions asked in the interview, and several of the main attitude and penal philosophy scales.

Urban magistrates attach less importance to reformation and more importance to deterrence and retribution. They have a less favourable attitude towards parole. In assessing information, they attach greater weight to the offence and criminal record than to the offender's background. If they perceive a conflict between the needs of the offender and the needs of the community they are more likely to resolve that conflict in the direction of community protection. Their policy in using probation is rather restrictive. When they do use probation, their purposes are likely to be supervision and surveillance rather than counselling or treatment. Consistent with this is the view held by more urban magistrates that few offenders are mentally ill.

Urban magistrates tend to simplify the decision-process by operating with a large number of presumptions which guide them in the exercise of discretion. Moreover, these presumptions are more likely to be in the direction of using imprisonment rather than probation or fines.

A significant number of urban magistrates are dissatisfied with the wide discretionary powers given to them in sentencing. The only magistrates who wanted the law to provide a larger number of minimum penalties were from urban areas. Similarly, the only magistrates who indicated that they would like to see the amount of discretion given to the court decreased through the reduction of maximum penalties, were from urban areas.

Urban magistrates also tend to have rather more negative feelings to "outsiders." Of the twelve magistrates who felt that their image in the community was not a good one, eleven were from urban areas. These magistrates also have less positive feelings towards their colleagues. They are more likely to define their own penal philosophy as being "different" from the majority, and they feel that the work of the Ontario Magistrates' Association to achieve uniformity in sentencing has not been helpful.

Turning to sentencing behaviour, a number of differences between urban and rural magistrates were observed.[5] Urban magistrates are less likely to use: (i) suspended sentence without probation, (ii) suspended sentence with probation, (iii) short-term ordinary imprisonment, or (iv) reformatory sentences. These magistrates are *more* likely to use: (i) fines, (ii) longer terms of ordinary imprisonment, and (iii) penitentiary sentences.

These findings may be partially accounted for by differences in the types of cases appearing before magistrates in the two areas, but it is also true that there are significant differences in the penal philosophies and attitudes of the two groups. Probably both factors operate.

The data show that the problems faced by magistrates in the court and in the wider community, their attitudes and beliefs, and their sentencing behaviour are organized in congruence with one another. One cannot tell from these data whether the attitudes and behaviour of magistrates are caused by the social situations in which sentencing takes place. One way to tease out the answer to this question is to examine differences among magistrates within each of the urban and rural areas. If there are significant differences in the attitudes and beliefs held by magistrates facing similar situations, then it can be said that situational factors are not likely to be the sole determinants of the way in which magistrates respond to crime.

In Table 71 the differences between urban and rural magistrates in penal philosophy and attitude scores are presented. It can be seen from Table 71 that urban magistrates tend to be rather more punitive, having higher justice and social defence scores on the attitude scales and higher general deterrence and lower reformation scores on the penal philosophy scales. It is significant that there is considerable variation (represented by standard deviations) in the attitude and penal philosophies of both groups. On examination, it was discovered that some magistrates in rural communities were more punitive in their attitudes and beliefs than many magistrates in urban areas. Similarly, some magistrates in urban areas were less punitive than many magistrates in rural communities. Therefore, one must reject the hypothesis that urban-rural differences can "explain" variation in the attitudes and beliefs of magistrates.

One additional fact emerged from Table 71. The amount of variation in attitude and penal philosophy scores among urban magistrates is considerably larger than that among rural magistrates.[6] This is not what one would expect. Magistrates in urban areas communicate with each other more frequently (in many instances they share offices), and through this inter-action it should be expected that they would come closer together in their attitudes and beliefs.

TABLE 71

Urban-rural differences in penal philosophy and attitudes

		Urban N = 34	Rural N = 36	Differ- ence	Level of significance
Penal philosophy					
General deterrence	Mean	8.372	5.861	2.511	0.05
	S.D.	4.914	3.289		
Individual deterrence	Mean	6.734	6.002	0.732	-
	S.D.	4.133	3.135		
Reformation	Mean	7.758	10.056	-2.946	0.01
	S.D.	3.384	2.116		
Punishment	Mean	4.592	3.874	0.718	-
	S.D.	3.905	3.156		
Incapacitation	Mean	3.578	2.803	0.775	-
	S.D.	1.890	1.006		
Attitudes					
Justice	Mean	-0.102	-0.689	0.587	0.02
	S.D.	0.994	0.700		
Punishment corrects	Mean	0.319	0.746	-0.427	-
	S.D.	0.947	0.653		
Intolerance	Mean	0.179	0.089	0.090	-
	S.D.	1.029	0.893		
Social defence	Mean	0.817	-0.103	1.920	0.01
	S.D.	1.074	0.932		
Modernism	Mean	-0.304	-0.109	0.195	-
	S.D.	1.470	0.888		

*Significance determined by the t-test.

To seek an explanation to this apparent contradiction, urban magistrates were divided into two groups around the median attitude scores on the main scales and an examination was made of the differences between the two groups. It was discovered that all but two of the urban magistrates on the non-punitive side of these scales were active participants in the Ontario Magistrates' Association. It was also learned that these magistrates attend more conferences and seminars about sentencing, do more reading, visit more institutions and clinics, and generally appear to make greater efforts to improve their knowledge about crime and the treatment of offenders. It appears from this that while the basic influences in the urban environment may be those which tend to encourage the development of punitive attitudes and beliefs, magistrates can insulate themselves from these influences through reading and social interaction with like-minded persons if they have the motivation to do so.

There is some recent experimental work in the psychology of attitude change which is relevant.[7] Research evidence suggests that where an individual is exposed to values and concepts related to deeply held feelings of his own, he is likely to assimilate only those that are very close to his private beliefs and reject all others. Continual exposure to values not held has either an "inoculation" effect or a "contrast" effect. Moreover, the evidence suggests that the greater the degree of personal involvement in the problem (called ego-involvement), the greater the tendency to reject any attempt at persuasion. Sentencing is indubitably very "ego-involving" for magistrates. This suggests that attempts to change attitudes through persuasion will be difficult.

It is the urban magistrates who are exposed to the greatest amount of pro-treatment "propaganda". These magistrates have more opportunities to attend seminars and lectures, they have more frequent contact with the universities, and they are exposed to a larger number of influences from the correctional and treatment community. Research suggests that both "contrast" and "assimilation" effects are likely under these conditions.[8] These magistrates who are treatment-oriented to begin with, are more likely to assimilate pro-treatment doctrines, and their sentencing behaviour is likely to shift in that direction. Those who initially hold strong anti-treatment views are likely not only to reject any attempt at persuasion, but also to become more extreme in the opposite direction. This is a possible explanation for the large variation in attitudes and beliefs among urban magistrates.

A number of policy implications suggest themselves. It would appear that conferences and group discussions, in themselves, do not promote uniformity in attitudes. Exposure to radical concepts is likely to promote further polarization in views. If efforts are to be made to change the attitudes of magistrates, it would appear to be more fruitful to attempt small shifts in attitudes and beliefs rather than to make a wholesale attack on them.

Age and Education Re-visited

It will be remembered that neither age nor education were significantly associated with any of the major attitude or penal philosophy scales. Because such large differences exist among magistrates in urban and rural areas, it was deemed advisable to have another look at the relationship between attitudes and beliefs and these two background characteristics, this time controlling for urban-rural differences.

Initially, magistrates were divided into two groups, consisting of those from large urban centres and those from small towns and rural communities. The two groups were then further divided in terms of age, consisting of those under fifty-five and those fifty-five and over. Finally, they were divided again, this time in terms of the median number of years at school. The scheme of classification created eight groups of magistrates. The penal philosophy and attitude scores of the eight groups of magistrates were compared. A number of statistical tests were calculated to determine whether the relationship of age and education to attitudes and penal philosophy were significantly different in urban or rural communities. The results are presented in Tables 72 and 73.

TABLE 72

Differences in penal philosophy of magistrates divided by age, education, and type of community

| | Under 55 | | 55 and over | |
Community	BA	No BA	BA	No BA
General deterrence scale*				
Urban	N=10	N=7	N=7	N=10
	13.078	8.001	12.578	7.372
Rural	N=7	N=7	N=9	N=10
	2.179	4.332	7.820	9.426
Reformation scale +				
Urban	N=10	N=7	N=7	N=10
	5.224	9.376	5.933	9.2126
Rural	N=7	N=7	N=9	N=10
	12.997	11.343	8.004	8.578

*Kruskal Wallis Test: H=43.59; significant at 0.001
+Kruskal Wallis Test: H=18.58; significant at 0.01

The rather surprising fact which appears is that the most punitive magistrates, represented by high general deterrence and low reformation scores on the penal philosophy scales, and high justice and social defence scores on the attitude scales, are young, well-educated, *urban* magistrates. The least punitive magistrates are young, well-educated, *rural* magistrates. Age and education appear to operate in opposite directions in urban and rural communities.

The explanation offered is that social conditions in the two types of community are so vastly different that the position of magistrates in these communities is likely both to attract different types of persons, and to encourage the development of different sets of attitudes and beliefs. Moreover, it will be argued that selective and socializing influences are likely to be most pronounced among young, well-educated lawyers.

TABLE 73

Differences in attitudes of magistrates divided by age, education, and type of community

Community	Under 55		55 and over	
	BA	No BA	BA	No BA
Justice scale*				
Urban	N=10	N=7	N=7	N=10
	0.021	-0.480	-0.278	-0.132
Rural	N=7	N=7	N=9	N=10
	-1.015	-0.650	-0.679	-0.204
Social defence scale+				
Urban	N=10	N=7	N=7	N=10
	1.052	0.332	0.933	0.864
Rural	N=7	N=7	N=9	N=10
	-0.230	-0.164	-0.249	-0.056

*Kruskal Wallis Test: H=14.11; significant at 0.05.
+Kruskal Wallis Test: H=16.98; significant at 0.01.

The situations facing magistrates in the larger urban centres are considerably more difficult. Magistrates in larger centres deal with an average of two hundred more Criminal Code cases each per year than magistrates in small towns and rural areas (the actual numbers are 929 and 728 cases respectively).[10] Until recently, courtroom facilities and other amenities were considerably less favourable in most urban centres. While there are no salary differentials in Ontario, the cost of living is substantially higher in larger centres. Most importantly, the status of the magistrate, among the professional bar and in the community generally, is considerably different in the two types of community. Small town and rural magistrates enjoy enormous prestige. They are more likely to be called upon to be members of police commissions, charitable boards, and other community organizations, which gives them a sense of participation in the life of the community. They are likely to be on a first name basis with most professional people who can be of assistance to the court in sentencing, and in the smaller communities particularly, they are likely to know many of the older families.

For all these reasons, it can be expected that the position of magistrate is likely to attract quite different people in the two types of community. Moreover, there is reason to expect that the selective process will be particularly pronounced among young, well-educated lawyers. They are familiar with conditions in magistrates' courts, and in large urban areas they are not likely to seek this position unless they are willing to put up with the low status, inadequate facilities, and heavy work-load of a city magistrate. As far as sentencing is concerned, they must have a set of attitudes and beliefs that do not conflict too greatly with having to dispose of a large number of cases in a routine and somewhat superficial way. In short, young, well-educated persons who seek the position of magistrate in large urban centres are not likely to be typical of young, well-educated people generally.

In contrast, young, well-educated persons in rural and small town areas are likely to feel that they can do some "good" for the community as magistrates. They are likely to be familiar with treatment and other resources available locally, and they have the time to give proper consideration to each case. They are also more protected from punitive influences in the community by reason of the enormous respect they enjoy. It is significant that nine out of twelve magistrates who held executive positions in the local Bar association prior to appointment were rural and small town magistrates.

It is also likely that it is the young, well-educated magistrate who feels greater pressure to change his attitudes and beliefs to coincide with the demands of the situation. Young people are likely to be rather more flexible and have a greater need to find a suitable rationale to justify their behaviour. The same holds true for more educated people, particularly those with legal training, as this form of training stresses rationality and consistency. If the situation calls for a punitive approach in sentencing, young, well-educated magistrates may experience greater pressure to re-organize their attitudes and beliefs in the direction of congruence with the demands of the situation. In seeking a convenient rationale to justify what they are forced to do, they are likely to find in the doctrines of justice, deterrence, and social defence, ways of legitimizing their conduct on the bench. In contrast, rural and small town magistrates find it easier to justify their sentences in terms of reformation. It can, therefore, be expected that the processes of socialization and change operate in different directions in urban and rural areas, and that these processes are likely to have a greater impact on young, well-educated magistrates.

NOTES TO CHAPTER 13

1   See, for example, S. Lipset, "Democracy and Working Class Authoritarianism," *American Sociological Review*, 24 (1959), 482-501; S. Miller and F. Reisman, "Working Class Authoritarianism: A Critique of Lipset," *British Journal of Sociology*, 12 (1961), 265- 76; W. Lentz, "Social Status and Attitudes toward Delinquency Control," *Journal of Research in Crime and Delinquency*, 3 (1966), 147-54; and, E. McDill, "Anomie, Authoritarianism, Prejudice and Socio-economic Status - An Attempt at Clarification," *Social Forces*, 39 (1961), 239-45.

2   *Reg.* v. *Holden* (1962), 39 Crim. Rep. 288; and *Reg.* v. *Roberts* (1963), 1 C.C.C. 27.

3   Included in the group were magistrates with experience as crown attorneys, justices of the peace, and clerks of the court. The latter two groups were included because of their close working relationships with the police.

4   See, for example, P.J. Giffen, "Rates of Crime and Delinquency," in *Crime and its Treatment in Canada* (Toronto, 1965), 74-5; and G. Rose, "The Artificial Delinquent Generation," *Journal of Criminal Law, Criminology, and Police Science*, 59 (3) 370-85.

5   For the purpose of analysis, all magistrates appointed for judicial districts in which the court house was situated in a town of at least 50,000 population were called "city" magistrates - the others were called "rural" magistrates. It would be more accurate to call this latter group rural and small town magistrates.

6   If one uses s.d.^{2} as a measure of variance, there is at least twice as much variance among urban magistrates in their attitude scores.

7   See, for example, C. Hovland, I. Janis, and H. Kelley, *Communication and Persuasion* (New Haven, 1953).

8   *Ibid.*, 191-211.

9   The Kruskal-Wallis Test of one way analyses of variance from ranks was used. For a description of this test see S. Siegel, *Non-Parametric Statistics* (New York, 1956), 184-92.

10 In the larger cities justices of the peace deal with most of the cases involving contravention of city by-laws and provincial statutes. This means that small town and rural magistrates may actually handle many more cases than city magistrates. But they do not deal with as many serious cases.

14

The Search for Information

Introduction

The analysis presented so far attempted to relate certain characteristics of magistrates, in terms of their social backgrounds, attitudes and beliefs, to the end product of the sentencing process, the decision itself. The next five chapters will attempt to fill in the intermediate stages, namely, the way in which magistrates search for and use information in the process of coming to decisions.

Research has shown that people develop characteristic ways of adapting and responding to information.[1] Moreover, there is evidence to suggest that once an individual has developed a pattern of information-use, he tends to resist change and copes with new problems, and new sets of information in similar ways.[2] Over time, much of an individual's decision-behaviour becomes routine and habitual, lending both consistency and predictability to it.

March and Simon point out that, in the search for information, human decision-makers do not seek "optimum" solutions to problems, but rather "satisficing" solutions.[3] Schroder, Driver, and Streufert describe a similar process which they call "adaptive orientation."[4] They, as well as Garfinkel who shows it experimentally, suggest that people operate according to a set of rules which arise from past experience and training.[5] These rules affect both the selection of information and the subsequent organization of it.

One of the most important mechanisms by which individuals order and structure the world around them is the mechanism of selectivity. Three types of *selectivity* have been shown to characterize how people deal with complex facts and situations. They are *selective exposure*,[6] *selective interpretation*,[7] and *selective memory*.[8]

Selectivity is generally considered to be one of the psychological mechanisms operating in the direction of certain needs, the most important of which is the need for certainty and consistency in one's conceptions.[9] A wealth of research evidence has demonstrated that individuals tend to interpret information in ways that minimize inconsistency.[10] The general finding obtained from these studies is the simple one that people are more satisfied by "consistent" arrangements of facts than by "inconsistent" arrangements. Included in these studies are a number of investigations based on Festinger's "Dissonance Theory,"[11] Heider's "Theory of Inter-Personal Perception,"[12] Newcomb's "Theory of Communicative Acts"[13] and Osgoode's and Tannenbaum's "Congruence Approach."[14] None of these separate theories will be discussed here except to say that they all support the general conclusion that in certain circumstances, when individuals experience discrepancy or a conflict between different facts about a problem, a process is set in motion which leads to reorganization or reinterpretation of the facts in the direction of congruency.

More recently, a flurry of research reports have demonstrated that the strain towards consistency is by no means absolute. Certain intervening variables are likely to reflect the degree to which an individual will attempt to resolve inconsistent beliefs by avoiding, misinterpreting or forgetting information. Thus, it has been shown that tolerance of inconsistency varies with differences in personality.[15] It has also been shown that differences in information processing and decision-making can be induced in the same individual as a result of experimental alteration of the conditions under which decisions are made, such as speeding up the task.[16] Finally, factors such as the amount of confidence the individual has in his own opinions,[17] the credibility of the sources from which information is received,[18] and the degree to which consistency is demanded by the social situation in which the individual functions,[19] have been shown to affect the way in which information is used.

In the scheme of analysis presented in the next few chapters, the decision-making process is viewed as follows: a magistrate forms certain initial impressions of the case from information available during the trial and immediately after the issue of guilt is determined. He then may decide to seek additional information from a variety of sources. This information is organized and integrated with other information and interpreted in the light of past experience in similar or analogous situations. In doing so the magistrate identifies the "issues" involved. Finally he examines the alternatives available, and selects the sentence that appears to be the one most consistent with the facts as he interprets them.

Given the same information, different magistrates may have different ways of interpreting it, integrating it, attaching meaning to it and organizing it in relation to other information. Although membership in the legal profession and common experience on the bench may dispose towards a common conceptual system, some variation can be expected among magistrates in the way in which they approach sentencing problems. In similar situations, variations in judgement can be expected and these variations can be viewed as functions of the individual's particular attitudes to the problem at hand. Judicial attitudes can thus be revealed by systematic differences in the way in which information is used in sentencing.

This chapter will first of all deal with the strategies magistrates consciously employ in the search for information. The data were derived from interviews with magistrates and are limited to the discovery of the deliberate and conscious policies of magistrates in seeking and evaluating information relevant to the problems of sentencing as they define them. Later in the chapter additional data will be presented dealing with the sources of information actually used by magistrates in a sample of cases. Subsequent chapters will deal with the pre-sentence report as a medium of communication, the impact of information on magistrates' assessments of cases, the organization and integration of information in the process of judgement, the complexity of thought processes in sentencing and the relationships between perceived "facts" and sentencing decisions.

Identification of Relevant Information

A piece of information is not likely to be "effective" unless it belongs to a category that the magistrate deems important. The first problem is to identify the categories of information magistrates consider "relevant" to problems in sentencing as they define them. To probe this area magistrates were asked the following two questions.

1. Suppose for the moment that the probation service could no longer provide the court with full pre-sentence reports, but it agreed to provide a much shortened version of the existing report. What instructions would you give your probation officers concerning the kinds of information that must be included in this shortened report?

2. If a new crown attorney were appointed to your court, and he requested instructions from you concerning the kind of information about offences that should be read to you on pleas of guilty, what instructions would you give?

The answers given to these questions are presented immediately below in Table 74.

TABLE 74

Information considered relevant to sentencing

	Essential	Not essential
Information about offenders		
Family background	61	10
Criminal record	51	20
Employment record	42	29
Intelligence	26	45
Marital status	26	45
Ties in community	24	47
Mental condition	19	52
Attitude to rehabilitation	19	52
Use of alcohol or drugs	12	3
Other	3	68
Information about offences		
Planning and premeditation	62	9
Culpability in other respects	32	39
Degree of personal injury or violence	29	42
Damage or loss to property	12	59
All circumstances must be considered	12	59
Offender's present attitude to the offence	8	63
Other	3	68

With respect to the offender, the majority of magistrates considered family background, criminal record, and employment record as "essential." It is interesting that family background was picked more often than any other factor. It is a very broad category and one that is difficult to assess. Moreover, it is very difficult to know what to do with this information once it is received. Factors related to the family life of the offender are not generally good predictors of whether the offender will commit a further offence.[20] Perhaps this information is not used for prediction, but rather as an assessment of the offender as a person. Information of this type can be used to determine whether the offender "needs" treatment or it can be used to determine whether the offender "deserves" punishment.

While a majority considered family background, criminal record, and employment record essential, there was little agreement among magistrates concerning other areas of the offender's life. This is not surprising in view of the fact that while a great deal of information is made available to the court, no guide-lines are provided as to how magistrates are to assess it. This makes it necessary for magistrates to establish their own criteria for assessing the relevance of and weight to attach to different types of information.

The ten magistrates who did not consider family background to be essential had higher general deterrence and incapacitation scores, and lower reformation scores on the penal philosophy scales, and higher social defence scores on the attitude scales.[21]

Concerning the offence, it is evident that most magistrates consider the "moral quality" of the criminal act to be more important than the actual harm incurred by the victim. Nearly two out of three magistrates considered information about planning and premeditation or culpability in other respects, to be essential. In contrast, only about one in four considered the degree of personal injury or violence or the damage or loss to property to be essential. None of the penal philosophy or attitude scales distinguished magistrates in terms of the kinds of information about offences that were considered essential. Perhaps the explanation lies in the fact that each of the factors selected can be considered as indicators of the extent of the offender's criminality, either for purposes of treatment or for purposes of punishment. It may also be true that there is a tendency for magistrates to consider all kinds of information as being "essential" in the abstract, but in the actual process of judgement tend to rate one category of information higher than another. The next section will explore this possibility.

Ordering of Priorities among Information

Magistrates were asked to rate, in order of importance, information concerning the offender, the criminal record and the offence. The results are presented in Table 75.

Two out of three magistrates rated the nature and circumstances of the offence above the criminal record and the background and history of the offender. Almost half ordered the na-

TABLE 75

Magistrates' views as to the relative importance of information concerning the offence, the criminal record and the background and history of the offender

Order of priority among categories of information	Number	Per cent
First: nature and circumstances of offence Second: criminal record Third: background and history of offender	31	43.7
First: nature and circumstances of offence Second: background and history of offender Third: criminal record	17	23.9
First: background and history of offender Second: criminal record Third: nature and circumstances of offence	7	9.9
First: background and history of offender Second: nature and circumstances of offence Third: criminal record	3	4.1
First: criminal record Second: background and history of offender Third: nature and circumstances of offence	-	-
First: criminal record Second: nature and circumstances of offence Third: background and history of offender	2	2.9
All three equal	11	15.5
Total	71	100.0

ture and circumstances of the offence first, the criminal record second, and the background and history of the offender last. This is a fairly clear indication of the importance of the offence in sentencing. Only one in seven gave the background and history of the offender priority over the offence or the criminal record. This suggests that regardless of differences in penal philosophy or attitudes among magistrates, there is a fair degree of agreement about the pre-eminence of the offence in determining sentence. Even among magistrates who espouse a treatment or reformative penal philosophy, most will make an assessment of the offender and his chances of successful treatment primarily through a consideration of the nature and circumstances of the offence committed. We see in these data the degree to which the traditional role of the court to punish crime is being maintained in spite of the verbal commitment given to reformation and treatment by increasing numbers of judges and magistrates.

While there was a reasonable degree of uniformity among magistrates concerning the relative importance of information concerning the offence compared to information about the criminal record or background of the offender, some variations among individual magistrates was evident. It was discovered that this variation was closely associated with differences among magistrates in penal philosophy and attitudes. For each magistrate, each category of information was given a score of three, two, or one, depending upon his rating of it. These scores were then correlated with the penal philosophy and attitude scores of the magistrates concerned. The results are presented in Table 76.

Magistrates who rate the offence higher tend to have higher justice scores on the attitude scales, and higher general and individual deterrence scores but lower reformation scores on the

TABLE 76

Correlations of penal philosophy and attitude scores with importance given to different categories of information

	Offence	Criminal record	Background of offender
Penal philosophy			
Reformation	-0.286	-0.270	0.451
General deterrence	0.291	0.271	-0.456
Individual deterrence	0.266	-	-
Punishment	-	-	-
Incapacitation	-	-	-
Attitudes			
Justice	0.273	-	-0.250
Punishment corrects	-	-	-
Intolerance	-	-	-
Social defence	-	0.393	-0.464
Modernism	-	-	

penal philosophy scales. Magistrates who rate the criminal record higher tend to have higher social defence scores on the attitude scales, and higher general deterrence but lower reformation scores on the penal philosophy scales. In contrast, those who rate the background of the offender higher have higher reformation scores on the penal philosophy scales and lower justice and social defence scores on the attitude scales.

It can be concluded, therefore, that the identification of "essential" information, and the relative weights attached to different categories of information is, to a large extent, consistent with the penal philosophies and attitudes of the magistrates concerned. We now turn to the way in which different magistrates assess information within each of the main categories.

Discrimination Within Categories of Information

Apart from identifying the relative weights attached to a category of information, it is important to know how carefully individual magistrates assess information within each category. A good indication of the importance of a category of information to an individual is the number of differentiations he makes within the category. If a magistrate seeks answers to a large number of questions about a particular aspect of a case, it can be expected that he attaches great importance to it.[22]

Magistrates were divided into three groups on each of the main penal philosophy and attitude scales. For each scale, they were further divided into those with high scores, those in the middle, and those with low scores. There were twenty-three magistrates in each group. The mean number of factors about the offence and the offender considered essential by magistrates in each group was determined. Correlations between penal philosophy and attitude scores and the number of factors considered essential were then calculated. The results are presented in Table 77.

Magistrates primarily concerned about reformation make more discriminations concerning the offender and fewer concerned about deterrence and social defence. It appears, therefore, that the amount and kind of information brought to bear on sentencing problems depends, at least in part, on the purpose to which it will be put. There is no evidence in these data to suggest that magistrates with "punitive" attitudes and beliefs are inherently less subtle in their thought processes. Rather, it appears that the style of information-use is the one most suited to the objectives of the magistrates concerned.

Frequency of Information Requests

Having specified the kinds of information that magistrates consider to be essential in sentencing, and the number of perspec-

TABLE 77

The mean number of factors considered essential by magistrates with high,
moderate, and low scores on penal philosophy and attitude scales

Scale	Mean number of factors	
	About the offence	About the offender
Reformation		
High scores	2.27	4.75
Moderate scores	2.69	3.71
Low scores	3.71	3.00
	$(r = -0.317; p = 0.01)$	$(r = 0.383; p = 0.01)$
General deterrence		
High scores	3.92	2.83
Moderate scores	3.51	3.11
Low scores	3.01	4.09
	$(r = 0.302; p = 0.01)$	$(r = -0.367; p = 0.01)$
Social defence		
High scores	3.89	2.22
Moderate scores	3.57	3.01
Low scores	3.11	4.16
	$(r = 0.355; p = 0.01)$	$(r = -0.392; p = 0.01)$

tives generated in assessing this information, we now turn to an
examination of the situations which prompt magistrates to seek
information of various kinds.

Magistrates were asked several questions concerning the reasons for requesting pre-sentence and psychiatric reports. The results indicated that regardless of penal philosophy, most magistrates (sixty-five out of seventy-one) will ask for reports from
probation officers when considering the possibility of probation.
Significant differences exist, however, among magistrates who
use pre-sentence reports for other purposes. Slightly more than
half (thirty-seven out of seventy-one) will seek reports when
considering an institutional sentence. Four magistrates stated
that they did not have a great deal of confidence in the pre-
sentence report, but requested them occasionally in order to
ensure that the Ontario Court of Appeal would be satisfied that
sufficient care was taken in determining the appropriate sentence.

Once again, differences in information-use are associated with
penal philosophies and attitudes. Magistrates who use pre-
sentence reports when considering institutional sentences, are
likely to have higher than average reformation and lower than average general deterrence scores on the penal philosophy scales.
At the same time, they are likely to have higher than average pun-

ishment corrects and lower than average social defence scores on the attitude scales. In each case the differences were significant at 0.01 or better.[23]

A similar pattern emerged with respect to the use of the psychiatric report. The majority of magistrates (sixty-two out of seventy-one) would use psychiatric reports when "fitness to stand trial" was "an issue" at the trial. A smaller number (forty-nine out of seventy-one) would request psychiatric reports when there was evidence of emotional disturbance that might require psychiatric treatment. A yet smaller group (twenty-four out of seventy-one) would request reports when the offence was committed in a bizarre or unusual way, or when there were other circumstances requiring an explanation. Only twenty magistrates would request reports in all three situations.

Magistrates who restrict the use of psychiatric reports to cases in which fitness to stand trial is the only issue, tended to have higher general deterrence and lower reformation scores on the penal philosophy scales, and higher justice and lower punishment corrects scores on the attitude scales. The differences were statistically significant at 0.01 or better.[24]

These data suggest that magistrates concerned about the treatment of offenders are more active in their search for information than magistrates concerned to punish crime for deterrent or retributive purposes. But in each case, the type of information sought after, the amount of information used, and the way in which it is assessed appear to depend on the highly individual ways in which particular magistrates define their objectives in sentencing.

Faults Found in the Format of the Pre-Sentence Reports

Certain insights can be gained from the criticisms expressed by magistrates concerning the pre-sentence report. Two out of three magistrates expressed general satisfaction with the report. Faults mentioned by those magistrates who were unhappy with it are listed in Table 78.

The faults mentioned seem to express a desire on the part of some magistrates to avoid having to deal with offenders as persons, and/or displeasure with the "excessive" length and non-legal style of the report. Magistrates who find fault with the pre-sentence report are distinguishable in terms of having significantly higher general deterrence, retribution, and justice scores, and significantly lower reformation and punishment corrects scores.[25]

These data provide further confirmation that magistrates tend to respond to information in ways consistent with their personal motivations and subjective ends. Magistrates who express negative attitudes towards the pre-sentence report tend also to have

TABLE 78

Faults found by magistrates in the format and content of the pre-sentence report

Fault	Number	Per cent
Too long	14	19.9
Too many technical words	9	14.1
Not specific enough in recommendations	8	11.4
Too much information on offender's early life	6	8.4
Not enough information about offence	6	8.4
Other	4	5.7

negative attitudes towards the rationale underlying it, namely, the individualization of justice and the treatment of offenders.

The next section will deal with the information-seeking strategies actually followed by magistrates. This time the data will not be restricted to self-reports from magistrates, but rather will be derived from a sample of cases dealt with by magistrates over a specified time period.

Sources of Information Actually Used

A sample of 2354 cases was drawn consisting of all offenders dealt with in the sample by magistrates over an eighteen-months' period, who were convicted of any one of seven indictable offences. The offences concerned covered a wide range of different sentencing problems and were comprised of: robbery, breaking and entering, taking a motor vehicle without consent, fraud, assault occasioning bodily harm, indecent assault, and dangerous driving. Information was collected from magistrates with respect to each of these cases concerning, among other things, the number and kind of information sources used. The development of the instrument used to collect this data and other findings based on it are described in Chapter 16.

In Table 79 the frequencies in which different sources of information were used are listed. The list does not include information concerning the offence, which can be assumed to have been received in all cases.

It is interesting to see that the crown attorney participated in sentencing by making a statement in nearly three out of four cases, while defence counsel did so in less than half the cases in

TABLE 79

Sources of information received as to sentence

Source of information		Number	Per cent
Statement of offender		1293	54.9
Statement of crown		1704	72.4
Statement by defence counsel		565	24.0
Probation report: (a) written	914		
(b) oral	82		
(c) total		996	42.3
Psychiatric report		101	4.3
Criminal record of offender		828	35.2
Statement by parents		212	9.0
Statement by employer		63	2.7
Statement by other relatives		64	2.7
Statement by priest or minister		27	1.1
Other		149	6.3

which the accused was represented.[26] The degree of participation by the crown attorney was somewhat greater than that indicated by magistrates in interviews. It will be remembered that the majority of magistrates stated that crown attorneys participated only on request from a magistrate, and that such requests were only occasionally made.

Use of the Pre-Sentence Report

Perhaps the most important fact which emerges from Table 79 is that in less than half the cases was a pre-sentence report requested.

Certain insights can be gained from knowledge of the kinds of cases which prompt magistrates to seek pre-sentence reports and from the relationship between the use of these reports and the kinds of sentencing decisions made.

In Table 80 a breakdown is provided of the proportion of requests for a pre-sentence report by type of offence.

The general pattern which emerges from Table 80 is that pre-sentence reports were usually requested in more serious types of cases. This is a fairly good indication that these reports are not requested only when non-institutional sentences are being consid-

TABLE 80
Proportion of requests for pre-sentence reports by type of offence

Type of case	Number of cases	Number of requests	Proportion (per cent)
All offences	2354	1077	44.1
Robbery	136	76	55.9
Breaking and entering	916	610	66.6
Taking a motor vehicle	235	134	57.0
Fraud	171	52	30.4
Assault and bodily harm	405	65	16.2
Indecent assault	125	53	42.3
Dangerous driving	378	44	11.6

ered. Even in cases of robbery, where over eighty-six per cent of the cases resulted in institutional sentence, pre-sentence reports were requested in over half the cases. In contrast, the two offences for which institutional sentences are rarely imposed, namely assault occasioning bodily harm (23 per cent) and dangerous driving (18 per cent), were the least likely to involve the use of a pre-sentence report by the magistrate concerned.

The relationship between the use of the pre-sentence report and the choice of sentence selected can be seen from Table 81. For each offence, in turn, cases were divided into four groups: pre-sentence report, no pre-sentence report, institutional sentence, and non-institutional sentence. Chi square tests were calculated on the resulting two-by-two contingency tables. The results are rather interesting.

It appears that while in general the use of pre-sentence reports was associated with a tendency to select institutional sentences, different patterns emerge with respect to individual offences. Thus, with respect to serious cases such as robbery and breaking and entering, where the rate of committal to penal institutions is rather high, the use of pre-sentence reports was associated with the more frequent selection of non-institutional sentences. In contrast, with respect to relatively minor offences such as dangerous driving, where the rate of committal to penal institutions is relatively low, the use of the pre-sentence report was associated with a greater proportion of committals to penal institutions. It appears from this that pre-sentence reports are requested in cases for which magistrates are considering sentences that are not normally or usually given for that type of offence. This may mean that the cases themselves are somewhat unusual and magistrates request pre-sentence reports to satisfy themselves that atypical sentences are justified, or it may mean that the contents of these reports themselves lead magistrates to conclude that somewhat unusual sentences are warranted. In any event, it cannot be said that the use of pre-sentence reports is associated with lenient sentencing practice.

The use of pre-sentence reports was also associated with differences in the lengths of institutional sentences imposed. For each offence in turn, comparisons were made between the lengths of institutional sentences given in cases where pre-sentence reports

TABLE 81

Impact of pre-sentence report on choice of sentence

		Institutional sentences	
		Yes	No
All offences,[a] N = 2316	Yes	514	523
Pre-sentence report	No	595	722
Robbery,[b] N = 136	Yes	62	14
Pre-sentence report	No	56	4
Breaking and Entering,[c] N = 916	Yes	323	287
Pre-sentence report	No	230	76
Taking a motor vehicle,[d] N = 235	Yes	25	109
Pre-sentence report	No	25	76
Fraud,[e] N = 171	Yes	31	21
Pre-sentence report	No	69	50
Dangerous driving,[f] N = 378	Yes	15	29
Pre-sentence report	No	47	287

a   Yates chi square = 4.308 (continuity corrected) significant at 0.038
b   Yates chi square = 4.034 (continuity corrected) significant at 0.045
c   Yates chi square = 41.102 (continuity corrected) significant at 0.001
d   Yates chi square = 0.940 (continuity corrected) not significant
e   Yates chi square = 0.001 (continuity corrected) not significant
f   Yates chi square = 9.950 (continuity corrected) significant at 0.002

were received and cases where this information was not used. The results indicated that in cases of robbery, the use of pre-sentence reports was associated with significantly shorter institutional sentences. The average difference was 646 days and the results were statistically significant. Similarly, in breaking and entering, the average institutional sentence where pre-sentence reports were requested was 88 days less than in cases where pre-sentence reports were not received. Again the differences were statistically significant. In contrast, in cases of fraud and indecent assault the use of pre-sentence reports were associated with longer sentences of imprisonment (Table 82).

These data show that the pre-sentence report does not necessarily lead to lenient sentencing practice. Rather, it appears that magistrates in Ontario use pre-sentence reports in "difficult" cases. In fact, it would appear that pre-sentence reports can serve

TABLE 82

Impact of pre-sentence report on length of institutional sentences imposed

Type of case	Mean length of sentence (days)				Level of significance
	Report	No report	Difference	t	
Robbery	814	1460	646	2.06	0.041
Breaking and entering	392	480	88	2.32	0.021
Taking motor vehicle	129	172	43	1.13	0.265
Fraud	380	250	-140	2.05	0.051
Assault and bodily harm	175	115	-60	1.63	0.106
Indecent assault on female	503	320	-183	2.16	0.025
Dangerous driving	88	66	-22	0.74	0.463

to justify sentences that would appear punitive if based solely on the offence. The data, however, do not provide any information as to the actual impact of the pre-sentence report on the image the magistrate forms of the offender. The whole of Chapter 16 is devoted to this issue.

Number of Different Information Sources Used

Magistrates also differ in the amount of information received prior to sentence. Some magistrates appeared content to base their sentences on the offence and possibly the criminal record of the offender. Others were more active in the search for information, and not only frequently requested pre-sentence and psychiatric reports, but also appeared to encourage lawyers on both sides, parents, employers, and others to make verbal statements in court concerning the offender. The average number of different information sources used by magistrates was 2.7. Individual magistrates varied in the number of sources of information habitually used from a low of 1.5 sources for one magistrate to a high of 3.7 sources for another.

It was discovered that variation in the number of sources of information used was closely associated with variations in the penal philosophy and attitude scores of the magistrates concerned. Magistrates who used more sources of information tended to have significantly higher reformation and significantly lower general deterrence and retribution scores, on the penal philosophy scales. These same magistrates tended to have significantly higher punishment corrects and modernism scores and significantly lower justice, intolerance, and social defence scores, on the attitude scales.[27]

It appears that the "styles" of information-search actually used approximate closely to self-reported "styles" revealed from interviews. In each case, the number of sources of information used and the type of information relied upon are consistent with the personal values and subjective goals of the magistrates concerned.

In Chapter 6 judicial attitudes in sentencing were defined as pre-dispositions to evaluate offenders in particular ways. The data presented in this section suggest that the selective use of information enables magistrates to maintain their original attitudes intact. Magistrates tend to seek information consistent with their preconceptions (which are the essence of attitudes). At the same time, they tend to avoid information which is likely to present a picture of the offender that may conflict with their expectations. The evaluative nature of judicial attitudes is thus revealed.

NOTES TO CHAPTER 14

1   For a good review of the literature see C. Hovland, I. Janis, and H. Kelley, *Communication and Persuasion* (New Haven, 1953); and S. Feldman, ed., *Cognitive Consistency, Motivational Antecedents and Behavioral Consequents* (New York, 1966).
2   The best known recent work in this field includes: H. Schroder, M. Driver, and S. Streufert, *Human Information Processing: Individuals and Groups Functioning in Complex Social Situations* (New York, 1966); and M. Rokeach, *The Open and Closed Mind* (New York, 1960).
3   J. March and H. Simon, *Organization* (New York, 1958), 41.
4   Schroder, *et al.*, *Human Information Processing*, chap. 1.
5   H. Garfinkel, *Studies in Ethnomethodology* (New Jersey, 1967), 76-103.
6   Selective exposure represents one of the most consistent findings in the entire field of communications. See, for example, Lazarfeld's famous voting

study which showed that people are likely to expose themselves to information which tends to support policy stands already taken. P. Lazarfeld, B. Berelson, and B. Gaudet, *The People's Choice* (New York, 1944).

7 See, for example, the study of Cooper and Jahoda which showed that prejudiced subjects could not get the point of jokes lampooning prejudice. E. Cooper and M. Jahoda, "The Evasion of Propaganda," *Journal of Psychology*, 23 (1947), 15-25.

8 The classical Levin and Murphy experiment demonstrates this well. Pro-communist students were more likely to remember pro-communist arguments, while anti-communist students were more likely to remember anti-communist arguments. J. Levine and G. Murphy, "The Learning and Forgetting of Controversial Material," *Journal of Abnormal and Social Psychology*, 38 (1943), 507-17.

9 For an excellent discussion see M. Rosenberg, "Psychological Selectivity in Self-Esteem Formation," in M. Sherif, ed., *Attitude, Ego-Involvement and Change* (New York, 1967), 26-50.

10 Most of the significant work in this field is discussed in C. Hovland and M. Rosenberg, eds., *Attitude Organization and Change* (New Haven, 1960); and Feldman, ed., *Cognitive Consistency*.

11 L. Festinger, *A Theory of Cognitive Dissonance* (Evanston, 1957).

12 F. Heider, *The Psychology of Interpersonal Relations* (New York, 1958).

13 T. Newcomb, "An Approach to the Study of Communicative Acts," *Psychological Review*, 60 (1953), 393-404.

14 C. Osgoode and P. Tannenbaum, "The Principle of Congruity and the Prediction of Attitude Change," *ibid.*, 62 (1955), 42-55.

15 For a review of the literature see S. Shauger and J. Altracchi, "The Personality of the Perceiver as a Factor in Person Perception," *Psychological Bulletin* 5 (1965), 289-308; and O. Harvey and R. Ware, "Personality Differences in Dissonance Resolution," *Journal of Personal and Social Psychology, 7* (1967), 227-30.

16 See, for example, K. Gergen and R. Bauer, "Interactive Effects of Self-Esteem and Task Difficulty on Social Conformity," *Journal of Personal and Social Psychology*, 6 (1) (1967), 16-22.

17 The best known work in this field includes J. Freedman and D. Sears, "Selective Exposure," in *Advances in Experimental Social Psychology* (New York, 1965), 57-97; and A. Lowin, "Approach and Avoidance," *Journal of Personal and Social Psychology*, 6 (1967) 1-9.

18 See, particularly: Lowin, "Approach and Avoidance," and C. Hovland and W. Weiss, "The Influence of Source Credibility on Communication Effectiveness," *Public Opinion Quarterly*, 15 (1951), 635-50. More generally, see I. Janis, *et al.*, *Personality and Persuasibility* (New Haven, 1959).

19 Hovland and Rosenberg, "Theoretical Issues," in *Attitude Organization and Change*, 220.

20 A good review of predictive factors is to be found in D. Gottfredson, "Assessment of Prediction Methods in Crime and Delinquency," in President's Commission, *Task Force Report: Juvenile Delinquency and Youth Crime* (Washington, 1967), 171-87.

21 See Technical Appendix 7 for supporting statistics.

22 For a review see W. McGuire, in Feldman, ed., *Cognitive Consistency*, 22-63.

23 See Technical Appendix 7 for supporting statistics.

24 *Ibid.*

25 *Ibid.*

26 Defence counsel were present in approximately 1100 out of 2350 cases.

27 See Technical Appendix 7 for supporting statistics.

15

Communication of Information

Rationale and Use of the Pre-Sentence Report

The pre-sentence report has been hailed as "one of the most important developments in Canadian criminal law during the twentieth century."[1] It is seen as "individualizing" the sentencing process by enabling the court to select the sentence that is most likely to suit both the needs of the offender and the protection of society.[2] Over the years it has become the most important medium through which magistrates and judges obtain information about offenders, and it is being relied on more and more heavily.[3]

In 1938 the *Archambault Report* strongly recommended the use of the pre-sentence report by Canadian courts whenever probation was being considered.[4] At that time, however, probation officers served only a few of the courts in some of the larger urban areas, and some provinces were without probation services of any kind.[5] After the war, probation services became established in most provinces, and by 1956 the *Fauteux Report* was able to recommend that pre-sentence reports should be made mandatory in a wide range of situations, including certain cases in which institutional sentences were likely.[6] More recently, the Sentencing Committee of the Ontario Magistrates' Association specified additional situations in which the courts should obtain pre-sentence reports before passing sentence.[7]

Many judges and magistrates have publicly stated that the pre-sentence report has become an "essential" document without which a proper determination of sentence would be impossible.[8] A leading Ontario magistrate recently wrote: "the court, in some instances, fails in its duty if it refuses to accept the pre-sentence report. It then usurps the function of the skilled probation officer and could be delinquent in not accepting the service of this specialist."[9] The learned magistrate went so far as to state that to a large extent sentencing has now become "scientific, definitive, and clinical in its application," and that "just as in medicine or surgery" the court makes use of many specialized diagnostic services, the most important of which are the probation services.[10]

In the light of such favourable comments it is not surprising that a senior official of the Ontario Probation Services was recently prompted to write that the pre-sentence report has made a "major contribution to the Administration of justice," and he confidently claimed that the report "took the subjective hunch out of sentencing."[11] The growing confidence on the part of judges and magistrates in the usefulness of these reports is evidenced by the fact that requests for them by Ontario magistrates increased steadily over the years from 3880 in 1956 to 6648 in 1966.[12]

While such unbounded confidence in the pre-sentence report is understandable and to some extent laudable, it must be stated that there is little proof that the report actually lives up to the extravagant claims made for it. It is taken for granted that "in order to impose sentence which will fit the needs of the offender and meet the demands of society, the judge must know the offender and his background."[13] It is also assumed that the pre-sentence report fulfils this function. But certain questions must be asked: What need a court know about the offender to make effective decisions? Can this information be communicated to the court through the medium of pre-sentence reports?

Format and Content of the Report

The pre-sentence report is prepared at the request of the presiding magistrate after the finding of guilt and before sentence is passed. The use of pre-trial reports, common in England, is not frequently employed in Canada.[14] The usual practice is for the magistrate to remand the case for a week or more, during which the probation officer interviews the accused (on one or more occasions), the spouse or parents of the accused, and possibly other relatives, employers, friends, or other people who may know the offender. Because of pressures of work many probation officers find it necessary to restrict their pre-sentence investigations to the offender, his wife, and, possibly, his mother (the father usually being away at work). In the end the probation officer writes a report containing various social, psychiatric, and environmental details about the offender and his circumstances. The policy in Ontario is for probation officers to indicate to the court the likely response of the offender to probation, if granted. Probation officers are not permitted by law or policy to suggest a particular sentence.

The probation officer's handbook provides general guidelines for probation officers in completing pre-sentence reports. It states that the following areas are to be included:[15] (1) basic information (age, sex, etc.); (2) family and personal history; (3) educational history; (4) employment history; (5) marital history; (6) financial status; (7) leisure time activities; (8) health; (9) religious affiliation; (10) the offender as a person; (11) extenuating circumstances surrounding the commission of the offence; (12) conclusion - including the offender's likely response to probation if granted.

In addition to this list probation officers usually include the criminal record of the offender as revealed by the RCMP Fingerprint File.[16]

The model upon which the pre-sentence report is based is essentially a mental health model. Pre-sentence reports are very close in both content and structure to social workers in mental health settings. Criminological research has challenged the relevance of mental health concepts and methods of the treatment of crime and delinquency, but so far correctional practice has been largely resistant to such influences. In dealing with information use in corrections Carter and Wilkins state: "in essence, it appears that the increasing problems of crime and delinquency are being addressed by the application of principles and practices which have not been substantially modified, or even questioned (authors' emphasis), since their inception."[17] The assumption that the pre-sentence report is an effective medium of communication of information about offenders will be tested in this chapter.

Previous Research

There is some research evidence from both England[18] and the United States[19] that the courts tend to "follow" the recommendations of probation officers contained in pre-sentence reports, but in both instances the researchers were not sure about the extent to which some probation officers may have "second guessed" the court by making recommendations which they thought to be those desired. Moreover, in the study of the use of pre-sentence reports in Northern California, Carter and Wilkins demonstrated that most probation officers tended to develop highly individual ways of preparing reports, and tended to base their recommendations on different types and amounts of information, depending on their own background of experience, thus "contributing to the problems of disparities in sentencing."[20] Hood reports several studies which tend to show that the increased use of the pre-sentence report by English magistrates leads to both an increase in the use of probation at the expense of fines and detention and, in one case, a reduction in the number of offenders re-convicted after sentence.[21] However, the evidence on this last point was equivocal and, was found to be in conflict with the results of both earlier and later studies.[22] In another study, Hood found that magistrates tend to change their minds about the appropriate sentence after reading reports.[23]

In none of these studies was any evidence provided as to the actual impact of the report on the image of the offender held by the magistrate. The crucial question is: how is information communicated, and what factors help or hinder in this process? The studies described in this chapter are directed to this question.

Research Design

The pre-sentence report is studied as a medium of communication between the probation officer (the communicator) and the magistrate (the recipient), about a third person (the offender). If the communication process is effective it can be expected that the magistrate will change his perception of the offender by having read the report. Moreover, the magistrate should alter his perception of the offender in the direction of agreement with the probation officer.

A number of experiments were designed in which magistrates and probation officers on a sample of cases appearing before the courts provided identical information to the research team concerning various aspects of offenders' backgrounds and their chances for rehabilitation. In one half of the cases the magistrate read a pre-sentence report from the probation officer. In the other half, this information was not received. In both instances, magistrates and probation officers sent information to the research team independently. The sample was a time sample and included all offenders convicted by the magistrates concerned of breaking and entering over an eighteen-month time period.

The purpose of the analysis was to test the *a priori* assumption that: "there would be more agreement between probation officers and magistrates concerning the offender if there was a pre-sentence report than if there was not."

Information was collected on two forms: the sentencing study sheet completed by the magistrate, and the offender assessment guide completed by the probation officer. The identical sections in these two documents related to the following areas.

The offender's present attitude to his offence. There were seven possible descriptions of the offender's attitude towards his involvement in the offence. They ranged from being "remorseful" and "accepting full responsibility," to being "indifferent" and "defiant."

The assessment of the offender. On both forms, ten characteristics of the offender, in terms of problem areas in his life, were rated on a series of five-point scales.

Categorizing the offender. Both magistrates and probation officers were asked to indicate whether the offender fitted any of the following descriptions: (*a*) a dangerous mentally ill offender; (*b*) a persistent offender; (*c*) a professional criminal.

Treatment factors. Both the sentencing study sheet completed by magistrates and the offender assessment guide completed by probation officers require ratings on a number of built-in scales concerning factors thought to be useful in the possible treatment planned. In all, ten areas of treatment were explored.

Adequacy of resources. Magistrates and probation officers were asked to indicate whether or not they felt their present resources were adequate to deal with a particular offender. A second question asked if they would suggest any changes in the law or resources at present available.

Method

A stratified random sample of eighty-four cases of breaking and entering was selected. The pre-sentence report was requested and received in forty-two of these cases but not requested in the remainder. Half the group (twenty-one) were rural and half were urban. The amount of agreement between probation officers and magistrates was operationalized as the absolute differences between the scores on the sentencing study sheet and the offender assessment guide.

The method of analysis was two-way analysis of variance.[24] The design was orthogonal, i.e., there were an equal number of cases in each cell. In all, some twenty-one analyses of variance problems were dealt with.

Analysis of variance is a statistical technique which allows the investigator to determine relationships among a complex set of variables. The technique can demonstrate that a relationship between two variables is caused by the "inter-action" of one of the variables with a third. It determines the relationships between all possible combinations of independent variables with the dependent variable. In this case, it was used because the research problem was one of discovering whether the degree of agreement between the probation officer and the magistrate (the dependent variable) was affected, not only by the existence or non-existence of a pre-sentence report (the first independent variable), but also by whether the pre-sentence report had different "effects" in urban and rural areas (the second independent variable).

Results

The results indicated that, ignoring urban-rural differences, the pre-sentence report was not associated with greater agreement between probation officers and magistrates concerning any of the areas examined. In fact, it appeared that, in some aspects of the offender's life, the use of a pre-sentence report was associated with *less* agreement between the probation officer and the magistrate. However, when one examined the inter-action between the use of the pre-sentence report and the type of community in which the probation officer and magistrate live, a number of contrasting trends emerged.

Rural magistrates tended to be *closer* to probation officers in their perception of the offender and the possibilities of treatment if they had received pre-sentence reports from them. But, where pre-sentence reports were requested in urban areas, magistrates and probation officers tended to be *further* away from each other, in both their perceptions of the offender and their assessment of treatment possibilities. These results are pictured graphically below. The statistical work supporting them is provided in full in Technical Appendix 8.

Offender's Present Attitude to his Involvement in the Offence

The amount of agreement between magistrates and probation officers concerning the degree of remorse expressed by the offender after the commission of the offence did not appear to be affected by the pre-sentence report. Moreover, the degree of agreement or disagreement between magistrates and probation officers did not appear to be significantly different in urban or rural areas. In absolute terms, probation officers tended to see slightly more remorse on the part of offenders than did magistrates. The degree of remorse was rated on a five-point scale. The average distance between magistrates and probation officers on this scale was 0.81. This is not a large difference, and it suggests that a fair degree of uniformity exists between magistrates and probation officers concerning the assessment of this area. This uniformity persisted whether or not there was a pre-sentence report and whether or not the case arose in an urban or rural environment.

Assessment of the Offender's Problems

Considerably less agreement exists between magistrates and probation officers concerning the amount of pathology seen in various areas of the offender's life. In the ten areas of the offender's life examined the average distance between magistrates and probation officers on a series of five-point scales was 1.75. The differences were in the expected direction. Probation officers tend to see more pathology than magistrates, but the pattern was not entirely uniform.

For each area considered, correlations were calculated between ratings given by magistrates and ratings given by probation officers. In tests of this kind, it is generally considered that inter-rater agreement (represented by the correlation) should exceed 0.9.[25] If correlations fall much below 0.9, it must be concluded that there is an excessive amount of inconsistency in the ratings or, in other words, the ratings are unreliable. Over the ten areas concerned, inter-rater agreement ranged from a low of 0.36 to a high of 0.85, with a mean of 0.67. This means that not only are there systematic differences in the amount of pathology seen by the two groups, but also that there are discrepancies which are unsystematic, i.e., some of the ratings given by magistrates and probation officers bear no relationship to each other. This has important implications for the role of the probation officer in sentencing. If there are marked discrepancies in perceptions of offenders, even after magistrates have read the pre-sentence reports, then questions are raised about the effectiveness of these reports as a medium of communication.

Ignoring urban-rural differences, the only area where the pre-sentence report appeared to have led to more agreement between magistrates and probation officers was "alienation from the community." In five of the remaining nine areas, the amount of agreement between magistrates and probation officers did not appear to be associated with either the existence or non-existence of a pre-sentence report, or with urban-rural differences. Null results were derived in the following areas: "family and personal relationships," "attitudes towards authority," "the use of alcohol," "present adjustment in employment or school," and "present financial setting."

In the remaining four areas: "the use of drugs," "anti-social behaviour," "association with delinquents or criminals," and "pattern of criminal behaviour," the amount of agreement between magistrates and probation officers appeared to be solely due to "interaction effects." In these cases, *rural* magistrates appear to be *closer* to probation officers in their perception of the offender if a pre-sentence report was received. In contrast, *urban* magistrates tended to be further away from the probation officer's view of the case if they had read a pre-sentence report prepared by him. These results are demonstrated in Figures 9 to 12, which show the advantage of two-way analysis of variance. These contrasting trends would not have been revealed by univariate methods. It appears that rural magistrates are influenced by the pre-sentence report as expected, while urban magistrates tend to move in the opposite direction. Possible explanations for this phenomenon will be presented later in this chapter.

Assessment of Treatment Factors

In none of the ten treatment areas rated by magistrates and probation officers were there statistically significant differences in the amount of agreement between them depending on whether or not there was a pre-sentence report. This held true in both urban and rural areas. In order to maximize variance, an over-all "agreement" score was calculated over the ten treatment areas, and a prediction of this variable using the categories of pre-sentence report, no pre-sentence report, rural, and urban, was made. No statistically significant differences were obtained.

It appears from these data that the pre-sentence report does not have an impact on magistrates' assessments of factors that could be used in treatment plans.

Magistrates and probation officers rated the strength of the treatment factors on a series of threepoint scales ranging from "strong" through "moderate" to "weak." In terms of absolute differences between magistrates and probation officers, the average differences between the two groups was slightly over 1.0. Proba-

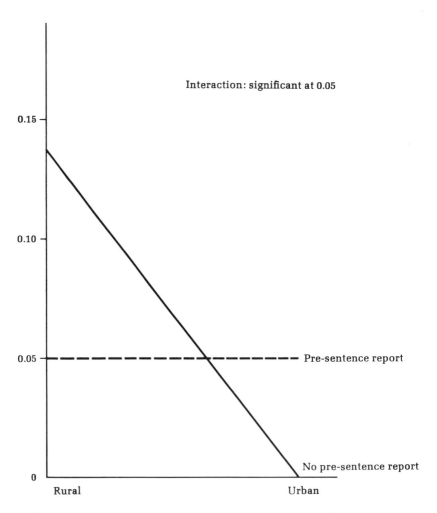

Figure 9. Agreement between magistrates and probation officers concerning their perception of the offender: (a) the use of drugs

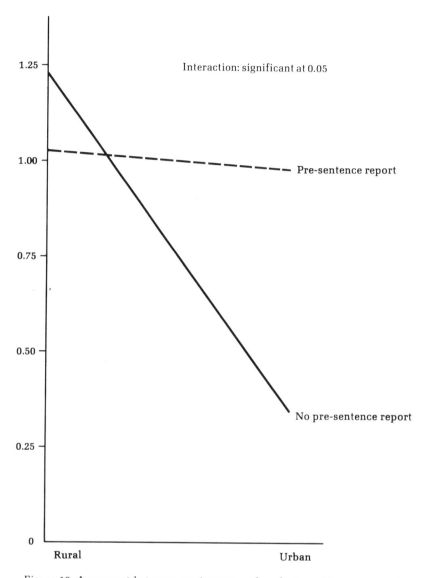

Figure 10. Agreement between magistrates and probation officers concerning their perception of the offender: (b) patterns of anti-social behaviour

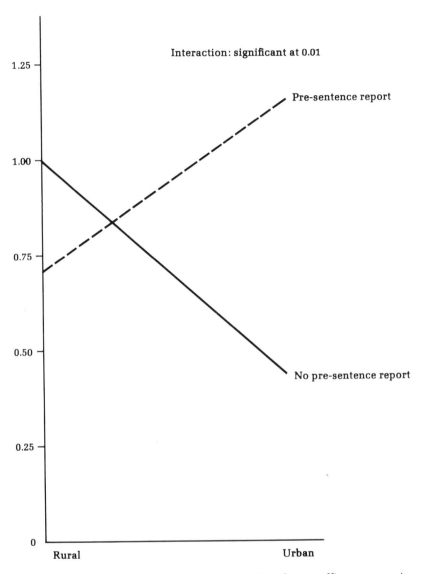

Figure 11. Agreement between magistrates and probation officers concerning their perception of the offender: (c) association with delinquents

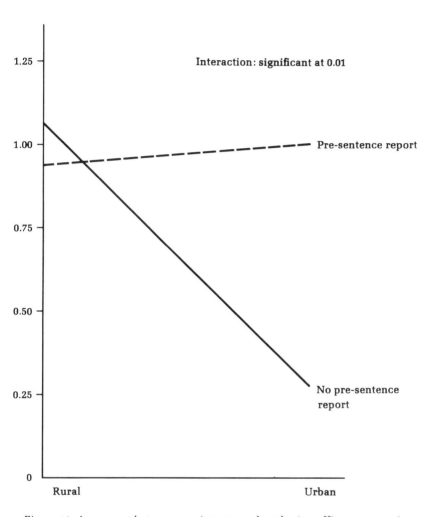

Figure 12. Agreement between magistrates and probation officers concerning their perception of the offender: (d) patterns of criminal behaviour

tion officers consistently rated the possibility of treatment in the community higher, while magistrates appeared to be somewhat more sceptical. The variation between magistrates and probation officers was quite large. It appears from the data that probation officers, by and large, are not very successful in communicating to magistrates the strength of the community resources available to deal with offenders.

Perceived Adequacy of the Law and Existing Resources

Contrasting results were achieved in urban and rural areas concerning the amount of agreement between magistrates and probation officers about the adequacy of the law and existing resources to deal with the case. Magistrates in urban areas appeared to be further away from probation officers concerning this issue if they had read a pre-sentence report than if they had not. The opposite holds true in rural areas. These contrasting trends are graphically presented in Figure 13. It appears that rural probation officers are much more effective in convincing the magistrate about the degree to which existing resources can cope effectively with the problem at hand.

Categorizing the Offender

Ignoring urban-rural differences, there does not appear to be any relationship between the existence of a pre-sentence report and the amount of agreement between magistrates and probation officers concerning whether or not the offender is a "dangerously mentally ill offender," a "persistent offender," or a "professional criminal." However, when one takes into account the interaction between urban-rural differences and the existence or non-existence of a pre-sentence report, contrasting trends emerge once again. It can be seen from Figure 14 that the amount of agreement between magistrates and probation officers in rural areas concerning the category in which the offender falls is not greatly affected by the existence or non-existence of a pre-sentence report. However, urban magistrates agree with their probation officers concerning the category in which the offender falls only if they have not received a pre-sentence report concerning him. Marked disagreement exists where the probation officer has communicated his views concerning the offender to the court.

It appears that rural magistrates and probation officers can come independently to similar judgements concerning the classification of the offender. However, in urban areas there is agree-

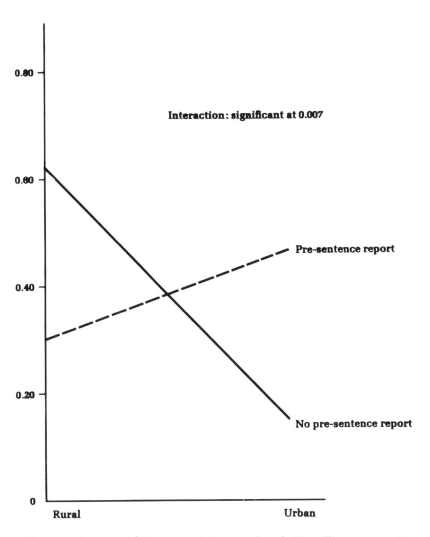

Figure 13. Agreement between magistrates and probation officers concerning the adequacy of existing resources

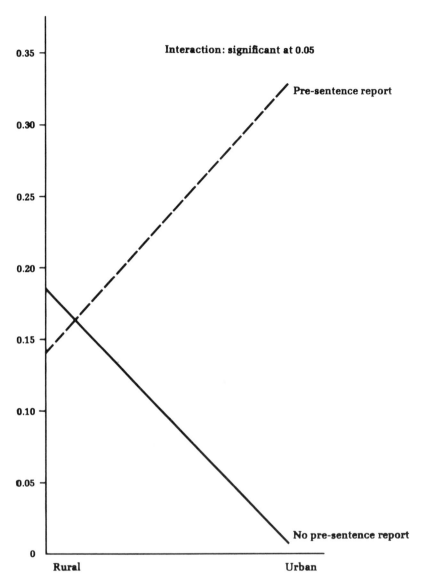

Figure 14. Agreement between magistrates and probation officers concerning the classification of the offender

ment between magistrates and probation officers only if they did not communicate with each other concerning the case. Once the probation officer communicates his view of the case to the magistrate, considerable discrepancy arises.

Discussion

These data tend to reject the *a priori* hypothesis that the pre-sentence report will lead a magistrate to come closer to the probation officer's view of the case. In fact, in a number of instances it was demonstrated that the opposite held true. In urban areas, if a magistrate read a report from a probation officer he was more likely to disagree with him concerning the offender and the possibility of treatment than if he did not. One is tempted to conclude that urban magistrates not only fail to assimilate the contents of the report but appear to react negatively to it, and in doing so obtain a picture of the offender which is opposite to that communicated to him by the probation officer. Rural magistrates, on the other hand, appear to accept the probation officer's view of the case.

There is evidence presented in other parts of the study which may help the reader to interpret these apparently odd results. It will be recalled that rural magistrates have better relationships with probation officers.[26]

They seek pre-sentence reports more often, they are more willing to allow the probation officer to participate in the decision-process through making recommendations, and they find fewer faults with the format and content of the pre-sentence report. Moreover, the work load in rural areas is more conductive to communication between probation officers and magistrates. In these areas, magistrates and probation officers usually know each other personally. This is likely to make it easier for magistrates to interpret more accurately the written communications from probation officers. Magistrates in rural areas have higher status, both in the community and in the court. This means that they are not likely to feel that their role in sentencing is being usurped by accepting the probation officer's view of the offender. The less onerous workload of rural magistrates gives them time to read pre-sentence reports carefully, and, if necessary, they can ask probation officers to discuss their contents with them informally.

Contrasting conditions exist in urban areas. Relationships between magistrates and probation officers are characterized by formality and social distance. Many magistrates read reports from probation officers whom they do not know. The workload of

many magistrates makes it difficult for them to give proper attention to pre-sentence and psychiatric reports. Very often urban
magistrates find it necessary to "skim" reports, and in some instances they read only the summary at the end. It is also true that
urban magistrates tend to be more concerned about "justice" and
less concerned about "treatment" than rural magistrates.[27] This
means that information concerning the offender is not as salient
for them, and there is considerable research evidence to suggest
that if a category of information is not considered important to
the individual, he is less likely to assess it accurately.[28]

These factors lead to the conclusion that if the pre-sentence
report is to have the impact on sentencing that was originally intended, and indeed often assumed, certain favourable conditions
for its proper use must exist. Magistrates must have the time to
read reports carefully. They must also have the opportunity,
when the need arises, to discuss their contents informally with
probation officers. Most important, they must have a set of attitudes and beliefs which are consistent with the rationale underlying the use of the pre-sentence report, namely, the individualization of justice.

A note of caution should be sounded concerning the nature of
the data upon which these conclusions are based. It must be
pointed out that in selecting the sample no attempt was made to
match the kinds of cases in each cell apart from ensuring that all
cases involved breaking and entering. Selection was random, but
since the sample was restricted to breaking and entering, the generality of the findings must be somewhat limited. Different patterns may emerge with respect to individual offences, but further
studies will be required to determine whether this is so.

Since urban magistrates tend to use pre-sentence reports less
frequently, it may be true that the kinds of cases in which reports
are requested are somewhat more complex and difficult to interpret. This would suggest that there is likely to be more disagreement between probation officers and magistrates in urban areas
concerning these cases. However, a comparison of the types of offences and the kinds of offenders committing them in the urban
and rural cases used yielded no significant differences that could
be determined. The cases were roughly similar in terms of the
severity of the offences and the criminal records, ages and occupational status of the offenders concerned.

It should also be pointed out that there are certain limitations
to "after the fact" analysis. It would have been better to use a
design in which the magistrate rated the case before and after

receiving a pre-sentence report. In this way, one could be more certain that differences in perception were due solely to the contents of the pre-sentence report. However, it was not administratively possible to use this technique, and the results must be interpreted in the light of the weaknesses in the methods used.

Another factor concerning the way in which the experiment was handled must be considered. While probation officers completed the offender assessment guide independent of the magistrate, this form was completed before sentence only if a pre-sentence report was requested. In cases where pre-sentence reports were not requested, the probation officer completed the document shortly after sentence. The sentence pronounced by the magistrate is a form of indirect communication to the probation officer concerning the case. The type and severity of sentence is an indication to the probation officer of the magistrate's thinking concerning that case. The fact that there was considerably more agreement between urban probation officers and magistrates in cases where no pre-sentence report was received by the court may be due, in part, to the fact that these probation officers tended to alter their perception of cases in the direction of conformity to their estimates of the magistrates' views. But this explanation is only tenable if the tendency for probation officers to be influenced in this way by the sentence imposed only occurs in urban areas.

Lorge[29], Sherif[30], and others[31] have demonstrated that the persuasive effect of communications is likely to be enhanced when the communicator has higher status than the recipient. The status differences between magistrates and probation officers are considerably greater in urban areas. This may mean that in these areas probation officers tend to accept the magistrates' views of the cases, while magistrates would resist any effort of persuasion from probation officers.

Hovland, Janis, and Kelley present evidence showing that communication tends to be more effective when the receiver does not feel that the communicator is trying to convince him.[32] The pre-sentence report can be viewed as an attempt by the probation officer to affect the magistrate's decision. It was interesting to note that during the course of the interviews, the only magistrates to indicate that probation officers were attempting to do this were urban magistrates.[33]

On the other hand, the probation officer is not likely to feel that the magistrate is attempting to alter his view of the case. The only piece of information a probation officer gets from a magistrate is the sentence itself. This is simply "information" in contrast to "propaganda" and is, therefore, more likely to affect opinion change.[34]

Subject to the qualifications mentioned above, there is sufficient consistency in the data presented to challenge the assumption that the pre-sentence report is an effective form of communication between the probation officer and the magistrate concerning the offender. The data suggest that certain intervening variables, many of which are associated with urban-rural differences, affect the degree to which probation officers can communicate effectively to the courts through the medium of pre-sentence reports. For the moment, the potential of the pre-sentence report seems to be far greater than can be shown to be realized in fact.

NOTES TO CHAPTER 15

1 The Report of a Committee Appointed to Inquire into the Principles and Procedures Followed in the Remission Service (the Fauteux Report) (Ottawa, 1956), 26.
2 For example, see S. Glueck, Ventures in Criminology (New York, 1954).
3 C. McFarlane, "Theory and Development of Pre-Sentence Reports in Ontario," Canadian Journal of Corrections, 10(1968), 152-78.
4 The Report of the Royal Commission to Investigate the Penal System (Ottawa, 1938).
5 Ibid., 13-14.
6 The Fauteux Report, 26.
7 Report of the Sentencing Committee of the Ontario Magistrates' Association (1962), mimeo.
8 See, for example, E. Kendrick, "The Role of the Adult Court in Corrections," Canadian Journal of Corrections, 10(1968)152-78.
9 Ibid., 158.
10 Ibid., 157.
11 McFarlane, "Theory and Development of Pre-Sentence Reports in Ontario," Canadian Journal of Corrections, 7 (1965), 201-24.
12 This was based on information kindly supplied by the Director of the Ontario Probation Service.
13 P. Tappan, Contemporary Corrections (New York, 1951), 11-12.
14 For a discussion of the issues see Report of the Inter-Departmental Committee on the Business of the Criminal Courts (Streatfeild Report) (London, 1961), 98-101.
15 W. Outerbridge, Handbook for Provincial Probation Officers (Toronto, 1965).
16 Fingerprints are taken under authority provided by the Identification of Criminals Act, Stats. of Canada, 1952, and s.574 of the Criminal Code.
17 R. Carter and L.T. Wilkins, "Some Factors in Sentencing Policy," Journal of Research in Crime and Delinquency, 4(1967),503-14.
18 R.G. Hood, "A Study of the Effectiveness of Pre-Sentence Investigations," British Journal of Criminology, 6(1966), 303-10, and with I. Taylor, ibid., 7 (1967), 431-7.
19 R. Carter, "The Pre-Sentence Report and the Decision-Making Process," Journal of Research in Crime and Delinquency, 4 (1967), 203-11.
20 Carter and Wilkins, "Some Factors in Sentencing Policy," 514.
21 Hood, "Pre-Sentence Investigations."

22 Since the second report contradicts the first, further validation seems necessary.

23 In a third (as yet unreported) study, Hood found that the use of pre-sentence reports led to an increase in fines at the expense of detention. The consistent finding from his studies, therefore, appears to be that detention is used less frequently if reports are used. My data indicate that Ontario magistrates use reports in "difficult" cases and these reports are more likely to be associated with the use of sentences that are not usually given for the particular offence (see Chapter 14).

24 For an easy to follow description of two-way analysis of variance, see S. Diamond, *Information and Error* (New York, 1959), 120-42 and especially 132-8.

25 See L. Cronbach, *Essentials of Psychological Testing* (New York, 1960), 126-42.

26 See Chapter 11.

27 See Chapter 13.

28 H. Kelley and C. Woodruff, "Member's Reactions to Apparent Group Approval of a Counternorm Communication," *Journal of Abnormal and Social Psychology*, 52(1956), 67-74; and Kelley's contributions to C. Hovland, ed., *Communication and Persuasion* (New Haven, 1953).

29 I. Lorge, "Glen-Like: Halo or Reality," *Psychological Bulletin*, 34 (1937),545-6.

30 H. Sherif, M. Sherif, and R. Nebergall, *Attitude and Attitude Change* (Philadelphia, 1965).

31 The classic Asch study is important in this context. S. Asch, "Studies in the Principles of Judgement," *Journal of Social Psychology*, 12 (1940), 433-65. See also A. Lowin, "Approach and Avoidance," *Journal of Personal and Social Psychology*, 6(1)(1967), 1-9.

32 C. Hovland, J. Janis and H. Kelley, *Communication and Persuasion* (New Haven, 1953).

33 See Chapter 11.

34 Hovland et al., *Communication and Persuasion*.

16

The Assessment of Information

Research Problem

This chapter deals with the way in which magistrates interpret information in the process of judgement. An attempt will be made to reveal the number, kind, and organization of dimensions employed by magistrates in their perceptions and evaluations of the "facts" upon which their decisions are based. Just listing the sources of information is not sufficient. Much information presented to the court may be overlooked, perceived as redundant, or in some other way may add nothing to the subjective facts involved in the decision. For example, a magistrate may receive a long pre-sentence report from a probation officer but may be interested only in one or two parts of it. He may read only the summary or he may feel that certain aspects of the probation officer's impressions of the offender are too unreliable to be considered. On the other hand, he may consider information in a report but misunderstand its meaning or react negatively to it.

The basic document used to reveal the manner in which information is assessed in sentencing was the "sentencing study sheet." This was an instrument completed by magistrates at the time of sentencing. It was designed to assist magistrates to determine the appropriate sentences to impose, as well as to reveal the mental processes involved. It was hoped that the document would reveal four properties of information-use. They were: (i) the amount and kind of information used in sentencing; (ii) the impact of information on magistrates' interpretations of cases; (iii) the ways in which information is organized and integrated by magistrates in the thought processes leading to decisions; (iv) the relationship of fact patterns to the decisions made, as perceived by magistrates.

The next section will describe the design of the sentencing study sheet and subsequent sections will describe some of the main findings derived from this instrument.

Design of the Sentencing Study Sheet

After experimenting with a number of formats, an instrument was designed and piloted twice. The first draft of the instrument contained a number of open-ended categories related to the following areas: assessment of the offender, assessment of the offence, determining factors in the decision, and purposes of the sentence imposed.

In the first pilot, seven magistrates completed the instrument with respect to ten cases each. As a result, it was possible to specify the number of response categories, within each area, that were required to cover adequately the different kinds of cases appearing before the courts. A new version of the instrument was drafted and the procedure was repeated. A number of minor changes were made, and a final version of the instrument was drawn.

Every effort was made to ensure that the instrument required little change from the normal and traditional processes of coming to sentencing decisions. The categories were derived empirically, that is, derived strictly out of the responses of magistrates who participated in the two pilot experiments. Various features of the case were presented in the "natural" order in which information is usually collected and evaluated by magistrates. Thus, the circumstances of the offence were considered first. Magistrates were then directed to a section requiring them to indicate their assessment of the offender under a number of different headings. Following this magistrates were asked to identify the features of the case that were considered to be of over-riding importance in the decision reached. The next section of the document was concerned with the purposes of the sentence, in which magistrates were asked to indicate the primary and secondary purposes involved under the classical headings of reformation, individual deterrence, general deterrence, punishment, and incapacitation. If a magistrate indicated that reformation was the main purpose, he was then asked to specify the features of the case which led him to conclude that reformation was likely to succeed. The penultimate section dealt with the adequacy of present law and resources to deal with cases of this kind. The final section solicited magistrates' views as to the desirability of early release on parole.

A copy of the sentencing study sheet is reproduced in Technical Appendix 9, together with instructions to magistrates in the use of it.

How Sentencing Study Sheets Were Used

Starting 1 February 1966, magistrates in Ontario began completing sentencing study sheets with respect to every case in which an offender was convicted of any of the seven named offences on the document, or an attempt to commit any one of those offences.

Study sheets were completed on each case as it appeared before the court. Magistrates were instructed not to select cases for which this document was to be used. Originally, the project was to proceed for twelve consecutive months, but because an insufficient number of cases had been collected during that time it was extended for an additional six months.

No magistrate was asked to complete more than one hundred sentencing study sheets in all, or more than twenty-five sentencing study sheets for any one offence category. Once a magistrate had completed twenty-five sentencing study sheets for offenders convicted of any one of the seven named offences, the magistrate was notified and that offence was struck off his remaining study sheets. Magistrates continued to complete the instrument with respect to offenders convicted of other offences until they had completed one hundred study sheets in all, or until the time period lapsed, whichever was the lesser.

Magistrates were asked to complete the instrument during the period of time when they were considering the appropriate sentence to impose, and prior to the time that sentence was actually imposed. If this was not possible, the magistrate was asked to complete the study sheet on the day that sentence was passed, while the case was fresh in his mind.

The average length of time taken to complete the document was ten minutes. No writing was involved except the marking of a printed form. Requests were not made for magistrates to seek information that was not placed before them and considered by them when imposing sentence. Each part of the document contained a "not known" category and magistrates were advised that a "not known" response was a perfectly appropriate and satisfactory one if they did not have the necessary information to complete the section.

Self-addressed, stamped envelopes were provided for the return of sentencing study sheets to the Centre of Criminology. These returns were submitted monthly.

The Sample

In choosing cases for which sentencing study sheets were to be completed, the research was guided by both theoretical and practical considerations. It was necessary to select offences which occurred relatively frequently so that a sufficient number of cases of each type would be dealt with by each magistrate. It was also desirable to select cases which represented different kinds of decision-problems, varying along certain theoretically important dimensions. In the end, it was decided to examine the decision-process with respect to seven indictable offences. They were: (i)offences against property involving force: breaking and entering; (ii) offences against property involving deceit: fraud; (iii) offences similar to theft where the property involved was of a reasonably high value: taking a motor vehicle without consent; (iv)offences against the person with an economic motive: robbery; (v)offences against the person involving bodily harm: assault and bodily harm; (vi)offences against the person with a sexual motive: indecent assault on a female; (vii)serious motoring offences: dangerous driving.

The obvious omission from this list is theft. It was decided to leave it out because there were many different legal definitions for offences resembling theft, making it administratively difficult to ensure that instructions were followed carefully throughout the province. Moreover, the majority of theft cases are relatively minor, and it could be expected that the sentencing process would be rather routine. It was decided that "taking a motor vehicle without consent" would be an adequate substitute for theft, having the additional advantage of being a fairly serious offence in terms of the value of property taken.

The number of sentencing study sheets received, classified by offence, is indicated in Table 83.

The main characteristics of the offenders concerned were as follows: nearly all were males (approximately ninety-seven per cent); most were young, the largest single group belonging to the sixteen to nineteen age category, while the mean age of the total

TABLE 83

Number of sentencing study sheets received by offence

Type of offence		Number	Per cent
Breaking and entering		913	38.1
Assault and bodily harm		405	16.9
Dangerous driving		383	16.0
Taking motor vehicle		244	10.2
Fraud		176	7.3
Robbery		150	6.3
Indecent assault on a female		125	5.2
	Total	2,396	100.0

sample was twenty-three point five years; and about half (fifty-four per cent) were appearing in court for the first time.

Less than half of the offenders concerned (forty-four per cent) were represented by legal counsel. Nearly four out of five offenders pleaded guilty to the charges. Eighty-five per cent of the cases concerned one charge. In seven per cent of the cases there were two charges per offender, and in the remaining eight per cent the number of charges ranged between three and sixty-one.

Less than half [forty-one per cent] were remanded prior to sentence, the remainder being sentenced on the day of conviction. Of those remanded, seventy-two per cent were remanded in custody, eight per cent had original bail continued and twenty per cent were released on their own recognizance of good behaviour. The breakdown of sentences imposed by magistrates in all cases is shown in Table 84.

TABLE 84

Distribution of sentences given

Type of sentence		Number	Per cent
Suspended sentence without probation		103	4.3
Suspended sentence with probation		595	24.8
Fine		552	23.0
Institution		1068	44.6
Other and combinations		78	3.3
	Total	2396	100.0

Response Rate

A total of 2426 usable sentencing study sheets were returned during the eighteen-month period.[1] The average number of sentencing study sheets completed per magistrate was thirty-three. However, one magistrate completed only eleven, while six others completed the maximum number required, i.e. one hundred. The response rate varied from one hundred per cent (in six instances) to less than twenty per cent (in four instances), with an average response rate of sixty-eight per cent.

Compared to the one hundred per cent response rate from magistrates with respect to the interview and attitude questionnaire, the results were disappointing. A sixty-eight per cent rate created problems not only with respect to the size of the sample, but also increased the likelihood of "bias." A researcher must assume that cases for which information was not provided are in some significant way different from cases for which information was given.[2] In this case, it was also assumed that magistrates who diligently provided information according to the instructions given were in some significant way different from magistrates who were less co-operative. Steps were taken to determine the nature and extent of possible bias in the sample.

Problem of Bias in the Sample

In comparing "co-operative" and "unco-operative" magistrates, it was discovered that there were no statistically significant differences between them on any of the main penal philosophy or attitude scales. It was also discovered that while one of the more common reasons given for not completing sentencing study sheets in all cases for which this information was required was pressure of work, some of the most diligent magistrates were among the busiest in the province. The only variable in terms of background characteristics which distinguished "co-operative" from "unco-operative" magistrates was the degree of participation in the Ontario Magistrates' Association. A greater proportion of defaulting magistrates did not participate actively in association activities. This is not particularly surprising, as the Magistrates' Association was a joint sponsor of the project, and on several occasions its senior members implored magistrates to give full support to it.

There were no discernible differences in the types of cases for which information was and was not provided. Certain information was collected from the police (for which a ninety-eight per cent response rate was achieved), with respect to all cases for which sentencing study sheets were required. It appeared that there were no significant differences between cases with respect to either the type or the severity of the crimes committed. It may be, however, that a number of more subtle differences exist between the cases which were not revealed from the comparisons made. The possibility of bias, while not as great as originally believed, remained. There were also problems concerning the small number of sentencing study sheets received for offences occurring relatively infrequently. Certain steps were taken to deal with these problems which will be discussed in the analysis section.

The Analysis

Two initial problems had to be overcome in the analysis. The first related to the representativeness of the sample, and the second to the small number of sentencing study sheets received from some magistrates concerning infrequently occurring offences. Under these conditions, certain limitations were imposed on the kinds of analysis that could be conducted.

Two kinds of analysis were based on the sentencing study sheet. In the first type the basic unit was the case, and in the second, the magistrate. In the former, the analysis sought to determine similarities among magistrates in their approach to cases. The purpose was to reveal general patterns common to magistrates. In these analyses the problem of numbers and the problem of representativeness was not as great.

The second type of analysis attempted to determine the degree to which there were *differences* among magistrates in the way in which they used information in coming to decisions. For these analyses the basic unit was the magistrate. The variables used were the mean scores given by magistrates to various features of the cases as revealed from sentencing study sheets. Differences in mean scores represented variation among magistrates in their perceptions of information upon which decisions were based. The problem to overcome was that some magistrates dealt with an insufficient number of cases with respect to some of the infrequently occurring offences. One solution to the problem was to omit certain magistrates if they did not complete a specified number of cases. Of twenty-four hundred sentencing study sheets received by seventy-one magistrates, over two thousand were completed by fifty magistrates. These fifty completed an average of forty-four cases each. A rule of thumb was adopted which held that no magistrate would be included in this part of the analysis unless he had completed at least twenty-five sentencing study sheets in all, or at least ten sentencing study sheets with respect to each individual offence studied. This meant that the number of magistrates included in the analysis differed dependng upon the type of case considered. Analysis directed towards decision-making with respect to all offences (combined) included fifty magistrates. A similar number were included in analysis of decision-making with respect to frequently occurring offences such as breaking and entering, while for the less frequently occurring offences (e.g., robbery and indecent assault on a female) the number of magistrates was reduced to as little as twenty-nine.

There was another solution to the problem. Using the Sellin-Wolfgang Severity Scale, it was possible to include each offence, regardless of the legal category in which it fell.[3] For each offence a simple severity score was calculated, thus reducing all offences to a common base.

Magistrates' Assessments of Offences

The sentencing study sheet required magistrates to rate four dimensions of the offence along a number of built-in scales. The dimensions were: (a) the gravity of the act committed, (b) the offender's participation in the act (where multiple offenders were concerned), (c) the degree of premeditation and planning, and (d) the offender's present attitude to his involvement. For the seven offences, in turn, analyses were performed to determine similarities and differences among magistrates in their assessments of these areas. The distribution of responses to this part of the sentencing study sheet is included in Technical Appendix 9.

Nearly all the criminal acts concerned were rated as being at least "moderately serious" by magistrates. Only ten cases were deemed "insignificant." Most of the offenders concerned (eighty-three per cent) were considered to have participated either alone or with others as the leader or equal participant in the crime. In a small number of cases (seventeen per cent) magistrates believed that the offender was led into the commission of the crime by another person.

In nearly half the cases magistrates felt that the act was "impulsive," and in a small proportion of cases (nine per cent) magistrates concluded that the act was committed under stress of provocation, threat, or inducement. In approximately one third, magistrates felt that the crime committed was planned and premeditated by the offender concerned. It was interesting to note that, despite the difficulties that might be involved in drawing conclusions concerning the degree of planning and premeditation on the basis of evidence available to the court, only in twelve per cent of cases did magistrates answer "not known" to this section.

There were wide variations in the conclusions drawn by magistrates concerning the offender's present attitude to his involvement in the offence. In about half the cases, the magistrate felt that the offender concerned was "remorseful" or otherwise accepted responsibility for his involvement in the act. In the other half, magistrates concluded that the offender was "indifferent," "defiant," "tended to blame others," or continued to "dispute his guilt." Once again, in only a small number of cases (eighteen per cent) were magistrates unable to draw a conclusion in this regard.

On the basis of these data alone, one cannot be sure whether a magistrate's perceptions of the offence are accurate. It can certainly be expected that the gravity of crime will vary from case to case, and so will the offender's participation, premeditation, and present attitude towards his involvement. At the same time, it can be expected that some magistrates will tend to rate some offences as being more serious than others, and in addition, there may be differences among magistrates in the amount of premeditation and remorse perceived.

For each magistrate, three variables were created representing the characteristic way he perceives the offence. They were: a mean "perceived gravity" score, a mean "perceived degree of premeditation" score, and a mean "perceived attitude" score. Correlations were then calculated between these scores and the main penal philosophy and attitude scores of the magistrates concerned.

The results indicated that neither the penal philosophy nor the attitude scales distinguished magistrates in terms of the ratings given to the severity of criminal acts. It appears that there was either a high level of agreement among magistrates concerning the severity of crime, or the penal philosophy and attitude measures used did not measure the significant differences.

On the other hand, penal philosophy and attitude scores were closely associated with the amount of premeditation seen in the commission of offences, and in the perceptions magistrates formed about offenders' attitudes toward their involvement. Thus, magistrates who saw a great deal of premeditation in the commission of offences tended to have high general deterrence, incapacitation and punishment penal philosophy scores. They also had high scores on the social defence attitude scale. Similarly, magistrates also perceived the offender's present attitude as being "indifferent" or "defiant" tended to have relatively high general deterrence, retribution, and incapacitation scores and relatively low reformation scores on the penal philosophy scales. These magistrates also tended to have relatively high justice and social defence scores and relatively low punishment corrects scores on the attitude scales.

It was of particular interest to note that the attitudes and penal philosophies of magistrates appear to be closely associated with how they perceive offenders' premeditation and present attitudes, while not being associated with how they perceive the severity of the acts committed. A physical act is relatively easy to assess. Not only is the evidence "hard" and readily available to the court, but there is also some guidance for assessing the seriousness of different crimes to be gleaned from the decisions of the appeal courts. In contrast, it is much more difficult to assess either the premeditation of the offender or his present attitude toward involvement in the crime, and no specific criteria are provided to assist magistrates in making these determinations. If selective interpretation is likely to occur, it is more likely to occur in these areas.

Magistrates' Assessments of Offenders

Ten areas of the offender's life were assessed by magistrates on a series of five-point scales, ranging from "very severe" to "no problem," or "not known." The distribution of responses to this section of the sentencing study sheet is included in Technical Appendix 9. The striking feature which emerged was the large number of "no problems" and "not knowns." These two categories (between them) accounted for over one-half of the responses in each of the ten areas.

It is also evident that magistrates, as a group, tend to see more problems in the area of "family and personal relationships" and "attitude towards authority" than any of the other areas examined. The relative importance attached to these areas is possibly an accurate reflection of the type of pathology exhibited by offenders, but it may also be a reflection of the importance attached to these areas by the magistrates concerned. It is interesting that the degree of pathology seen in offenders as revealed in the sentencing study sheet follows very closely the importance attached to information of various kinds revealed through the interview material presented earlier in this study.[4]

As with the assessment of offences, variation exists among magistrates in the way in which they perceive offenders. For each magistrate a "mean perceived pathology score" was calculated. This score represented the average score over all ten areas of the offender's life as indicated by responses to the sentencing study sheet. Correlations were then calculated between this score and the penal philosophy and attitude scores of the magistrates concerned. None of the penal philosophy or attitude scores distinguished magistrates in this respect. The analysis then turned to individual dimensions of the offender's life. This time it was learned that magistrates who see a great deal of pathology in the area of family and personal relationships tended to have relatively high reformation and punishment corrects scores and relatively low general deterrence, retribution, and justice scores. A contrasting pattern emerged with respect to the attitude toward authority dimension. Magistrates who rated this area as "severe" or "very severe" tended to have relatively low reformation and relatively high justice scores.

It seems that the degree of pathology seen in certain areas of the offender's life is associated with selective interpretation of data in the interests of resolving conflict which may arise between the facts of the case and what the magistrate would like to do by way of sentence. It is difficult to impose a deterrent or punitive sentence if the offender is seen as having serious problems in his family or personal life. In such cases, the sentence called for is one directed towards his rehabilitation. At the same time, a magistrate identifying with a punitive or deterrent philosophy would find it more satisfying to perceive offenders as having negative attitudes towards authority, which may be corrected through the imposition of punishment. The attitudes and penal philosophies of magistrates appear to function as filters through which information is perceived selectively.

An interesting fact emerged at this stage. In comparing the amount of agreement among magistrates concerning different aspects of the cases appearing before them, it was discovered that considerably more agreement existed with respect to the offence than with respect to the offender. This fact is demonstrated strikingly in Table 85, which indicates that there is at least twice the variation in magistrates' perceptions of offenders than in their perceptions of offences.[5]

There are a number of factors that help explain this. Over the years, the courts have established fairly clear guide-lines for assessing criminal acts.[6] The criteria are simple, comprehensive, and relatively easy to apply. In contrast, there is little coherence in judicial pronouncements concerning the criteria that should be used in assessing offenders.[7] Moreover, the impact of reports from eye-witnesses to a crime is likely to be greater than the dry words of a pre-sentence report. It should also be noted that the magistrate receives information about the crime first and may be expected to interpret information about the offender in the light of what he deems significant about his offence. This last point will be explored more fully in the next chapter. Finally, it must be said that there is little agreement, even among the so-called "experts," concerning the kind of information about offenders that it is useful to have for the purpose of sentencing. Until these issues are resolved there are bound to be differences in the way in which information is interpreted and used in sentencing.

TABLE 85

Variations in magistrates' perceptions of offences and offenders
($N = 50$ magistrates)

	Mean	*Standard deviation*	*Variance (S.D.)²*
The offence			
Gravity	2.414	0.800	0.641
Premeditation	1.400	0.701	0.492
Offender's participation	1.459	0.645	0.420
Offender's attitude	2.525	0.789	0.622
The offender			
Personal relationships	2.280	1.697	2.880
Attitude to authority	2.220	1.505	2.266
Use of alcohol	1.850	1.505	2.264
Direction from community	1.768	1.398	1.955
Adjustment at work or school	2.008	1.527	2.333
Financial	1.893	1.550	2.402
Anti-social behaviour	1.866	1.491	2.222
Criminal associates	1.883	1.505	2.266

NOTES TO CHAPTER 16

1   Seventy-three sentencing study sheets were rejected as being unusable because of errors in completion (28 cases), or completion on the wrong cases (45 cases).
2   See C. Moser, *Survey Methods in Social Investigation* (London, 1958), 56-72.
3   M. Wolfgang and T. Sellin, *The Measurement of Delinquency* (New York, 1964).
4   See Chapter 14.
5   The standard deviations are at least twice as large and the S.D.^{2} are four to five times as large. In each case the ratings were based on five-point scales permitting comparability.
6   See, for example, the judgement of Mr Justice Schultz in the well-known case, *Reg. v. Inaniev* (1959), 32 *Crim. Rep* 389.
7   In *Reg. v. Inaniev* the learned judge lists seven specific factors about the offence and only one general factor about the offender. See, more generally, for England, D. Thomas, "Theories of Punishment in the Court of Criminal Appeal," *Modern Law Review*, 27 (1964), 546-76; and for Canada, J. Decore, "Criminal Sentencing," *The Criminal Law Quarterly*, 6 (1964), 324-80.

17

The Organization and Integration of Information

In this chapter sentencing is studied as a cognitive process in which information concerning the offender, the offence, and the surrounding circumstances is read, organized in relation to other information, and integrated into an over-all assessment of the case. Each assessment can be defined in terms of two properties: (a) the units of information or "facts" perceived by the magistrate as being relevant to the problem at hand, and (b) the magistrate's perceptions of the relationships between these "facts."

The first problem is to reveal the number of *separate* dimensions to the information perceived by the magistrate. Before information presented to a court can be said to have made an *independent* contribution to the decision, it must be shown to have been perceived by the magistrate as being important.[1] If it is perceived as trivial, meaningless, irrelevant, or unreliable, it cannot be said to have played a conscious role in the decision.

The second problem is to reveal the manner and the degree of the integration of information. Facts are not considered independently, but rather in relation to each other. Magistrates can be expected to ascribe particular importance to one or more pieces of information and minimize the importance of others. Moreover, information is interpreted in the light of the alternatives available and the magistrate's purposes in sentencing. The research problem is one of revealing the ways in which magistrates combine information in the process of coming to decisions.

This chapter will present evidence showing that magistrates tend to organize information in ways which minimize inconsistency between different facts and between facts and purposes. Towards the end of the chapter it will be argued that there are a number of features of the system in which magistrates find themselves which make selective interpretation almost a necessity. Eleven such features will be discussed.

The Determining Factors in the Decision

Magistrates were asked to indicate the factors in the case which were of over-riding importance in their decision. A list of twenty-five possible factors was included in the sentencing study sheet. This list was empirically derived from the pilot studies, in which magistrates themselves indicated the factors which were "controlling." Magistrates were asked to indicate the three most important factors and to place them in order of importance. While the twenty-five factors covered a number of diverse areas, they can be placed into six main categories: those related to the offence, those related to the criminal record of the offender, those related to a diagnosis of the offender's problems, those related to a prognosis or estimate concerning the possibility of further crime, those related to supervision and control of the offender, and a "miscellaneous" category.

In Table 86 the twenty-five individual factors are ranked in order of times selected. The mean weights given to each of the six main categories of items are presented in Table 87. These data were based on a total sample of 2355 cases.

Taking magistrates as a whole, it appears that the most important individual determining factor is the degree of culpability of the offender. This factor was selected by magistrates in four out of five cases as being of over-riding importance in their decisions. It is interesting that culpability was picked more frequently than the degree of harm incurred by the victim. This is a fairly clear indication of the extent to which magistrates are still committed to assessing the moral quality of a crime rather than its physical nature.

The second fact which emerges is that when they are grouped together into categories, factors associated with the offence were given greater weight in sentencing than any other group. Factors concerning the criminal record of the offender were ranked second, with those associated with social control close behind. Treatment factors were quite clearly last. The one treatment factor given the highest rating by magistrates was "the offender's need for supervision" which is capable of being interpreted as a factor more concerned with social defence or punishment than with treatment.

TABLE 86

Rank order of determining factors in the disposition

Determining factor	Times picked	Per cent
Culpability of the offender in this offence	1867	79.3
Absence of a significant criminal record	1401	59.5
Offender's need for supervision	1142	48.5
Probability that the offender will not commit further offences if released	866	36.8
Number of offences that the offender now stands convicted of	739	31.4
Offender's need for counselling in personal or family problems	647	27.5
The minor nature of the act committed	574	24.4
Degree of personal injury resulting from this offence	527	22.4
Prevalence of this type of offence in the community	520	22.1
Length of offender's criminal record	494	21.0
Offender is likely to respond to treatment	493	20.9
Recency of offender's last conviction	401	17.0
Probability that offender will commit further offences if released	362	15.4
Failure of offender to respond to treatment in the past	316	13.4
Value of property stolen, damaged, or destroyed	314	13.3
Demand made by community that this offence be punished	285	12.1
Other	277	11.8
Offender is not likely to respond to treatment	243	10.3
Offender's need for educational, vocational, or occupational training	170	7.2
Lack of culpability of offender in this offence	164	7.0
Absence of any real problems needing help	156	6.6
Offender's need for psychiatric treatment	125	5.3
Serious nature of offences that the offender might commit if released	61	2.6
Availability of appropriate treatment services	42	1.8
Lack of appropriate treatment services	40	1.7

It is quite clear from these data that the shift in emphasis from the offender to the offence, which became obvious during the interview as questions moved from the general to the specific, is confirmed when one looks at the actual decision-behaviour of magistrates on the bench as revealed by responses to the sentencing study sheet.[2]

TABLE 87

Mean weights given by magistrates to six main categories of determining factors

Category	Mean weight
Offence factors	1.927
Record factors	1.097
Control factors	1.058
Diagnosis factors	0.649
Prognosis factors	0.474
Miscellaneous factors	0.157

Relationships of Attitudes and Penal Philosophy to Identification of Determining Factors

On examination of the determining factors selected by individual magistrates it was discovered that some magistrates tended to select factors of a particular type to the total exclusion of others. It seemed that each magistrate had a fairly consistent way of isolating from the total body of information presented to him those individual factors which would be of over-riding significance in his decision. In order to determine whether differences among magistrates in the types of factors selected were associated with attitudes and beliefs, mean scores for each of the twenty-five determining factors were calculated for each magistrate. A high mean score indicated that the magistrate frequently gave importance to that particular factor. Correlations were then calculated between these mean scores and the attitude and penal philosophy scores of the magistrates concerned.

The results indicated that the penal philosophies and attitudes of magistrates were closely associated with the type of factors selected. The statistical work upon which these conclusions are based is to be found in Technical Appendix 10.

Magistrates with high general deterrence scores tended to give greater weight to "the probability that the offender will commit further offences if released" and to "the number of previous convictions." On the other hand, they gave less weight to the "culpability of the offender" and to "the offender's need for counselling." This illustrates, in a rather interesting way, that magistrates concerned primarily with general deterrence do not attach importance either to retributive punishment or to treatment. In achieving a deterrent purpose, it is necessary for a magistrate sometimes to sacrifice both quantitative retribution (that is, proportioning the sentence in strict accordance with the severity of the crime and the offender's culpability), and the treatment needs of the individual offender before the court.

Magistrates with high Individual Deterrence scores tended to give great weight to "the prevalence of the offence in the community," "the availability of appropriate treatment" and "the offender's need for psychiatric treatment." It appears that these magistrates have a great deal of confidence in the efficacy of existing correctional methods as a treatment for offenders.

As one would expect, magistrates with high reformation scores tended to give great weight to the factors concerned with the treatment of offenders. They gave less weight to "the prevalence of the offence in the community" and more weight to "the offender's need for supervision."

Magistrates with high punishment scores are distinguishable from those with low scores on this scale in a number of ways. Treatment factors were generally ranked low by this group, while record and offence factors were ranked high. Turning to attitudes, high scores on the punishment corrects scale were associated with the selection of both offence and record factors, and a tendency to select factors concerning the availability of appropriate treatment. It appears that these magistrates respond primarily to the offence and criminal record in assessing the type of "corrective" punishment that should be applied.

Concern for social defence was associated with attaching low weight to both treatment and record factors. Magistrates with high scores on this scale responded primarily to the offence.

The intolerance scale distinguished magistrates only with respect to a tendency for those with high intolerance scores to give greater weight to "the offender's need for supervision" and less weight to "the degree of personal injury." This is a difficult pattern to interpret. It will be recalled that high intolerance scores were associated with a tendency to impose relatively severe sentences in minor cases, and relatively lenient sentences in serious cases.[3] The explanation offered was that magistrates with high intolerance scores did not discriminate as well among offences of greater or lesser severity. This may explain the relatively low weight attached to "the degree of personal injury." The selection of "supervision" rather than "counselling" among the treatment factors is not surprising.

"Modernism" appeared to be associated with giving more weight to "the prevalence of the offence in the community" and the "offender's need for conselling," and less weight to "the value of property taken." This appears to be consistent with a modern view of sentencing.

These data suggest that magistrates tend to develop characteristic ways of isolating, from the total body of information placed before them, certain "facts" which will be controlling in their decisions. By emphasizing one or more features of the case and by minimizing the others, they are able to interpret selectively cases consistent with their objectives. Let us take a closer look at the way in which this operates with respect to magistrates with high, moderate, and low scores on the justice scale.

Each of the twenty-five determining factors was grouped into one of four main categories. These categories related to the offence, the record, social defence, and treatment. Magistrates were divided into three equal groups on the justice scale: those with high scores, those with moderate scores, and those with low scores. In Table 88 the mean rank position of the main categories of factors for each group of magistrates can be seen.

TABLE 88

Mean rank position of four groups of determining factors for magistrates with high, moderate, and low justice scores

Group	Factor	Mean rank position
High group (N = 21)	Offence	6.0
	Record	6.6
	Social defence	13.5
	Treatment	17.8
Middle group (N = 219)	Record	3.3
	Offence	11.0
	Social defence	15.0
	Treatment	15.5
Low group (N = 21)	Record	10.0
	Offence	11.5
	Social defence	15.0
	Treatment	13.2
Total population (N = 63)	Offence	9.3
	Record	11.3
	Social defence	13.0
	Treatment	16.3

Magistrates as a group tended to rank factors on a high-low

continuum from offence through record to social defence and finally to treatment. When one examines the relative rank positions of these categories for magistrates with high, moderate, and low justice scores, different patterns emerge.

Factors concerning the offence have a mean rank position of six for the high group. However, for the moderate and low groups these factors rank considerably lower, at approximately eleven. Treatment factors are given a very low rank position by both the high and moderate groups, and a somewhat higher rank position by magistrates in the low group. The moderate group appears to be more record-oriented than either the high or low groups, since record factors are given a very high mean rank score (3.3) by these magistrates, compared with the high group (6.6), and the low group (10.0).

It can also be observed that the high and moderate groups have a greater tendency to select certain factors to the exclusion of others. The range in rank positions of these two groups is approximately twelve. In contrast, magistrates with low scores on the justice scale tended to give more equal weight to each of the four groups of factors. For these magistrates the range of rank positions from highest to lowest is only five. From this it can be concluded that magistrates with low justice scores tend to consider the four groups of factors as being relatively important, with record and offence factors being only slightly more important than treatment and social defence factors. However, magistrates with higher scores on this scale tend to attach great importance to factors concerning the offence and the criminal record, and very little importance to the others. This suggests that there is a greater tendency for magistrates with high scores on the justice scale to simplify the decision-process by excluding from consideration all but certain selected elements in the case. In other words, magistrates with low scores on the justice scale tend to perceive essential information multi-dimensionally (they use more information), while magistrates with high scores on this scale tend towards a uni-dimensional perception of the facts upon which the decisions are based (they use less information).

Discriminating Variables

The relationship between the attitudes of magistrates and the factors considered to be of over-riding importance in their decisions was not always a simple one. A number of curvilinear relationships appeared, i.e., relationships that could not be represented, or even approximated, by a straight line. Thus, magistrates with high and low scores on the same scale would sometimes give similar weights to a particular factor, while magistrates occupying middle positions on the scale would give it quite a different weight. Figure 15 demonstrates a number of relationships between justice scores of magistrates and weights attached to particular types of factors. In particular, it can be seen that while for many factors there is a strong positive-negative (straight line) relationship between attitudes and the weights attached to particular factors, in many cases the relationships were curvilinear.

Let us now examine some of the more complex relationships. Determining factor sixteen - "the availability of appropriate treatment services" - clearly discriminates between magistrates with high and low scores from those with moderate scores on the justice scale. The high and low groups of magistrates on this scale ranked this factor twenty-fourth (out of twenty-five), while the moderate group ranked it eleventh. Similarly, factor nine - "the recency of the offender's last conviction" - was ranked tenth by the high group, eleventh by the low group, and third by the moderate group. In the same way, factor eight - "the length of the offender's criminal record" - was ranked eighth by the high group, fourteenth by the low group, and fifth by the moderate group. Finally, factor five - "lack of culpability of the offender" - was given more importance by both the high and low groups (seventeenth in each case) than the moderate group (twenty-third).

It appears that in some respects magistrates occupying extreme positions on the justice scale are more alike in the way in which they respond to certain types of information than magistrates occupying middle positions. What is the explanation for this? An examination of the content of factors that discriminated among magistrates in complex ways will reveal that each of them were more subtle and required more interpretation than the others. The use of these factors indicated a more discriminative use of information in sentencing. While magistrates occupying middle positions on the justice scale do not attach as much overall importance to "treatment" as magistrates with low scores on this scale, they are willing to consider treatment in cases where it is available and is likely to work. Similarly, in responding to information concerning the criminal record, they are not concerned simply with the existence or non-existence of the record, but rather with its length and the recency of the last conviction. This

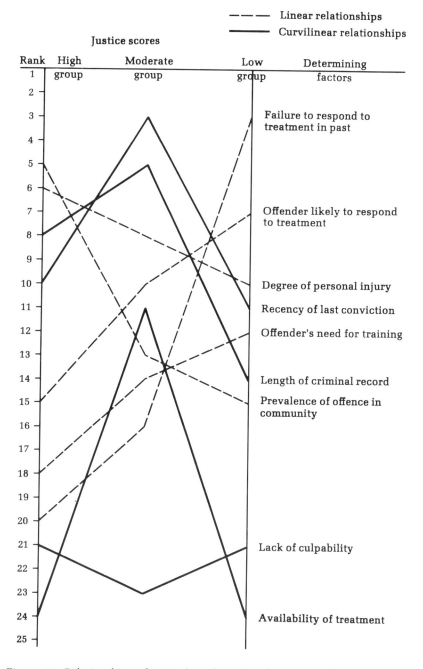

Figure 15. Relationships of attitudes of magistrates to weight given to determining factors (N= 63)

suggests that there may be a dimension, independent of the attitudes of magistrates, which relates to subtlety of thought in assessing information. It was data such as these which led the research into explorations of the complexity of judicial thinking in sentencing, a topic which will be dealt with in some detail in the next chapter.

The Selection of Purposes

The next section of the sentencing study sheet required magistrates to indicate what their purposes in sentencing were, giving five points to the main purpose and up to five points for any secondary or tertiary purposes. They selected among five main purposes: to deter potential offenders, to deter this offender, to reform this offender, to punish this offender, and to prevent further crime by removing this offender into custody.

The mean scores for each of these purposes are listed in Table 89. Mean scores are given for all offences, as well as for each of

TABLE 89

Mean weights given to different purposes

Type of offence		Purpose in sentencing				
		To deter potential offenders	To deter this offender	To reform this offender	To punish this offender	To remove this offender from society
All offences	N = 2355	1.465	2.554	1.986	1.815	0.414
Breaking and entering	N = 916	1.345	2.331	2.860	1.503	0.643
Robbery	N = 141	2.298	2.532	1.823	1.871	0.777
Fraud	N = 230	1.294	3.250	1.753	1.780	0.562
Taking a motor vehicle without consent	N = 252	1.171	2.663	2.785	1.151	0.263
Assault and bodily harm	N = 388	1.473	2.868	1.265	2.442	0.253
Indecent assault on a female	N = 185	1.667	2.423	2.526	1.385	0.346
Dangerous driving	N = 376	2.029	2.971	.595	2.851	0.112
Institutional sentences only						
All offences	N = 1110	1.867	2.759	1.566	2.198	0.855

the seven individual offences for which sentencing study sheets were completed.

There was a general tendency for individual deterrence to be given the highest weight. This was true not only for all offences (combined), but also for the specific offences of fraud, assault and bodily harm, and dangerous driving. Reformation achieved the second highest weight over-all, and was highest in cases of breaking and entering, taking a motor vehicle without consent and indecent assault on a female. It was given a very low rating, as one would expect, in cases of dangerous driving. General deterrence was given a consistently high rating, never falling below fourth among the five purposes. It is not surprising to learn that incapacitation was generally ranked low, as it can only be a factor in cases where institutional sentences were used. However, it is interesting to note that it was also ranked low in cases where institutional sentences were used. It is somewhat surprising to see punishment (which was defined as retributive punishment), being given such a high ranking. In cases of assault occasioning bodily harm, and fraud, it was given the second highest weight behind individual deterrence. Retribution is not dead in Ontario Courts.

The purposes of sentencing as revealed from the sentencing study sheet appear to differ somewhat from the self-reports of purposes as given by magistrates during the course of interviews. It will be recalled that most magistrates defined their personal penal philosophy in terms of giving great weight to reformation, some weight to general deterrence, less weight to individual deterrence, and very little weight to incapacitation and punishment.[4] Individual deterrence and retributive punishment appear to assume greater significance in the actual decision-behaviour of magistrates than in magistrates' images of their behaviour.

On examination of sentencing study sheets completed by individual magistrates, it was discovered that regardless of the type of sentence imposed, or the type of case dealt with, some magistrates were consistent in giving great weight to one or more of the purposes to the exclusion of others. A significant group of magistrates tended to view their purposes in sentencing as being directed towards the reformation of offenders, regardless of the type of case, or indeed the length or severity of the sentences imposed. Thus, there was a significant minority of magistrates who always gave maximum weight to reformation and little, if any, to the other purposes, even in cases of long terms of imprisonment in the penitentiary. On the other hand, a significant minority of magistrates consistently gave great weight to punishment, regardless of the type of disposition imposed. It appeared that different magistrates can achieve similar sentences through quite

TABLE 90

Distribution of weights given to different purposes

	Minimum 0	1	2	3	4	Maximum 5
To punish this offender						
All sentences	1264	49	122	251	117	552
Institutional sentences	497	23	69	126	74	321
To deter potential offenders						
All sentences	1326	125	132	313	173	286
Institutional sentences	525	42	66	191	105	181
To reform this offender						
All sentences	1295	31	138	76	766	49
Institutional sentences	691	14	29	82	50	244
To deter this offender						
All sentences	853	56	112	322	291	721
Institutional sentences	338	28	51	188	157	348
To incapacitate this offender						
All sentences	2093	23	27	60	42	110
Institutional sentences	856	20	27	60	40	107

different mental routes.

Evidence for this can be found in Table 90, which shows the distributions of weights attached to various purposes in cases where institutional and non-institutional sentences were imposed.

Several things are evident from this table. First, there is a general tendency for magistrates to give maximum weight to a particular purpose, or no weight at all. In each case, the zero and five scale positions are more frequently checked than the intermediate ones.[5] Secondly, a significant number of magistrates will give maximum weight to the reformation of offenders, even in cases in which institutional sentences are used. These magistrates must believe that institutions can, and do, reform offenders.[6]

It was also interesting to note that the incapacitation of offenders was given relatively little weight, even in cases where institutional sentences were used. In only about one quarter of the cases in which institutional sentences were imposed did incapacitation appear as a factor in the magistrate's mind. This is somewhat surprising, as short-term protection of society is the only absolutely certain gain that can be achieved from institutional sentences.

The attitudes and penal philosophies of magistrates were associated with the types of purposes selected in sentencing. Magistrates with high reformation scores tended to give greater weight to reformation as a purpose in sentencing than those with low scores on this scale. Similarly, magistrates with high general deterrence scores tended to give greater weight to punishment than those with low scores on this scale. However, the expected pattern did not always appear. High scores on the retribution, incapacitation, and individual deterrence scales were not associated with a tendency to select the corresponding purpose in completing the sentencing study sheet. This may be due to the unreliability of self-reports of penal philosophy concerning these areas. It will also be remembered that the reformation and general deterrence scales discriminated better among magistrates in a variety of other ways, indicating that these scales are rather more valid.[7]

Turning to attitudes, concern for justice was associated with a tendency to give greater weight to punishment, and less weight to reformation in the purposes selected. Punishment corrects scores were positively associated with giving great weight to both reformation and incapacitation. The other three attitude scales did not distinguish magistrates in terms of the weights attached to any of the five purposes in sentencing.

So it appears that the purposes magistrates seek to achieve through sentencing are fairly consistent with their attitudes and penal philosophies. Considerable variation exists among magistrates as a group, but individual magistrates appear to have worked out a fairly consistent, rational, sentencing policy. Consistency appears to have been achieved through the mechanism of selectivity.

Magistrates choose selectively certain kinds of information, they interpret it selectively, they selectively ascribe importance to certain features of the case to the exclusion of others, and they select among the purposes in sentencing those which are most consistent with their personal values and subjective ends.

Relationships among Perceptual Dimensions

So far, the data presented dealt with relationships between magistrates' perceptions of individual aspects of the cases appearing before them, and certain background characteristics of the magistrates concerned, such as attitudes and penal philosophy. This section will examine the way in which magistrates organize and integrate their perceptions of various aspects of the cases.

The major variable in the analysis is the manner and degree of integration of information. The purpose of the analysis is to identify the links or connections between different perspectives. For example, the analysis seeks to determine the relationship between a magistrate's perception of the offence and his perception of the offender. It is also directed towards revealing relationships between perceived facts and purposes.

The consistency theories mentioned above would suggest that magistrates are likely to interpret information in ways which minimize inconsistency between various features of the case and between these features and their objectives in sentencing.[8] We have already seen that nearly all magistrates rated information concerning the offence as being more important than information either concerning the criminal record or about the background and history of the offender. Because of the pre-eminent position of the offence, it can be expected that all other information would be interpreted in the light of the assessment made of it.

In order to test this assumption, correlations between magistrates' assessments of offences, their perceptions of offenders' problems, their selection of the determining factors, and their purposes were calculated.

Correlations were based on a sample of eleven hundred cases.[9] Since cases, not magistrates, were the units of analysis, the results are indications of the amount of consistency among magistrates, as a group, in their perceptions of various aspects of the case.

The general finding which emerges (Table 91) is that the way in which magistrates assess the gravity of a criminal act is associated with their perceptions of problems in the life of the offender and the purposes they attempt through sentencing. Correlations were statistically significant (at 0.01) in nine out of the ten offender problem areas. The only correlation which was not significant was between perceived gravity of the act and the amount of pathology seen in the area of drug use. Since drug use, while a significant problem in some cases, only affects a minority of offenders, a null result in this area is to be expected.

The second fact which emerges is that the correlations between perceived gravity of the offence and perceived pathology in the offender are all positive. This means that if magistrates assess the criminal act as being more severe they are more likely to see a greater degree of pathology in the life of the offender. While it is possible that these perceptions are accurate, there is a considerable body of research evidence which raises some doubt about it.[10] Research suggests that personal pathology is more likely to be seen among petty, inadequate offenders rather than among offenders who commit serious offences. But magistrates are moti-

TABLE 91

Correlations between assessment of the crime and perceptions of offender, selection of determining factors and purposes attempted (N = 1103 cases)

	Assessment of the offence			
	Gravity of the act	Premeditation of offender	Offender's participation	Offender's attitude
Assessment of offender's problems				
Personal relationships	0.145	-	-	-0.082
Attitude to authority	0.216	-	-	-0.245
Use of alcohol	0.112	-0.115	-0.201	-
Use of drugs	-	-	-	-
Alienation from community	0.190	-	-	0.156
Adjustment at work or school	0.110	-	0.093	0.118
Financial situation	0.163	-	0.114	-
Anti-social behaviour	0.136	-	-	0.116
Delinquent associates	0.165	-0.161	-0.099	0.156
Criminal record	0.199	-	-	0.115
Determining factors				
Offence	-	-	-	-
Record	-	-	-	-
Diagnosis	-	-	-	0.083
Prognosis	-	-	-	-0.100
Control	0.092	-	-	-0.087
Miscellaneous	-	-	-	-
Purposes attempted				
To deter potential offenders	0.187	-	-	-
To punish this offender	0.104	-	-	-
To reform this offender	-	-0.088	-0.081	-
To deter this offender	-	-	-	-
To incapacitate this offender	0.195	-	-0.121	-0.113

All correlations are significant at at least 0.01

vated to perceive cases in the ways indicated by Table 90. If offenders "deserve" punishment on the basis of the crime committed, and at the same time "need" treatment, a long prison term to a "correctional" institution is indicated. If, on the other hand, offenders who have committed serious crimes neither need nor can benefit from correctional treatment, magistrates are placed in some difficulty as to the appropriate sentence to impose.

Magistrates' ratings of the degree of premeditation in the commission of the offence are associated with seeing fewer problems in the areas of alcohol-use and delinquent associates. Both the use of alcohol and the influence of delinquent friends tends to be exculpatory. It is difficult to blame a person who committed an offence through alcoholism or through "bad companions." Since premeditation is evidence of moral blameworthiness, the more premeditated the crime, the greater the motivation to perceive the offender as a fully responsible agent.

A similar pattern emerges with respect to the relationship between magistrates' perceptions of offenders and their rating of offenders' participation in offences. If magistrates feel that offenders have participated fully in offences, they are less likely to perceive them as having problems in the area of alcohol-use or delinquent companions. At the same time they are more likely to see these offenders as having problems in adjustment at work or school, and money problems.

An interesting pattern emerges with respect to the relationship of magistrates' assessments of the offenders' attitudes towards their involvement in offences, and their perceptions of offenders' problems. If magistrates feel that the offender is remorseful, they are less likely to believe that he has problems in the areas of personal and family relationships, or attitudes to authority. At the same time they are more likely to believe that he suffers because of alienation from the community, maladjustment at work or school, ant-social behaviour, delinquent associates, and a criminal record.

Without independent evidence it is impossible to test the validity of these impressions, but the consistency in the patterns which emerged suggest that there is a tendency for magistrates to organize and integrate various pieces of information received about the offender in a way which leads to a rather consistent, clear-cut picture of him. It is suggested that the motivation for doing so is to simplify the sentencing task.

There were only a few significant correlations between magistrates' assessments of the offence and the type of determining factors selected as being of over-riding importance in the case. However it must be pointed out that the determining factors used in the analysis were grouped under a number of main headings. There might be relationships between individual factors and specific aspects of the offence as perceived by magistrates, but the correlations of these were not calculated.[11] However, the few correlations that were statistically significant are interesting. If magistrates rate the offence as being particularly grave, they are more likely to select factors concerning social control than any of the others. Further, if magistrates feel that the offender is remorseful, they are more likely to select factors concerned with the diagnosis of the problem, and less likely to select factors concerning prognosis or social control. It appears from this that if magistrates feel that the offender is "sorry for what he did," they are more likely to select treatment rather than supervision or control as the determining factor in the case.

There were a number of statistically significant correlations between magistrates' assessments of the offence and the purposes attempted in the cases. Thus, if magistrates rate the offence as being particularly grave, they are more likely to give greater weight to the deterrence of potential offenders, punishment, and the removal of the offender from society, than either reformation or the deterrence of the particular offender. If magistrates feel that the act was premeditated, they are less likely to be concerned about reformation. Similarly, if magistrates feel that the offender participated fully in the act, they are less likely to be concerned with reformation or incapacitation. Finally, if magistrates feel that the offender is remorseful they give less weight to incapacitation.

A fairly consistent pattern emerges from these findings. Taking magistrates as a whole, it appears that the perception of the offence is closely associated with the perception of the offender, and to a lesser extent to the purposes attempted, and the factors considered to be of over-riding importance in the case. It must be pointed out, however, that the correlations, while statistically significant, are fairly low. There are two likely reasons for this. First, with the case as the basic unit, the analysis ignores individual differences among particular types or groups of magistrates in the way in which they integrate information of various kinds in sentencing. Second, a magistrate's assessment of the case is made up of the perception, organization, and integration of many different units of information. The analysis described above was restricted to the examination of the relationships between individual variables taken two-by-two. Later, when the analysis turns to an examination of the inter-relationships among all the facts of the case as perceived by magistrates and the decisions they make, we shall see a remarkable degree of consistency. But the data presented in this section are sufficient to conclude that there is a tendency for magistrates to organize and integrate information concerning a case around their assessment of the offence.

Relationships Between "Facts" and "Purposes"

We will now examine the degree to which the magistrates' perceptions of the facts of a case are consistent with the purposes they attempt in sentencing. This time the unit of analysis will be the magistrate.

For each area related to the offence - the offender's problems, the determining factors, and the purposes attempted - mean

TABLE 92

Correlations between purposes in sentencing and perceptions of the offence, the offender, and the factors considered of over-riding importance

Variable	Direction	Size	Level of significance
Purpose: to deter this offender, correlated with:			
Determining factor 4: culpability of the offender in this offence	Negative	-0.303	0.05
Determining factor 8: length of the offender's criminal record	Positive	0.360	0.01
Determining factor 20: probability that the offender will commit further offences if released	Positive	0.311	0.05
Determining factor 21: serious nature of offences that the offender might commit if released	Positive	0.297	0.05
Determining factor 22: prevalence of this type of offence in the community	Positive	0.266	0.05
Determining factors (grouped): record	Positive	0.348	0.01
Determining factors (grouped): control	Positive	0.406	0.01

TABLE 92 continued

Variable	Direction	Size	Level of significance
Purpose: to reform this offender correlated with:			
Determining factor 12: offender's need for educational, vocational, or occupational training	Positive	0.318	0.05
Determining factor 13: offender's need for supervision	Positive	0.367	0.01
Determining factor 24: absence of any real problems needing help	Negative	-0.253	0.05
Perceived pathology in offender	Positive	0.272	0.05
Perceived attitude of offender	Positive	0.406	0.01
Perceived premeditation of offender	Negative	-0.537	0.01
Purpose: to deter this offender correlated with:			
Perceived pathology in offender	Negative	-0.379	0.01
Determining factors (grouped): record	Positive	0.252	0.05
Purpose: to deter this offender correlated with:			
Determining factor 4: culpability of the offender in this offence	Positive	0.376	0.01
Determining factor 10: offender's need for psychiatric treatment	Negative	-0.259	0.05
Determining factor 13: offender's need for supervision	Negative	-0.327	0.05
Determining factor 20: probability that the offender will commit further offences if released	Positive	0.309	0.05
Determining factors (grouped): offence	Positive	0.256	0.05
Purpose: to prevent crime by placing this offender in custody correlated with:			
Determining factor 9: recency of the offender's last conviction	Positive	0.264	0.05
Perceived pathology in offender	Positive	0.454	0.01
Perceived premeditation of offender	Positive	0.663	0.01

scores were calculated for each magistrate. A high mean score indicates that the magistrate, over all his cases, tends to attach great weight or importance to that particular item. Correlations were then calculated between the mean weights given by magistrates to each of the five purposes attempted and those given to various aspects of the offence, the offender, and the determining factors. The results are presented in Table 92.

A consistent pattern emerges from this table. Magistrates who usually attach great weight to the deterrence of potential offenders tend to emphasize factors associated with both social control and the past criminal behaviour of the offender. Interestingly enough, they minimize factors associated with the culpability of the offender, thus confirming once again that magistrates concerned with social control through deterrence are not concerned with retributive punishment.[12]

Magistrates who consistently give great weight to the reformation of offenders tend to see a great deal more pathology in the life of the offender, they view offenders as being remorseful and they perceive less premeditation in the commission of offences. In selecting determining factors they are likely to emphasize the offender's need for supervision, educational, and vocational training and they tend to feel that most offenders have problems needing help.

Magistrates who often give great weight to the deterrence of the offender before the court tend to see less pathology in his life, and respond primarily to his past criminal record.

Magistrates frequently concerned about punishment, for retributive purposes, of the offender tend to attach great importance to the offence. They emphasize the culpability of the offender and tend to believe that he will commit further offences if released in the community. They de-emphasize the offender's need for psychiatric treatment and supervision.

Magistrates who rely often upon the prevention of crime through incapacitation have a strong tendency to perceive a great deal of premeditation in the way in which the crime was committed. Interestingly, they also see a great deal of pathology in the life of the offender, and respond primarily to the recency of the offender's last conviction.

These data show clearly that there is an association between the purposes magistrates tend to emphasize in sentencing and those factors which they isolate, ascribe importance to, and use as the basis for determining the appropriate sentence to impose. To a lesser extent, the purposes of magistrates are associated with their perceptions of the gravity of the crime committed and the amount of pathology they perceive in the life of the offender. A number of distinct "styles" of information-use are identified. Each style is characterized by the way in which magistrates interpret information selectively in ways consistent with their objectives in sentencing. In doing so they resolve any conflict or discrepancy between the facts upon which their decisions are based and their objectives.

Conclusions

The data presented so far support the view that magistrates tend to interpret the "facts" of the cases before them in such a way as to minimize inconsistency. In doing so, they rearrange the facts to fit the types of sentences they use habitually. It may be said that rather than "seeking a punishment to fit the crime," magistrates, through selective interpretation, "seek an offender to fit the punishment." The findings confirm the results of research in other areas of human judgement, and only go to show that magistrates are human. No criticism of individual magistrates is intended or implied. Indeed, there are many features of the system in which magistrates are enmeshed which makes selective interpretation of information almost a necessity. Eleven such features will be discussed below. Others could probably be added and the list is not intended to be exhaustive.

Lack of Agreement as to the Proper Principles in Sentencing

It is common knowledge that there are inconsistencies, not only in sentencing practices but also in the principles that the courts apply. These differences reflect not only divisions among judges and magistrates as to the principles of sentencing, but also deep contradictions within society as to what the proper basis should be for dealing with crime. As the *Streatfeild Report* points out clearly, the type of information which enables a court to assess culpability for the purposes of punishment is not necessarily the information which indicates how the offender should be reformed, much less how potential offenders should be deterred.[13] Data presented earlier indicated that there were enormous differences among magistrates in the degree to which they identify with the classical purposes in sentencing.[14] Until these fundamental contradictions in principle are resolved, differences are bound to exist in the kinds of information different judges and magistrates consider relevant to the cases before them.

The Social Value Placed on Consistency in Judicial Decision-Making

In every social group there exists a standard calling for a measure of consistency in the words and actions of its members. In discussing this phenomenon, Hovland and Rosenberg stated: "To be sure, few social or cultural settings impose so strongly or exhaustively as the special sub-cultures of the court of law or the philosophy seminar."[15] The law, and the norms and values associated with it, demand a high level of rationality on the part of judges. Whatever private doubts a judge or magistrate may have about his decisions, they must appear to be the logical, rational, and almost inevitable outcome of legal reasoning.

The Special Nature of Legal Training and Experience

Many devices which are built into the legal process allow a judge to reconcile incompatible elements in the facts before him. Training as a lawyer and experience as an advocate impart skills in the selective presentation and interpretation of a set of facts. Moreover, experience as a judge enhances these skills even further. While the doctrine of precedent requires a court to make decisions which are consistent with previous decisions made by courts of equal or superior status, a number of well-known mechanisms are available to the court to avoid the rigidity that would result from a slavish adherence to precedent.[16] The analytical tools of judicial reasoning allow an experienced judge or magistrate to deal with conflict between what he wants to do and what precedent suggests should be done, by making subtle distinctions among similar fact situations, by re-interpreting previous decisions consistent with subjective motives, or simply by avoiding direct dealing with the problems involved in the cases. Thus, legal training and experience on the bench disposes towards a conceptual system trained in the sophisticated use of selective interpretation of information.

The Public Nature of the Decision-Process

A number of writers, McGuire[17], Rosenberg[18], and Abelson[19] among them, have stated that the more public and visible an individual's expression of his thoughts, the more likely he will find the need to appear consistent. It is difficult to imagine a situation where the individuals are more visible and receive more attention from the mass media than the participants in the court room drama. Magistrates are aware that evaluations of their decisions will be made by a large number of people - the accused, counsel on both sides, the press and the public, and possibly the appeal courts. To the degree that they are concerned that all, or any, of these people accept the validity of the decisions they make, they are under strain to explain the rationale lying behind them in terms that will be accepted. This puts the judges and magistrates under considerable pressure to avoid logical flaws in the reasons underlying their decisions, and to appear consistent in the decisions they make.

The Amount of Unguided Discretion in Information-use
Given by the Law

The law does not, and properly cannot, specify what factual considerations ought to be considered in particular kinds of cases. Of all existing and proposed penal statutes, the American Law Institute's Model Penal Code probably makes the greatest effort to identify broad considerations that ought to cover a selection of particular kinds of sentences.[20] But even in the Model Penal Code, the criteria laid down are stated in terms of broad conclusions of fact, rather than in terms of the specific items of information on which a court can properly base these conclusions. For example, the Code asks the court to consider whether the offender is a "professional criminal," and whether the offender "intended serious harm."[21] But enormous problems exist in making these determinations on the basis of evidence normally available to the courts.

The Canadian Criminal Code not only fails to provide guidelines to the courts as to the proper principles or purposes of sentencing, but leaves it entirely to the courts' discretion to determine the amount and kind of information it should use in sentencing. As we have seen, there are marked differences among the courts in the degree to which they avail themselves of pre-sentence and other reports, the reasons for obtaining them, and the use put to them.[22] Without specific guidance in the law, such differences are inevitable.

In a recent study, Morris Rosenberg states that "the selective use of information is particularly free to operate under two conditions: (1) When a situation is unstructured or ambiguous, and (2) where the range of options are wide."[23] These two conditions characterize Canadian law as it affects sentencing.

Inadequacies in the Sentencing Alternatives Available

The scope of the discretionary power given to the court is more apparent than real. While most courts, and Canadian magistrates' courts in particular, are given wide powers in the length or amount of sentence, the number of genuine *alternatives* is rather restricted. Frequently, the courts deal with cases for which the penal system does not provide an opportunity to give the type of sentence that is considered to be appropriate in the circumstances. Often a magistrate or judge must choose sentences from among imperfect alternatives. This can place him in a dissonance situation.[24] If the needs and circumstances of the offender do not fit any of the sentencing alternatives available to the court, the magistrate or judge is forced to admit that the criminal justice system, of which he is a part, is inadequate. The consistency theories mentioned above suggest that unless the individual judge or magistrate can tolerate the feeling of personal inadequacy resulting from this situation, he is under considerable pressure, either to alter his perceptions of the offender to coincide with the alternatives available in law, or to alter his perceptions of the penal system so that it can be seen to be adequate to the needs of the offender.[25] If offenders can be seen either as "sick" and in need of the kind of correctional treatment available, or "evil" and in need of punishment, the decision-making problems are simplified. And if prisons can be seen as "hospitals," sentencing becomes a relatively easy task. It is much more difficult to accept the harsh realities that most offenders are neither "sick" nor "evil" in terms of the normal definitions of these words, and that on the evidence available, prisons are not places where effective treatment is being carried out, despite the best efforts of some people to make them so.

Information-Overload

There is considerable research evidence suggesting that in human decision-making the capacity of individuals to use information effectively is limited to the use of not more than five or six items of information.[26] In many cases, depending on the kind of information used, the purposes to which it is put, and the capacity of the individual concerned, the limit is much less.[27] Despite this evidence there is a noticeable tendency for pre-sentence reports to become longer. One of the most unfortunate myths in the folk-lore concerning sentencing, is the notion that the courts should know "all about the offender." Quite apart from whether much of the information is likely to be reliable, valid or even relevant to the decision possibilities open to the court, the burden of a mass of data can only result in information-overload and the impairment of the efficiency in which relevant information is handled. This suggests that if probation officers wished to improve the effectiveness of their communications to magistrates they would be advised to shorten their reports.

The Poor Quality of Information

Elsewhere this writer commented that, to be of practical value to a court, pre-sentence information should pass four tests: namely, reliability, validity, relevance, and efficiency.[28] Information ought to be reliable in the sense of being reproducible by different people over different periods of time, valid in the sense of representing what it purports to represent, relevant to the objectives of the court and the alternatives available in law, and efficient in the sense of not duplicating the contribution of other information already received. The thought was expressed that if research was conducted as to the quality of information commonly presented to the courts through the medium of pre-sentence and psychiatric reports, a number of profound and terrible truths would be revealed, but the point was not pressed.

In Chapter 14, the research was focused primarily on the degree of confidence magistrates have in the quality of information presented to them. We saw that there were significant differences in the weight that different magistrates attached to different types or categories of information, particularly in relation to the relative weights given to information concerning the offender, the offence, and the criminal record.[29] Moreover, a significant minority of magistrates felt that pre-sentence reports were not objective, but were rather biased in favour of the offender.[30] This allowed those magistrates to dismiss the reports, or at least those parts of them considered to be objectionable. In this way, magistrates were able to maintain consistency between their decisions and the facts of the cases deemed relevant to sentencing problems involved.

The Subjective Nature of the Decision-Process

Sentencing is not only difficult intellectually, it is demanding emotionally. Decisions are not made in a neutral, clinical atmosphere. The drama of the trial, the rituals and ceremonies acted out in the court-room, the adverse nature of the proceedings, and the concepts of crime, punishment and evil with which the court grapples, all lend an atmosphere of emotion to the proceedings which is likely to have some impact on the participants.

Magistrates are deeply and subjectively involved in the

decision-process. It is not a task that they take lightly and, compared to the trial of guilt, many find it an intellectually and emotionally draining experience. Recently, Sherif and Hovland presented evidence showing that the greater the degree of personal involvement (ego-involvement) in the decision-making process, the more rigid a person will be in the way in which he uses information.[31] Specifically, these writers suggest that the more subjectively involved an individual is in the process of judgement, the more likely he will be to reject information as not being relevant to the problem as he defines it.[32]

The Sequence in which Different Kinds of Information is Provided

Both in trials, and in pleas of guilty, the first piece of information a magistrate gets about a case concerns the offence. He is then presented with facts concerning the criminal record, if any, and finally he may receive information about the offender. This suggests that, as a general rule, the first impressions a magistrate gets are negative ones which may be contradicted later by the image of the offender revealed from the pre-sentence report. In such a situation, the order of presentation has an important bearing on how conflict will be resolved. Early studies on the order of presentation in the communication of information, for example, the pioneering study of Lund in 1925, indicated that the impression presented first will have greater effectiveness than subsequent impressions. Lund enunciated a "Law of Primacy in Persuasion," and for many years it was felt that first impressions were the more lasting ones.[33] Subsequent experiments, however, have not always obtained this outcome. Cromwell, for example, found that in certain circumstances the side of an issue presented last is likely to predominate.[34] This investigator obtained a "recency" effect rather than a "primacy" effect. Later work by Hovland, Mandell, and others, tends to show that primacy effects are usually more persuasive, but that a number of mediating variables must be considered.[35] In any event, the order of presentation of information appears to be a significant variable that must be considered in understanding how magistrates respond to information in sentencing.

Status Differences Between "Information-Givers" and "Information-Receivers"

In a volume entitled *Communication and Persuasion*, Hovland and Kelley describe a number of experiments which suggest that an individual is more likely to be influenced by communications received from high rather than from low status sources.[36] Moreover, the degree of persuasion depends upon the degree of confidence the individual has in his own opinions. Later, Hovland suggested that it may be predicted that the higher the communicator's perceived credibility, i.e., the greater the extent to which he is judged to be a trustworthy source of reliable information, the lower the threshold for response to inconsistency aroused by his communications.[37]

Magistrates and judges have considerably higher status than any other official involved in the decision-process. This suggests that it is easier for them to reject information if they should wish to do so. On the other hand, the degree to which a magistrate is influenced by information inconsistent with his private beliefs will depend upon the credibility he gives to the communicator. It has been demonstrated in this study that different patterns of relationships exist between probation officers, crown attorneys, defence counsel and magistrates in different communities.[38] Accordingly, it can be expected that the weight attached to information received from these individuals will depend upon the nature of face-to-face relationships, and the degree of confidence the magistrate has, both in his own opinions and in those of the other people concerned.

NOTES TO CHAPTER 17

1   Schroder *et al.* call this quality "functional uniqueness." See H. Schroder, M. Driver, and S. Streufert, *Human Information Processing* (New York, 1966).
2   Compare the data presented in Chapters 5 and 14 to these data.
3   Chapter 9.
4   Chapter 5.
5   This may be due, in part, to the instructions, which allowed them to pick only 3 factors out of 5.
6   Further data supporting this conclusion can be seen in Chapter 5.
7   *Ibid.*
8   See Chapter 14, ns. 1-10.
9   There were 1100 cases of institutional sentences for which sentencing study sheets were received.
10 See, for example, D.J. West, *The Habitual Prisoner* (London, 1963), 12-20, 100-8.
11 These correlations could not be calculated because only 3 out of 25 factors were picked in any one case. They were, therefore, grouped in one of several broad categories.
12 This is consistent with findings, presented earlier, of zero or negative correlations between high social defence and deterrence scores and the assessment of the seriousness of the offence; see Chapter 16.
13 *Report of the Interdepartmental Committee on the Business of the Criminal Courts* (London, 1961), 77-83.
14 Chapter 5.
15 C. Hovland and M. Rosenberg, *Attitude Organization and Change* (New Haven, 1960), 220.

16   In a recent book, Cross describes how judges use the doctrine of precedent. R. Cross, *Precedent in English Law* (Oxford, 1968).
17   W. McGuire, "A Syllogistic Analysis of Cognitive Relationships," in Hovland and Rosenberg, *Attitude Organization and Change,* 65-111.
18   M. Rosenberg and R. Abelson, "An Analysis of Cognitive Balancing," *ibid.,* 112-63.
19   *Ibid.* More generally see W. McGuire, "Current Status of Cognitive Consistency Theories," in S. Feldman, ed., *Cognitive Consistency* (New York, 1966).
20   American Law Institute, *Model Penal Code,* Proposed Official Draft (Philadelphia, 1962).
21   *Ibid.,* ss. 7.01-7.04.
22   See Chapters 14 and 15.
23   M. Rosenberg, "Psychological Selectivity in Self-Esteem Formation", in M. Sherif, ed., *Attitude, Ego-Involvement and Change* (New York, 1967), 31.
24   For a discussion of dissonance see L. Festinger, *A Theory of Cognitive Dissonance* (Evanston, 1957).
25   *Ibid.;* see also Chapter 14, ns. 1-10.
26   See, for example, Schroder et al., *Human Information Processing.*
27   *Ibid.*
28   J. Hogarth, "Towards the Improvement of Sentencing in Canada," *Canadian Journal of Corrections,* 9 (1967), 122-36.
29   Chapter 14.
30   *Ibid.*
31   M. Sherif and C. Sherif, "The Own Categories Procedure in Attitude Research," in M. Fishbein, ed., *Attitude Theory and Measurement* (New York) 190-8 and especially at 194.
32   *Ibid.,* 194-5.
33   F. Lund, "The Law of Primacy in Persuasion," *Journal of Abnormal and Social Psychology,* 20 (1925), 183-91.
34   H. Cromwell, "The Relative Effect on Audience Attitude of the First Versus the Second Argumentative Speech," *Speech Monographs,* 17 (1950), 105-22.
35   C. Hovland, W. Mandel, et al., *The Order of Presentation in Persuasion* (New Haven, 1957).
36   C. Hovland, I. Janis, and H. Kelley, *Communication and Persuasion* (New Haven, 1953).
37   *Ibid.*
38   Chapter 11.

18

The Complexity of Thought Processes in Sentencing

The Concept of Cognitive Complexity

Even if magistrates interpret information in similar ways they may differ in the way in which they combine it in coming to a decision. A sharp distinction must be made between *what* a magistrate perceives and *how* he perceives. Some magistrates may have fairly simple and concrete rules for organizing information, while others may use it in more complex and subtle ways. If a magistrate appraises a great body of information characteristically it can be expected that his mechanisms for integrating and organizing it in the process of coming to decisions are likely to be more complex. But there may be magistrates who receive a great deal of information but have rather rigid and simple rules for dealing with it. Their thought processes may be characterized by stereotyped or departmentalized thinking. Regardless of the kind or amount of information used, the individual pieces of information may be organized in a relatively fixed way with little or no integration.

There is research evidence to suggest that the capacity of an individual to deal with information in complex, problem-solving situations relates to a basic personality trait, and is therefore relatively fixed.[1] Much of this evidence relates to research built around the concept of "cognitive-complexity." Cognitive-complexity is generally conceived as a measure of the capacity of an individual to view the persons and objects in his social world in a complex or differentiated fashion. The best known work in this area is by Harvey, Hunt, and Schroder.[2] These writers formulated a theory which postulated a continuum or conceptual functioning ranging from "very simple"(concrete) to "very complex" (abstract).[3] In complex, problem-solving tasks, it was postulated that cognitively complex individuals would be able to bring a greater number of dimensions to bear on a given problem and generate more perspectives that link specific dimensions to task considerations. In short, he takes a more perceptive and subtle approach to complex problem-solving tasks.

From a series of experiments, Harvey and Ware found greater concreteness in contrast to greater abstractness to be reflected in several ways, the most relevant to the present study being (a) a simpler cognitive structure, that is, one of fewer differentiations and more incomplete integration of information, (b) a tendency towards extreme and polarized evaluations, namely, good-bad, right-wrong, etc., (c) a greater intolerance of ambiguity, expressed in higher scores in such measures as the F- and D-scales,[4] and a tendency to form judgements of novel situations more quickly, (d) a greater tendency to form and generalize impressions of other people from incomplete information, (e) a greater inability to change "set," and hence a greater tendency to stereotype in the solution of more complex and changing problems, (f) a greater insensitivity to subtle and minimal cues and hence a greater susceptibility of false but salient cues, (g) a higher score on the factor of dictatorialness (reflected in such behavioural characteristics as a high need for structure, low flexibility, high rule orientation, high frequency of the usage of unexplained rules, and low diversity of activities).[5] Greater abstractness was found to be accompanied by reverse qualities on the above dimensions.

Cognitive-complexity can be seen as a measure of the information processing ability of an individual. It is closely linked to intelligence. The formulations of Harvey, Hunt, Schroder, *et al.* seem to be particularly applicable to studies of information-use in sentencing. Fortunately, it was possible to operationalize most of the variables postulated from these theories from responses to various parts of the sentencing study sheet. The purpose of the analysis was to determine whether cognitive-complexity is a generalized trait, underlying the way in which magistrates process and interpret information in the course of coming to sentencing decisions.

The Creation of Cognitive-Complexity Variables

Seventeen variables, thought to be associated with the concept of cognitive-complexity, were created primarily from magistrates' responses to sentencing study sheets. They will be described briefly below and basic data statistics concerning them will be found in Technical Appendix 11.

Variable 1 measures the number of different information sources characteristically employed by the magistrate in sentencing. It represents the average number of sources of information used by each magistrate over all the cases for which he returned sentencing study sheets.

Variable 2 relates to the total number of perceptual dimensions employed by each magistrate in coming to decisions. It consists simply of the proportion, on average, of "known" to "not-known" responses to all areas of the sentencing study sheet.

Variable 3 is concerned with the number of *different* perceptual dimensions employed by magistrates in coming to decisions. Information in the section dealing with determining factors in the case were classified in terms of "offence," "record," "diagnosis," "prognosis," "control," and "other." Some magistrates characteristically restricted themselves to items falling within only one of these, whilst others tended to use items in several categories. The variable derived was the mean number of perceptual categories used by each magistrate.

Variable 4 measures the degree to which magistrates found the sentencing study sheet to contain a number of categories insufficient for them to indicate the way in which they dealt with the case. It was felt that magistrates who used the "miscellaneous" and "other" categories frequently are more likely to be cognitively complex. This variable was the proportion of cases in which these categories were used.

Variable 5 represents the degree to which magistrates prefer simple to complex information. For example, when considering the criminal record, magistrates who prefer simple information would tend to think in terms of the existence or non-existence of a record rather than the number of previous convictions, the recency of the last conviction, the nature and pattern of criminal behaviour revealed, or gaps of freedom from criminal activity. The variable derived was the proportion of simple versus complex information used by each magistrate.

Variable 6 relates to the degree to which magistrates label or stereotype offenders into specific categories. Magistrates indicated whether the offender before them fell within one of the following categories: a "persistent offender," a "professional criminal," or a "dangerous mentally ill offender." The variable derived represented the proportion of cases perceived as falling within these three categories.

Variable 7 measures the ability of magistrates to perceive offenders differently from case to case. It was derived from the responses to the section of the sentencing study sheet dealing with the perception of offenders. There were ten independent areas of the offender's life that were rated by magistrates on five-point scales. On each dimension a standard deviation score was determined for each magistrate. A high standard deviation indicates that the magistrate tends to alter, from case to case, his perception of the amount of pathology seen in that particular area of the offender's life. The variable used was the mean standard deviation over the ten characteristics studied.

Variable 8 is concerned with the degree to which magistrates view the determining factors in their decisions as being different from case to case. The variable was derived in much the same way as variable 7. For each of the twenty-five possible determining factors, magistrates were given standard deviation scores. Over the twenty-five factors, mean standard deviation scores were calculated. A high mean standard deviation score indicates that the magistrate tended to view the determining or over-riding considerations as different from case to case.

Variable 9 deals with the degree to which the purposes magistrates have in mind differ from case to case. The variable was derived similarly to variables seven and eight. For each of the five purposes in sentencing a standard deviation score was calculated. The variable created was the mean or average standard deviation over the five purposes in sentencing. A high score indicates that the purposes which a magistrate has in mind tend to change from case to case depending on the circumstances. It represents the ability to change "set," i.e., the ability to change one's approach to a problem depending upon the facts of the case.

Variable 10 measures the capacity of magistrates to take several aspects of the offender's life into account at the same time. For each magistrate a mean score was calculated for each of the ten dimensions dealing with problem areas in the offender's life. The standard deviation of these mean scores was determined. A low standard deviation indicates that the magistrate characteristically takes a larger number of factors into account, whilst a high score indicates that he perceives problems in only a few of these areas.

Variable 11 was created in a similar way to variable 10, but was concerned with the number of determining factors that the magistrate characteristically takes into account at one time. For each of the twenty-five determining factors a mean score was calculated and the standard deviation of these means was determined. A low score indicates that the magistrate tends to consider a larger number of determining factors depending on the case before him.

Variable 12 is similar to 10 and 11, but is based on the degree to which magistrates shift from case to case in the purposes hoped for in sentencing. A low score indicates that the magistrate tends to select the same purposes in sentencing, regardless of the legal or factual make-up of the cases. The variable represents the ability of magistrates to avoid rigidity in the solution of problems.

Variable 13 measures the range of discrimination a magistrate makes within a category of information. In using five-point scales in the sentencing study sheet, magistrates tended to differ in the number of scale positions used. Some magistrates tended to use all five positions, while characteristically others selected one or two. The variable derived is the number of scale positions actually used as a proportion of those that could have been used. This variable measures the number of discriminations that the magistrate tends to make within a category of information.

Variable 14 is a simple one. It is the time taken to make decisions. It is represented by the period of time (in days) from the finding of guilt to the determination of sentence.

Variable 15 was obtained from the interview. It consists of a composite score of the number of social and legal constraints that the magistrate feels exist over his behaviour. The score represents the degree to which a magistrate feels that his discretion is controlled by legal precedent, by the doctrine of uniformity, by public opinion, and by the views of the Department of the Attorney-General, the probation officer, and the crown attorney.

Variable 16 was derived from the section of the sentencing study sheet requesting magistrates to indicate whether they felt that existing legal provisions, facilities, and resources were adequate to deal with the case before them. A variable was created which represented the proportion of each magistrate's cases in which he felt existing legal provisions and treatment resources were adequate to deal with the case. One would expect that magistrates who are more cognitively complex, and thus more likely to be creative in attempts to solve problems, would feel that the law and existing resources were inadequate.

Variable 17 is concerned with the actual sentencing behaviour of magistrates. An effort was made to look at the way in which sentencing alternatives are used rather than what alternatives are used. A variable was derived which represented a tendency towards extreme sentencing behaviour. An extreme sentence is one that is particularly lenient or particularly severe, and a moderate sentence is one that falls within the mid-range of sentences given. A variable was created which represented the ratio of non-institutional sentences and sentences of more than two years (i.e., extreme sentences) to sentences of imprisonment of less than two years (i.e., moderate sentences). Research suggests that magistrates whose decision-behaviour is characterized by cognitive simplicity are more likely to be extreme in their sentencing behaviour.[6] That is, they are more likely to be both extremely lenient and extremely punitive.

The Analysis

The seventeen variables hypothesized as being related to a cognitive-complexity dimension of decision-making were factor analysed using the principal component method developed by Hotelling and Kelley.[7] The analysis was based on a total sample of fifty magistrates who completed an average of forty-four sentencing study sheets each. The purpose of the analysis was to determine if the variables "hang together" in some meaningful way. If they do, factor analysis would yield one or more interpretable factors (or dimensions) which account for a significant proportion of the variance.

Factor analysis yielded three interpretable factors, accounting for over forty-four per cent of the total variance. Rotation distributed the amount of variation explained almost equally among the three factors and led to easier interpretation of them. On the basis of similarity to content of variables with high loadings on each factor, it was possible to label the factors as follows: factor 1, discrimination; factor 2, size of information space; and factor 3, effort in problem solving. The loadings of the variables on each rotated factor are included in Technical Appendix 11. Table 93 contains the items with the highest loading on each factor, ranked in order of importance.

TABLE 93

Cognitive-complexity variables: ranked rotated factor loadings $(N=50)$

Variable number	Loading	Positive scores indicate	Negative scores indicate
Factor 1: discrimination			
13	0.820	Wide category width on 5-point scales	Narrow category width on 5-point scales
10	0.811	Gives equal weight to all areas of offender's life	Gives unequal weight to all areas of offender's life
11	0.713	Large no. of categories used	Small no. of categories used
2	0.642	Large no. of perceptual dimensions	Small no. of perceptual dimensions
8	0.618	Determining factors seen as different from case to case	Determining factors seen as similar from case to case
7	0.424	Perceives offenders differently from case to case	Does not perceive offenders differently from case to case
	0.391	Does not stereotype offenders	Stereotypes offenders
9	0.356	Has different purposes from case to case	Does not have different purposes from case to case
4	0.232	Uses miscellaneous categories	Does not use miscellaneous categories
Factor 2: size of information space			
11	0.761	Gives equal weight to different determining factors	Gives unequal weight to different determining factors
5	0.566	Prefers complex information	Prefers simple information
12	0.544	Gives equal weight to different purposes	Gives unequal weight to different purposes
16	0.456	Not satisfied with existing conditions	Satisfied with existing conditions
15	0.447	Does not feel his behaviour is externally controlled	Feels his behaviour is externally controlled
17	0.401	Extreme sentencing behaviour	Moderate sentencing behaviour
4	0.391	Uses miscellaneous categories	Does not use miscellaneous categories
8	0.317	Determining factors seen as different from case to case	Determining factors seen as similar from case to case
9	0.279	Has different purposes from case to case	Does not have different purposes from case to case
3	0.221	Large no. of categories used	Small no. of categories used
6	0.194	Does not stereotype offenders	Stereotypes offenders

TABLE 93 continued

Cognitive-complexity variables: ranked rotated factor loadings (N = 50)

Variable number	Loading	Positive scores indicate	Negative scores indicate
Factor 3: effort in problem solving			
1	0.705	Large no. of information sources	Small no. of information sources
2	0.621	Large no. of perceptual dimensions	Small no. of perceptual dimensions
14	0.521	Makes decisions slowly	Makes decisions quickly
15	0.483	Does not feel his behaviour is externally controlled	Feels his behaviour is externally controlled
5	0.448	Prefers complex information	Prefers simple information
9	0.443	Has different purposes from case to case	Does not have different purposes from case to case
3	0.379	Large no. of categories used	Small no. of categories used

The Interpretation of Cognitive-Complexity Factors

Factor 1: Discrimination

Factor 1 appears to represent differences among magistrates in the degree to which they can discriminate in a complicated fact situation. The variable with the highest loading on this factor is the one related to the number of scale positions used by magistrates in rating the offender and the offence along a series of five-point scales. Magistrates with high scores on this factor tend to make finer distinctions within a category of information.

The variable with the second highest loading appears to measure the ability of magistrates to perceive offenders in multidimensional terms. Magistrates with high scores on this factor tend to see problems in all areas of the offender's life, while magistrates with low scores on this factor tend to be concerned with a smaller number of problem areas.

The variable with the third highest loading is concerned with the number of determining factors that magistrates bring to bear on sentencing problems. Magistrates with high scores on this factor tend to apply a large number of determining factors depending on the circumstances of the case.

The variable with the fourth highest loading on the factor of discrimination appears to measure the number of perceptual dimensions that the magistrates are capable of using in coming to a decision. Magistrates with high scores on the factor tend to bring a large number of perceptual dimensions to bear on a given problem. That is, they tend to see the problem in a more complex way than do magistrates with low scores on this factor.

Variables 9, 10, and 11 have high loadings on this factor. These variables relate to the degree to which magistrates are capable of shifting their approach to the case when the circumstances change. Magistrates with high scores on this factor tend to perceive offenders differently from case to case, and to identify different determining factors, depending upon the circumstances and shift in the purposes hoped for, in response to changing combinations of facts as they perceive them.

Finally, magistrates with high scores on the factor of discrimination tend to avoid stereotyping offenders, and, consistent with this, they tend to use miscellaneous categories more frequently.

Factor 1 is fairly easy to interpret. It appears to be clearly related to the fineness or subtlety of distinctions that magistrates can make within a category of information. At the same time, it appears to measure the capacity of magistrates to change "set," i.e., to respond to information in a variety of ways depending upon the facts as they interpret them.

Factor 2: The Size of Information-Space

This factor is somewhat more difficult to interpret. It appears to be related not to the fineness or subtlety of distinctions made within a category of information, but rather to the amount of information a magistrate is capable of bringing to bear on a given problem.

Variables with high loadings on this factor include three variables related to the degree to which magistrates tend to approach each case in a fairly similar fashion. Magistrates with low scores on this factor tend to restrict themselves to viewing the determining factors and the purposes as fairly similar from case to case. They prefer simple to complex information. They have a tendency to stereotype and they do not use miscellaneous categories. Their sentencing behaviour is marked by inflexibility. In using sentencing alternatives they appear to exercise great caution and appear to be unwilling to innovate. They are satisfied with existing conditions despite feeling that their behaviour is controlled by law, the doctrine of uniformity, public opinion, and precedent. These magistrates appear to have a rigid and relatively fixed way of approaching sentencing problems. Information either fits into existing categories or departments of thought, or is excluded from consideration. They appear to have difficulty in thinking creatively when faced with novel fact situations and they tend to reduce the dissonance that is aroused, by perceiving or interpreting the facts selectively to fit a pre-determined structure.

This factor appears to measure the number of different ways a magistrate can perceive the problems involved in sentencing. It relates to the number of perceptual dimensions that he is capable of bringing to bear in dealing with the cases before him. It can be distinguished from factor 1 in terms of a distinction between the amount of information brought to bear on a given problem (size of information-space) and the way in which this information is handled once it is perceived (discrimination).

Factor 3: Effort in Problem Solving

Factor 3 is fairly easy to interpret. It appears to measure the amount of effort that magistrates expend in solving a problem or achieving a goal through sentencing. The variables with high loadings on this factor include the number of information sources, the number of perceptual dimensions brought to bear on a given problem, the time taken to make decisions, the degree of autonomy and social responsibility felt for decisions, a preference for complex as opposed to simple information, and the capacity to shift in both purposes and determining factors from case to case.

Magistrates with high scores on this factor appear to expend more effort in problem solving. They tend to make decisions slowly, they use more information, they prefer complex information, and they tend to feel that they have responsibility for their decisions. Magistrates with low scores on this factor appear to be less involved in the decision-process. These magistrates do not appear to have a concept of self as an autonomous agent. They do not feel they have freedom of choice and, accordingly, they feel less responsible for what they do.

Cognitive-Complexity as a Multidimensional Concept

The analysis demonstrates that magistrates differ not only in *what* they perceive but also in *how* they perceive. Magistrates vary in the amount of information they are capable of bringing to bear on a given problem, the fineness or subtleties of distinctions made with information once it is perceived, and the effort expended in problem solving. These three dimensions of information-use appear to be largely independent of one another. Thus, regardless of the amount of information brought to bear on a given problem, the rules that are used for organizing and structuring it in relation to other information may be fairly simple or rather complex. Moreover, the amount of information used and the fineness or subtleties of distinctions made are independent of the amount of effort expended in attempting to resolve a problem or achieve a goal through sentencing.

The data presented tend to confirm the cognitive-complexity concept postulated by Harvey *et al.* However, it appears that, as far as magistrates are concerned, cognitive-complexity must be seen as a multidimensional concept. Later it will be shown that these variables are significantly associated with the decision-behaviour of magistrates on the bench. In the meantime, let us examine the relationship of cognitive-complexity to personal characteristics of magistrates in terms of their backgrounds, attitudes and penal philosophies.

Relationship of Cognitive-Complexity to Personal Characteristics of Magistrates

Each magistrate was given three scores representing his ability to discriminate within a category of information, the amount of information he is capable of bringing to bear on a problem, and the effort he expends on problem solving. These scores were then correlated against certain background characteristics of the magistrates concerned, as well as against their scores on the main penal philosophy and attitude scales. In addition, correlations were calculated between the three cognitive-complexity variables and certain variables concerning the types of communities in which the courts are situated. The results are presented in Table 94.

None of the background characteristics of magistrates were significantly correlated with the complexity of thought-processes in sentencing. Thus, the age of the magistrate, the number of years spent at school, the number of years experience on the bench, and the number of cases dealt with, were not associated in any significant way with use of information in sentencing.

On the other hand, the complexity of thought-processes in sentencing was closely associated with the attitudes and penal philosophies of magistrates and to a lesser extent to certain demographic characteristics of the communities in which they work.

Urban magistrates, particularly in the larger centres, tend to be less discriminative in the way in which they use information and they expend less effort in problem solving than do magistrates in smaller communities or rural areas. Magistrates in high growth-

TABLE 94

Correlations of cognitive complexity variables with personal characteristics of magistrates (N = 50)

	Cognitive complexity variables		
Characteristic	Discrimination	Size of information space	Effort in problem solving
Social background and experience			
Age	n.s.	n.s.	n.s.
Education	n.s.	n.s.	n.s.
Years employed	n.s.	n.s.	n.s.
Attitudes			
Concern for justice	-0.314*	-0.322*	-0.392†
Punishment corrects	0.289*	n.s.	n.s.
Intolerance	n.s.	n.s.	n.s.
Social defence	n.s.	n.s.	-0.314*
Traditionalism	n.s.	n.s.	n.s.
Penal philosophy			
General deterrence	n.s.	n.s.	n.s.
Individual deterrence	n.s.	n.s.	n.s.
Reformation	0.318*	n.s.	0.555‡
Punishment	n.s.	-0.393†	-0.323*
Incapacitation	n.s.	-0.321*	n.s.
Community characteristics			
Density (urbanization)	-0.309*	n.s.	-0.326*
Growth rate	n.s.	0.280*	n.s.
Crime rate	n.s.	n.s.	n.s.
Caseload size	n.s.	n.s.	n.s.

*Significant at 0.05
†Significant at 0.01
‡Significant at 0.001

rate areas, i.e., those areas characterized by a quickly expanding population, prosperity, a low crime-rate, and a predominantly British population, tend to utilize more information in sentencing than do magistrates in areas not having these characteristics.[8]

The explanation for these findings probably lies in the different ways in which demographic characteristics of communities affect the work of magistrates as described earlier. The relative inefficiency of magistrates' courts in the urban areas, the atmosphere of rush, the general feeling of frustration and the lowering of morale which results from this, all militate against a dispassionate and sophisticated use of information in sentencing.

Other elements of the social situation faced by magistrates in large urban centres are likely to affect the way in which they use information. It will be recalled that magistrates in urban areas tend to feel that their standing in the community is low, they tend to have rather negative relationships with those who provide information to them, and they seem to have less confidence in themselves.[9] It would appear, therefore, that certain factors in the social structure within which the court functions impinge upon the effectiveness of information-use in sentencing. More importantly, there are significant differences in the attitudes and beliefs of magistrates in urban and rural communities. The attitudes and penal philosophies of urban magistrates tend to support a simple and more rigid way of approaching cases.

There are a number of significant correlations between the complexity of thought processes of magistrates and their penal philosophies and attitudes. Magistrates with high reformation scores on the penal philosophy scales appear to be more discriminative in the use of information, and they expend greater effort in problem solving than do magistrates with low scores on this scale. Magistrates with high retribution scores tend to employ little information in sentencing and expend relatively little effort in problem solving. A similar pattern emerges with respect to the incapacitation scale. Magistrates with high scores on this scale employ few perceptual dimensions and utilize little information in coming to decisions.

Turning to attitudes, it can be seen that magistrates with high scores on the justice scale employ little information in coming to decisions, are relatively rigid in the way in which this information is used and expend little effort in problem solving. On the other hand, magistrates who feel that "punishment corrects" tend to be more discriminative in the way in which information is used. Magistrates with high social defence scores expend relatively little effort in problem solving.

It would appear from this that punitiveness in attitudes and beliefs is associated with a fairly simple (concrete) way of organizing information in the process of judgement. The thought processes of punitive magistrates appear to be characterized by stereotyped or compartmentalized thinking. Individual bits of information are organized in a relatively fixed way with little or no integration. In contrast, non-punitive magistrates appear to use information in a more complex and subtle way. Their thought processes are characterized by flexibility, autonomy, and creativity. Their tolerance for conflict and ambiguity are higher, and their capacity for abstract thought or conceptualization is enhanced. They appear to be much more involved in the sentencing process and find it a more difficult and demanding task.

From the data provided it is impossible to say whether the attitudes and penal philosophies of magistrates cause them to deal with information in the way they do, or whether they tend to develop attitudes and beliefs which are consistent with their capacity for abstract thought. A review of the literature indicates that cognitive-complexity is generally viewed as an innate psychological trait pervading all realms of cognitive functioning.[10] This view would support the hypothesis that the attitudes and beliefs of magistrates tend to develop out of their capacity for subtle and abstract thought. On the other hand, there is some evidence in the data presented in this study which suggests that the subtlety of information-use is affected by the social conditions in which decisions are made.[11] Without further data the safest interpretation would allow for both factors. Social situations demanding a rigid, concrete, and simple set of rules for information use are likely to attract magistrates whose attitudes and beliefs are consistent with this way of processing information and at the same time socialize them into using information in ways consistent with the demands of the situation. If this proposition is tenable it means that it may be possible to improve the quality of information use through creating conditions which would attract individuals with greater capacities to handle information in subtle and complex ways, and at the same time, encourage them to be rather more sophisticated in how they use it. The final chapter will deal with some of the changes that might be made in this direction.

NOTES TO CHAPTER 18

1   For a review of early studies see S. Shraugher, and J. Altracchi, "The Personality of the Perceiver as a Factor in Person Perception," *Psychological Bulletin* 5 (1964), 289-308; more recently, see O. Harvey and R. Ware, "Personality Differences in Dissonance Reduction," *Journal of Personality and Social Psychology*, 72 (1967), 227-30.
2   O. Harvey, D. Hunt, and H. Schroder, *Conceptual Systems and Personality Organization* (New York, 1961); and, H. Schroder, M. Driver, and S. Streufert, *Human Information Processing* (New York, 1966).

3 *Ibid.*
4 The F-scale is the "authoritarianism" scale in the California Personality Inventory based on the work of T. Adorno *et al, The Authoritarian Personality* (New York, 1950). The D-scale is the "dogmatism" scale based on the work of M. Rokeach, *The Open and Closed Mind* (New York, 1960).
5 For a fuller description see Harvey and Ware, "Personality Differences."
6 *Ibid.*
7 See H. Harman, *Modern Factor Analysis* (Chicago, 1960). For a non-technical description see Chapter 7.
8 See Chapter 13 for a comparison with the attitudes of magistrates in these areas.
9 *Ibid.*
10 Harvey and Ware, "Personality Differences"; Harvey, Hunt, and Schroder, *Conceptual Systems;* and, Schroder, Driver, and Streufert, *Human Information Processing.*
11 Several writers have challenged the notion that cognitive-complexity is a general personality trait which exists apart from the social conditions in which information is used. See, for example, J. Vannoy, "The Generality of Cognitive Complexity - Simplicity as a Personality Construct," *Journal of Personality and Social Psychology,* 2 (3) (1965), 385-96.

19

The Prediction of Sentencing Behaviour from Fact Patterns Perceived by Magistrates

The Research Problem

If the sentencing study sheet reveals accurately the mental processes involved in decision-making, there ought to be a high level of consistency between magistrates' perceptions of facts and the decisions they make. In this chapter, the amount of consistency between "what magistrates perceive" and "what they decide" is tested by means of prediction equations. In the scheme of analysis, two types of prediction problems are dealt with. The first relates to predicting the type of sentence that will be imposed in qualitative terms, i.e., will it be a fine, suspended sentence, probation, or an institutional sentence? The second relates to the amount, length, or severity of the sentence imposed in quantitative terms. Different statistical models were required for these respective tasks. For the first set of problems the statistical technique used was multiple discriminant analysis and for the second, regression analysis. The theory of regression analysis was described earlier. Discriminant analysis will be briefly described below.[1]

This chapter also deals with predicting sentencing behaviour from "how magistrates perceive," in terms of cognitive-complexity. An attempt will be made to see whether knowledge of the complexity of thought processes in sentencing adds significantly to the power of prediction equations which already incorporate variables concerned with the attitudes of magistrates and their definitions of the operative social and legal constraints in the situations facing them. Towards the end of the chapter, an attempt will be made to draw together various aspects of the overall research scheme.

The Rationale for Multiple Discriminant Analysis

Multiple discriminant analysis is a technique to test the degree to which a battery of test scores concerning an individual will successfully predict the group to which that individual belongs. To give an example: suppose one wished to know whether a battery of psychological, aptitude, and ability tests used by employment counsellors were good predictors of the career choices eventually made. One could test the relationship of career choices to the scores on each test, but this would be a time-consuming task, and it would likely yield both complex and equivocal results. In its simplest form, discriminant analysis can transform the scores on all these tests to a single "discriminant score," which places each individual on a line which best separates all the individuals concerned into the careers which were eventually chosen. Discriminant analysis has the advantage of vastly simplifying the analysis, usually without leading to a substantial loss of information. Since one "best" line may not exhaust the predictive power of a battery of different tests, additional discriminant functions, all mutually independent of one another may be fitted. The maximun number of discriminant functions that may be derived is one less than the number of groups in which the individual may be placed (in the example, one less than the number of career choices that could have been made).

The technique first of all determines whether or not the relationship between the scores of individuals on the tests used and the groups to which they belong could have occurred by chance. If there is a statistically significant relationship between the tests and separations into groups, the next step is to calculate the number of discriminant functions which best describe group separations. Each discriminant function derived is then tested to determine both the statistical significance of its contribution to group separation and the proportion of explained variance that "it accounts for."

Additional refinements are often added. It is usual to obtain correlations between the original test scores and the discriminant functions derived. By examining the "loadings" of original scores on each discriminant function it is possible to determine which of the tests used are the "best" discriminators. Moreover, these loadings may be interpreted in much the same way as factor loadings are used to identify or label the factors derived from factor analysis. By examining the loadings of the original scores on each discriminant function derived, it is possible to give a name to each discriminant function in terms of similarity of content among the original variables with high loadings on it. Finally, it is sometimes desired to determine which of the original scores best discriminate among individuals in terms of group separation. This is usually done by an analysis of variance approach, in which the significance of group separation for each original variable is calculated by means of an F-test.

In this study, the problem is to predict the separation of cases into types of sentence, on the basis of the perceptions magistrates have of these cases. There are four types of sentence into which the case can fall: fine, suspended sentence, probation, and institution. In all, some 2340 cases were used in the analysis. The original variables used were magistrates' perceptions of various features of the cases as revealed from sentencing study sheets. Twenty-five variables were used in the analysis. They relate to the magistrate's assessment of the offence, his perception of the offender, his assessment of the determining or over-riding considerations in the case, and his purpose.

The analyses were based on the case rather than on the magistrate. Differences among magistrates were controlled for by accepting their individual interpretation of the cases as revealed by relevant sections of the sentencing study sheet.

Results

Discriminant analysis was first performed with respect to the total population of indictable cases for which magistrates completed sentencing study sheets. Additional analyses were then performed with respect to each of the seven individual offences. In each case, discriminant functions were extracted which were highly significant in both a statistical and a theoretical sense. Since the patterns which emerged from these analyses were roughly similar with respect to each offence studied, a detailed discussion of the findings with the main analysis only will be presented below. The remaining analyses are summarized in Technical Appendix 12.

At the first step, the computer program used calculated "Wilk's

Lambda" and determined the statistical significance of it. Wilk's Lambda represents the significance of group separations.[2] The value obtained was 1.287 and the F-ratio for statistical significance was 47.851. The chance of obtaining an F-ratio this high was calculated at less than 0.0001. Thus, it can be concluded that there are significant relationships between the facts of the cases as perceived by magistrates and the decisions they make.

The programme then extracted three discriminant functions which accounted for one hundred per cent of the explained variance, distributed as follows. Discriminant function 1 explained 64.37 per cent of the variance. The chi square value for this function was 1755.48, and the significance of this function was greater than 0.0001.

Discriminant function 2 accounted for 33.99 per cent of the variance, and the chi square value for this function was 1086.06 with a significance of greater than 0.0001. Discriminant function 3 accounted for only 1.64 per cent of the variance, but the chi square value was 66.02 and once again the significance of this value was greater than 0.0001. From this it can be concluded that three discriminant functions significantly accounted for the separation of cases into four categories of sentence.

The next step was to determine what these functions were. This was done by examining the original items with the highest loadings on each discriminant function. Immediately below are tables containing the loadings of original variables on each discriminant function, ranked in order of significance. In each case only the "best" items are included.

TABLE 95

Ranked correlations between original sentencing study sheet variables and discriminant function 1

Rank order	Original variable	Correlation coefficient
1	Assessment of offender's problems: criminal record	0.68
2	Purpose: to reform this offender	-0.60
3	Purpose: to punish this offender	0.50
4	Assessment of offence: lack of remorse	0.47
5	Determining factors (grouped): offence	-0.46
6	Determining factors (grouped): diagnosis	0.41
7	Assessment of offence: gravity of the act	0.40
8	Purpose: to deter potential offenders	0.39
9	Purpose: to remove this offender from society	0.39
10	Assessment of offender: attitude to authority	0.32

TABLE 96

Ranked correlations between original sentencing study sheet variables and discriminant function 2

Rank order	Original variables	Correlation coefficient
1	Purpose to reform this offender	0.59
2	Assessment of offence: degree of premeditation	-0.53
3	Assessment of offender: criminal record	0.52
4	Assessment of offence: gravity of the act	0.46
5	Assessment of offender: adjustment at work or school	0.45
6	Assessment of offender: personal relationships	0.43
7	Purpose: to punish this offender	-0.40
8	Assessment of offender: alienation from community	0.39
9	Assessment of offender: attitude to authority	0.36
9	Assessment of offender: financial	0.36

TABLE 97

Ranked correlations between sentencing study sheet variables and discriminant function 3

Rank order	Original variables	Correlation coefficient
1	Purpose: to punish this offender	0.40
2	Purpose: to deter this offender	-0.39
3	Assessment of offence: gravity of the act	0.36
4	Assessment of offender: personal relationships	-0.22
5	Determining factors (grouped): criminal record	0.21
5	Determining factors (grouped): prognosis	0.21
5	Purpose: to deter potential offenders	0.21
8	Assessment of offender: criminal record	0.20
9	Determining factors (grouped): control	-0.17
9	Assessment of offender: use of alcohol	-0.17

The first two discriminant functions are relatively easy to interpret and are quite distinct from one another. It appears that the first discriminant function relates to a punishment-control dimension and is labelled as such. Items with high loadings on this factor concern the offence rather than the offender. The only factor concerning the offender's background that appears among the ten factors with the highest loadings relates to the criminal record. As far as determining factors are concerned, there are high positive loadings with respect to the offence and high negative loadings with respect to the diagnosis of the offender's problems. With respect to purposes hoped for, items with high loadings on this function are: punishment, general deterrence, and incapacitation (all positive), and reformation (negative). Since this discriminant function accounts for nearly two-thirds of the variance, it can be concluded that variation among magistrates in the degree to which they interpret information in the direction of a punishment-control objective determines to a large extent the type of sentence that will be selected among the four main sentences available to them.

The second discriminant function extracted appears to relate to a treatment-reformation dimension. Since the statistical method used guarantees that all discriminant functions are independent of one another, it is rather interesting to note that the degree to which information is interpreted in a punishment direction bears no relationship to the degree to which magistrates interpret information in a treatment direction. The original variables with high loadings on this function are those related to magistrates' assessments of various problems in the life of the offender, failure to see premeditation in the commission of offences (but at the same time perceiving considerable gravity in the act itself), the attempt to achieve reformation and the denial of punishment as a purpose.

Discriminant function 3 is more difficult to interpret. Items with high loadings on this function also appear to relate to a punishment dimension. The distinguishing feature from discriminant function 1 appears to be the absence of items with high positive loadings concerning the control of crime through punishment. Negative loadings or very low loadings on original variables relating to social control and deterrence distinguish this function from the first one extracted. Accordingly, this discrimination function was labelled punishment-retribution. It accounted for less than two per cent of the explained variance, and because of this it was not used in subsequent analyses.

The interpretation of these discriminant functions becomes clearer when one examines the degree to which the original variables discriminate among the four types of sentence selected. Dealing with over-all discrimination first, it appears that magistrates' ratings of the criminal record are the best predictors of the type of sentence that will be selected. The second best predictor relates to the weight attached to "reformation" as a purpose. The third best predictor relates to the weight given to "punishment." The next best predictor relates to magistrates' assessments of the gravity of the crime committed. Other significant discriminators concern the degree of premeditation perceived in the commission of the offence, the degree to which magistrates respond to factors concerning the diagnosis of the offender's problems, the degree of remorse perceived and the degree to which magistrates believe the offender to have problems with respect to attitudes towards authority.

It would appear from the above that the type of sentence selected depends primarily on the magistrate's assessment of the offence and the criminal record of the offender. The weight he attaches to both reformation and punishment in the purposes hoped for are also highly significant.

Now let us see the way in which these discriminant functions distinguish among the sentences selected by magistrates. Table 98 contains the loadings of discriminant functions 1 and 2 on each type of sentence. A high loading on a particular type of sentence indicates that the selection of that type of sentence is associated with a tendency to interpret information in a way which emphasizes punishment or treatment as the case may be. The results are pictured graphically in Figure 16.

A rather interesting pattern emerges from Table 98. The selection of fines is associated with high punishment and low treatment loadings, the selection of probation is associated with low punishment and high treatment loadings and the selection of suspended sentence is associated with low punishment and low treatment loadings. This is roughly what could be expected for these types of sentence. What is surprising, however, is that the selection of institutional sentences appears to be associated with interpretations of facts which emphasize both punishment and treatment. It appears that magistrates believe that in using institutional sentences they can punish and treat offenders at the same time.

TABLE 98

Discriminant function loadings on particular types of sentence

Discriminant function	Type of sentence			
	Institution	Fine	Suspended sentence	Probation
Punishment-control	3.73	2.64	1.20	0.67
Treatment-reformation	1.92	-0.07	1.09	1.98
Punishment-retribution	2.39	2.47	1.66	2.49

It will be remembered that the majority of magistrates believe that the experience of institutions can be, and often is, beneficial to most offenders.[3] We also saw that, regardless of the length of institutional sentence imposed, many magistrates indicated that

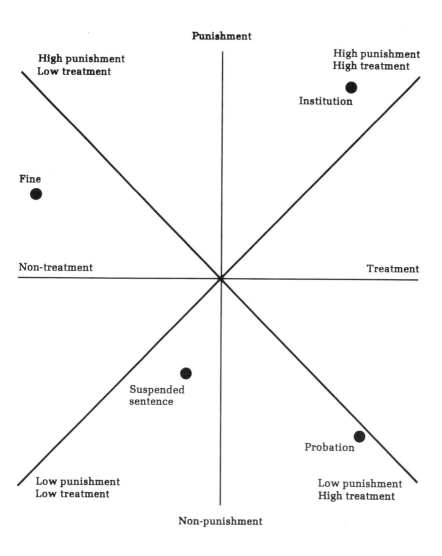

Figure 16 Type of sentence plotted against discriminant functions 1 and 2
(N = 2340 cases)

their prime purpose was to "reform" the offender. Other magistrates frequently indicated that punishment was their prime purpose in using institutional sentences, while few gave incapacitation much weight. One must therefore conclude that magistrates have successfully resolved, at least to their own satisfaction, the dilemma of reconciling punitive and rehabilitative aims in sentencing. Any attempt to show that institutional "treatment" has little rehabilitative impact is likely to be resisted by magistrates, as this would make it more difficult for them to sentence.

The analysis described above was repeated with respect to each individual offence for which sentencing study sheets were provided. Remarkably consistent results were achieved. For each offence, two main dimensions were extracted. These dimensions appeared to be associated with a tendency to interpret information in ways that emphasized punishment and treatment, respectively. Once again, the use of institutional sentences was associated with interpretations which emphasized both punishment and treatment. Interpretations which emphasized punishment and minimized treatment usually led to fines, interpretations which emphasized treatment and minimized punishment usually led to probation, and interpretations which emphasized neither punishment nor treatment usually led to suspended sentences.

The findings suggest that in the selection of sentences among alternatives available a high level of consistency exists among magistrates once variation in perceptions have been accounted for. This means that once magistrates perceive cases in a particular way there is a strong tendency for them to select the same type of sentence. The difficulty arises from the fact that different magistrates tend to perceive similar cases differently. But the data suggest that if means could be found to develop greater uniformity among magistrates in the way in which they assess information in sentencing, a great deal more consistency in sentencing practice could be achieved.

Prediction of Length of Sentence

Having demonstrated that there appears to be a high level of consistency between magistrates' perceptions of facts and the *types* of sentences they select, the analysis now turns to an examination of the degree to which these perceptions are associated with the length or severity of sentences imposed. First of all, correlations between perceived facts and lengths of institutional sentence were calculated. A series of regression equations were then calculated which regressed magistrates' perceptions of the facts and their purposes against the length of institutional sentences imposed (in days). Seven equations were derived, one for each type of offence for which sentencing study sheets were completed.

Correlational Analysis

The results of initial correlational analysis indicated that there was significant association between the lengths of institutional sentence imposed and most aspects of magistrates' assessments of the cases. Magistrates' assessments of offences, their perceptions of offenders, their selection of determining factors, and the purposes attempted were all found to be significantly associated with the severity of the penalties imposed.

While there were slight differences with respect to individual offences, the general pattern which emerged was of a tendency to select longer sentences if the crime was assessed as being serious, if the offender was seen to have participated fully in it and to lack remorse, if the offender was seen to have a great many problems in his background, and if the magistrate attached particular importance to the factors concerning the offence, the criminal record, and social control.

Different patterns with respect to purposes attempted appeared for each offence. In cases of robbery, long sentences were associated with giving emphasis to punishment and to incapacitation. In cases of breaking and entering, long sentences were associated with giving great weight to general deterrence and incapacitation and little weight to reformation. In cases of fraud, long sentences were associated with giving great weight to general deterrence and incapacitation. On the other hand, long sentences for taking a motor vehicle without consent were associated with attaching little weight to punishment and great weight to both reformation and incapacitation. Lengthy sentences in cases of assault occasioning bodily harm were associated with attaching great weight to incapacitation. Over all, the pattern which emerged is that the longer the sentence, the more likely was the magistrate concerned with preventing crime by removing the offender from society, and the less likely was he concerned with reformation or individual deterrence.

In Table 99 correlations between magistrates' assessments of cases and the lengths of institutional sentences imposed are presented for all seven offences (combined). In Technical Appendix 12 correlations between these factors for specific offences will be found.

While there were many statistically significant correlations between various features of the cases as perceived by magistrates and the length of sentence imposed, they were not particularly high. The highest correlations achieved were with respect to magistrates' assessments of the gravity of the acts committed and their assessments of the length of the offender's criminal record. Even in these areas, however, correlations ranged from a low of 0.3 to a high of 0.7. One should not expect correlations between these individual factors and the sentences imposed to be much higher. Sentences are based on the combination of a great many

TABLE 99

Correlations of length of institutional sentence with magistrates' assessments of the offence, the offender, the determining factors, and the purpose of the disposition (N = 1103)

All offences, length of institutional sentence (in days) correlated with:	Correlation	Level of significance
Assessment of offence		
Gravity of the act	0.311	0.01
Premeditation of offender	-	-
Degree of participation by offender	0.217	0.01
Offender's present attitude	-0.086	0.01
Assessment of offender's problem		
Family and personal relationships	0.161	0.01
Attitude to authority	0.197	0.01
Use of alcohol	-	-
Use of drugs	-	-
Alienation from community	0.235	0.01
Adjustment at work or school	0.184	0.01
Financial situation	0.219	0.01
Antisocial behaviour	0.159	0.01
Criminal or delinquent associates	0.190	0.01
Criminal record	0.299	0.01
Determining factors in the case		
Offence factors (grouped)	0.095	0.01
Record factors (grouped)	-	-
Diagnosis factors (grouped)	-	-
Prognosis factors (grouped)	-	-
Control factors (grouped)	0.154	0.01
Miscellaneous factors (grouped)	-	-
Purposes attempted		
To deter potential offenders	-	-
To punish this offender	-	-
To reform this offender	-0.080	0.01
To deter this offender	-0.099	0.01
To incapacitate this offender	0.304	0.01

facts as perceived and understood by magistrates. While individual correlations shed some light on the decision-making process, the appropriate statistical model is one that allows for an assessment of the magistrate's total response to various features of the case. This is a situation which calls for multivariate procedures, and in this case step-wise multiple regression was used.

Regression Analysis

In the analysis the dependent variable in all cases was the length of institutional sentence given (in days). Seven regression equations were calculated, one for each offence for which sentencing study sheets were completed. A computer was instructed to roam freely among the independent variables, selecting those which best predicted the severity of the penalty given. The seven regression equations derived can be seen in Table 100.

The size of the correlation coefficients range from a low of 0.638 to a high of 0.834 with an average of 0.716. This means that about fifty per cent of the total variation in length of institutional sentences imposed can be accounted for by variations in magistrates' perceptions of the facts in the cases.

It is interesting to see the variables which appear frequently in the regression equations. As far as magistrates' assessments of offences are concerned, their assessments of the degree of premeditation appears in five out of seven regression equations, the gravity of the criminal act in three, the offender's present attitude towards his involvement in only two, and the degree of participation in none. From this it would appear that the degree of premeditation is a somewhat more important factor in the determination of length of sentence than any other aspect of the offence.

As far as assessments of offender's problems are concerned, the length of criminal record appears in each of the seven regression equations. Moreover, in each case it is the first variable selected by the computer. This means that it explains more variance than any other factor. Adjustment at work and school appears in three equations, criminal associates and financial standing appear in two each, family relationships and attitude to authority appear only once and the other four factors appear in nine. It would seem from this that, as far as length of institutional sentences is concerned, a small number of factors related to the background and the history of the offender are relevant, the most important being the criminal record.

As far as the determining factors in the case are concerned,

TABLE 100
Regression of lengths of institutional sentences (in days) against
magistrates' assessments of cases

Constant	Assessment of offence	Assessment of offender	Determining factors	Purposes
1 Robbery (r at final step = 0.705)				
-2140.7	+394.4 gravity	+375.2 criminal record	+414.4 control	+ 87.5 incapacitation
				+158.7 punishment
				-182.0 deter potential offender
				-121.6 deter this offender
2 Breaking and entering (r at final step = 0.668)				
-255.1	+147.1 gravity	+100.9 criminal record		+55.9 incapacitation
	+70.7 premeditation	-25.6 criminal associations		+15.9 deter potential offender
				- 23.2 reform
				- 14.2 deter this offender
3 Fraud (r at final step = 0.828)				
-1000.8	+220.4 gravity	+36.4 criminal record	-58.7 diagnosis	+ 34.5 incapacitation
	+101.5 participation	+100.5 criminal associations		+ 26.6 deter potential offender
		-34.8 adjustment at work		
4 Assault and bodily harm (r at final step = 0.728)				
-284.7	+94.1 gravity	+42.6 criminal record	+50.8 diagnosis	+30.2 incapacitation
	+25.2 premeditation		+12.5 control	- 9.3 punishment
5 Indecent assault on a female (r at final step = 0.834)				
+123.14	+157.3 premeditation	+173.3 criminal record	+41.4 control	+99.0 incapacitation
		+217.8 finance		+60.5 punishment
		-131.4 adjustment at work		
6 Take motor vehicle (r at final step = 0.638)				
122.9	+64.2 participation		- 20.5 offence	+ 25.3 incapacitation
				+177.7 reformation
	+37.7 premeditation			- 6.6 punishment
	+25.1 lacks remorse			- 7.7 deter this offender
7 Dangerous driving (r at final step = 0.809)				
177.7		+47.4 criminal record	+26.9 offence	+64.8 incapacitation
		- 27.9 attitude to authority		+15.1 reformation
		- 27.3 family relations		
		+48.1 finance		

different patterns emerge with respect to individual offences. For cases of assault occasioning bodily harm, indecent assault on a female and robbery (both serious offences against the person), lengths of institutional sentences are positively associated to the weights attached to variables concerning the control of further criminal behaviour by the offender. With respect to dangerous driving and taking a motor vehicle without consent, lengths of institutional sentences are associated with weights given to variables concerning the offence, and in cases of fraud long sentences are associated with a tendency to minimize factors concerning a diagnosis of the offender's problems. This shows that magistrates will not impose long sentences of imprisonment on offenders convicted of relatively minor offences unless they ascribe particular importance to the severity of the offence and minimize the importance of the offender's problems.

Turning to purposes in sentencing, it is interesting that the prevention of crime through incapacitation appeared in all seven regression equations, whilst punishment appeared in four, the deterrence of potential offenders in three, and both the deterrence of the individual offender and reformation in only two. This suggests that while magistrates tend to give low over-all weights to retributive punishment and incapacitation, these two purposes play a more important role in the actual behaviour of magistrates than do any of the others. It would appear, therefore, that despite verbal support given to the more acceptable purposes, such as reformation and deterrence, sentencing is to a significant extent centred around the more traditional purposes of retribution and short term protection of society through incapacitation.

The relationships between purposes and length of institutional sentences is rather complex. In regression equations, each variable makes an independent contribution to the prediction equation, i.e., a separate contribution to that of other variables already in the equation. Thus, it can be seen that after controlling for the other purposes involved, attaching weight to reformation is negatively associated with length of institutional sentences in cases of breaking and entering, while being positively associated with length of institutional sentences in cases of dangerous driving and taking a motor vehicle without consent. Similarly, attaching great weight to punishment is positively associated with length of institutional sentences in cases of robbery and cases of indecent assault on a female (serious cases), while being negatively associated with length of institutional sentences in cases of assault occasioning bodily harm, and taking a motor vehicle without consent (less serious cases). In all cases, the weights attached to incapacitation and the deterrence of potential offenders are positively associated with the length of institutional sentences imposed.

It is interesting to note that in relatively minor cases long institutional sentences are associated with attaching great weight to reformation and individual deterrence and little weight to punishment. In serious cases, severe sentences are associated with attaching great weight to incapacitation and general deterrence. This suggests that when the offence itself does not warrant a severe penalty, magistrates will only impose such a penalty if they can justify it on the grounds of preventing further crime in the individual through reformation or intimidation.

The general conclusion that one can draw from this section is that there is a high level of consistency among magistrates in the lengths of institutional sentences imposed once variation in their perceptions of cases is controlled for.

The Relationship of How Magistrates Perceive to What They Decide

Having demonstrated that the relationship between magistrates' perceptions of the facts and their decisions is a close one, the analysis now returns to the complexity of thought processes in decision-making. In the analyses described below, the basic unit is the magistrate. Each magistrate received three scores representing his level of cognitive-complexity. These scores related to his capacity to discriminate in a complicated fact situation, the amount of information he is capable of bringing to bear on a given problem, and the effort he expends in problem solving. The purpose of the analysis was to determine the degree to which knowledge of these three factors could lead to successful prediction of sentencing behaviour. Sixty-seven different measures of sentencing behaviour were used. They represented the proportion of sentences of particular kinds given for specific types of offence. Thus, the analysis begins with an examination of the general breakdown of sentences for all indictable cases. The cases are then divided into specific types and finally an examination is made of the sentencing behaviour of magistrates with respect to individual offences.

It will be recalled that the cognitive-complexity variables were created from magistrates' responses to sentencing study sheets with respect to seven offences dealt with over an eighteen-month period. These cases were not used in this part of the analysis. It was deemed desirable to test the validity of the cognitive-complexity concept against further data, independent to that from which the original variables were derived. In a sense, the use of new behavioural variables provides an opportunity to validate the original study and thus strengthens the cogency of the findings.

The judicial section of the Dominion Bureau of Statistics provided a special print-out of sentencing behaviour by magistrates in the Province of Ontario for the year 1965. For each magistrate the proportion of his sentences falling within the main categories of fine, suspended sentence, probation, and institution were determined. The mean lengths of institutional sentences imposed were also calculated. These variables became the dependent variables. The first step in the analysis was to calculate correlations between the three complexity scores and the sentencing behaviour of magistrates. The next step was to determine the degree to which knowledge of the complexity of thought processes adds significantly to the prediction equations which already took into account the attitudes of magistrates, and their definitions of the operative constraints in their social environments.

Results

Correctional Analysis

A large number of statistically significant correlations were found between cognitive-complexity and sentencing behaviour (see Table 101). Magistrates who use suspended sentence frequently in indictable cases, particularly suspended sentence with probation, tend to discriminate better in complicated fact situations, are capable of bringing a larger body of information to bear on a given problem and expend more effort in problem solving. In contrast, magistrates who rely heavily on fines do not appear to be as subtle in discriminating among information. Magistrates who use institutional measures frequently tend to bring less information to bear on sentencing problems and are rather more rigid in their approach to sentencing problems.

Cognitive-complexity was associated not only with the *frequency* with which institutional sentences were used, but also with the *type* of institutional sentence selected. Thus, magistrates who rely heavily on short-term institutional sentences expend less effort in problem solving. Magistrates who tend to use gaol as opposed to reformatory or penitentiary sentences do not discriminate so well in assessing information, and magistrates

TABLE 101

Correlations of sentencing behaviour against cognitive-complexity variables
(N = 50 magistrates)

Sentencing behaviour	Cognitive-complexity variables		
	Discrim-ination	Size of information space	Effort
All indictable			
Suspended sentence with probation	0.310	-	0.278
Suspended sentence without probation	0.453	-	-
Suspended sentence combined	0.643	0.335	-
Fine	-0.57	-	-
Institution	-	-0.287	-
Average gaol sentence (days)	-0.509	-0.332	-
Average reformatory (days)	-	-	-
Average penitentiary (days)	-	-	0.284
Average all institutions (days)	-0.257	-0.515	0.239
Gaol: percentage of total disposition	-	-	-
Less than 6 months	-	-	-0.316
More than 6, less than 24 months	-0.303	-	-
Total gaol	-	-	-
Reformatory: percentage of total disposition	-	-	-
Less than 12 months	0.327	-	-
More than 12, less than 24 months	0.332	-	-
Total reformatory	0.382	-	-
Total penitentiary: percentage of total disposition	-	-0.383	-
Gaol: percentage within all institutions	-	-	-
Less than 6 months	-	-	-0.241
More than 6, less than 24 months	-0.377	-	-
Total gaol	-0.327	-	-
Reformatory: percentage within all institutions	-	-	-
Less than 12 months	0.320	-	-
More than 12, less than 24 months	0.321	0.264	-
Total reformatory	0.381	-	-
Total penitentiary: percentage within all institutions	-	-0.438	-

who rely heavily on penitentiary sentences tend to bring less information to bear on sentencing problems. In contrast, magistrates who use reformatory sentences frequently tend to have a greater capacity to discriminate.

The main conclusion that can be drawn is that the frequent use of both very short and very long institutional sentences is associated with a simpler and more rigid way of dealing with information.

Turning to specific offences, a number of different patterns emerge. While it is generally true that magistrates whose decision-behaviour is characterized by cognitive-complexity tend to rely more heavily on suspended sentence and less heavily on fines and institutions, different patterns emerged with respect to individual offences. The most striking fact which appeared is that there is a tendency for magistrates who often give sentences which depart from the norm to be rather more complex in their thought processes. Thus, the use of both probation and suspended sentence in serious cases is associated with cognitive-complexity. On the other hand, the more frequent use of these sentences in relatively minor cases is associated with cognitive-simplicity. These data confirm the proposition of Harvey, Hunt, Schroder, and others that cognitive-complexity is associated with a willingness to innovate on the part of the individuals concerned.[4]

It would appear, therefore, that cognitive-complexity is associated with a number of characteristics of sentencing behaviour. The more cognitively complex the magistrate, the more likely he is to avoid fines and institutional sentences, particularly those involving common gaol and penitentiary commitments. It will be remembered that cognitive-complexity was associated with high reformation and low punishment scores on the penal philosophy scales, and high punishment corrects, low justice and low social defence scores on the attitude scales.[5] It seems, therefore, that punitiveness in both attitudes and behaviour, is associated with cognitive-simplicity. The only qualification that must be made is that due to an apparent willingness to innovate, cognitively complex magistrates sometimes appear relatively punitive with respect to minor offences. They do not feel constrained by the doctrine of uniformity, they attach less weight to the concept of justice, and therefore they are sometimes willing to impose sentences which are rather more severe than the offence itself would warrant. However, in doing so they tend to avoid penitentiary and common gaol sentences, preferring to use reformatory sentences, which, according to accepted doctrine, provide a greater opportunity for the offender to benefit from the institutional experience he will receive.

The general conclusion that can be drawn from this chapter is that subtlety in information-processing is associated with subtlety in decision-behaviour.

NOTES TO CHAPTER 19

1   See Chapter 9, for a non-technical description of regression. For multiple discriminant analysis see W. Cooley and P. Lohnes, *Multivariate Procedures for the Behavioral Sciences* (New York, 1966), 116-33.
2   *Ibid.*, 119.
3   Chapter 5.
4   Chapter 18.
5   *Ibid.*

20

Towards a Model of
Sentencing Behaviour

The studies so far described in this book attempted to show how judges make sentencing decisions. The perspective was phenomenological, i.e. it started with a deliberately naïve position and built a model of the decision process, straw by straw, guided primarily by an effort to understand sentencing as magistrates themselves experience it. All the data upon which the eventual model was built concerned the "meanings" that magistrates attached to the facts of the cases and those surrounding circumstances which they deem significant, including how they define self in relationship to those facts and circumstances.

The approach taken differs in several respects from classical research orientations in this area, all of which assume that the only significant variables affecting sentencing are those externally visible "facts" available from judicial records. This is the familiar stimulus-response or input-output model of behaviour in which the facts of the case comprise the stimulus or input and the sentencing decision the output or response. It should also be noted that this approach is consistent with the traditional legal view of the process which makes the assumption that the only "legally significant" variables governing judicial decisions, within a given legal framework, are differences in the factual makeup of the cases, the law being a constant and the personality of the judge being legally irrelevant. The black box or legal model is schematically presented in Figure 17.

The point of departure in this study is in its attempt to show

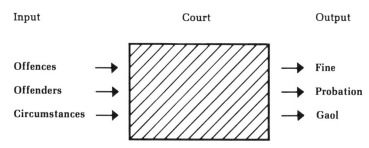

Figure 17   Black box model

how magistrates interpret their factual, legal, and social environments. It was demonstrated that magistrates tend to interpret their environments differently, depending on their personal values and subjective ends. In a variety of ways it was shown that the decision-making process in sentencing is not a neutral or mechanical one. It is highly charged affectively and motivationally. It is not neutral because it relates to matters touching on each magistrate's values, sentiments and commitments; in short, the very material out of which his self-identity is composed. The centre of the social space of a magistrate, therefore, is seen as his concept of self, expressed in his attitudes.

As Murphy observes: "Whatever the self is, it becomes a centre, an anchorage point, a standard of comparison, an ultimate real. Inevitably it takes its place as the supreme value."[1]

The concept of self as the centre of the social space of the magistrate leads to these propositions: (i) the development of relationships to judicial task that are consistent and enduring, including sets of attitudes which define their relationships to that task, is an integral aspect of the development of a judicial self concept; (ii) there is a tendency for magistrates to maintain adequate self images in their perceptions and responses to the objects and persons they define as being significant; and (iii) self is a valued object and is protected and enhanced in the face of influences which are perceived as tending to destroy or minimize it.

It was shown in this study that considerable mental energy is expended by magistrates in protecting their self-concepts from all threatening influences. This was done primarily through the mechanisms of selective perception. Magistrates interpret the law, the expectations of others, and the facts of the cases in selective ways which maximize concordance with their concept of self. The medium through which the world is selectively perceived (and the self-concept protected) is the attitudes of magistrates. Attitudes were studied as information-processing structures and it was shown that these attitudes were closely associated with all aspects of the sentencing process. The end result is a remarkably high level of internal consistency between magistrates' perceptions of the world and their behaviour on the bench.

The model which emerges from the analysis is one that sees sentencing as a dynamic process in which the facts of the cases, the constraints arising out of the law and the social system and other features of the external world are interpreted, assimilated, and made sense of in ways compatible with the attitudes of the magistrate concerned. In the process of judgement, the objective, external world is transformed into a subjective, definitional world. The results are sentencing decisions which are consistent with magistrates' definitions of the situations facing them. Relationships between the external world, magistrates' interpretation of that world, and their behaviour on the bench is presented schematically below.

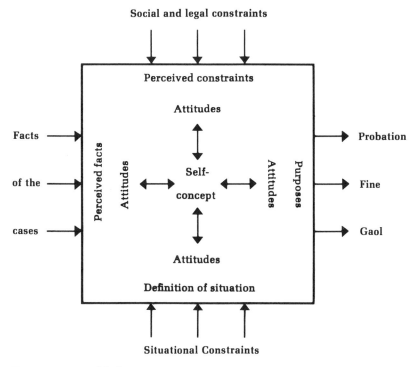

Figure 18   A model of sentencing behaviour

It would be interesting to compare the above model with one that ignored the conscious definitions, intentions and purposes of magistrates, concentrating on "objectively" defined facts concerning the cases and situations faced by magistrates, i.e., a black box model. Data for such a comparison have been collected, and the findings will be described immediately below.

Two Models of Sentencing

The Black Box Model

The first step in testing the black box model was to collect as much information as possible concerning the facts of the cases (the input or stimulus) coming before the court. In choosing variables the research was guided by findings in previous studies, particularly those of Green[2] and Hood[3], which showed statistical relationships between certain fact patterns and sentencing decisions. We also added additional variables in the hope that they might add to the predictive power of the model. These additional variables were not available to previous researchers and it was felt that fair test of the black box model would require a more complete analysis of the differences in fact patterns of cases appearing before the courts. The following list of twelve variables were eventually included.

1 The severity of the crime is measured by the Sellin-Wolfgang severity scale.
2 The type of victim categorized as (a) a private person; (b) a private business or corporation; (c) a government agency or department, and (d) the public at large.
3 The sex of the victim.
4 The offender's relationship to the victim, classified as: related by marriage, known to victim, and unknown to victim.
5 Number of separate counts or charges.
6 The plea.
7 The age of the offender.
8 The sex of the offender.
9 The marital status of the offender.
10 The occupation of the offender.
11 The length of the offender's criminal record.
12 The recency of the offender's previous conviction.

Variables were created representing each of these factors and analyses were performed to determine the relationship of these factors, both individually and collectively, to the sentencing behaviour of the courts.

The first set of analyses concerned the relationship between objectively defined facts of the case and the choice of sentence, in qualitative terms. The purpose was to reveal the extent to which different fact combinations affect the type of penalty. The statistical technique was multiple discriminant function analysis, described in Chapter 19. The second set of analyses concerned the relationship between objectively defined variables and the lengths or amount of sentence given in quantitative terms. The statistical techniques included correlational analysis and multiple regression.

The Relationship between Fact Patterns and Type of Sentence

Discriminant function analysis revealed that there were statistically significant relationships between fact patterns in individual cases and the types of sentence selected by the court. This held true for the total population of indictable cases for which magistrates completed sentencing study sheets and for each of the seven individual offences. The pattern which emerged was roughly similar with respect to each offence studied and the detailed findings of the analyses are summarized in Technical Appendix 13. A summary of the findings with respect to all offences (combined) is included below.

On a sample of approximately 1500 cases, the computer program extracted three discriminant functions, the first two accounting for over 90 per cent of the explained variance. The probability that these functions could have occurred solely by chance was less than one in a thousand. From this it was concluded that among various fact patterns in the cases two underlying factors relate to the choice of sentence selected by the court.

In order to determine what these factors are, an examination was made of the loadings of each original variable on each of the discriminant functions. Tables 102 and 103 contain such loadings, ranked in order of significance.

Original variables with high loadings on discriminant function 1 include: length of criminal record, recency of previous conviction, type of victim, occupation of offender, and number of counts, in that order. This function appears to measure the criminality of the offender as expressed by the nature of his crime and his previous criminal activity.

Original variables with high loading on discriminant function 2 include: the plea of the offender, the age of the offender, the sex of the victim, the offender's relationship to the victim, the number of counts, the marital status of the offender, and the severity of the crime. This discriminant function appears to measure the culpability of the offender in the particular offence charged. It would appear, therefore, that the choice of sentence among alternatives available is influenced by (a) whether or not the background and history of the offender reveal a pattern of criminality, and (b) whether the facts surrounding the commission of the offence suggest a high level of culpability or moral blameworthiness on the part of the offender.

TABLE 102

Ranked correlations between objectively defined variables and discriminant function 1

Rank order	Original variable	Correlation coefficients
1	Length of criminal record	0.85
2	Recency of previous conviction	0.80
3	Type of victim	0.24
4	Occupation score	-0.24
5	Number of counts	0.22
6	Age	0.14
7	Sex of offender	-0.14
8	Relationship to victim	0.09
9	Severity score	0.09
10	Plea	-0.06
11	Marital status	-0.05
12	Sex of victim	0.03

TABLE 103

Ranked correlations between objectively defined variables and discriminant function 2

Rank order	Original variables	Correlation coefficients
1	Plea	0.76
2	Age	0.67
3	Sex of victim	0.35
4	Relationship to victim	-0.28
5	Number of counts	-0.27
6	Marital status score	0.27
7	Severity score	0.23
8	Type of victim	-0.08
9	Occupation score	0.06
10	Sex of offender	0.03
11	Recency of previous conviction	-0.02
12	Length of criminal record	0.00

The analyses then turned to an examination of the degree to which the original variables discriminated among the four types of sentence selected. Dealing first with over-all discrimination, it appeared that the length of the criminal record was the most important factor influencing a court in the choice of sentence. The second was the recency of the last conviction. The third was the age of the offender, followed by the type of victim and the severity of the crime as measured by the Sellin-Wolfgang Scale.

Now let us turn to the way in which the two general functions discriminate among sentences selected. Table 104 contains loadings on discriminant functions 1 and 2 for each type of sentence. A high loading indicates that the selection of this type of penalty is associated with fact patterns suggesting a history of criminality or a high level of culpability in the commission of the offence, as the case may be.

TABLE 104
Discriminant function loadings on types of sentence

| Discriminant function | Centroids | |
Type of sentence	Previous criminality	Culpability
	1	2
Institution (1393 cases)	3.75	5.33
Fine (533 cases)	2.67	6.15
Suspended sentence (204 cases)	2.60	3.50
Probation (775 cases)	2.44	4.92

The results showed that the selection of institutional sentences was associated with fact patterns which revealed both a background of previous criminality and a high level of culpability in the commission of the offence. The selection of fines was associated with backgrounds which revealed no previous pattern of criminality but at the same time a high level of culpability of the offender in the present offence. The selection of suspended sentence with and without probation was linked to no previous history of criminality and low culpability in the present offence. A similar pattern emerged with each individual offence studied, and a full description of the analyses is included in Technical Appendix 13.

These data suggested that in the selection of sentences among alternatives available, fact patterns in the cases are significant, at least in a statistical sense. It remains to be determined whether or not these "objectively defined" facts are more powerful predictors of sentencing than the facts of the cases as perceived by magistrates. It was not possible to compare the predictive power of the two kinds of variables to predict choice of sentence in qualitative terms, as the statistical techniques used would not allow for such a comparison. All that can be said is that both classes of variables are closely enough associated to the decisions of the courts to make highly remote the possibility of such associations being due solely to chance. When we turn, however, to predicting the length or amount of sentence in quantitative terms, an adequate test of strength between the two models becomes possible. The next section will deal with this.

Relationship between Objectively Defined Facts and
Lengths of Sentence Imposed

The analyses began with simple correlations between the twelve objectively defined variables and the lengths of sentence imposed for each of the seven indictable cases examined. It was immediately discovered that the correlations between these variables and length of sentence (in days) were, in all instances, either non-significant or very low. Dealing with all offences (combined) only two variables were statistically at the 0.05 level. These were severity of the crime and the length of the criminal record. The size of these correlation coefficients were 0.201 and 0.231, respectively. None of the other variables was significantly associated with the length of sentence imposed. Turning to the individual cases, in no instance were more than three variables significantly associated with the length of sentence imposed and in no case did the correlations exceed 0.4. Individual correlation coefficients for each offence are included in Technical Appendix 13. Table 105 shows the correlations between lengths of institutional sentences and these variables for the total sample of cases studied.

The following conclusions may be drawn. Correlational analysis indicates that the facts most closely associated with length of sentence are the length of criminal record and the severity of the crime. Occasionally the age of the offender, his occupation, and the number of counts in the indictment were associated with the length of the sentence imposed. However, none of these variables accounts for very much of the variation in lengths of sentence im-

TABLE 105

Correlations of lengths of institutional sentence with objective variables

Number of cases= 771	Correlation coefficient
Occupational variable	-0.033
Marital status	-0.028
Age	0.089
Sex	-0.052
Plea	-0.066
Number of counts	0.100
Sex of victim	0.088
Relationship to victim	0.071
Type of victim	0.142
Severity of crime	0.201
Recency of previous conviction	0.050
Length of criminal record	0.231

posed and in no case did the contribution of any one variable exceed 6 per cent.

Turning to regression analysis, we sought to determine the combined predictive power of these variables. Regression equations were calculated for all offences (combined) and for each of the seven indictable offences concerned. The computer program selected the best combination of variables and weighted them to maximize their predictive power. The results indicated that in no case was the computer program able to develop an equation that could account for more than 23 per cent of the total variation in length of sentence imposed. Individual correlation coefficients of the resulting equations ranged from a low of 0.17 in cases of taking a motor vehicle without consent, to a high of 0.485 in cases of breaking and entering with an average correlation of approximately 0.3. On average, the facts of the cases account for 9 per cent of the variation in practice. This means that while these facts bear some relationship to the decisions of the court they do not account for very much of the total variation in sentencing practice. Using tests of significance one may be tempted to conclude that one has "explained" sentencing through an exhaustive analysis of the facts before the court. However, in using measures of association it must be concluded that this type of analysis gives only a partial and inadequate explanation of the processes involved. Let us compare the predictive and explanatory power of the black box model to that of the phenomenological model upon which the bulk of our research was based.

The Phenomenological Model

We have already seen that correlations between the facts of the cases as perceived and understood by the judge and their sentencing behaviour on the bench yielded correlation coefficients ranging from a low of 0.638 to a high of 0.834 with an average of 0.716. This means that about 50 per cent of the total variation in length of institutional sentence imposed could be accounted for by variations among magistrates in their perceptions of the facts of the cases. It can therefore be concluded that analysis based on "facts" as perceived and understood by judges is 5 or 6 times more powerful in the predictive sense than analysis based on "facts" as defined by the researcher himself. Of course, it may be expected that both classes of variables make an independent contribution to these decisions and that better prediction could be achieved by combining them. This was done and it was learned that, in most instances, the size of correlation coefficients were not significantly increased, while in a few a marginal improvement was achieved. From this it was concluded that once one knows how a magistrate defines the case before him, it becomes unnecessary to seek additional information about that case. In fact, it appears from the analysis that one can explain more about sentencing by knowing a few things about the judge than by knowing a great deal about the facts of the case. The next section will deal with this.

We have seen that while the attitudes of magistrates were closely associated with their sentencing behaviour, a significantly greater proportion of variation in sentencing could be explained by incorporating into the analysis the way in which magistrates define the operative constraints in their social environments. In this section a further element will be added: namely, the subtlety of thought processes in handling information. In doing so, the analysis draws together various elements of the over-all research design and a model of judicial behaviour begins to emerge.

Sixty-seven regression equations were calculated, each one attempting to predict the sentencing behaviour of some fifty magistrates.[4] The independent variables consisted of five attitude scores, ten perceived constraint scores and three cognitive-complexity scores.

We have already seen that there is a large measure of inter-correlations among these variables. Thus, the attitudes of magistrates were associated both with how they define the operative constraints in their social situations and with the subtlety of thought processes in sentencing.[5] This poses an interesting research problem once the analysis turns to the prediction of behaviour, as some of the variables may add little to the predictive power of an equation already incorporating other variables closely associated with them. Multiple regression analysis is particularly well suited to this type of problem, as it can determine the degree to which each variable makes an independent contribution to the prediction once the contribution of all other significant variables have been accounted for. In order to avoid capitalizing on chance, the computer was instructed not to include a variable if the statistical significance of its contribution to the equation was less than 0.01. However, once in an equation, a variable could stay as long as its contribution did not fall below 0.05.

The results indicated that the cognitive-complexity variables do make an independent contribution to prediction equations already including variables associated with the attitudes of magistrates and their definitions of the constraints in their social environments. Out of sixty-seven regression equations, the computer program selected one or more cognitive-complexity variables, fifty-three times. Moreover, the cognitive-complexity variables did not replace variables related to the attitudes and perceived constraints of magistrates. Thus, out of sixty-seven equations, the computer selected at least one variable from each of the three main types, forty-one times. This means that the attitudes of magistrates combine with their definitions of social constraints and with the subtlety of their thought processes to produce certain consequences in the form of sentencing decisions. The correlation coefficients for these equations range from a low of 0.55 to a high of 0.85, with an average correlation of approximately 0.7. About 50 per cent of the variation in sentencing behaviour could be accounted for by knowing nothing about the cases and relying solely on three pieces of information about the magistrate. The actual equations calculated are included in Technical Appendix 13. In Tables 106 and 107 the results of seven equations relating to the sentences given for all indictable offences (combined) and for the most frequently occurring single offence, theft, are presented in a non-statistical form.

TABLE 106

Regression of sentencing behaviour against perceived constraints,
attitudes and cognitive-complexity, all indictable cases (N = 50 magistrates)

Dependent variable	Step	Attitude (factor scores)	Perceived constraints	Cognitive-complexity	r
Independent variables					
Suspended sentence (with and without probation)	1	Lacks concern for justice			0.679
	2			Discriminates among information	0.782
	3	Tolerance of deviance			0.814
	4		Respects magistrates who lack concern for justice		0.829
	5			Expends effort in problem solving	0.841
Fine	1			Does not discriminate among information	0.577
	2		Respects magistrates not concerned for justice		0.660
	3	Does not feel punishment corrects			0.716
	4	Modernism			0.735
Institution	1			Uses less information	0.287
	2		Positive relationship with crown		0.386
	3		Considers community punitive		0.471
	4	Feels punishment corrects			0.598

TABLE 106 continued

		Independent variables			
Dependent variable	Step	Attitude (factor scores)	Perceived constraints	Cognitive-complexity	r
Average length of institutional sentence	1			Uses less information	0.515
	2	Concern for social defence			0.581
	3		Sees other magistrates as punitive		0.620
	4			Does not discriminate among information	0.646

The pattern which emerges from these tables, and indeed, from the other equations calculated, shows the rather interesting way in which the variables combine together to predict the sentencing behaviour of magistrates. While slightly different patterns emerge with respect to individual offences, there is a high level of over-all consistency in the findings. Certain broad conclusions may be drawn. They are summarized below.

Magistrates who rely heavily on probation tend to be tolerant of social deviance, to attach little weight to justice or social defence, and to feel that punishment corrects. At the same time, they tend to have positive relationships with probation officers and negative relationships with crown attorneys, they see the law as flexible and tend to respect magistrates concerned about justice. In addition, these magistrates tend to discriminate better among information and expend greater effort in problem solving.

Magistrates relying on suspended sentence without probation tend to be tolerant of social deviance, lack concern for justice and social defence, and, most interestingly, do not feel that punishment corrects. They tend to feel that public opinion supports a lenient sentencing policy, although they define public opinion as being unimportant in their decisions. They do not have positive relationships with probation officers or with crown attorneys and they tend to respect magistrates who lack concern for social defence. In terms of cognitive-complexity, magistrates who rely heavily on suspended sentence tend to discriminate well among

TABLE 107

Regression of sentencing behaviour against perceived constraints,
attitudes, and cognitive-complexity, theft (N = 50 magistrates)

		Independent variables			
Dependent variable	Step	Attitude (factor scores)	Perceived constraints	Cognitive-complexity	r
Suspended sentence (with and without probation)	1			Discriminates among information	0.464
	2		Respects magistrates concerned for justice		0.616
	3	Feels punishment corrects			0.690
	4		Respects traditional magistrates		0.723
Fine	1			Does not discriminate among information	0.497
	2		Respects magistrates who lack concern for justice		0.569
	3	Does not feel punishment corrects			0.633
	4	Modernism			0.684
	5			Expends effort in problem solving	0.730
Institution	1			Uses less information	0.431
	2	Lacks concern for justice			0.596
	3			Does not discriminate among information	0.643
	4	Concern for social defence			0.673
	5	Feels punishment corrects			0.698
	6	Traditionalism			0.722

information, but generally use less information in sentencing and do not expend as much effort in problem solving.

Magistrates who rely heavily on fines tend to be rather modern in outlook and do not feel that punishment corrects. They are likely to have positive relationships with crown attorneys, to conform to other magistrates, and to respect magistrates who are both tolerant of social deviance and lack concern for justice.

Magistrates who rely heavily on institutional measures tend to feel that punishment corrects offenders, are concerned for justice and for social defence, and are rather traditional in outlook. They tend to have positive relationships with crown attorneys, they feel the community supports a punitive sentencing policy and they believe that their own sentencing practice is different from that of other magistrates. With respect to cognitive-complexity, these magistrates tend to use less information in problem solving, do not discriminate so well among information, and expend less effort in problem solving.

Slightly different patterns emerge with respect to individual offences. It appears that with respect to relatively minor offences, magistrates who are rather severe in their sentencing behaviour tend to minimize the concept of justice and maximize the concept of punishment corrects. Moreover, there is a tendency for magistrates who use sentences which depart from the normal sentence given for a particular offence to be rather more discriminative in the use of information and to expend more effort in problem solving.

One begins to get a picture of the decision-process in sentencing. Magistrates have attitudes which predispose them to respond in particular ways to certain types of crime. However, their actual responses will depend, in part, on how they define the operative social and legal constraints in the situation and, in part, on their capacity to use information in subtle and complex ways. Their attitudes, their definitions of the situation and the complexity of their thought processes all affect the way in which they interpret information in the process of judgement. The data demonstrate in a variety of ways that magistrates interpret cases, the law, and the expectations of others in ways which minimize inconsistency. Through selective interpretation of the world and their relationship to it, magistrates protect themselves from acknowledging the harsh realities that there are fundamental contradictions in the criminal justice system and that it is frequently impossible for them to resolve them.

So it would appear from these analyses that one cannot understand sentencing without examining the particular ways in which magistrates respond to their social environments. Essentially it is an environment of facts, laws, ideas, and people. Since selective interpretation was shown to be such a central feature of judicial thinking in sentencing, it becomes necessary to know how each judge defines his environment for himself.

Sentencing is not a rational, mechanical process. It is a human process and is subject to all the frailties of the human mind. Hence, the title of this book.

NOTES TO CHAPTER 20

1 G. Murphy, *Personality* (New York, 1947), 498; Rosenberg defines self as: "simply an attitude or a cluster of attitudes towards an object": H. Rosenberg, "Psychological Selectivity in Self-Esteem Formation," in M. Sherif, ed., *Attitude, Ego-Involvement and Change* (New York, 1967), 27; see also R. Wylie, *The Self Concept* (Lincoln, 1961); A. Rose, *Human Behavior and Social Processes - an Interactionist Approach* (New York, 1961); G. Mead, *Mind, Self and Society* (Chicago, 1934); J. Campbell, "Studies in Attitude Formation," in Sherif, ed., *Attitude, Ego-Involvement and Change*, 18-9.

2 E. Green, *Judicial Attitudes in Sentencing* (London, 1961).

3 R. Hood, *Sentencing in Magistrates' Courts* (London, 1962).

4 All magistrates who completed at least 40 sentencing study sheets were included.

5 These findings are to be found in Chapters 8, 9, and 18.

21

Summary of Principal Findings

Introduction

In order to provide the reader with an overview of the main findings which emerged from the analysis, a list of some of the principal findings are included below. The reader is warned, however, that a summary of findings cannot do justice to the complexities of the problems dealt with. It is for this reason that he is strongly advised to use the summary only as a guide to the material contained in previous chapters.

The Jurisdiction and Sentencing Power of Magistrates

The magistrates' court in Canada has a broader jurisdiction to try cases, and wider sentencing powers, than that given to any other lower court exercising criminal jurisdiction in the world. Over ninety-four per cent of indictable cases are dealt with by magistrates. Sentencing powers given to magistrates are unusually broad. Wide discretionary powers in sentencing are provided by the Criminal Code. Maximum penalties are very high, leaving more scope in matters of sentence than is actually used. Depending upon the maximum penalty provided by the Code for a particular offence, a magistrate sitting alone may: sentence to life imprisonment, commit to preventive detention, impose whipping, order forfeiture, fine any amount. In short, he may impose any penalty except death. No lower court judge sitting alone in any other country is given this power.

Imprisonment is used more frequently by Canadian courts than equivalent courts in most other countries. Canada appears to have one of the highest rates of imprisonment in the world. While traditionally there has been a heavy reliance on imprisonment as a penalty in this country, the trend is away from the use of this type of measure. Fines are being used more frequently, particularly for less serious offences which previously resulted in short-term institutional sentences.

Wide variation in sentencing practice appears to exist between courts in different provinces and between courts within particular provinces. In 1964, courts in Ontario varied in using probation, from one court using this form of disposition in nearly half the cases coming before it, to another never having used it. Similarly, use of suspended sentences without probation ranged from 0 to 34 per cent, fines from 2 to 39 per cent, short-term gaol sentences from 4 to 60 per cent, reformatory sentences from 1 to 37 per cent, and long-term penitentiary sentences from 0 to 32 per cent. On their face, these differences appear to be too large to be explained solely in terms of differences in the type of cases appearing before the courts in different areas. Apparent inconsistency was the first "fact" about sentencing in Ontario that this study attempted to explain.

Background Characteristics of Magistrates

For the most part, magistrates come from stable, successful protestant families. More than half come from business or professional families and most of the rest have fathers who were skilled wage earners. There was only one whose father was in the unskilled wage-earner category. Over-representation in the professional category becomes even more pronounced in the magistrates' generation. Thus, over one-half of the brothers and brothers-in-law of magistrates are professional people, compared to slightly more than one-twentieth of the total labour force. Together with the business category, over three-quarters of the family contemporaries are in the top fifteen per cent of the labour force. Not one of these family members was in the unskilled wage-earner category, and only 14 per cent were in the skilled wage-earner category, compared to 24 per cent and 34 per cent in these respective categories in the general population. A pattern of rapid upward mobility among family members of magistrates was evident.

Magistrates range in age from thirty-four to seventy-one with a mean age of fifty-five. They are considerably younger than judges of superior, district, and county courts, and somewhat younger than English magistrates. Nearly all magistrates were born in Canada and spent all of their adult lives (apart from school) in the local community where they reside at present. Most have strong contacts with the local community through memberships in clubs and organizations of various kinds.

Over 75 per cent of magistrates in Ontario are protestant. Compared to the general population, Anglican, United Church, and Presbyterian backgrounds are all over-represented by magistrates while "other" protestants and Roman Catholics are greatly under-represented. Roman Catholics comprise over 30 per cent of the general population but only 12 per cent of magistrates are of the Catholic faith. Out of a sample of 71 magistrates, 56, or approximately 70 per cent, were lawyers. Of the 15 lay magistrates, 9 were previously employed as justices of the peace or clerks of the court, and one was a former police chief. This means that many "lay" magistrates came to the bench with a certain amount of technical knowledge of the rules of procedure in criminal courts.

Marital stability is a striking feature of magistrates as a group. All but six were married, and of the remainder 5 were widowers and only 1 was in each of the divorced or single categories.

Dealing with past work experience, all legally-trained magistrates had at least ten years' practice at the Bar prior to appointment. Of these, forty-nine, approximately 87 per cent, acted as defence counsel, while eight (13 per cent) were full-time attorneys for most of their prior legal experience. However, among forty-six magistrates with some experience as defence counsel, only eight devoted 20 per cent or more of their practice to this type of work. Like most lawyers in Ontario, these magistrates earned the greater part of their income from the civil side of their law practices.

A significant group of magistrates had military experience. Most of them ended their military careers as either commissioned or non-commissioned officers.

A pattern of occupational stability in the employment record of magistrates was evident. The majority of magistrates did not change jobs frequently, forty-three holding one or two previous jobs, and only eleven holding four or more.

Appointments to the bench in Canada are "political," in the sense that most appointments are made from supporters of the party in power. Since the Conservative Party has been in power in Ontario for more than twenty-five years, most magistrates are, or were, Conservative Party supporters.

Magistrates range in length of judicial experience from one to thirty-six years, with a mean of approximately fourteen years. Very few magistrates move on to higher judicial appointments.

In summary, a study of the background characteristics of magistrates revealed a pattern of stability and success in family, economic, and community life.

Penal Philosophy

Penal philosophy was studied as a strategy for making decisions. Interviews probed the priorities, strategies, and rules of thumb applied consciously by magistrates in dealing with cases.

As far as the classical doctrines of sentencing are concerned, nearly all magistrates believe that it is their role to prevent crime through sentencing. They differ widely, however, in the ways in which this purpose should be achieved. Magistrates as a group tend to rate reformation highest, followed by general deterrence, individual deterrence, incapacitation, and punishment in that order. Few magistrates would rule out any of the classical purposes in sentencing, but it was evident that they varied widely in the relative merits attached to each. Marked inconsistency in the principles of sentencing among magistrates was revealed. The majority of magistrates believe in the efficacy of the penal measures they apply, but considerable disagreement exists among them as to the relative effectiveness of particular measures. They also differed in the criteria applied in deciding between different kinds of sentences, the way in which conflict between the offender's needs and community protection is resolved, the amount of informational support they have for their views, and the kind of situations in which they experience difficulty in sentencing.

It did appear, however, that the differences among magistrates were not random, but followed certain patterns due primarily to the weights attached to the various doctrines of sentencing. While it appeared that there were wide variations in penal philosophy among magistrates, it was also evident that individual magistrates had a fairly consistent and coherent set of beliefs bearing on their penal philosophies. While magistrates were inconsistent with each other, they were consistent within themselves.

Interviews revealed the relative simplicity of the purpose, concepts, and beliefs of those who espoused a deterrent or retributive penal philosophy. Reformation-oriented magistrates, on the other hand, appeared to be much more involved in the sentencing process, and find it to be a more complex and demanding task. There was a considerable amount of internal consistency in the thinking of magistrates. Once one knew the social purpose that a magistrate attempted to achieve through sentencing, the whole of the penal philosophy unfolded as a logical extension of it.

Judicial Attitudes

Judicial attitudes in sentencing were defined as a set of evaluative categories used by magistrates in assessing crime and in determining the appropriate judicial response to it. Two sets of attitude scales were developed, one based upon Likert procedures and the other on factor analysis. Both scales consisted of statements concerning crime, sentencing, and related issues with which magistrates and others were asked to agree or disagree. Considerable effort was made to determine the reliability and validity of the two procedures. Both had reliability coefficients well in excess of minimum requirements for research purposes, and in most instances approached the requirements of tests used for individual diagnostic work. As far as validity is concerned, both procedures produced scales that were able to distinguish adequately between different population groups tested. It seemed, therefore, that reliable and valid results could be achieved from both scale construction procedures. However, a major weakness in Likert procedures was revealed. In developing scales through Likert procedures it was assumed that they would measure different things. However, inter-correlations between different scales were found to be very high. Moreover, there was a striking similarity on each scale in the way in which the mean scores for each population group tested were ordered. This meant that it was possible through item analysis to develop reliable and valid scales, at least in terms of agreed criteria. At the same time it seemed that instead of having a number of different scales, the procedure ended up with one scale in several broadly equivalent forms. For this reason Likert scales were abandoned at this stage, and all further attitude work was based on scales derived through factor analysis. These were not only easier to interpret, but were clearly independent of one another.

Five factorially-derived scales were constructed. The first factor was labelled "justice." It related to the concept of "just deserts." Items with high factor loadings on this scale were offence- rather than offender-oriented. These items were usually not related to hatred of offenders or desire for vengeance, but to a concern that crime be punished in proportion to its severity.

The second factor was labelled "punishment corrects." This factor was associated with the notion that offenders deserve and need punishment, in order to prevent them from committing further crime. It represented a desire to stop crime at almost any cost to the offender, including, if necessary, capital punishment. This factor was distinguishable from the first in that punishment was directed more to the offender than to the offence.

The third factor was labelled "intolerance." Items with high factoral loadings did not relate specifically to crime but rather to other forms of social deviance. Concepts of "evil," "morality," and "sin" were found among items with high factoral loadings.

The fourth factor was labelled "social defence." Most of the items with high factoral loadings appeared to be related to the concept of general deterrence. These items were associated with the view that crime poses a threat to the social order and that potential offenders should be intimidated from committing crimes by the threat of punishment. It was distinguishable from factors 1 and 2 in that punishment was directed primarily to potential offenders in the community at large.

The last factor was labelled "modernism." It appeared that this factor measured differences among individuals in the degree to which they identify with what is commonly known as "new-world puritanism." People holding these values tend to look upon failure through alcoholism, crime or any other cause, as being "sinful." At the opposite end of the continuum were values associated with the modern welfare state.

Samples of persons drawn from five population groups were selected. They included magistrates, law students, social work students, police officers, and probation officers. Probation officers were divided further into those with and those without university degrees, making a total of six criterion groups.

On the justice scale, police officers had the highest mean score. Law students came next and then came a big drop to magistrates, social work students, and finally probation officers. On the punishment corrects scale, magistrates scored the highest. Police officers came second and then there was a substantial drop to probation officers without degrees, law students, and probation officers with degrees. Social work students had by far the lowest mean score. More than any other group, magistrates were shown to believe that punishment is "good for offenders." This notion seems to make it possible for them to resolve the contradictory demands made on them in sentencing as it enables them to believe that they can punish and treat offenders at the same time.

The intolerance scale was anchored at either end by police officers (the most intolerant) and law students (the most tolerant). After police officers came probation officers without degrees, magistrates, probation officers with degrees, and social work students.

Magistrates scored highest on the social defence scale, as one might expect. It was somewhat surprising to see the relatively low mean score for police officers on this scale, which suggested that their underlying attitudes relate to more deeply seated feelings of "justice" and intolerance of deviance. Law students had a fairly high mean score, as did social work students. This probably reflects the view of students in general that the courts should, and can be, instruments of social control.

On the modernism scale, social work students had the highest score, and probation officers without degrees had the lowest. Interestingly enough, magistrates had the second lowest score. Police officers and law students occupied middle positions. It seems that both probation officers without degrees and magistrates uphold the traditional values of hard work and self-discipline.

Returning to magistrates, the most interesting configuration of attitudes was revealed by plotting the mean scores of each criterion group on a graph measuring punishment corrects against social defence. Here we saw magistrates clearly isolated from all other groups. On both these scales they occupied relatively extreme positions which were diametrically opposite to those of probation officers with and without degrees. Armed with a philosophy which emphasized both protection of the community and the correction of offenders through punishment, magistrates are in a position to impose rather severe penalties without any sense of guilt about sacrificing the offender for the good of the community. The way in which the demands of one's occupational role affect one's attitudes was thus revealed.

Data were obtained about the sentencing behaviour of all Ontario magistrates during the years 1966 and 1967. These data included the frequency with which sentences of different kinds were given by individual magistrates for each Criminal Code offence, as well as the lengths or amounts of such sentences.

Scores on the justice scale were significantly associated with most of the behavioural measures used. Dealing with indictable cases in general, concern for justice was associated with: the less frequent use of probation, the more frequent use of fines and institutions, longer sentences to institutions, and a preference for penitentiary and gaol sentences as opposed to reformatory sentences. In general terms, high justice scores were found to be associated with relatively severe sentencing behaviour. Different patterns emerged when one considered specific offences. For offences of a severe nature, such as offences against property with violence and offences against the person, concern for justice was positively associated with the frequent use of institutional sentences. In contrast, with respect to minor offences such as theft, concern for justice was associated with a low rate of imprisonment. It seemed from this that the concern for justice not only demands that crime be punished,but also ensures that the punishment given is only as severe as the offence itself warrants.

High punishment corrects scores were associated with a greater use of reformatory sentences, and the avoidance of both ordinary gaol sentences and penitentiary sentences. There appears to be a relationship between the view that punishment is "good for offenders" and the selection of institutional sentences that can provide education, training, self-discipline, and work. Magistrates with high scores in this scale tend not only to use reformatory-type institutional sentences but also to give longer sentences to these institutions. Sentences given by magistrates with high scores in this scale would probably be considered unfair by those with high scores on the justice scale.

Concern for social defence was associated with the use of long-term imprisonment. Magistrates with high scores on this scale appear in general to prefer penitentiary sentences, as opposed to reformatory or gaol sentences. Dealing with specific offences, it was shown that magistrates with high social defence scores use suspended sentences, fines, and institutions more frequently than probation for minor offences against property. On the other hand, fines were used less frequently for serious offences against property and for offences against the person. It appears that the social defence scale measures the degree to which magistrates are willing to sacrifice the interest of the offender for the sake of community protection.

High modernism scores were associated with a greater use of fines and the use of longer terms of reformatory sentences when institutional sentences were used. This scale seems to measure differences among magistrates with respect to the degree to which they identify with a "progressive" correctional policy.

This is a policy which encourages fines for minor offences, the use of reformatory-type sentences of substantial length when institutional dispositions are used, and the restriction of probation to cases where it may be expected to be effective.

Relationships between scores on the intolerance scale and sentencing behaviour were somewhat puzzling. Magistrates with high scores on this scale used suspended sentences more frequently than did those with low scores for serious offences such as breaking and entering, and institutions more frequently for minor offences such as causing a disturbance. The explanation offered was that magistrates with high intolerance scores tend to be less discriminative and more rigid in dealing with offences.

The most interesting finding which emerged from this analysis was an apparent relationship between "punitive" behaviour and "modern" thinking. One could not describe either the attitudes or the behaviour of magistrates in terms of a simple punitive, non-punitive dimension. The relationship between attitudes and judicial behaviour was found to be a complex one. Depending on the offence, severe sentencing practice, characterized by lengthy institutional sentences, could be associated with high scores on any of the scales. It is particularly interesting to note that magistrates with high scores on the justice scale used less severe sentencing in relatively minor cases than did those with high scores on either the modernism or punishment corrects scales. In practical terms, a person who has committed a fairly minor offence should consider himself fortunate to come before a magistrate concerned with "justice" rather than one concerned with either his "correction" through punishment or with being "modern."

With use of multiple regression methods it was possible to demonstrate that the sentencing behaviour of magistrates (for every offence considered) was significantly associated with their attitudes. In all sixty-seven different measures of sentencing behaviour used there was found to be a statistical relationship between the attitudes and behaviour. This was strong enough to exclude the possibility that this relationship could have occurred solely by chance to less than one in a thousand. Many different combinations of attitude scores were associated with the behaviour of magistrates, depending upon the type of case considered.

The fact that variation in sentencing behaviour was found to be associated with variation in the attitudes of the magistrates concerned indicates that the judicial process is not as uniform and impartial as many people would hope it would be. Indeed, it would appear that justice is a very personal thing.

Legal and Social Constraints on Sentencing

Analyses were conducted to determine the degree to which the legal and social framework within which sentencing takes place imposes constraints or otherwise influences the discretion of the court.

As far as the law is concerned, the data presented led to the conclusion that the law expressed in legislation and reported cases offers little guidance to or control over magistrates' behaviour.

Those magistrates who found the law restrictive resorted to a number of devices which enabled them to achieve their objectives in sentencing without fear of criticism or judicial review. There was a tendency for magistrates to interpret the demands made of them by the law in ways which minimized discrepancy between those demands and their personal values. Punitive magistrates interpreted the law as demanding punitive behaviour and non-punitive magistrates did the opposite. But this is not to say that the law exercises no control over the behaviour of magistrates on the bench. It was suggested that experience on the bench has an important influence in the development of standards, values and sentiments associated with the law and the professional role of the judge. To the extent that magistrates adopt them, they form part of his personal penal philosophy and attitudes. The general conclusion drawn was that the socializing and educative influence of legal experience was far more important in controlling judicial behaviour than were the formal rules laid down by parliament and the appeal courts.

As far as social constraints on sentencing are concerned, analyses were conducted to determine the degree to which magistrates are influenced by other people in their environment whom they define as "significant" including: their colleagues, probation officers, crown attorneys, the Department of the Attorney-General, and the public at large. Two sets of questions were asked concerning each constraining influence. The first set of questions asked magistrates to indicate what they felt other people expected of them in sentencing. The second set of questions concerned the degree to which the magistrates felt obliged to take these expectations into account.

It was found that the operative constraints in the social world of magistrates were both punitive and non-punitive in nature. The degree to which they actually influence sentencing seemed to depend not so much on the existence of such constraints, but rather on how magistrates define them. Non-punitive magistrates tend to view the social influences in their environment as being supportive of a non-punitive sentencing policy. The reverse was true for punitive magistrates and this held true for each area examined. It appeared that magistrates selectively define the expectations of others in ways that maximize concordance with their private beliefs. The only qualification to the general pattern which emerged was that punitive magistrates appeared to be somewhat more socially isolated and were more likely to deny the influences of others in their sentencing behaviour.

Certain analyses were done on the impact of perceived sociolegal constraints on sentencing. Thirteen variables were created out of interviews with magistrates, measuring how they define the expectations of others. Simple correlational analysis yielded very low or non-significant relationships between sentencing behaviour and perceived constraints. These variables were then included in a series of multiple regression equations which regressed both attitudinal and perceived constraint variables against the sentencing behaviour of the magistrates concerned. The results indicated that statistically significant relationships between attitudes and perceived constraints on the one hand, and sentencing behaviour on the other, were achieved in nearly all cases. Correlations ranged from a low of 0.33 to a high of 0.74 with a mean correlation of approximately 0.6. In 63 out of 67 equations, the computer selected one or more perceived constraint variables in addition to certain attitudinal variables. It appeared from this that constraints operating in the social world of magistrates assumed significance in both a statistical and theoretical sense only when the attitudes of magistrates had been accounted for. From this it was concluded that the operative constraints of the social world of a magistrate, as perceived and defined by him, while closely related to his attitudes, do make an independent contribution to sentencing behaviour. The degree to which a magistrate will allow his personal attitudes to find expression in his behaviour depends, in part, on how he defines the expectations of the law and of "significant others" in his social environment. This means that whilst attitudes of magistrates act as filters through which the world is perceived selectively, these filters can only partially screen out what is objectionable in that world. Certain reality aspects of the social environment of a magistrate do penetrate his consciousness, resulting in a modification of his behaviour on the bench.

The Relationship of Social Characteristics to Attitudes and Beliefs

Analyses were carried out to determine the relationship of the attitudes and beliefs of magistrates, as well as of their sentencing behaviour, to their social background characteristics.

There were no statistically significant relationships between the ages of magistrates and their scores on any of the attitude or penal philosophy scales. There were, however, a number of significant relationships between specific beliefs and age. The general picture which emerged was one of a relationship between greater age and a feeling of independence, self-reliance, and moderation in attitudes and beliefs.

A professional family background was found to be associated with being treatment-oriented in attitudes and beliefs. Magistrates from working-class backgrounds appeared rather more punitive in their views, a finding which is in accordance with those reported in a number of studies.

The number of years a magistrate spent at school was not found to be associated with his attitudes or beliefs. However, there were a number of significant relationships between the type of educational experience and these factors. Most of these differences showed up between legally-trained and lay magistrates. Legally-trained magistrates tend to be less punitive in their outlook. They also show a greater degree of sophistication and subtlety in the way in which they assess crime, taking more factors into consideration. It was particularly interesting to note that lay magistrates appeared more "legalistic" in their approach to sentencing. In contrast, legally-trained magistrates were found to interpret the law more flexibly, responding more to what they believed to be a true meaning and spirit. A factor of personal confidence also distinguished between lay and legally-trained magistrates. Lay magistrates were less willing to allow others to participate in the decision-process, and expressed greater concern about the possibility of political interference in their work. They tended to have a somewhat more hostile view towards "outsiders." Taken together, these data suggested that legal training yields a more creative and flexible approach to the law, a somewhat more offender-oriented penal philosophy, and a great deal more confidence in self. These findings give empirical support to the view that legal training should be a pre-requisite to an appointment to the bench.

There are a number of significant differences in the attitudes and beliefs of magistrates of different religious denominations.

As a group, Roman Catholic magistrates had lower justice scores than magistrates of other faiths. At the same time most of these magistrates had higher intolerance scores. Among the protestant magistrates, those of the United Church and Presbyterian faiths usually tended to have higher justice and lower intolerance scores. Most Anglican magistrates occupied middle positions on the scales.

The type of work experience that magistrates had prior to their appointment was closely associated with their attitudes and beliefs. Magistrates who were employed as crown attorneys, clerks of the court, or justices of the peace tended to be more offence-oriented in their attitudes and somewhat more punitive in their behaviour. Magistrates who acted as defence counsel tended to be more offender-oriented than those who acted primarily for the Crown. But the longer the individual spent at either type of work the more likely he was to have a punitive approach to sentencing.

Length of experience on the bench appeared to be associated with a more moderate and coherent penal philosophy. Moreover, length of judicial experience on the bench was associated with the degree of confidence a magistrate had in his ability to discharge his sentencing responsibilities and a greater feeling of independence from political or social pressures.

The work-load of a magistrate was found to have a direct influence on the way he makes decisions. The greater his workload, the more likely was the magistrate to have negative attitudes toward both his colleagues and other professional people with whom he comes in contact. Busy magistrates tend to use fines in Criminal Code cases more frequently. They tend to have a more restrictive policy with the use of probation and they operate with a larger number of presumptions, or rules of thumb, which control the exercise of discretion. Significantly, these presumptions were found to be in favour of imprisonment rather than community-based treatment. A heavy work-load was reflected in both a rigid, expedient penal philosophy and in punitive behaviour

In their attitudes and beliefs, magistrates were found to reflect the types of communities in which they lived. Those with high justice scores were more likely to be found in communities that were characterized by a high degree of urbanization, a high crime rate, and a highly mixed ethnic composition. Magistrates who believe that punishment corrects were found to come from prosperous, high growth-rate communities with a predominantly British population and a low crime rate. Magistrates with high intolerance scores were more likely to come from rural, stable French-speaking communities with a high crime rate. High social defence scores were found among the magistrates in urban, high crime-rate environments. Magistrates identifying with the so-called "modern" doctrines tended to come from communities that consist of a large population of British and a small proportion of French people. These communities were also rather stable in terms of growth-rate, and the crime rate was not particularly high. Further evidence was thereby found to support the view that judicial attitudes are not isolated from external influences.

The most important demographic characteristic which distinguished magistrates in terms of attitudes and beliefs was the degree of urbanization of the community in which they lived. On the whole, urban magistrates were considerably more punitive in their approach to sentencing than were rural and small town magistrates. This held true not only for their attitudes, as expressed in scores on scales, but also in responses to questions asked in interviews and in their behaviour on the bench. However, a significant minority of urban magistrates were relatively non-punitive and treatment-oriented in their approach. It was found that nearly all of these were active in the Ontario Magistrates' Association. These magistrates also attended more conferences and seminars about sentencing, did more reading, and visited more institutions than did their colleagues. It appeared from this that while the basic influences in an urban environment may be those which tend to encourage the development of punitive attitudes and behaviour, magistrates can, if they have the motivation to do so, insulate themselves from these influences through reading and through social interaction with like-minded persons.

Profiles of the attitudes and beliefs of magistrates were drawn, dividing them into groups based on age, education, and urban-rural differences. Magistrates were divided into two groups consisting of those from large urban centres and those from small towns in rural communities. These two groups were then divided further in terms of age, those under fifty-five and those fifty-five and over. Finally, they were divided again, this time in terms of the median number of years in school. The scheme of classification created eight groups of magistrates. An examination of the attitudes and beliefs of these eight groups yielded a number of surprising findings. The most punitive groups, represented by high general deterrence and low reformation scores on the penal philosophy scales, and high justice and social defence scores on the attitude scales, were found to be young, well-educated urban magistrates. The least punitive group were young, well-educated rural magistrates. Age and education appeared to operate in opposite directions in urban and rural communities. The explanation offered was that the position of magistrate was likely to attract quite different people in the two types of community and that the selective process would be particularly pronounced among young, well-educated lawyers. Moreover, it was felt that it would be the young, well-educated magistrate who would feel greater pressure to change his attitudes and beliefs to coincide with the demands of the situation. It was, therefore, suggested that the processes of socialization and change operate in different directions in urban and rural areas, and that these processes are likely to have a greater impact on younger, well-educated magistrates.

The Search for Information

Six chapters deal with how magistrates use information in sentencing. One chapter is concerned with the strategies they employ consciously in the search for information. Another deals with the pre-sentence report as a medium of communication, followed by chapters analysing the mental processes involved in coming to sentencing decisions.

First of all we identified the categories of information that magistrates considered "relevant" to the problems in sentencing as they defined them. With respect to information about the offender, the majority of magistrates considered family background, criminal record and employment record as "essential." There was little agreement among magistrates concerning other areas of the offender's life. The identification of relevant information was closely associated with the attitudes of the magistrates concerned. Each magistrate seemed to establish his own criteria for assessing the relevance of, and the weight to attach to, different types of information concerning the background of the offender. Concerning the offence, it was evident that most magistrates considered "moral quality" of the criminal act to be more important than the actual harm incurred by the victim.

Magistrates were asked to rate the following in order of importance: information concerning the offender, the criminal record, and the offence. Two out of three magistrates rated the nature and circumstances of the offence above both the criminal record and the background and history of the offender. There was a fair degree of agreement among magistrates about the pre-eminence of the offence in determining sentence, and this was so even for magistrates who espoused a treatment or reformative penal philosophy.

Magistrates who rated the offence higher, however, tended to have higher justice scores on the attitude scales and higher general and individual deterrence scores, but lower reformation scores, on the penal philosophy scales. In contrast, those who rated the background of the offender higher had higher reformation scores on the penal philosophy scales, and lower justice and social defence scores on the attitude scales. It was concluded, therefore, that the identification of "essential" information and the relative weights attached to different categories of information are, to a large extent, consistent with the penal philosophies and attitudes of the magistrates concerned.

Certain analyses were carried out to determine the degree of discrimination within categories of information made by magistrates. If a magistrate seeks answers to a larger number of questions about a particular aspect of a case, it can be expected that he attaches greater importance to it. It was found that magistrates primarily concerned about reformation make more discriminations concerning the offender and fewer concerning the offence. The reverse was true for magistrates primarily concerned about deterrence and social defence. It appeared, therefore, that the amount and kind of information brought to bear on sentencing problems depends, at least in part, on the purpose to which it will be put. There was no evidence in the data to suggest that magistrates with "punitive" attitudes and beliefs were inherently less subtle in their thought processes. Rather, it appeared that the style of information-use was the one most suited to the objectives of the magistrates concerned.

Magistrates were asked several questions concerning the reasons for requesting pre-sentence and psychiatric reports. The results indicated that, regardless of penal philosophy, most magistrates (65 out of 71) will ask for reports from probation officers when considering the possibility of probation. Significant differences existed, however, among magistrates who use reports for other purposes. Magistrates who use pre-sentence reports when considering institutional sentences were found to have higher than average reformation, and lower than average general deterrence scores on the penal philosophy scales. At the same time they had higher than average punishment corrects and lower than average social defence scores on the attitude scales. A similar pattern emerged with respect to the psychiatric reports.

The data suggested that magistrates who are concerned about the treatment of offenders were more active in their search for information than were those concerned to punish crime for deterrent or retributive purposes. But in each case, the type of information sought after, the amount used, and the way in which it was assessed, appeared to depend on the highly individual way each particular magistrate defined his objectives in sentencing.

Certain insights were obtained from the criticisms expressed by magistrates concerning the pre-sentence report. Two out of three expressed general satisfaction with reports. Those who found fault expressed unhappiness with the length and technical language of the report. Some also expressed reservations about emphasis in the report on the background and history of the offender, as opposed to the offence. Magistrates expressing negative attitudes toward the report tended to have negative attitudes towards its underlying rationale, namely the individualization of justice and the treatment of offenders.

Analyses of the actual information-seeking behaviour of magistrates on the bench were then conducted. The general pattern which emerged was that pre-sentence reports were usually requested in more serious types of cases.

The relationship between the pre-sentence report and the choice of sentence selected was interesting. It appeared that while, in general, the use of pre-sentence reports was associated with a tendency to select institutional sentences, different patterns emerged with respect to individual offences. With respect to serious cases such as robbery, and breaking and entering, use of the pre-sentence report was associated with the more frequent selection of non-institutional sentences. In contrast, with respect to relatively minor offences such as dangerous driving, the use of the pre-sentence report was associated with a greater proportion of committals to penal institutions. It appeared from this that pre-sentence reports were requested in cases for which magistrates were considering sentences that are not normally or usually given for that type of offence. It could not be said that the use of pre-sentence reports were associated with lenient sentencing practices.

The use of pre-sentence reports was also associated with the differences in the lengths of institutional sentences given. Data once again showed that the pre-sentence report did not necessarily lead to lenient sentencing practice. Rather, it appeared that magistrates in Ontario use these reports in difficult cases. Where the offences themselves usually led to long terms of institutional sentence, the pre-sentence report was associated with shorter sentences. In contrast, where the offences usually warranted short sentences the use of the pre-sentence report was associated with longer sentences. It appeared from this that the use of pre-sentence reports was associated with a shift away from sentencing based solely on the offence.

Dealing with the number of information sources used, wide variation among magistrates was evident. The average number of different information sources used by magistrates was 2.7. Individual magistrates varied the number of sources of information used habitually from a low of 1.5 for one magistrate to a high of 3.7 for another. It was discovered that this variation was closely associated with variation in the penal philosophy and attitude scores of the magistrate concerned. In each case, the number of sources of information used and the type of information relied upon was consistent with the personal values and subjective goals of the particular magistrate. It appeared that the selective use of information in sentencing enabled magistrates to maintain their original attitudes intact. Magistrates tended to seek information consistent with their preconceptions (which are the essence of their attitudes). At the same time, they tended to avoid information which was likely to present a picture of the offender that was in conflict with their expectations. The evaluative nature of judicial attitudes was thus revealed.

The Communication of Information

The pre-sentence report was studied as a medium of communication between the probation officer (the communicator) and the magistrate (the recipient) about a third person (the offender). A number of experiments were designed in which magistrates and probation officers, in a sample of actual cases appearing before the courts, provided identical information to the research team concerning various aspects of the offender's background and his chances of rehabilitation. If the communication process was effective, it could be expected that the magistrate would change his perception of the offender after having read the report. The results indicated that the pre-sentence report was not associated with greater agreement between probation officers and magistrates concerning any of the areas examined. In fact it appeared that in some areas of the offender's life the use of the pre-sentence report was associated with less agreement between the probation officer and the magistrate. However, when one examined the interaction between the use of the report and the type of community in which the probation officer and magistrate lived, a number of contrasting trends emerged. As a rule, rural and small town magistrates tended to be closer to probation officers in the perception of the offender and the possibilities of treatment if they had read a pre-sentence report. But, where the presentence reports were requested in urban areas, magistrates and probation officers tended to be further away from each other, both in their perception of the offender and in their assessments of treatment possibilities. These data tended to reject the hypothesis that a pre-sentence report will lead a magistrate to come closer to the probation officer's view of the case.

Evidence from other parts of the study was used to interpret these apparently odd results. Differences in the work-loads of urban and rural magistrates, in the nature of relationships between probation officers and magistrates, in the attitudes of the two groups of magistrates toward the rationale of the report, as well as differences in the actual mechanisms of reading and evaluating them, were all associated with differences in the impact of the report on the magistrates' perceptions of the cases. These factors led to the conclusion that, if the pre-sentence report was to have the impact on sentencing that was originally intended, and indeed often assumed, certain favourable conditions for its proper use must exist. Magistrates must have the time to read reports carefully. They must also have the opportunity, when the need arises, to discuss their contents informally with probation officers. Most importantly, they must have a set of attitudes and beliefs which are consistent with the rationale underlying the report.

The Assessment of Information

Data were presented which showed the ways in which magistrates interpret information in the process of judgement. These data showed the number, kind, and organization of dimensions employed by magistrates in perception and evaluation of the "facts" upon which the decisions are based. The data came from the sentencing study sheet, a document completed by the magistrate at the time of disposition. The results showed that, while there was a high level of agreement among magistrates concerning the severity of the crime, there was considerable disagreement among them in their perception of the offender and in the possibilities for treatment. Magistrates tended to interpret information in these areas in a way consistent with their personal attitudes. Selective interpretation of data was evident, and these mechanisms appeared to operate in the direction of resolving conflicts which may arise between the facts of the case and what the magistrate would like to do by way of sentence. The magistrates holding strong views about the necessity of deterrence and punishment did not see offenders as having serious problems in their family or personal lives. At the same time they tended to perceive offenders as having negative attitudes towards authority, and little remorse for their crimes. They also tended to believe that the resources available in the community were not adequate to deal with most cases appearing before them. In contrast, reformation-oriented magistrates tended to minimize the severity of the crime, found an element of remorse in the offender's attitude toward his offence, and found a great deal of pathology in the personal history and background of the offender. They were also more likely to find community based resources as adequate to deal with most cases appearing before them.

The Organization and Integration of Information

Data were presented in a chapter which showed the way in which information about the offender, the offence, and the surrounding circumstances is organized in relationship to other information and integrated into an over-all assessment of the case.

Taking magistrates as a whole, it appeared that the most important individual determining factor in their decisions was the degree of culpability of the offender in the offence. The second fact which emerged was that when grouped together into categories, information associated with the offence was given greater weight in sentencing than was any other kind, and this held true regardless of the penal philosophy of the magistrates concerned. The one treatment factor given the highest rating by magistrates was the offender's need for supervision, which is capable of being interpreted as a factor more concerned with social defence or punishment than with treatment. It was quite clear from these data that the shift in emphasis from the offender to the offence, which became obvious during interviews as questions moved from the general to the specific, was confirmed when one looked at the actual decision behaviour of magistrates on the bench as revealed by responses to the sentencing study sheets.

Another important factor which emerged at this stage was that each magistrate seemed to have a fairly consistent way of isolating from the total body of information presented to him those individual factors which would have over-riding significance in his decisions. Different styles of information-use were identified, and these styles were closely associated with the attitudinal and penal philosophy scores of the magistrates concerned. By emphasizing one or more features of the case and minimizing the others, they were able to interpret cases selectively consistent with their objectives.

It was also interesting to note that magistrates occupying extreme positions on the attitude scales tended to be somewhat similar in the way in which they used information in sentencing. It appeared that magistrates holding extreme attitudes at either end of each scale tended to be somewhat more rigid in the way in which they approached the decision-making problem, and preferred to deal with simple information rather than complex information requiring interpretation. Thus, while magistrates occupying middle positions on the justice scale do not attach much overall importance to factors associated with treatment, they are willing to consider treatment in cases where it is available and likely to work. Similarly, in responding to information concerning the criminal record, they were concerned not simply with the existence or non-existence of the record, but rather with its length and the recency of the last conviction. These data suggest the existence of a dimension, independent of the attitudes of the magistrates, relating to the subtlety of thought in assessing information, a matter which was explored later.

The selection of purposes in sentencing as revealed from sentencing study sheets appeared to be somewhat different from self-reports of purposes as given by magistrates during the course of the interviews. On examining sentencing study sheets completed by magistrates, it was discovered that, regardless of the type of sentence imposed or the type of case dealt with, some magistrates consistently gave great weight to one or more of the purposes of sentencing to the total exclusion of others. It appeared that different magistrates can achieve similar sentences through quite different mental routes. A significant number of magistrates would give maximum weight to the reformation of offenders in cases where lengthy institutional sentences were used, while in similar cases another group would give maximum weight to punishment or deterrence. It was interesting that incapacitation was given relatively little weight, even in cases where institutional sentences were used.

The actual weight accorded to particular purposes and individual cases was closely associated with the attitudes and penal philosophies of magistrates concerned. Considerable variation was found to exist among magistrates as a group, but individual magistrates appeared to have worked out a fairly consistent, rational sentencing policy. Consistency was achieved, however, through the mechanism of selectivity. Magistrates chose certain kinds of information selectively, interpreted this information selectively, ascribed importance to certain features of the case to the exclusion of others, and selected among the various purposes in sentencing those which were most consistent with their personal values and subjective ends.

It is also interesting to note the way in which magistrates resolved conflict among various pieces of information presented to them. There was a strong tendency to interpret the background history of the offender in the light of the seriousness of the offence that he committed. There was also a tendency to filter out those particular pieces of information which might be inconsistent with the sentence that the magistrate had in mind. The data presented supported the view that magistrates tend to interpret the facts of cases before them in such a way as to minimize inconsistency. In doing so, they rearrange the facts to fit the type of sentences they use habitually. The findings confirm the results of research in other areas of human judgement and only go to show that magistrates are human. Many features of the system in which magistrates are trapped make selective interpretation of information almost a necessity. Eleven such features were discussed. They were: (i) lack of agreement as to the proper principles in sentencing; (ii) the social value placed on consistency in judicial decision-making; (iii) the special nature of legal training and experience; (iv) the public nature of the decision process; (v) the amount of unguided discretion in information-use given by the law; (vi) inadequacies in the sentencing alternatives available; (vii) information overload; (viii) the poor quality of information available to the courts; (ix) the subjective nature of the decision-process; (x) the sequence in which different kinds of information is provided; (xi) status differences between "information givers" and "information receivers."

The Complexity of Thought Processes in Sentencing

A number of studies were conducted to determine "how" magistrates perceive facts rather than "what" they perceive. These studies were built around the concept of "cognitive-complexity." Cognitive-complexity was conceived as a measure of the capacity of the individual to view the persons and objects in a social order in a complex or differentiated fashion. It is a measure of the information-processing ability of an individual and is closely linked to intelligence.

Seventeen variables thought to be associated with the concept of cognitive-complexity were created primarily from the magistrates' responses to sentencing study sheets. These variables were factor analysed, and three interpretable factors, accounting for over 44 per cent of the total variance, emerged. The first factor was labelled "discrimination" and represented differences among magistrates in the degree to which they can discriminate in a complicated fact situation. The second factor was entitled "size of information space" and measured differences among magistrates in the amount of information that they are capable of bringing to bear on a given problem. The third factor was labelled "effort in problem solving" and measured the expenditure of energy by magistrates in solving the problem of achieving a goal through sentencing. It was found that magistrates with high justice scores tend to be cognitively-simple in using information while those with high punishment corrects scores tended to be somewhat more complex. Similarly, magistrates concerned about reformation tended to be cognitively-complex while those magistrates concerned primarily about punishment or incapacitation were rather less complex.

Certain social structural factors affecting the work of the magistrate appeared to be associated with the complexity of his thought processes in sentencing. Thus urban magistrates, particularly in the larger centres, tended to be less discriminative in the way in which they used information and expended less effort in problem solving than did magistrates in smaller communities or rural areas. Magistrates in prosperous high growth rate areas with a low crime rate, tended to utilize more information in sentencing than did magistrates in areas without these characteristics. It appeared from these data that certain factors in the social structure within which the court functions impinge upon the effectiveness of information used in sentencing. The data as a whole showed that punitiveness in attitudes and beliefs was associated with a fairly simple way of organizing information in the process of judgement. The thought processes of punitive magistrates appeared to be characterized by stereotyped or compartmentalized thinking. Individual bits of information were organized in a relatively fixed way with little or no integration. In contrast, non-punitive magistrates appear to use information in a more complex and subtle way. Their thought processes were characterized by flexibility, autonomy, and creativity. Their tolerance of conflict and ambiguity was higher and their capacity for abstract thought or compartmental conceptualization enhanced. They appear to be much more involved in sentencing, and, while finding it a difficult and demanding task, appear to have responded to the challenge.

Prediction of Sentencing Behaviour from Fact Patterns as Perceived by Magistrates

The amount of consistency between "what magistrates perceive" and "what they decide" was tested by means of prediction equations. In the scheme of analysis two types of prediction problems were dealt with. The first relates to predicting the type of sentence that will be imposed in qualitative terms, i.e., will it be a fine, suspended sentence, probation, or institutional sentence? The second relates to the amount, length, or severity of the sentence imposed in quantitative terms. Different statistical models were required for these respective tasks. Dealing with the selection of sentence in qualitative terms, it was found that the selection of fines was associated with a tendency to interpret information which emphasized punishment and de-emphasized treatment, selection of probation was associated with an interpretation which de-emphasized punishment and emphasized treatment, and the selection of suspended sentence was associated with de-emphasizing both punishment and treatment. What was interesting, however, was that the selection of institutional sentences appeared to be associated with interpretations of facts which emphasized both punishment *and* treatment. It appeared from this that magistrates, in using institutional sentences, believe that they can punish and treat offenders at the same time.

The findings suggested that, in the selection of sentences among the available alternatives, a high level of consistency exists among magistrates once variation perceptions have been accounted for. This means that once magistrates perceive cases in a particular way, there is a strong tendency for them to select the same type of sentence. The difficulty arises from the fact that different magistrates tend to perceive similar cases differently. But the data suggested that if means could be found to develop greater uniformity among magistrates in the way in which they assess information in sentencing, a great deal more consistency in sentencing practice could be achieved.

Analyses were then conducted to determine the relationship between magistrates' perception of facts and the length or severity of sentences imposed. A series of equations were calculated which regressed the magistrates' perception of facts, and their purposes, against the length of institutional sentence (in days). Seven equations were derived, one for each type of offence for which sentencing study sheets were completed.

The results indicated that there were significant associations between length of institutional sentence and most aspects of magistrates' assessment of cases. Magistrates' assessment of crimes, their perceptions of offenders, their selections of determining factors, and the purposes attempted, were all found to be significantly associated with the severity of penalties imposed. In regressing these factors against the length of sentence imposed, correlation coefficients range from a low of 0.64 to a high of 0.83 with an average correlation of more than 0.7. This meant that about 50 per cent of the total variation in length of institutional sentences could be accounted for by variations in magistrates' perceptions of the facts of the cases. The general conclusion drawn was that while different magistrates have different ways of processing information, their individual decision-behaviour was highly consistent with their definition of the facts of the cases as understood by them.

The analysis then turned to the relationship of decision-behaviour to cognitive-complexity. Results showed that magistrates who used suspended sentence frequently in indictable cases, particularly suspended sentence with probation, tended to discriminate better in complicated fact situations; were capable of bringing a larger body of information to bear on a given problem, and expended more effort in problem solving. In contrast, magistrates who relied heavily on fines did not appear to be as subtle in discriminating among information. Magistrates who used institutional measures frequently tended to bring less information to bear on sentencing problems, and were rather more rigid in their approach to the task.

Cognitive-complexity was associated not only with the frequency with which institutional sentences were used, but also with the type of institutional sentence selected. The main conclusion that was drawn was that frequent use of both very short and very long institutional sentences was associated with a simpler and more rigid way of dealing with information. It seemed, therefore, that punitiveness in both attitude and behaviour was associated with cognitive-simplicity. The only qualification that was necessary was that, due to an apparent willingness to innovate, cognitively-complex magistrates sometimes appeared to be relatively punitive with respect to minor offences. The general conclusion that subtlety in information processing was associated with subtlety in decision-behaviour was drawn from these analyses.

Towards a Model of Sentencing Behaviour

Two models of sentencing behaviour were described and tested in terms of their power to predict decisions. The first was the classical, input-output model which assumed that the only "legally significant" variables governing judicial decisions are the facts of the cases, the law being a constant and the personality of the judge being legally irrelevant. The second model was a phenomenological model, built straw by straw, in the course of the study. It was based on the "meanings" that judges attach to these facts, laws, ideas, and people that they deem significant.

It was shown that the phenomenological model was considerably more powerful in predicting sentence than was the black box model. Between five and six times as much variation in sentencing practice could be accounted for by knowing the ways in which judges themselves experience sentencing. In fact, only about 9 per cent of the variation in sentencing could be explained by objectively defined facts, whilst over 50 per cent of such variation could be accounted for simply by knowing certain pieces of information about the judge himself. Once one incorporated into the analyses the magistrate's definition of the situation, a still fuller and more meaningful explanation of the judicial process was possible.

The model which finally emerged was one that viewed sentencing as a dynamic process in which the facts of the cases, the constraints arising out of the law and the social system, and other features of the external world are interpreted, assimilated, and made sense of in ways compatible with the attitudes of the magistrates concerned. Sentencing was shown to be a very human process.

An Afterword

Implications
for the Improvement
of Sentencing

Differences in Outlook Between Researchers and Practitioners

Practitioners often claim, sometimes with justification, that while researchers may be competent at critical analysis, they rarely put forward practical suggestions for change. At the root of the problem appears to be the age-old split between men faced with practical problems of having to do something "here and now" and men whose efforts are primarily directed to the pursuit of knowledge.[1] While most practitioners will admit certain weaknesses in matters of detail, they are likely to feel that these are due mainly to a failure to apply what is already known, due to pressures of work and economic constraints, rather than any fundamental weakness in the system itself. "Give us a chance to do the job properly before evaluating it," is a plea often made. The results of research in sensitive areas, such as in sentencing, which may appear to challenge not just the techniques used but the basic assumptions and goals of the system as a whole, are likely to be perceived as a threat by the individuals concerned, and it can be expected that some of them will be tempted to dismiss all conclusions, regardless of content, as impractical.

On the other hand, researchers are likely to claim that the premature search for immediate solutions to complex problems, which are not only misunderstood but also undefined, will not only fail to yield valid knowledge but, in the long run, will fail to contribute to the successful handling of practical problems. Most researchers claim that their relationship to their subject matter must be one of detachment and scepticism, and many demand the right to pursue knowledge wherever it may lead. While the "disinterested" nature of such social research is more apparent than real (value positions being obscured by apparently objective methods of analysis) it is true that the researcher does not have the same degree of emotional, economic, or other commitment to the system as does the practitioner. In fact, he may have a negative identification with the system, and may use research as a vehicle for expressing his hostility towards it. The problem is exacerbated when researchers give way to the temptation to oversell their research, or indeed misrepresent its objectives in an effort to gain co-operation.

This writer feels an enormous debt of gratitude to magistrates in Ontario for co-operating so splendidly in this project. The fact that they agreed to participate, despite the full knowledge that the study was primarily aimed at evaluating their behaviour on the bench, is a testimony to their courage, confidence, and social concern. If for no other reason than to express appreciation, an effort to deal with some of the policy implications posed by the research is called for. In any event, any weakness in sentencing that may appear from the analysis would not seem to be so much the responsibility of individual magistrates as of the system in which they are all enmeshed. As a result of the enquiry, respect for magistrates, both individually and collectively, was enhanced.

The Problem of Values

The main difficulty in making practical suggestions arises from the fact that the fundamental problems in sentencing are not scientific ones, but rather questions of competing values.[2] Suggestions made which are designed to maximize the reformative aims of sentencing, for example, are not necessarily those that would maximize the deterrent or punitive goals. The studies presented in this book were primarily directed towards a description and explanation of the sentencing process as it now exists. Being primarily concerned with "what is" they do not provide a solid basis for a discussion of "what ought to be."

At the same time, it is recognized that there is a relationship between "what is" and "what ought to be."[3] Our understanding of "what is" in the area of sentencing was found to be helpful in identifying and making more explicit some of the underlying value positions taken by the judges concerned. Moreover, our analysis of the characteristics of the sentencing process in all its complexity revealed certain inherent limitations not only to our existing system but also to any future system of decision-making which may attempt to achieve a number of contradictory goals. Armed with some knowledge of how this system functions we are in a better position to predict how a modified system may work.

It must be admitted, however, that our evaluation of the data presented in this volume was intimately linked with certain implicit value assumptions. There was no escape from this, as one cannot evaluate any set of social data without having at least an implicit model of how society should order its affairs in the area touched upon by the enquiry.

While we took great pains to avoid becoming enmeshed in arguments about what social purposes sentencing should serve, we were prepared to assume that in any rational system the courts should try to make the most effective use of available information. It is because we took this position that so much of this book deals with information use, and it is also because of this that most of the suggestions put forward at this time deal with strengthening the way in which information is used in sentencing. That is not to deny the importance of questions of social purpose and criminal policy, but simply to admit that these questions are far too important to be dealt with in an afterword to an empirical study and are beyond the scope of this particular enquiry.

It was also assumed that an evenhanded administration of justice requires a measure of consistency in the way in which different judges approach sentencing tasks. While recognizing that complete uniformity is not possible, and probably undesirable, underlying our research was the assumption that it is in the public interest for the courts to strive towards uniformity in both purpose and method.

Areas in which Changes might be Considered

The most obvious fact which emerges from the findings is that there are enormous differences among magistrates in nearly every aspect of the sentencing process. Magistrates differ in their penal philosophies, in their attitudes, in the ways in which they define what the law and the social system expect of them, in how they use information, and in the sentences they impose. In a variety of ways it was demonstrated that magistrates interpret the world selectively in ways consistent with their personal motivations and subjective ends. Regardless of what position one takes with regard to the social purposes that sentencing should serve, it is likely to be repugnant to the average man's sense of justice if such differences are allowed to persist.

It is unlikely that a simple solution will be found, as the problem has many facets requiring action on a number of levels. It is well to recognize that effecting real change will be difficult, and that superficial change, i.e., a change in the words used to describe current practice or in other forms of "tinkering" with the system, will not only fail to yield the desired results but also will mask the realities of the situation. All this suggests that if sentencing is to be improved a massive attack on the problem is required. For the sake of convenience, the areas in which change might usefully be considered are classified below under the headings: legislation, selection, training, information-use, and research.

Legislative Changes

Inconsistency in sentencing begins with vagueness in the law. Many different types of conduct are lumped together under one legal definition, and the maximum penalty provided is necessarily very high to allow for various combinations of factual circumstances that might occur. It would be helpful if many offences in the Criminal Code (theft and robbery, to give but two examples), were simplified and redefined so that each would relate to a narrower range of conduct. This would permit the maximum penalty provided to bear a closer relationship to the type of conduct proscribed. The American Law Institute, in its Model Penal Code, takes an imaginative and constructive approach to simplifying and standardizing the grading of offences for sentencing purposes.[4] It is not suggested that the actual provisions in this Code should form the basis of Canadian legislation, but rather that a great deal is to be learned from the thinking that went into the drafting of it.

If it is felt that the rate of imprisonment is too high, then certain legislative changes are indicated. For many offences maximum penalties could be drastically reduced to be more in line with prevailing public sentiment and court practice. It seems absurd that for some offences, breaking and entering for example, the maximum penalties are so high that less than one per cent of the sentences actually imposed are in excess of one half the maximum provided.[5]

Legislation could also discourage the use of imprisonment by clearly indicating that it is to be used as a last resort. In the present scheme of punishment in the Code, imprisonment is the basic penalty provided, with fines, probation, and suspended sentence as exceptions. Within the present legislative framework courts are placed in the position of having to justify the use of non-institutional measures. This could be reversed. Legislation could clearly state that fines, suspended sentence, and probation are the appropriate dispositions to make, unless the court can show that the circumstances of the case justify imprisonment. This would necessarily involve providing for fines as an independant penalty rather than, as at present, a penalty to be used in lieu of, or in addition to, imprisonment. It would also mean giving probation independent legal status, with specific penalties for its breach, freeing this form of disposition from its ancient tie to the recognizance of suspended sentence.

Perhaps the most important legislative change that could be made relates to the establishment of criteria for the selection of particular types of sentences in specific types of situations. One cannot determine what information should be placed before the courts until one knows what purpose it is to serve. The data presented in this study indicate that if it is left to individual magistrates to determine what the proper basis of sentencing ought to be, marked inconsistency is likely to result. Statutory criteria provide a way of directing the judge's attention to those factors which the legislature determines to be relevant to sentencing decisions. Both the Model Penal Code and the Model Sentencing Act employ such criteria.[6] However, the development of proper standards to guide the court to determine the proper disposition is only in the elementary stages. Standards employed in the Model Penal Code and in the Model Sentencing Act are somewhat imprecise, as they have been formulated on the basis of limited ability to predict behaviour. These standards will be revised, however, as the behavioural sciences develop more improved ways of identifying specific types of offenders in ways relevant to the sentencing alternatives available. The advantage of the approach taken by the Model Penal Code and the Model Sentencing Act is that they provide a vehicle for incorporating improved criteria into the basic sentencing structure. There is an urgent need to establish a criminal policy in this country, expressed in part by legislative criteria to guide the courts in sentencing.

Effort towards drafting specific legislation will undoubtedly act as a stimulant to further thinking, and it may inject a note of realism into discussions about specific changes that are both desirable and practical. It would be wrong to make specific suggestions at this time about the machinery that could be used for drafting a model statute, except to say that this task is large enough to warrant a permanent commission. The drafting committee should be composed not only of lawyers, but also of people representing a broader range of professional skills and lay experience. Because of the wide-ranging implications of major changes in the penal law, the draft proposals should be given the widest publicity so that full debate will be possible. No doubt there will be differences of opinion as people directly concerned are likely to take up positions reflecting their particular professional interests and social concerns. However, it should not be beyond the wit of the drafters to come up with a statute that represents a sensible balance of informed opinion. While the framing of statutory standards is a complicated and laborious task, it is an undertaking of great importance, and it is one that is likely to produce valuable results.

The Selection of Judges

In the final analysis, good sentencing depends on good judges. The data presented in this study indicate that magistrates of different backgrounds tend to approach similar sentencing situations in remarkably different ways. Age, religion, education, social class background, and previous employment experience all were shown to have a relationship to magistrates' behaviour on the bench. If flexibility, self-confidence and independence are important assets to a sentencing magistrate, the advantage of legal training in developing these qualities has been demonstrated. We now have in these findings a body of empirical evidence which can guide the selection process. With the recent establishment of a judicial council to advise the Attorney General on appointments, it should be possible to select from a list of possible candidates those that are best equipped in both ability and temperament to discharge effectively the formidable responsibilities of sentencing judges.

The creation of a new sentencing authority composed of experts in the behavioural sciences does not appear to be a satisfactory answer. If the sentencing process were solely concerned with the prevention of crime through the rehabilitation of offenders, the proposal for the creation of a new sentencing authority would seem to have more merit. But most people would agree that sentencing cannot be concerned solely with one purpose. It inevitably involves the balancing of a diversity of interests and the harmonizing of the conflicts which emerge. One of the norms rooted in the law, judicial precedent, and in the professional role of the judge is the sanctity and dignity of the individual. The State must have clear, unequivocal grounds for interfering when the liberty of the subject is involved. One of the values in the present system that might be sacrificed by the introduction of an administrative board would be the protection afforded by an independent judiciary acting as a brake on a possibly over-zealous administration.

If decision-making in sentencing must involve an inevitable balancing of competing values, then it would appear that training in law and experience at the Bar and bench are valuable assets to the decision-maker. A good judge or magistrate should be a master in the art of fairness, imbued with the doctrine of reasonableness, and he should have a keen sense of what is practical in the circumstances. It is not suggested that the data in this study show that legal training and practical experience help develop them. The solution does not appear to be to replace lawyers with behavioural scientists, but rather to provide lawyers with the training and knowledge required to make the best use of information derived from the behavioural sciences. The next two sections will deal with this.

Training

The data presented here show that most magistrates sentence without a great deal of background information concerning the cause of crime or the results of research concerning the efficacy of different types of correctional methods. Few do any significant reading in this field and only a minority have visited penal institutions. No effective mechanism exists at present for bringing new information to the attention of the courts, and, unless this is corrected, judges and magistrates are likely to continue to sentence "in the dark."

There appears to be an urgent need to provide initial and ongoing training for judges and magistrates. One way of doing this is to establish a federal-provincial institute which will provide short-term initial training (approximately three months or less) for newly-appointed magistrates, and judges. In addition, periodic refresher courses might be provided for practising judges and magistrates, and consideration might be given to making this a requirement of continued appointment. Short-term study leave every three or four years is another possibility. The expansion of knowledge in this field is so rapid that it will become increasingly difficult for judges and magistrates to keep up with current developments unless they are provided with time to read, attend lectures and seminars, and take formal courses, if necessary. If we are serious about the need for training, it should not be something that is considered a frill that can be dispensed with in times of economic stress or pressures of work. The content of courses and seminars for judges and magistrates must be carefully developed. While "little knowledge is dangerous" for most people, it would appear that this is particularly so for sentencing judges and magistrates. Improperly handled, formal training can lead to the development of more sophisticated rationalizations for essentially punitive practices. Because of this, training should not be directed solely to providing information about sentencing procedures or the content of institutional programmes available for offenders (important as these matters are), but primarily to enhancing the perceptual skills, human sensitivity, and critical abilities of judges and magistrates in handling information and in assessing the results of research concerning the effectiveness of different types of penal measures. The purpose of such a course would be to develop a greater level of sophistication among judges and magistrates in their approaches to sentencing problems. This will undoubtedly make sentencing more complicated and difficult for them, but at the same time it is likely to create an atmosphere in which sentencing can be improved.

Information-Use

Perhaps the most significant findings in this study, as far as the improvement of sentencing is concerned, relate to the proper use of information. We can no longer assume that magistrates are likely to interpret information in similar ways. The evidence also shows that the pre-sentence report is not likely to be an effective medium of communication of information unless certain favourable conditions for its proper use exist. The notion that magistrates can sentence better if they know "all about" offenders has been shown to be a myth. All this underlines the urgent need to give attention to providing the courts with better information in a form that can be more easily used.

Providing Better Information to the Courts

The sentencing problem can be divided into two parts. The first relates to determining the risk involved in taking one of several courses of action open to the court, and the second to whether that risk should be taken. In determining the risk involved in choosing a particular sentence, the judge or magistrate is, in effect, addressing himself to the problem of prediction. Whether done systematically and deliberately, or haphazardly and intuitively, these predictions are made by relating information concerning the offender before the court to previous experience of similar offenders. The difficulty arises from the fact that the human mind has a very limited capacity to deal with a large body of information. Due to limited experience, faulty memory, or memory of an exceptional case, the predictions that magistrates make are likely to be fallible. There is also likely to be variation among them in the degree to which they can predict from past experience, due to the fact that they vary enormously in information-processing ability, as we have already seen.

The determination of risk is, essentially, an empirical question in which the use of all modern decision-making aids, including mathematical prediction and computers, are likely to be helpful. Prediction devices can do no more than summarize experience, but they can do this quite objectively and efficiently. They have the additional advantage of a virtually unlimited capacity to handle information. It can be shown that these methods are usually much superior in predicting than are individual judgements.[7]

Determining what risks should be taken is, essentially, a policy question that can only be determined by the court guided by both legislative criteria and the best evidence available. Research cannot provide answers to these policy questions, but it can provide data crucial to making informed policy judgements.

Modern technology now makes it possible to provide courts with immediate access to information concerning the results of sentencing decisions made by other courts in similar situations. Information retrieval systems have been used with advantage in many commercial, scientific and governmental fields, and there is now a considerable body of experience with the use of them in criminology.[8] The essential point is that it is within the capacity of *existing* knowledge to provide courts with a computerized system of information retrieval which will enable them to make the best use of existing knowledge concerning the likely impact of contemplated sentences on offenders before them. While providing a systematic information retrieval system available to all courts in Ontario is not a small undertaking, it appears to be a feasible one which would probably reap immediate benefits in terms of effectiveness and efficiency, and in the long run it should prove to be more economical than the present time-consuming and highly inefficient way of obtaining information relevant to the sentencing task.

The scheme envisioned would work roughly as follows. Once an offender is convicted, a court officer (possibly the probation officer) would feed certain information concerning the offence and the background and criminal record of the offender to a large, centrally located data bank through a terminal located in the court-house. Additional hardware for such a system is not required, as all court-houses in Ontario are at present linked with Government of Ontario central computers.[9] Immediately, the computer would provide a print-out indicating: (a) the sentences given by other courts for cases of a similar kind, (b) the results of those sentences in terms of the number of persons reconvicted after specified periods of time, (c) a probability score that the offender at present before the court will be reconvicted within a specified period of time and for a specific type or types of offence, and (d) the probability that the chances of reconviction would be altered by choosing one form of disposition over another.

Each user would add information of his experience to the central bank so that it could be shared with others. Data collected in the course of this and other studies could form the initial data bank, and, as additional experience is collected, it can be expected that the efficiency of prediction would improve. As new methods of correctional treatment are introduced they would automatically be evaluated and the results made available to all courts and correctional agencies concerned.

The advantages of the system outlined above are obvious. It would ensure that magistrates get the best information available in a simplified and standardized form, and would thus help to avoid the inconsistency that presently obtains in information use. It would also help the court to check the results of its own decisions and provide a useful source of information for research.

There are dangers, however, in using the computer in sentencing. The problems of confidentiality of information, the possibility of abuse or misuse by the courts and a host of other legal, technical and social issues are involved.[10] But none of these appears insurmountable.

Perhaps the most frequent criticism made of proposals to use mathematical prediction devices in sentencing is that they would make unwarranted inroads into the discretionary power at present enjoyed by the courts, and would, therefore, "dehumanize" sentencing.[11] In the opinion of the writer, such concern is unnecessary and is grounded on a mistaken conception both of the meaning of discretion and the human element in sentencing. Real discretion can only be exercised in full awareness of pertinent information. Computers can never take risks, they can only determine what they are. Determining what risks shall be taken and the actual taking of risks in the light of the evidence are, fundamentally, value judgements. This aspect should always be a matter of the personal judgement of the court, bearing in mind the need to effect a balance between concern for the individual as a person and concern for community protection. Decision-making in ignorance of pertinent information is not the exercise of discretion, it is pure speculation. Information provided by the computers can only widen the scope of possible alternatives open to the court and thereby increase its real discretionary power. Judicial decision-making is, therefore, in no way threatened by scientific sentencing aids. By making it easier for the courts to settle the scientific issues quickly and effectively, it will be possible for them to concentrate a greater proportion of their time and effort to coping with the far more difficult human aspects of the problem.

These considerations have a bearing on the true value of the pre-sentence report. Perhaps the greatest impact which probation has had on the penal system has been in the degree to which it has humanized the sentencing process. Whether or not pre-sentence reports have always contained the most useful predictive information is not the whole story; they have enabled judges and magistrates to see offenders as ordinary individuals, in many ways more like their fellow human beings than the stereotype of the "typical criminal." It is, therefore, not suggested that the statistical prediction technique should take the place of the pre-sentence report, but rather that it become a supplement to it. The prognostic aspect of pre-sentence reports is likely to be better effected by actuarial methods, and this would leave the probation officer free to concentrate his efforts on writing straightforward descriptions of offenders and in developing better treatment plans for them. If this were done the pre-sentence report would become less of a scientific document and more of a summary of the offender as a person, written in ordinary language.

It would seem, therefore, that it would be worthwhile to conduct a feasibility study to determine the practicality, cost, and implications of introducing a computerized information retrieval system.

Creating Conditions Conducive to Effective Information-Use

We saw in this study that the effective use of information is to some extent determined by the conditions under which information is used and decisions are made. In particular, it was evident that the work-load of a magistrate appears to effect the quality of information-use. The analysis showed that if magistrates become over-burdened with work they use less information, adopt rigid rules for assessing it, and expend less effort in problem solving. There were striking differences between magistrates in urban and rural areas in this regard. It would appear, therefore, that particular attention should be paid to improving the working conditions of magistrates in large urban centres. A great deal has already been done to improve the status and salary of magistrates. The next step would appear to be to improve working conditions in such a way that a more professional and dispassionate approach to sentencing decisions will be made possible.

Promoting the Best Use of Information: The Need for a New Decision-Making Structure

Getting better information before the court in a more usable form is only part of the answer. Equally important is the problem of encouraging the courts to make the best use of the information placed before them. The data presented in this study indicate that magistrates tend to use information in highly individual ways. Differences among magistrates are bound to persist, but some of the more extreme disparities might be reduced. It can be expected that the introduction of specific criteria in legislation, the provision of initial and on-going training for magistrates, and the use of modern prognostic aids, such as prediction devices, will go some way towards improving the way in which information is handled in sentencing.

Perhaps the findings most suggestive of change were those re-lating to the effectiveness of the pre-sentence report as a medium of communication. It was shown that the pre-sentence report is likely to be effective only if the relationship between the magis-trate and the probation officer is characterized by informality and mutual respect. The magistrates who take time to discuss the contents of reports with probation officers informally, and who know their probation officers personally, are likely to interpret written communication from them properly. This suggests that "arm's length" relationships between probation officers and mag-istrates are not suited to the sentencing problem. Serious com-munication problems exist between some magistrates and some probation officers. It would appear that these can be overcome, but only if the decision-making process is altered in a way that would maximize the free exchange of ideas between the parties concerned. It is suggested, therefore, that consideration be given towards holding separate, informal, sentencing hearings at which the magistrate, probation officer, crown attorney, defence counsel and, whenever possible, the offender himself would attend. While the ultimate decision would be that of the judge or magistrate concerned, all would contribute to the discussion bringing to bear their particular knowledge or expertise. Because of the nature of the information discussed it would be necessary for the sentencing hearing to be held in private and it should be informal in nature. On the other hand, the decision and reasons for judgement could be pronounced in open court; a complete transcript would be kept of the hearing which would be made available in the event of an appeal. This should go some way to-wards protecting both the interests of the offender and the public whilst reducing disparity in sentencing. At the same time it would ensure that the offender himself can participate in decisions affecting his liberty, to a greater extent than is now pos-sible. This may seem to be a far-reaching proposal, but the seri-ousness of the problem, as revealed by this study, suggests that significant changes in sentencing structure are necessary.

There is another possibility that might usefully be explored. The sentencing study sheet used in this study was designed as a research document with the main purpose of revealing the mental processes involved in utilizing information in sentencing. It was not intended to alter the decision process in any way. But, on the whole, magistrates found the document helpful to them in ensuring that all relevant aspects of the sentencing problem have been weighed and considered. Consideration might be given, therefore, to building in, on a more permanent basis, some form of sentencing assessment guide as a normal process of sentencing in serious or important cases. It can be expected that completing such an instrument will promote a conscious and deliberate approach to sentencing, and that it would encourage magistrates directly to confront and deal with conflicting interests in individual cases, and give specific reasons for the decisions they make. It is unlikely that the instrument will replace painful decision-making in sentencing, and its use may reveal complexities that were not fully recognized.

Good results have been reported from a number of jurisdictions in which judges have experimented with the use of assessment forms similar to sentencing study sheets.[12] While great care would have to be exercised in designing an instrument that would be practical for magistrates to use on a regular basis, continued experimentation is likely to produce a decision-making guide that will tend to rationalize the sentencing process.

Research

In its final report, the President's Crime Commission stated: "The Commission has found and discussed throughout this report many needs of law enforcement in the administration of criminal justice. But what it has found to be the greatest need is the need to know."[13]

Improvement in sentencing seems dependent on the provision of continuous research programmes into the effectiveness of different penal measures and on making the results of such research known to the courts and correctional agencies. At the present time in Canada it is estimated that approximately one-tenth of one per cent of the total public expenditure for law enforcement, judicial administration, and correction is spent on research of any kind.[14] At the same time, the Canadian government spends approximately ten per cent of its defence budget on research.[15] In the United States the figure is approximately fifteen per cent.[16] All major corporations allocate a significant proportion of their budgets to research and development, and it would be considered inefficient not to do so.

While crime is said to pose a serious threat to the community, only token expenditures are being allocated for the kinds of descriptive, operational, and evaluative research that are the pre-requisites of a rational programme of crime control. While research into complex phenomena such as crime and crime control is not likely to yield immediate, practical solutions, a modest beginning in the search for such solutions becomes a compelling need. It is not as if such knowledge is unobtainable; it has merely not been sought with anything like the energy and dedication that has been given to solving problems such as the reduction of disease, the development of new weapons, the raising of living standards, and the conquest of space.As the President's Commission reports, "there is probably no subject of comparable concern to which the nation is devoting so many resources and so much effort, with so little knowledge of what it is doing."[17]

The essential point is that research should become a normal and necessary part of the administration of criminal justice. In the absence of specific evidence of the efficacy of penal measures, it may be appropriate to label them all as "experiments" which remain to be proved. Sentencing offers a focal point around which much useful research can be built. It is also one of the more important areas of the criminal justice system in which research results can be used.

If there is to be the significant increase in research activity envisaged in this report, it seems desirable to establish some national body to act as a focus for research efforts, stimulating research activities in important areas, providing more effective communication between researchers and those asked to implement the results of research, and, generally, disseminating what is learned. It would serve as a clearing house of research and information for the benefit of governments, courts correctional agencies, and individuals.

If this study has shown anything, it has shown that we can no longer base our criminal policy in the area of sentencing on conventional wisdom. Nor can we operate on the naïve assumption that the judicial process, as constituted at present, is equipped with either the necessary knowledge or resources to discharge adequately the awesome tasks involved. Many judges recognize this fact, as the participation of Ontario magistrates in the study will testify. This recognition is the first and most important step in moving towards a more effective and more humane way of dealing with convicted offenders. If we are to move forward, the next step must be for government to allocate adequate human and financial resources to the task of initiating and implementing an ongoing process of evaluation, experimentation, re-evaluation, and, if necessary, legislative change. Only a few of the areas requiring change are suggested by this study. There will be many difficult problems involved both in formulating a practical criminal policy that can guide our courts and in providing the services needed to effect such a policy. But given the good will and social concern now being expressed by members of the legislatures, the judiciary, the criminal Bar, the correctional agencies, and the public, there is no reason to believe that significant improvement is beyond our grasp. While it is judges who must sentence, and offenders who must bear the brunt of such sentences, it is society itself that pays the price and reaps the results. A test of the depth of societal concern will be found in the response given to the publication of this study by those who have it within their power to do something about the problems revealed in the course of our research.

NOTES TO AFTERWORD

1 For an excellent discussion of this conflict see J. Rabow, "Research and Rehabilitation: The Conflict of Scientific and Treatment Roles in Corrections," *Journal of Research in Crime and Delinquency*, 1 (1) (1964), 67-79.
2 See Chapter 1 for a discussion of the opposing value positions taken by writers in this field, and Chapter 16 for a discussion of how the lack of agreement on these fundamental questions leads to inconsistency in sentencing.
3 As a researcher, the writer feels more confident in dealing with the "what is" questions rather than "what ought to be." Nonetheless, he recognizes that stating his assumptions of what ought to be is a necessary pre-requisite to drawing even tentative conclusions concerning implications arising out of this research for the improvement of sentencing.
4 American Law Institute, *Model Penal Code*, proposed official draft (Philadelphia, 1962), ss. 6.01, 6.02, 6.03, 7.01, 7.02, 7.03, 7.04; National Model Sentencing Act, National Council on Crime and Delinquency (New York, 1963); see also American Bar Association, *Standards Relating to Sentencing Alternatives and Procedures* (New York, 1967).
5 The data upon which this finding was based were obtained from sentencing study sheets completed by magistrates in Ontario over an eighteen-month period. The data showed that for none of the seven offences concerned did magistrates use the full range of discretionary power given to them. For each offence considered over 90 per cent of the sentences fell within one half of the maximum provided.
6 American Law Institute, *Model Penal Code*; National Council on Crime and Delinquency, *Model Sentencing Act*.
7 See, for example, P. Meehl, *Clinical versus Statistical Prediction* (Minneapolis, 1954); for an excellent survey of the use of prediction methods in crime and delinquency, see D. Gottfredson, "Assessment and Prediction Methods in Crime and Delinquency," in *Task Force Report: Juvenile Delinquency and Youth Crime* (Washington, 1967), 171-187.
8 "Assessment and Prediction Methods in Crime and Delinquency," Gottfredson, 171-87; see also *The Challenge of Crime in a Free Society*, President's Commission Report (Washington, 1967), 226-71.
9 A computerized system of information retrieval is currently in operation for the purpose of searching titles to property. For a description of how it works see *Computers and the Law: Conference Proceedings* (Kingston, 1968), 109-25.
10 A good discussion of these problems is contained in *Computers and the Law*, 181-218.

11 The danger of the courts becoming mesmerized by prediction scores has been commented on by a number ot writers.   See, for example: "The Selection of Offenders for Probation," in M.Paulsen, ed., *The Problem of Sentencing* (Philadelphia, 1965), 50-2; see also L. Wilkins, "The Effectiveness of Punishment," *Report of the Criminological Scientific Council* (Strasbourg, 1967), 9-104.

12 See, for example, T. Smith, "The Sentencing Council and the Problem of Disproportionate Sentences," *Federal Probation,* 27 (2) 1967, especially at 7-9.

13 *The Challenge of Crime in a Free Society,* 273.

14 "Preliminary Report on the Cost of Crime," prepared by the Centre of Criminology, University of Toronto (1967), mimeo.

15 *Ibid.*

16 *The Challenge of Crime in a Free Society,* 273.

17 *Ibid.*

Bibliography

Sentencing Research

American Bar Association, *Project on Standards of Criminal Justice, Appellate Review of Sentences* (April 1967).

American Bar Association, *Project on Standards of Criminal Justice, Sentencing Alternatives and Procedures* (December 1967).

American Bar Foundation, *The Administration of Criminal Justice in the United States*, Pilot Project, vol. III (1958), 89-107.

Balogh, J.K. and Mueller, Mary Ann, "A Scaling Technique for Measuring Social Attitudes toward Capital Punishment," *Sociology and Social Research*, 45 (October 1960).

Barrett, D.N., "Sentence Prediction and Penalties: A Sociological Approach," *Notre Dame Law*, 35 (May 1960), 305.

Blawie, J.L. and Blawie, M.J., "The Judicial Decision: A Second Look at Certain Assumptions of Behavioural Research," *Western Political Quarterly*, 18 (3) (1965), 179-93.

Bullock, H.A., "Significance of the Racial Factor in the Length of Prison Sentences," *Journal of Criminal Law, Criminology and Police Science*, 52 (1961) 411-17.

California University School of Criminology, *San Francisco Project Research Report*: Lohman, Joseph D., Wohl, Albert, and Carter, Hobert, M., "Three Hundred Pre-sentence Reports, Recommendations," no. 2 (1965); "Five Hundred Federal Offenders: Demographic Data," no. 3 (1965); "Federal Probationers and Prisoners: Statutary Sentencing Alternatives and Demographic Data," no. 4 (1965); "Presentence Report Recommendations and Demographic Data," no. 5 (1966); "Decision-Making and the Probation Officer: The Presentence Report Recommendations," no. 7 (1966).

Carter, R.M., "The Presentence Report and the Decision-Making Process," Journal of Research in Crime and Delinquency, 4 (1967), 203-11.

Carter, R.M. and Wilkins, L., "Some Factors in Sentencing Policy," Journal of Criminal Law, Criminology and Police Science, 58 (1967), 503-14.

Chandler, Ann and Wilkins, L., "Confidence and Competence in Decision-Making," British Journal of Criminology, 5 (1965), 22-35.

Christie, N.G., Paper Read to Research Symposium at National Institute of Mental Health (Washington, DC, 1963).

Cowan, T. A., "Decision Theory in Law, Science and Technology," Science, 140 (1965), 1065-75.

Eckoff, T., "The Mediator, The Judge and the Administrator in Conflict Resolution," Acta Sociologica, 10 (1966), 148-72.

Everson, G., "The Human Element in Justice," Journal of Criminal Law, Criminology and Police Science, 10 (1919-20), 90.

Fair, D., "An Experimental Application of Scalogram Analysis to State Supreme Court Decisions," Wisconsin Law Review, 2 (1967), 449-67.

Friedland, A., "Magistrates' Court: Functioning and Facilities," The Criminal Law Quarterly, 11 (1) (1968), 52-75.

Friedland, M., Detention Before Trial (Toronto, University of Toronto Press, 1966).

Fuller, L., "An Afterward: Science and the Judicial Process," Harvard Law Review, 79 (1966), 1604-28.

Gaudet, F. J., "The Differences Between Judges in the Granting of Sentences of Probation," Temple Law Quarterly, 19 (April 1946).

Gaudet, F. J., "Individual Differences in the Sentencing Tendencies of Judges," Archives of Psychology, 22 (June 1938).

Gaudet, F. J., "The Sentencing Behaviour of the Judge," V. C. Branham and S. B. Kutash, eds., Encyclopedia of Criminology (New York, Philosophical Library, 1949).

Gaudet, F. J., Harris, G. S., and St. John, G. W., "Individual Differences in the Sentencing Tendencies of Judges," Journal of Criminal Law and Criminology, 23 (January-February 1933).

Glaser, Daniel, The Effectiveness of a Prison and Parole System (Indianapolis, Bobbs-Merrill, 1964).

Gottfredson, D.M., "The Practical Application of Research," Canadian Journal of Corrections (October 1963).

Gottfredson, Don M. and Ballard, K.B., Jr., "Differences in Parole Decisions Associated with Decision-Makers," *Journal of Research in Crime and Delinquency,* 3 (1966), 112-19.

Green, E., "The Effect of Preceding Sentences on the Severity of Sentences Imposed on Criminal Offenders; The Influence of Stimulus Arrangements on Normative Judgments," *Current Projects* (Washington, DC, National Council of Crime and Delinquency, 1967).

Green, E., "Inter-and Intra-Racial Crime Relative to Sentencing," *Journal of Criminal Law, Criminology and Police Science*, 55 (1964), 348-58.

Green, E., *Judicial Attitudes in Sentencing: A Study of the Factors Underlying the Sentencing Practice of the Criminal Court of Philadelphia* (London, Macmillan, 1961).

Grossman, J.B., "Social Background and Judicial Decision-Making," *Harvard Law Review,* 79(1966), 1551-64.

Hagedern, R., "A Cross-Cultural Assessment of Official Reactions to Deviant Behavior," *British Journal of Criminology,* 7 (1967), 381-93.

Hall, Jay and Williams, Martha, *The Decision Making Grid* (President's Committee, Washington, 1968).

Hogarth, J., "Sentencing Research - Some Problems of Design," *British Journal of Criminology,* 7 (1967), 84-93.

Holtzoff, Alexander, "The Judicial Process As Applied to Sentencing in Criminal Cases,"*Federal Probation,* 12 (June 1950).

Hood, R., *Sentencing in Magistrates' Courts: A Study in Variation in Policy* (London, Stevens, 1962).

Hood, R., "Research into the Effectiveness of Punishments and Treatments," paper read to 2nd European Conference of Directors of Criminological Research Institutes, Strasbourg, November 1965 (Council of Europe, 1965).

Hood, R., "*Research on the Sentencing of Motor Offences in Magistrates' Courts,*" paper presented at the Second National Conference on Research and Teaching (Cambridge, 1966).

Hood, R., "A Study of the Effectiveness of Pre-Sentence Investigations in Reducing Recidivism," *British Journal of Criminology,* 6 (1966), 303-10.

Hood, R. and Taylor, I., "The Effectiveness of Pre-Sentence Investigations -- 2nd Report," *British Journal of Criminology,* 7 (1967), 431-7.

Jaffary, Stuart K., *Sentencing of Adults in Canada* (Toronto, University of Toronto Press, 1963).

Jobson, K.B., *Sentencing in Canada: Historical Aspects, 1892-1965*, unpublished LL.M. thesis (New York, Columbia University Law School, 1966).

Jobson, K.B., *Sentencing in Canada: Imprisonment*, unpublished LL.M. thesis (New York, Columbia University Law School, 1968).

Knight, D.W., "Punishment Selection as a Function of Biographical Information," *Journal of Criminal Law, Criminology and Police Science*, 56 (1965), 325-7.

Kort, F., "Quantitative Analysis of Fact-Patterns in Cases and their Impact on Judicial Decisions," *Harvard Law Review*, 79 (1966), 1595-603.

Krislov, S., "Theoretical Attempts at Predicting Judicial Behavior," *Harvard Law Review*, 79 (1966), 1573-82.

Ladinsky, Jack and Grossman, Joel B., "Organizational Consequences of Professional Consensus: Lawyers and Selection of Judges," *Administrative Science Quarterly*, 11 (1966), 78-106

Lane, H.E., "Illogical Variations in Sentences of Felons Committed to Massachusetts State Prison," *Journal of Criminal Law, Criminology and Police Science*, 32 (1941), 171-190.

Lodge, T.S., "Sentencing Research," Thirteenth Social Defence Colloquium Round Table Conference (London, 1965).

Makela, Klaus, "Public Sense of Justice and Judicial Practice," *Acta Sociologica*, 10 (1966), 42-67.

Mannheim, H., "Sentencing Revisited," in M. Wolfgang, ed., *Crime and Culture* (New York, Wiley, 1968), 349-74.

Mannheim, H., Spencer, J., and Lynch, G., "Magisterial Policy in the London Juvenile Courts, I and II," *British Journal of Delinquency*, 8 (1957), 13-33 and 119-38.

McClintock, F.H., *Crimes of Violence* (London, Macmillan, 1963).

McClintock, F.H. and Gibson, E., *Robbery in London* (London, Macmillan, 1961).

McCune, S.D. and Skoler, D.L., "Juvenile Court Judges in the United States," *Crime and Delinquency*, 11 (1965), 121-31.

McGuire, Matthew F. and Holtzoff, A., "The Problem of Sentencing in the Criminal Law," *Boston University Law Review*, 413 (1940), 724-33.

Mendelson, W., "The Neo-Behavioral Approach to the Judicial Process: A Critique," *American Political Science Review*, 57 (1963), 593-603.

Mohr, J.W., "The Contribution of Research to the Selection of Appropriate Alternatives for Sexual Offenders," *Criminal Law Quarterly*, 4 (1962), 317-328.

Morton, J.D., "Art of Sentencing," *Osgoode Hall, Law School Journal,* 1 (April 1959), 95.

Murphy, W.F., "Courts as Small Groups," *Harvard Law Review,* 79 (1966), 1565-72.

Nagel, S.S., "Ethnic Affiliations and Judicial Propensities," *Journal of Politics,* 24, 92.

Nagel, S.S., "Political Party Affiliation and Judges' Decisions," *American Political Science Review,* 55 (1961), 843.

Nagel, S.S., "Judicial Backgrounds and Criminal Cases," *Journal of Criminal Law, Criminology and Police Science,* 53 (1962), 331-9.

Nagel, S.S., "Off the Bench Judicial Attitudes," in G. Schubert, ed., *Judicial Decision Making* (Glencoe, Free Press, 1963).

Nagel, S.S., "Testing Relations Between Judicial Characteristics and Judicial Decision-Making," *Western Political Quarterly,* (September 1962).

Newman, D.J., *Conviction. The Determination of Guilt or Innocence Without Trial* (Boston, Little, Brown, 1966).

Outerbridge, W.R., *An Empirical Study of the Restrictions on Eligibility for Probation,* MSW thesis (Toronto, School of Social Work, University of Toronto, 1962).

Patchett, K.W. and McClean, J.D., "Decision-Making in Juvenile Cases," *Criminal Law Review,* 65 (1965), 699-710.

Radzinowicz, L., "The Assessment of Punishment by the Courts," in *The Modern Approach to Criminal Law* (Cambridge, 1945), 110-22.

Radzinowicz, L., ed., *Sexual Offences* (London, Macmillan, 1957).

Rose, Gordon, "An Experimental Study of Sentencing," *British Journal of Criminology* (1965), 314-19.

Schroeder, Theodore, "The Psychological Study of Judicial Opinions," *California Law Review,* 6 (January 1918), 89-113.

Schubert, G.A., "The Study of Judicial Decision-Making as an Aspect of Political Behaviour," *American Political Science Review,* 52 (1958), 1007-25.

Schubert, Glendon, "A Solution to the Indeterminate Factorial Resolution of Thurstone and Degan's Study of the Supreme Court," *Behavioral Sciences,* 7 (1962), 448-58.

Schubert, G., "The 1960 Term of the Supreme Court: A Psychological Analysis," *American Political Science Review,* 56 (1)(1962), 90-107.

Schubert, Glendon, *Judicial Decision-Making* (New York Free Press, 1963).

Schubert, Glendon, *Judicial Behaviour - a Reader in Theory and*

Research (Chicago, Rand McNally, 1964).

Schubert, Glendon, *The Judicial Mind* (Evanston, Ill., Northwestern University Press, 1965).

Schubert, Glendon, *The Political Role of the Courts - Judicial Policy-Making* (Glenview, Ill., Scott, Foresman, 1965).

Sellin, Thorsten, "The Negro Criminal: a Statistical Note," *Annals of the American Academy of Political and Social Science* (November 1928), 140.

Shoham, S., "Sentencing Policy of Criminal Courts in Israel," *Journal of Criminal Law, Criminology and Police Science,* 50 (1959), 327-37.

Shoham, S., "Suspended Sentences in Israel," *Crime and Delinquency,* 10 (January 1964), 74.

Shoham, S., "The Procedures and Sentencing Powers of the Criminal Courts in Israel," in *Crime and Social Deviation* (Chicago, Henry Regnery, 1966), 166-89.

Schmidhauser, J., "The Justice of the Supreme Court: A Collective Portrait," *Midwestern Journal of Police Science,* 3 (1959).

Schmidhauser, J., "Stare Decisis, Dissent and The Backgrounds of Justices of the Supreme Court," *Toronto Law Journal,* 14 (1962), 194.

Smith, Alexander B. and Blumberg, A., "The Problem of Objectivity in Judicial Decision-Making," *Social Forces,* 46 (1967), 96-105.

Spaeth, H.J., "An Approach to the Study of Attitudinal Differences as an Aspect of Judicial Behavior," *Midwestern Journal of Police Science,* 5 (1961), 165-80.

Spaeth, H.J., "Judicial Power as a Variable Motivating Supreme Court Behavior," *Midwestern Journal of Police Science,* 6 (1) (1962), 54-82.

Spaeth, H.J., "An Analysis of Judicial Attitudes in the Labor Relations Decisions of the Warren Court," *Journal of Politics,* 25 (1963), 290-311.

Spaeth, H.J., "Unidimensionality and Item Variance in Judicial Scaling," *Behavioral Sciences,* 10 (3) (1965), 290-304.

Sparks, R.F., "Sentencing by Magistrates: Some Facts of Life," in P. Halmos, ed., *Sociological Studies in the British Penal Services,* the *Sociological Review* monograph, no. 9 (Keele, 1965), 71-86.

Tannehaus, J., "The Cumulative Scaling of Judicial Decision," *Harvard Law Review,* 79 (1966), 1583-94.

Torgenson, U., "The Role of the Supreme Court in The Norwegian Political System," in Schubert, ed., *Judicial Decision Making* (Chicago, Glencoe, 1963), 221-4.

Ulmer, S., "The Analysis of Behavior Patterns on the United States Supreme Court," *Journal of Politics*, 22 (1960), 629-53.

Ulmer, S., "The Political Party Variable in the Michigan Supreme Court," *Journal of Public Law*, 11 (1962), 352.

Ulmer, S., "Public Office in the Social Backgrounds of Supreme Court Justices," *American Journal of Economic Sociology*, 57 (1962), 57.

Vann, Carl R., "Pre-trial Determination and Judicial Decision-Making: An Analysis of the Use of Psychiatric Information in the Administration of Criminal Justice," *University of Detroit Law Journal*, 43 (1965), 13.

Vasoli, R.H., "Growth and Consequences of Judicial Discretion in Sentencing," *Notre Dame Law Review*, 40 (June 1965), 404.

Walther, R.H. and McCune, S.D., "Juvenile Court Judges in the United States," *Crime and Delinquency*, 11 (1956), 384-93.

Walther, R.H. and McCune, S.D., "Judges Compared with Other Court System Personnel," *Juvenile Court Judges*, 17 (2) (1966), 74-7.

Wheeler, S., *et al.*, "Agents of Delinquency Control: A Comparative Analysis," in S. Wheeler, ed., *Controlling Delinquents* (New York, Wiley, 1968). 31-60.

Wilkins, L., "A Small Comparative Study of the Results of Probation," *British Journal of Delinquency*, 8 (1958), 201-9.

Wilkins, L. and Chandler, Ann, "Confidence and Competence in Decision-Making," *British Journal of Criminology*, 5 (1965), 22-35.

Wilkins, L., "The Effectiveness of Punishment," *Report of Criminological Scientific Council* (Strasbourg, Council of Europe, 1967), 9-104.

Williams, J.E.H., "The Use the Courts Make of Prison," *Sociological Review* Monograph, No. 9 (Keele, 1965), 49-70.

Winick, C., Gerver, I., and Blumberg, A.,"The Psychology of Judges," in H. Toch. ed., *Legal and Criminal Psychology* (New York, Holt, Rinehart and Winston, 1961), 121-45.

Non-Empirical Writings About Sentencing

Administrative Office of the United States Courts, Division of Probation. *The Presentence Investigation Report* (Washington, US Government Printing Office), 1965.

Alexander, M.E., "Hopeful View of the Sentencing Process," *American Criminal Law Quarterly*, 3 (Summer 1965), 189.

Alexander M.E. and Staub, *The Criminal, the Judge and the Public*, rev. ed. (Glencoe, The Free Press, 1956).

Allen, F., "Criminal Justice, Legal Values, and the Rehabilitative Ideal," *Journal of Criminal Law, Criminology, and Police Science*

50 (1959), 226-32.

Allen, F., *The Borderland of Criminal Justice* (Chicago, Chicago University Press, 1964).

Amicus Curiae, "A Guide to Sentencing," *Ontario Magistrates' Quarterly*, 4 (4) (1967), 6.

Andenaes, J., "The General Preventative Effects Of Punishment," *University of Pennsylvania Law Review*, 114 (1966), 949-83.

Asquith, L.J., "Problems of Punishment," *The Listener*, 43 (11 May 1950).

Bennet, James V., "Sentence - Its Relation to Crime and Rehabilitation," *University of Ill. Law Forum* (Winter 1960), 500.

Bennett, James V., "Countdown for Judicial Sentencing," *Federal Probation*, 25 (3) (1961), 22-4.

Bennett, James V., "Crime and the American Penal System: The Sentence and Treatment of Offenders," *Annals of American Academy of Politics and Social Science*, 339 (1962), 142-56.

Bigelow, S., "Problems of Sentencing," *Ontario Magistrates' Quarterly*, 3 (4) (October 1966) 6-7.

Bigelow, S., "Expunging Criminal Records," *Ontario Magistrates' Quarterly*, 4 (2) (1967), 7.

Bittner, E. and Platt, A., "The Meaning of Punishment," *Issues in Criminology*, 2 (1) (1966), 79-99.

Campbell, W.J., "Developing Systematic Sentencing Procedures," *Federal Probation*, 18 (September 1954).

"Canada, Brief of the Canadian Corrections Association on the Development of Probation in Canada," *Canadian Journal of Corrections*, 10 (1968), 151-78.

Canada, Report of a Committee Appointed to Enquire into the Principles and Procedures Followed in the Remission Service of the Department of Justice of Canada (Ottawa, Queen's Printer, 1956).

Canada, Report of the Royal Commission to Investigate the Penal System in Canada (Ottawa, Queen's Printer, 1938).

Canada, Report of the Royal Commission on the Revision of the Criminal Code (Ottawa, Queen's Printer, 1954).

Canada, Royal Commission Enquiry into Civil Rights, Report No. 1, vol.2 (Toronto, Queen's Printer, 1968).

Cardozo, B., *The Nature of the Judicial Process* (New Haven, Yale University Press, 1921).

Carter, R.M., "It is Respectfully Recommended ...," *Federal Probation*, 30 (2) (1966), 3842.

Cross, Rupert, "Paradoxes in Prison Sentences," *Law Quarterly Review*, 81 (1965), 20522.

Cross, Rupert, *Precedent in English Law*, 2nd ed. (Oxford,

Clarendon Press, 1968).

Decore, J.V., "Criminal Sentencing: the Role of the Canadian Courts of Appeal and the Concept of Uniformity," *Criminal Law Quarterly*, 6 (1964), 324-80.

Devlin, K.M., "Sentencing. The Theories in Practice," *Justice of the Peace and Local Government Review*, 131 (1967), 593-5.

Edwards, J. Ll. J., "Sentencing, Correction and the Prevention of Crime," *Canadian Journal of Corrections*, 8 (1966), 186-201.

Federal Rules Decisions, Institute on Disparity, 30 (1962), 449-54.

Fitzgerald, P.J., *Criminal Law and Punishment* (Oxford, Clarendon Press, 1962).

Flood, G., "Sentencing Function of the Judges," *Journal of Criminal Law, Criminology and Police Science*, 15(1955), 531-6.

Frank, J., *Courts on Trial* (Princeton, Princeton University Press, 1949).

Giles, Frances T., *The Magistrates' Courts* (London, Stevens, 1963).

Glaser, D., Cohen, F., and O'Leary, V., *The Sentencing and Parole Process* (Washington, US Department of Health, Education and Welfare, 1966).

Glueck, S., "Pre-Sentence Examination of Offenders to Aid in Choosing a Method of Treatment," *Journal of Criminal Law, Criminology and Police Science*, 41 (1951).

Glueck, S., "The Sentencing Problem," *Federal Probation*, 20 (4) (1956), 15-25.

Glueck, S., "Toward Improving Sentencing," in *Essays in Jurisprudence in Honor of Roscoe Pound* (Indianapolis, Bobbs-Merrill, 1967).

Grossman, J.B., *Lawyers and Judges; The ABA and the Politics of Judicial Selection* (New York, John Wiley, 1965), 7-81.

Guttmacher, M., "Individualization of Sentence," *Canadian Journal of Corrections*, 3 (1961), 226-35.

Hadden, T., "A Plea for Punishment," *Cambridge Law Journal* (April 1965), 117-36.

Hall, Jerome, *Theft, Law and Society*, 2nd ed. (Indianapolis, Bobbs-Merrill, 1952).

Hall, Jerome, *General Principles of Criminal Law*, 2nd ed. (Indianapolis, Bobbs-Merrill, 1960).

Hall-Williams, J.E., "Alternatives to Definite Sentences," *Law Quarterly Review*, 80, 41-62.

Hall-Williams, J.E., "Sentencing in Transition," in T. Grygier et al., eds., *Criminology in Transition* (London, Tavistock, 1965), 23-42.

Hart, H., Jr., "The Aims of the Criminal Law," *Law and Contemporary Problems*, 23 (1958), 401-41.

Hart, H.L.A., "Prolegomenon to the Principle of Punishment," presidential address to the Aristotelian Society (1959).

Hart, H.L.A., Punishment and the Elimination of Responsibility, L.T. Hobhouse Memorial Lecture no. 31 (London, The Athlone Press, 1962).

Hayner, Norman S., "Sentencing by an Administrative Board," Law and Contemporary Problems, 23 (Summer 1958).

Hays, Glenn, "Toward Uniformity of Sentence," Canadian Journal of Corrections, 9 (1967), 115-21.

Jackson, R.M., Enforcing the Law (London, Macmillan, 1967), 123-73.

Jarvis, F.V., "Inquiry Before Sentence," in T. Grygier et al., eds., Criminology in Transition (London, Tavistock, 1965), 43-63.

Joint Committee on Continuing Legal Education of the American Law Institute and the American Bar Association, The Problem of Sentencing (New York, 1964).

Kadish, S.H., "Legal Norm and Discretion in the Police and Sentencing Process," Harvard Law Review, 75 (1962), 904-31.

Kenrick, E.W., "The Role of the Adult Court in Corrections," Canadian Journal of Corrections, 10 (1968), 151-78.

Law and Contemporary Problems, Special Issue on Sentencing, 23 (1958), 401-582.

Legal Penalties, A Report by Justice (London, Stevens, 1959).

Lewis, C.S., The Humanitarian Theory of Punishment, Twentieth Century, Australia, vol. 3, no. 3.

MacLeod, A.J., "If a Penologist was the Sentencing Judge," Canadian Bar Journal (February 1966).

Madeley, St. John, "Probation," in W. McGrath, ed., Crime and its Treatment in Canada (Toronto, Macmillan, 1965).

Mannheim, H., Criminal Justice and Social Reconstruction (London, Kegan Paul, 1946).

Mannheim, H., "Comparative Sentencing Practice," Law and Contemporary Problems, 23 (Summer 1958).

Mannheim, H., "Some Aspects of Judicial Sentencing Policy," Yale Law Journal, 67 (1958), 971.

Mannheim, H., "This Sentencing Business," British Journal of Criminology, 4 (1964), 608-9.

Mannheim, H., "Sentencing Revisited," in M. Wolfgang, ed., Crime and Culture (New York, Wiley, 1968).

Matza, D., Delinquency and Drift (New York, Wiley, 1964).

McFarlane, G.G., "Theory and Development of Pre-Sentence Reports in Ontario," Canadian Journal of Corrections, 7 (1964), 201-25.

McRuer, J.C., "Sentencing," *Canadian Journal of Corrections*, 3 (1961), 207-25.

Mewett, Alan W., "The Suspended Sentence and Preventive Detention," *Criminal Law Quarterly*, 1 (1958), 268-82.

Mewett, Alan W., ed., *Proceedings of the Seminar on the Sentencing of Offenders* (Kingston, Queen's University, 1962).

Morris, N. and Buckle, D., *The Humanitarian Theory of Punishment: A Reply to C. S. Lewis*, Twentieth Century, Australia, vol. 6, no. 2.

Morris, N., "Impediments to Penal Reforming," *University of Chicago Law Review*, 33 (1966).

Morris, N., and Hawkins, G., *The Honest Politician's Guide To Crime Control* (Chicago, University of Chicago Press, 1970).

National Conference of Judges on Sentencing, *Proceedings* (Toronto, Centre of Criminology, University of Toronto, 1964).

National Probation and Parole Association Journal, Special Issue on Sentencing, 2 (1956), 305-92.

Newman, D., *Conviction: The Determination of Guilt or Innocence Without Trial* (Boston, Little, Brown, 1966).

Ontario Magistrates' Association, *Report on Sentencing* (1961, 1962), mimeo.

Page, Leo, *The Problem of Punishment* (London, The Clarke Hall Fellowship Lectures, 1946).

Page, Leo, *The Sentence of the Court* (London, 1948).

Packer, H., *The Limits of the Criminal Sanction* (Stanford, Stanford University Press, 1968).

Parker, Graham E., "Sentencing - Is It the Function of the Courts Alone?," *Criminal Law Quarterly*, 5 (1963), 405-9.

Parker, Graham E., "The Education of the Sentencing Judge," *International and Comparative Law Quarterly*, 14 (1965), 206-25.

Paulsen, M.G. and Kadish, S.H., *Criminal Law and its Processes* (Boston, Little, Brown, 1962).

Pound, R., "Individualization of Justice," *Crime and Delinquency*, 10 (October 1964), 467.

Radzinowicz, L., "The Assessment of Punishment by the Courts," in *The Modern Approach to Criminal Law* (Cambridge, 1945), 116-22.

Radzinowicz, L., "Changing Attitudes Toward Crime and Punishment," *Law Quarterly Review*, 75 (1959), 381.

Radzinowicz, L., *Ideology and Crime* (London, Heinemann, 1966).

Remington, F.J. and Newman, D.J., "The Highland Park Institute on Sentencing Disparity," *Federal Probation*, 26 (1) (1962), 3-9.

Roche, P., *The Criminal Mind* (New York, Farrar, Straus, 1958).

Rubin, S., "Sentencing Goals: Real and Ideal," *Federal Probation*,

21 (2) (1957), 51-6.

Rubin, S., *Crime and Juvenile Delinquency. A Rational Approach to Penal Problems* (New York, Oceana Publishers, 1961).

Rubin, S., "Developments in Correctional Law," *Crime and Delinquency*, 7 (1961) 64.

Rubin, S., "Sentencing Problems and Solutions," *Canadian Journal of Corrections*, 4 (2) (April 1962), 74-82.

Rubin, S., *The Law of Criminal Correction* (St. Paul, Minn., West, 1963).

Rubin, S., "Law Schools and the Law of Sentencing and Correctional Treatment," *Texas Law Review*, 43 (February 1965), 332.

Rubin, S., "Disparity and Equality of Sentences - A Constitutional Challenge," *Federal Rules Decisions*, 40, (July 1966), 55.

Scott, G.W., "Sentencing," *Canadian Journal of Corrections*, 1 (2) (April 1959), 6-14.

Sellin, T., "The Trial Judges' Dilemma: A Criminologist's View," in Sheldon Glueck, ed., *Probation and Criminal Justice* (New York, Macmillan, 1933).

Silvey, J., "The Criminal Law and Public Opinion," *Criminal Law Review* (1961), 349-58.

Silving, H., "Rule of Law in Criminal Science," in G.O.W. Mueller, ed., *Essays in Criminal Science* (London, Sweet and Maxwell, 1961), 77-154.

Smith, J.C., *Sentencing in the Superior English Courts*, Thirteenth Social Defence Colloquium, Round Table Conference (London, 1965).

Smith, Talbot, "The Sentencing Council and the Problem of Disproportionate Sentencing," *Federal Probation*, 27 (2) (June 1963), 5-9.

Sparks, R.F., "Sentencing by Magistrates. Some Facts of Life," in Peter Halmos, ed., *Sociological Studies in the British Penal Services* (Keele, University of Keele, 1965).

Sprott, "Sentencing Policy," in Peter Halmos, ed., *Sociological Studies in the British Penal Services* (Keele, University of Keele, 1965).

Stockdale, E., *The Court and the Offender* (London, Gollancz, 1967).

Stone, J., *Legal System and Legal Reasoning* (London, Stevens, 1964).

Street, T. George, "Problems of Sentencing," *Canadian Journal of Corrections*, 3 (1961), 236-7.

Thomas, D., "Sentencing - the Case for Reasoned Decisions," *Criminal Law Review* (1963), 243-53.

Thomas, D., "Theories of Punishment in the Court of Criminal

Appeal," *Modern Law Review,* 27 (1964).

Thomas, D., "Sentencing - the Basic Principles," *Criminal Law Review* (1967), 455-525.

The Training of Justices of the Peace in England and Wales (London, HMSO, 1964), Cmnd. 2856.

Ulman, Joseph N., "The Trial Judge's Dilemma," in S. Glueck, ed., *Probation and Criminal Justice* (New York, Macmillan, 1933).

United Kingdom, *Report of the Departmental Committee on the Probation Service* (London, HMSO, 1962), Cmnd. 1650.

United Kingdom, *Report of the Inter-Departmental Committee on the Business of the Criminal Courts* (London, HMSO, 1961), Cmnd. 128⁹

United Kingdom, Home Office, *The Sentence of the Court, a Handbook for Courts on the Treatment of Offenders* (London, HMSO, 1964).

United States, *The Challenge of Crime in a Free Society - A Report by the President's Commission on Law Enforcement and Administration of Justice* (United States Government Printing Office, 1967).

United States, *Task Force Report: The Courts* (Washington, US Government Printing Office, 1967).

United States Courts, *The Pre-Sentence Investigation Report,* Division of Probation, Publication no. 103 (1965).

United States Judicial Conference Committee on Administration of the Probation System, papers delivered at the Institute on Sentencing for United States District Judges, *Federal Rules Decisions,* 35 (1964), 381.

Walker, Nigel, *Crime and Punishment in Britain* (Edinburgh, Edinburgh University Press, 1965).

Walker, Nigel, *The Aims of the Penal System* (Edinburgh, Edinburgh University Press, 1966).

Watson, R.A., Downing, R.G., and Spiegel, F.C., "Bar Politics, Judicial Selection and the Representation of Social Interest," *American Political Science Review,* 61 (1) (1967), 54-71.

Webb, A.M.F., *The Training of Magistrates* (Cambridge, Second National Conference on Research and Teaching in Criminology, 1966).

Weihofen, Henry, *The Urge to Punish* (New York, Farrar, Straus and Cudahy, 1956).

Wilkins, Leslie T., *Social Deviance* (London, Tavistock, 1964).

Williams, D.G.T., "Suspended Sentence at Common Law," *Public Law* (Winter 1963), 441.

Williams, Glanville, "Authoritarian Morals and the Criminal Law," in *Criminal Law Review* (1966), 132-47.

Williams, Glanville, *The Proof of Guilt: A Study of the English*

Criminal Trial (London, Stevens, 1963).

Winick, C., Gewer, J., and Blumberg, A., "The Psychology of Judges," in H. Toch, ed., *Legal and Criminal Psychology* (New York, Holt, Rinehart and Winston, 1961).

Wootton, B., *Crime and the Criminal Law* (London, Stevens, 1963).

Sentencing Laws: Existing and Proposed

Advisory Council of Judges, "Model Sentencing Act - Text and Commentary," *Crime and Delinquency,* 9 (1963), 339-69.

American Bar Association, *Standards Relating to Sentencing Alternatives and Procedures* (New York, 1967).

The British North America Act, *Statutes of England* (30 and 31 Vic.) 1867, C.3.

The Criminal Code, *Rev. Statutes of Canada,* 1953-54, C.51.

Criminal Code Amendment Act, *Statutes of Canada,* 1921, C.25, s. 19. *Bill C195* (An Act to Amend the Criminal Code) (Ottawa, Queen's Printer, 1969).

Crime and Delinquency, "Symposium on Model Sentencing Act," 9 (1963), no. 4.

Criminal Justice Act, *Statutes of England,* 1948.

An Act Respecting the Criminal Law, *Statutes of Canada,* 1892, C.29.

An Act Respecting the Criminal Law, *Statutes of Canada,* 19534, C.51.

Flood, Gerald F., "The Model Sentencing Act - A Higher Level of Penal Law," *Crime and Delinquency,* 9 (1963), 370-80.

Gigeroff, A.K., "The Evolution of Canadian Legislation with Respect to Homo-Sexuality, Pedophilia, and Exhibitionism," *Criminal Law Quarterly,* 8 (1966), 445-54.

Hall, J. and Mueller, G., *Cases and Readings on Criminal Law and Procedure,* 2nd ed. (Indianapolis, 1965).

Identification of Criminals Act, *Statutes of Canada,* 1952.

Magistrates' Act, *Ontario Statutes,* 1961, C.226.

Mewett, A., ed., *Martin's Criminal Code* (Toronto, Canada Law Book, 1965).

Model Penal Code, Proposed Official Draft (Philadelphia, American Law Institute, 1962).

National Council on Crime and Delinquency, Advisory Council of Judges, *Model Sentencing Act* (New York, 1963).

National Probation and Parole Association, Advisory Council of Judges, *Guides for Sentencing* (New York, Carnegie Press, 1957).

Ohlin, L., and Remington, F., "Sentencing Structure: Its Effect Upon Systems for the Administration of Criminal Justice." *Law and Contemporary Problems* (Summer 1958).

Ontario Legal Aid Act, *Statutes of Ontario*, 1966, C.80.

Parole Act, *Statutes of Canada*, 1958, C.38.

Penitentiary Act, *Rev. Statutes of Canada*, 1960 -61, C.54.

Prisons and Reformatories Act, *Rev. Statutes of Canada*, 1952, C.217.

The Probation Act, *Rev. Statutes of Ontario*, 1960, C.308.

Provincial Courts and Judges Act, *Statutes of Ontario*, 1968, C.103.

Reg. v. Holden (1962) 39 Crim. Rep. 228.

Reg. v. Inaniev (1959) 127 C.C.C. 40.

Reg. v. Jones (1956) 115 C.C.C. 277.

Reg. v. Roberts (1963) 1 C.C.C. 27.

Reg. v. Switslishof (1950) 1 W.W.R. 918.

Reg. v. Willaert (1953) 105 C.C.C. 172.

Rubin, S., "Sentencing and Correctional Treatment Under the Law Institute's Model Penal Code," *American Bar Association Journal*, 46 (1960), 994.

Rubin, S., *The Law of Criminal Correction* (St. Paul, West 1963).

Rubin, S., "Federal Sentencing Problems and the Model Sentencing Act," *Federal Rules Decisions*, 41 (1967), 506.

Standards Relating to Sentencing Alternatives and Procedures (New York, American Bar Associations, 1967).

Supreme Court Act, *Rev. Statutes of Canada*, 1952, C.259.

Wechsler, H., "Sentencing, Correction and the Model Penal Code." *University of Pennsylvania Law Review*, 109 (1961), 465-93.

Concepts and Methods of Social Science Research: General

Anastasi, Anne, *Psychological Testing* (New York, Macmillan, 1963).

Anderson, Henry, "Toward a Sociology of Being," *Manas*, 21 (3) (17 January 1968).

Asch, S.E., *Social Psychology* (Englewood Cliffs, NJ, Prentice-Hall, 1952),

Becker, Howard S., *Outsiders: Studies in the Sociology of Deviance* (New York, Free Press, 1963).

Blumer, Herbert, "Society as Symbolic Interaction," in Arnold M. Rose, ed., *Human Behavior and Social Processes* (Boston, Houghton Mifflin, 1962).

Bogardus, E., "Measuring Social Distance," *Journal of Applied Sociology*, 9 (1925), 299-308.

Bolton, Charles D., "Is Sociology a Behavioral Science?," *Pacific Sociological Review*, 6 (Spring, 1963), 3-9. Reprinted in J.G. Manis and B.N. Meltzer, eds., *Symbolic Interaction* (Boston, Allyn and Bacon, 1967).

Brown, Robert, *Explanation in Social Science* (London, Routledge and Kegan Paul, 1963).

Bruyn, Severyn T., *The Human Perspective in Sociology: The Methodology of Participant Observation* (Englewood Cliffs, NJ, Prentice-Hall, 1966).

Cattell, R., *Factor Analysis* (New York, Harper, 1952).

Chein, I., "An Introduction to Sampling," Appendix B in Claire Sellitz, Marie Jahoda, Morton Deutsch, and Stuart W. Cooke, eds., *Research Methods in Social Relations* (New York, Holt, 1959).

Cooley, W. and Lohnes, P., *Multivariate Procedures for the Behavioral Sciences* (New York, Wiley, 1966).

Cronbach, L.J., *Essentials in Psychological Testing* (New York, Harper, 1960).

Diamond, S., *Information and Error* (Basic Books, New York, 1959).

Direnzo, Gordon J., ed., *Concepts, Theory, and Explanation in the Behavioral Sciences* (New York, Random House, 1966).

Duncan, Hugh D., *Communication and Social Order* (New York, Oxford University Press, 1962).

Edwards, A., *The Social Desirability Variable in Personality Assessment and Research* (New York, Dryden Press, 1957).

Eysenck, H., *The Structure of Human Personality* (London, Methuen, 1953).

Ferguson, L., *Personality Measurement* (New York, McGraw-Hill, 1952).

Festinger, L. and Katz, D., eds., *Research Methods in Behavioral Sciences* (New York, Dryden Press, 1953).

Fisher, R.A., *The Design of Experiments* (Edinburgh, Oliver and Boyd, 1947).

Garfinkel, H., *Studies in Ethnomethodology* (New Jersey, Prentice-Hall, 1967).

Guildford, J.P., *Psychometric Methods* (New York, McGraw-Hill, 1954).

Gulliksen, H., *Theory of Mental Tests* (New York, Wiley, 1950).

Hays, W.J., *Statistics for Psychologists* (New York, Holt, Rinehart and Winston, 1963).

Homans, George C., "Bringing Men Back In," *American Social Review*, 29(5) (1964), 809-18.

Hotelling, H., "Analysis of a Complex of Statistical Variables in Principal Components," *Journal of Educational Psychology*, 24 (1933), 417-41.

Hyman, H., et al., *Interviewing in Social Research* (Chicago, University of Chicago Press, 1957).

Kahn, R.L. and Cannell, C.F., *The Dynamics of Interviewing* (New York, Wiley, 1957).

Kendall, M.G., *Rank Correlation Methods* (London, Griffin, 1948).

Kluckhohn, Florence, "The Participant-Observer Technique in Small Communities, *American Journal of Sociology*, 46 (1940), 327-41.

Koch, Sigmund, "Psychology and Emerging Conceptions of Knowledge as Unitary," in T.W. Wann, ed., *Behaviorism and Phenomenology* (Toronto, University of Toronto Press, 1964).

Krech, D., Crutchfield, R.S., and Ballachey, E.L., *Individual in Society* (New York, McGraw-Hill, 1962).

Kuhn, Alfred, *The Study of Society - A Unified Approach* (Homewood, Ill., Richard D. Irwin, 1963).

Laing, R.D., *The Divided Self: An Existential Study in Sanity and Madness* (London, Tavistock, 1959).

Lazarsfeld, P., "Latent Structure Analysis," in Sigmund Koch, ed., *Psychology: A study of a Science*, vol. 3 (New York, McGraw-Hill, 1959).

Lewin, K., *Principles of Topological Psychology* (New York, McGraw-Hill, 1936).

Maciver, Robert M., *Social Causation* (New York, Harper Torchbooks, 1964).

Maslow, Abraham H., *The Psychology of Science* (New York, Harper and Row, 1966).

Maxwell, A.E., *Experimental Design in Psychology and the Medical Sciences* (London, Methuen, 1958).

Mead, George H., *Mind, Self and Society* (Chicago, University of Chicago Press, 1934).

Merton, Robert K., *Social Theory and Social Structure*, rev. ed. (New York, Free Press, 1957).

Moser, C.A., *Survey Methods in Social Investigation* (London, Heinemann, 1958).

Murphy, G., Murphy, L., and Newcomb, T., *Experimental Social Psychology* (New York, Harper, 1937).

Nagel, E., *The Structure of Science* (New York, Harcourt, 1961).

Newcomb, T.M., *Personality and Social Change* (New York, Dryden, 1943).

Newcomb, T.M., A Dictionary of the Social Sciences (London, Tavistock, 1964).

Newcomb, T.M., Turner, R.H., and Converse, P.E., Social Psychology: the Study of Human Interaction (New York, Holt, Rinehart and Winston, 1965).

Oppenheim, A.N., Questionnaire Design and Attitude Measurement (London, Heinemann, 1966).

Osgoode, C., Suci, G., and Tannebaum, P., The Meaning of Measurement (Urbana, University of Illinois Press, 1957).

Parsons, Talcott, The Structure of Social Action (New York, Free Press, 1949).

Payne, S.L., The Art of Asking Questions (Princeton, Princeton University Press, 1951).

Polanyi, M., Personal Knowledge (Chicago, University of Chicago Press, 1958).

Rose, Arnold M., Human Behavior and Social Processes - an Interactionist Approach (Boston, Houghton Mifflin, 1962).

Schutz, Alfred, Collected Papers, vol. I (The Hague, Martinus Nijhoff, 1967).

Seigel, S., Non-Parametric Statistics (New York, McGraw-Hill, 1956).

Sellitz, C., Jahoda M., Deutsch, M., and Cooke, S., Research Methods in Social Relations (New York, Holt, 1959).

Skinner, B.F., Science and Human Behavior (New York, Macmillan, 1953).

Smith, M.B., Bruner, J.S., and White, R.W., Opinions and Personality (New York, Wiley, 1956).

Stevens, S., "Mathematics, Measurement and Psychophysics," in S. Stevens, ed., Handbook of Experimental Psychology (New York, Wiley, 1951).

Tajfel, H., "Social Perception," in George Humphrey and Michael Argyle, eds., Social Psychology Through Experiment (London, Methuen, 1962).

Thomas, W.I. and Znaniecki, S., The Polish Peasant in Europe and America (New York, Knopf, 1927).

Thurstone, L.L., The Measurement of Values (Chicago, University of Chicago Press, 1959).

Tolman, E., Purposive Behavior in Animals and Men (New York, Appleton-Century, 1932).

White, Leslie A., "The Symbol: The Origin and Basis of Human Behavior," Philosophy of Science, 7 (1940), 451-63, reprinted in The Science of Culture (New York, Grove Press, 1949).

Winer, B.J., Statistical Principles of Experimental Design (New York, McGraw-Hill, 1962).

Wylie, Ruth C., *The Self-Concept - A Critical Survey of Pertinent Research Literature* (Lincoln, University of Nebraska Press, 1961).

Yates, F., *Sampling Methods for Censuses and Surveys* (London, Griffin, 1949).

Attitudes: Theory and Measurement

Adorno, T.W., Frenkel-Brunswik, Else, Levinson, D.J., and Sanford, R.N., *The Authoritarian Personality* (New York, Harper and Row, 1950).

Allport, G.W., "Attitudes," in C.A. Murchinson, ed., *A Handbook of Social Psychology* (Worcester, Mass., Clark University Press, 1935) 798-844.

Allport, G.W., *The Nature of Prejudice* (Glencoe, The Free Press, 1956).

Balogh, J. and Miller, M., "A Scaling Technique for Measuring Social Attitudes Toward Capital Punishment," *Sociology and Social Research*, 45 (1960), 24-6.

Bordua, David J., "Authoritarianism and Intolerance of Nonconformists," *Sociometry*, 24 (1961), 198-216.

Burke, W., "Social Perception as a Function of Dogmatism," *Perceptual and Motor Skills*, 23 (1966), 863-8.

Campbell, D., "The Indirect Assessment of Social Attitudes," *Psychological Bulletin*, 47 (1950), 15-38.

Campbell, Ernest A., "Scale and Intensity Analysis in the Study of Attitude Change," *Public Opinion Quarterly*, 26 (1962), 227-35.

Chein, I., "Behavior Theory and the Behavior of Attitudes," 55 (1948), 135-56.

Cohen, A., "Attitudinal Consequences of Induced Discrepancies Between Cognition and Behavior," *Public Opinion Quarterly*, 24 (1960), 297-318.

Cooke, S. and Sellitz, C., "A Multiple Indicator Approach to Attitude Measurement," *Psychological Bulletin*, 62 (1964), 36-55.

Crane, Wm. D., and Schroder, A.M. "Complexity of Attitude Structure and Processes of Conflict Reduction," *Journal of Personal and Social Psychology*, 5 (1967), 110-14

Cronbach, L. J., *Essentials in Psychological Testing* (New York, 1960).

Cronbach, L.J., "Response Set and Test Validity," *Educational and Psychological Measurement*, 6 (1946), 475-494.

De Fluer, M. and White, F., "Verbal Attitudes and Overt Acts," *American Sociological Review*, 23 (1958), 667-73.

Dicks, H.V., "Psychological Factors in Prejudice," *Race*, 1 (1959), 26-40.

Doob, L., "The Behavior of Attitudes," *Psychological Review*, 54 (1947), 135-56.

Dotson, Louis, "An Empirical Study of Attitude-Component Theory," *Public Opinion Quarterly,* 26 (1962), 64-76.

Dustin, D.S. and Davis, H., "Authoritarianism and Sanctioning Behaviour," *Journal of Personal and Social Psychology,* 6 (1967), 222-4.

Edwards, A., *Techniques of Attitude Scale Construction* (New York, Appleton- Century-Crofts, 1957).

Edwards, A. and Kenny, K., "A Comparison of the Thurstone and Likert Techniques of Attitude Scale Construction," *Journal of Applied Psychology,* 30 (1946), 72-83.

Epstein, R., "Authoritarianism, Displaced Aggression, and Social Status of the Target," *Journal of Personal and Social Psychology,* 2 (1965), 585-9.

Eysenck, H.J., "Personality and Social Attitude, " *Journal of Social Psychology,* 53 (1961), 243-8.

Eysenck, H.J., *Psychology of Politics* (London, Routledge and Kegan Paul, 1954).

Eysenck, H.J., "Response Set, Authoritarianism and Personality Questionnaires," *British Journal of Social and Clinical Psychology,* 1 (1962), 20-4.

Fishbein, M., "A Consideration of Beliefs, Attitudes, and their Relationship," in L.D. Steiner and M. Fishbein, eds., *Current Studies in Social Psychology* (New York, Holt, Rinehart and Winston, 1965), 107-20.

Fishbein, M., ed., *Readings in Attitude Theory and Measurement* (New York, Wiley, 1967).

Gerard, H., "Deviation, Conformity and Commitment," in L. D. Steiner and M. Fishbein, eds., *Current Studies in Social Psychology* (New York. Holt, Rinehart and Winston, 1965), 263-77.

Green, B., "Attitude Measurement," in Lindsey, ed., *Handbook of Social Psychology* (New York, Harper, 335-69).

Guildford, P. *Psychometric Methods* (New York, McGraw-Hill, 1958).

Guttman, L., "The Basis for Scalogram Analysis," in S. Stouffer. ed., *Measurement and Prediction* (Princeton, Princeton University Press, 1950).

Guttman, L. and Suchman, E., "Intensity and a Zero Point for Attitude Analysis," *American Sociological Review,* 12 (1947), 57-67.

Halbegwachs, Nancy C., "The Impossibility of Prediction Behavior From Attitudes." *Kansas Journal of Sociology,* 1 (13) (1964) 131-6.

Harvey, O.J., "Authoritarianism and Conceptual Functioning in Varied Conditions," *Journal of Personality,* 31 (1963), 462-70.

Heider, F., "Attitudes and Cognitive Organization," *Journal of Psychology*, 21 (1946), 107-12.

Hovland, C. and Sherif, M., "Judgmental Phenomena and Scales of Attitude Measurement: Item Displacement in Thurstone Scales," *Journal of Abnormal and Social Psychology*, 47 (1952), 822-32.

Katz, D., "The Functional Approach to the Study of Attitudes," *Public Opinion Quarterly*, 24 (1960), 163-204.

Katz, D. and Stotland, E., "A Preliminary Statement to a Theory of Attitude Structure and Change," in S. Koch, ed., *Psychology: A Study of a Science*, vol. 3 (New York, McGraw-Hill, 1959).

Kelman, Herbert C., "Processes of Opinion Change," *Public Opinion Quarterly*, 25 (1961), 57-78.

Kerlinger, F. and Rokeach, "The Factorial Nature of the F- and D-Scale," *Journal of Personal and Social Psychology*, 4 (1966), 391-9.

Kirscht, J.P., and Dillahay, R.C., *Dimensions of Authoritarianism: A Review of Research and Theory* (Lexington, University of Kentucky Press, 1967).

Koenig, Frederick W. and King, M.B., Jr., "Cognitive Simplicity and Prejudice," *Social Forces*, 40 (1962), 220-2.

Krech, D. and Crutchfield, R., *Social Psychology* (New York, Wiley, 1967).

Lawson, E.D., "Canadian Social Attitude Scores and Correlates," *Journal of Social Psychology*, 69 (1966), 327-35.

Leavitt, H.J., Hax, H., and Roche, J., "Authoritarianism and Agreement with Things Authorative," *Journal of Psychology*, 40 (1955), 215-21.

Lentz, William P., "Social Status and Attitudes Toward Delinquency Control," *Journal of Research in Crime and Delinquency*, 3 (1966), 147-54.

Lewis, E., "Attitudes: Their Nature and Development," *Journal of Genetical Psychology*, 21 (1939), 367-99.

Likert, R., "A Technique for the Measurement of Attitudes," *Archives of Psychology*, 140 (1932).

Lipetz, M. and Ossorio, P., "Authoritarianism, Aggression and Status," *Journal of Personal and Social Psychology*, 5 (1967), 468-72.

Lipset, Seymour M., "Democracy and Working-Class Authoritarianism," *American Sociological Review*, 24 (1959), 482-501.

Lipset, Seymour M., "Working-Class Authoritarianism. A Reply to Miller and Riessman," *British Journal of Sociology*, 12 (1961), 277-81.

Maccoby, N. and Maccoby, Eleanor, "Homeostatic Theory in Attitude Change," Public Opinion Quarterly, 25 (1961), 538-45.

MacKinnon, W. and Centers, R., "Authoritarianism and Urban Stratification," American Journal of Sociology, 61 (1956), 610-20.

Macleod, R., "The Logical Approach to Social Psychology," Psychological Review, 54, 193-210.

Manis, Meluin, "The Interpretation of Opinion Statements as a Function of Recipient Attitude and Source Prestige," Journal of Abnormal and Social Psychology, 63 (1961), 82-6.

Martin.J. and Westie, F., "The Tolerant Personality," American Sociological Review, 24 (1959), 521-8.

Martin, J. "Tolerant and Prejudiced Personality Syndromes," Journal of Intergroup Relations, 2 (1961), 171-6.

McDill, Edward L., "Anomie, Authoritarianism, Prejudice, and Socio-economic Status - An Attempt at Clarification," Social Forces, 39 (1961), 239-45.

McGuire, W.J., "Cognitive Consistency and Attitude Change," Journal of Abnormal and Social Psychology, 60 (1960),345-53.

McNemar, Q., "Opinion-Attitude Methodology," Psychological Bulletin, 43 (1946), 289-374.

Miller, S.M. and Riessman, F., "Working Class Authoritarianism: A Critique of Lipset," British Journal of Sociology, 12 (1961), 265-76.

Moranell, Gary M., "An Examination of Some Religious and Political Attitude Correlates of Bigotry," Social Forces, 45 (1967), 356-61.

Muthayya, V.C., "A Study of Autocratic-Democratic Attitudes," Journal of Psychological Research, 2 (1958), 9-17.

Newcomb, T., Experimental Social Psychology (New York, Harper, 1937).

Norris, E., "Attitude Changes as a Function of Open- or Closed-Mindedness," Journalism Quarterly, 42 (1965), 571-5.

Olsen, Marvin E., "Liberal-Conservative Attitude Crystallization," Social Problems, 3 (1962), 17-26.

Oppenheim, A., "Communication," in George Humphrey and M. Argyle, eds., Social Psychology Through Experiment" (London, Methuen, 1962).

Oppenheim, A., Questionnaire Design and Attitude Measurement (London, Heinemann, 1966).

Osgoode, C.E. and Tannenbaum, P.H., "The Principle of Congruity in the Prediction of Attitude Change," Psychological Review, 62 (1955), 42-55.

Peabody, D., "Attitude Content and Agreement Set in Scales of Authoritarianism, Dogmatism, Anti-Semitism and Economic Conservatism," *Journal of Abnormal and Social Psychology*, 63 (1961), 1-11.

Photiadis, J.D., "Education and Personality Variables Related to Prejudice," *Journal of Social Psychology*, 58 (1962), 269-75.

Rabinowitz, William, "A Note on the Social Perceptions of Authoritarians and Nonauthoritarians," *Journal of Abnormal and Social Psychology*, 53 (1956), 384-6.

Remmers, H.H., *Anti-Democratic Attitudes in American Schools* (Chicago, Northwestern University Press,) 1963.

Rhodes, A. Lewis, "Authoritarianism and Fundamentalism of Rural and Urban High School Students," *Journal of Educational Sociology*, 34 (1960), 97-105.

Rhodes, A. Lewis, "Authoritarianism and Alienation: The F-Scale and the S-Role Scale as Predictors of Prejudice," *Sociological Quarterly*, 2 (1961), 193-202.

Roberts, A.H. and Jessor, R., "Authoritarianism, Punitiveness and Perceived Social Status," *Journal of Abnormal and Social Psychology*, 56 (1958), 311-14.

Rokeach, Milton, *The Open and Closed Mind* (New York, Basic Books, 1960).

Rokeach, Milton, "Attitude Change and Behavioral Change," *Public Opinion Quarterly*, 30 (1966-7), 529-50.

Rose, Arnold M., "Prejudice, Anomie and the Authoritarian Personality," *Sociology and Social Research*, 50 (1966), 141-7.

Rosenberg, Milton J., "A Structural Theory of Attitudes Dynamics," *Public Opinion Quarterly*, 24 (1960), 319-40.

Scott, William A., "Cognitive Consistency, Response Reinforcement, and Attitude Change," *Sociometry*, 22 (1959), 219-29.

Sellitz, C. and Cooke, S., "Racial Attitude as a Determinant of Judgements of Plausibility," *Journal of Social Psychology*, 70 (1966), 139-47.

Sherif, C.W., Sherif, M., and Nebergall, R.E., *Attitude and Attitude Change; The Social Judgment-Involvement Approach* (Philadelphia, Saunders, 1965).

Sherif, Muzafer, ed., *Attitude, Ego-Involvement and Change* (New York, Wiley, 1967).

Simons, H.W., "Authoritarianism and Social Perceptiveness," *Journal of Social Psychology*, 68 (1966), 291-7.

Smith, M., Bruner, J., and White, R., *Opinions and Personality* (New York, Wiley, 1956).

Smith, P., "Attitude Changes Associated with Training in Human Relations," *British Journal of Social and Clinical Psychology,* 3 (1964), 107-12.

Stotland, E. and Hilmer, M., Jr., "Identification, Authoritarian Defensiveness and Self-Esteem," *Journal of Abnormal and Social Psychology,* 64 (1962), 334-42.

Sykes, A.J.M., "Myth and Attitude Change," *Human Relations,* 18 (1965), 323-37.

Tannenbaum, Percy H., "Initial Attitudes Towards Source and Concept as Factors in Attitude Change Through Communication," *Public Opinion Quarterly,* 20 (1956), 413-25.

Taylor, J., "What Do Attitude Scales Measure: The Problem of Social Desirability," *Journal of Abnormal and Social Psychology,* 26 (1961), 386-90.

Thurstone, L.L., "Theory of Attitude Measurement," *Psychological Review,* 36 (1922), 222.

Thurstone, L.L., "The Measurement of Social Attitudes," *Journal of Abnormal and Social Psychology,* 26 (1931), 249-69.

Thurstone, L.L. and Chave, E., *The Measurement of Attitudes* (Chicago, University of Chicago Press, 1929).

Tittle, G. and Hill, R., "Attitude Measurement and Prediction of Behavior: An Evaluation of Conditions and Measurement Techniques," *Sociometry,* 30 (1967), 199-213.

Torgerson, W., *Theory and Methods of Scaling* (New York, Wiley, 1958).

Triandis, Harry C., "A Note on Rokeach's Theory of Prejudice," *Journal of Abnormal and Social Psychology,* 62 (1961), 184-6.

Triandis, Harry C., "Exploratory Factor Analyses of the Behavioral Component of Social Attitudes," *Journal of Abnormal and Social Psychology,* 68 (1964), 420-30.

Vaughan, G. and White, K., "Conformity and Authoritarianism Re-Examined," *Journal of Personal and Social Psychology,* 3 (1966), 363-6.

Warner, L.G., "Verbal Attitudes and Overt Behavior," *Social Forces,* 46 (1967), 106-7.

Watson, J. and Lippitt, R., "Cross-Cultural Experience as a Source of Attitude Change," *Journal of Conflict Resolution,* 2 (1958), 61-6.

Wilkins, L., *Prediction of the Demand for Campaign Stars and Medals* (London, Central Office of Information, 1948).

Woolmansu, John J. and Cooke, S., "Dimensions of Verbal Racial Attitudes: Their Identification and Measurement," *Journal of Personal and Social Psychology,* 7 (1967), 240-50.

Wright, J. and Harvey, O., "Attitude Change as a Function of Authoritarianism and Punitiveness," *Journal of Personal and Social Psychology*, 1 (1965), 177-81.

Wright, Paul H., "Attitude Change Under Direct and Indirect Inter-personal Influence," *Human Relations*, 19 (1966), 199-211.

Information-Use and Decision-Making

Abelson, Robert P., "Modes of Resolution of Belief Dilemmas," *Journal of Conflict Resolution*, 3 (1959), 343-52.

Adorno, T.W., et al., *The Authoritarian Personality* (New York, Wiley, 1950).

Aronson, Elliott, Turner, Judith A., and Carlsmith, J. Merrill, "Communicator Credibility and Communication Discrepancy as Determinants of Opinion Change," *Journal of Abnormal and Social Psychology*, 67 (1963), 31-6.

Back, Kurt, W. and Davis, Keith E., "Some Personal and Situational Factors Relevant to the Consistency and Prediction of Conforming Behaviour," *Sciometry*, 28 (1965), 227-40.

Bassart, Philip and Di Vesta, Francis J., "Effects of Context, Frequency, and Order of Presentation of Evaluative Assertions on Impression Formation," *Journal of Personal and Social Psychology*, 4 (1966), 538-44.

Becker, G., "Ability to Differentiate Message from Source as a Curvilinear Function of Scores on Rokeach's Dogmatism Scale," *Journal of Social Psychology*, 72 (1967), 265-73.

Bernard, J., "Social Problems as Problems of Decision," *Social Problems*, 6 (1958-59), 212-21.

Binder, Arnold, et al., "Uncertainty and Stage of Decision," *American Journal of Psychology*, 79 (1966), 89-96.

Brehm, J.W., "Postdecision Changes in the Desirability of Alternatives," *Journal of Abnormal and Social Psychology*, 52 (1956), 384-9.

Brehm, J.W. and Cohen, A.R., *Explorations in Cognitive Dissonance* (New York, Wiley, 1962).

Brehm, J.W., *A Theory of Psychological Reactance* (New York, Academic Press, 1966).

Brock, Timothy C. and Balloun, Joe L., "Behavioral Receptivity to Dissonant Information," *Journal of Personal and Social Psychology*, 6 (1967), 413-28.

Chipman, A., "Conformity as a Differential Function of Social Pressure and Judgement Difficulty," *Journal of Social Psychology*, 70 (1966), 299-311.

Cooper, E. and Jahoda M., "The Evasion of Propaganda," *Journal of Psychology*, 23 (1947), 15-25.

Cromwell, A., "The Relative Effect on Audience Attitude of the First Versus the Second Argumentive Speech," *Speech Monographs*, 17 (1950), 105-22.

Darley, J.M., "Fear and Social Comparison as Determinants of Conformity Behavior," *Journal of Personal and Social Psychology*, 4 (1966), 73-8.

Davidson, Donald and Suppes, Patrick, in collaboration with Siegel, Sidney, *Decision-Making: An Experimental Approach* (Stanford, Stanford University Press, 1957).

Di Vesta, Francis J., "Effects of Confidence and Maturation on Susceptibility to Informational Social Influence," *Journal of Abnormal and Social Psychology*, 59 (1959), 204-9.

Di Vesta, Francis J., Meyer, Donald L., and Mills, Judson, "Confidence in an Expert as a Function of his Judgment," *Human Relations*, 17 (1964), 235-42.

Eagly, Alice H., "Involvement as a Determinant of Response to Favorable and Unfavorable Information," *Journal of Personal and Social Psychology*, 7 (1967), 1-15.

Feldman, S., ed., *Cognitive Consistency, Motivational Antecedents and Behavioral Consequences* (New York, Academic Press, 1966).

Festinger, Leon, *A Theory of Cognitive Dissonance* (Stanford, Stanford University Press, 1957).

Festinger, Leon, *Conflict, Decision and Dissonance* (London, Tavistock, 1964).

Festinger, Leon and Carlsmith, J.M., "Cognitive Consequences of Forced Compliance", *Journal of Abnormal and Social Psychology*, 58 (1959), 203-10.

Festinger, Leon and Maccoby, Nathan, "On Resistance to Persuasive Communications," *Journal of Abnormal and Social Psychology*, 68 (1964), 359-66.

Fillenbaum, Samuel and Jackman, Arnold, "Dogmatism and Anxiety in Relation to Problem Solving: An Extension of Rokeach's Results," *Journal of Abnormal and Social Psychology*, 63 (1961), 212-14.

Foulkes, David and Foulkes, Susan Heaxt, "Self-Concept, Dogmatism, and Tolerance of Trait Inconsistency," *Journal of Personal and Social Psychology*, 2 (1965), 104-10.

Freedman, J. and Sears, D., "Selective Exposure," in *Advances in Experimental Social Psychology* (New York, Academic Press, 1965), 57-97.

Gerard, H., "Choice Difficulty, Dissonance, and the Decision Sequence," Journal of Personality, 35 (1) (1967), 91-108.

Gergen, K. and Bouer, R., "Interactive Effects of Self-Esteem and Task Difficulty on Social Conformity," Journal of Personal and Social Psychology, 6 (1) (1967), 16-22.

Greenwald, Anthony G., "Behavior Change Following a Persuasive Communication: The Role of Commitment Prior to the Influence Attempt," Public Opinion Quarterly, 29 (1965-6), 595-601.

Gulliksen, H., "Measurement of Subjective Values," Psychometrika, 21 (1956), 229-44.

Harvey, O.J., Hunt, D.E., and Schroder, H.M., Conceptual Systems and Personality Organization (New York, Wiley, 1961).

Harvey, O.J., "Personality Factors in Resolution of Conceptive Incongruities," Sociometry, 25 (1962), 336-52.

Harvey, O.J. and Robert Ware, "Personality Differences in Dissonance Resolution," Journal of Personal and Social Psychology, 7 (1967), 227-30.

Heider, F., "Attitudes and Cognitive Organization," Journal of Psychology, 21 (1946), 107-12.

Heider, F., The Psychology of Interpersonal Relations (New York, Wiley, 1958).

Hollander, E.P., "Competence and Conformity to the Acceptance of Influence," Journal of Abnormal and Social Psychology, 61 (1960), 365-70.

Holmes, David and Berkowitz, Leonard, "Some Contrast Effects in Social Perception," Journal of Abnormal and Social Psychology, 62 (1961), 150-2.

Hovland, C.I. and Janis, I.L., eds., Personality and Persuasibility (New Haven, Yale University Press, 1959).

Hovland, C.I., Janis, I.L., and Kelley, H.H., Communication and Persuasion (New Haven, Yale University Press, 1953).

Hovland, C.I., Mandel, W., et al., The Order of Presentation in Persuasion (New Haven, Yale University Press, 1957).

Hovland, C.I. and Rosenberg, M., eds., Attitude Organization and Change (New Haven, Yale University Press, 1960).

Hovland, C.I. and Weiss, W., "The Influence of Source Credibility on Communication Effectiveness," Public Opinion Quarterly, 15 (1951), 635-50.

Hunt, Martin F., Jr. and Miller, Gerald R., "Open- and Closed-Mindedness, Belief-Discrepant Communication Behavior, and Tolerance for Cognitive Inconsistency," Journal of Personal and Social Psychology, 8 (1968), 35-7.

Janis, Irving L., "Decisional Conflicts: A Theoretical Analysis," Journal of Conflict Resolution, 3 (1) (1959), 6-27.

Janis, Irving L., "Motivational Factors in the Resolution of Decisional Conflicts," in M.R. Jones, ed., Nebraska Symposium on Motivation, 1959 (Lincoln, University of Nebraska Press, 1959), 198-231.

Jordan, Nehemiah, "The Resolution of Cognitive Conflict Under Uncertainty: A Critique," Human Relations, 15 (1962), 277-9.

Jordan, Nehemiah, "Cognitive Balance, Cognitive Organization and Attitude Change," Public Opinion Quarterly, 27 (1963), 123-32.

Karlins, Marvin and Lamm, Helmut, "Information Search as a Function of Conceptual Structure in a Complex Problem-Solving Task," Journal of Personal and Social Psychology, 5 (1967), 456-9.

Kelman, Herbert C. and Eagly, Alice H.,"Attitude Toward the Communicator, Perception of Communication Content, and Attitude Change," Journal of Personal and Social Psychology, 1 (1965), 63-78.

Kleck, Robert E. and Wheaton, Jerry, "Dogmatism and Responses to Opinion-Consistent and Opinion-Inconsistent Information," Journal of Personal and Social Psychology, 5 (1967), 249-52.

Kogan, Nathan and Wallach, Michael A., "Personality and Situational Determinants of Judgmental Confidence and Extremity," British Journal of Social and Clinical Psychology, 4 (1965), 25-34.

Lane, Robert E., "Familiarity and the Order of Presentation of Persuasive Communications," Journal of Abnormal and Social Psychology, 62 (1961), 573-7.

Lanzetta, John T. and Kanareff, Vera T. "Information Cost, Amount of Payoff, and Level of Aspiration as Determinants of Information Seeking in Decision Making," Behavioral Sciences, 7 (1962), 459-73.

Lasarfeld, P., Berelson, B., and Gaudet, B., The People's Choice (New York, Duell, Sloan and Pearce, 1944).

Lefton, Mark, Dinitz, Simon, and Pasamanick, Benjamin, "Decision-Making in a Mental Hospital: Real, Perceived, and Ideal," American Sociological Review, 24 (1959), 820-2.

Levine, J. and Murphy, S., "The Learning and Forgetting of Controversial Material," Journal of Abnormal and Social Psychology, 38 (1943), 507-17.

Levy, Leon H., and Steinmayes, Charles H.,"Variance Matching in Information-Source Preference and Judgment in Social Perception," Journal of Personal and Social Psychology, 7 (1967), 260-5.

Lewin, K., "Behavior as a Function of the Total Situation," in K. Lewin, ed., *Field Theory in Social Science* (New York, Harper and Brothers, 1951).

Linder, Darwyn E., Cooper, Jael, and Jones, Edward E., "Decision Freedom as a Determinant of the Role of Incentive Magnitude in Attitude Change," *Journal of Personal and Social Psychology*, 6 (1967), 245-54.

Lowin, Caron, "Approach and Avoidance: Alternative Modes of Selective Exposure to Information," *Journal of Personal and Social Psychology*, 6 (1967), 1-9.

Luce, R. Duncan and Raiffa, H., *Games and Decisions: Introduction and Critical Survey* (New York, Wiley, 1957).

Lund, F., "The Law of Primacy in Persuasion," *Journal of Abnormal and Social Psychology*, 20 (1925), 183-91.

Maier, Norman R.F., and Burke, Ronald J., "Response Availability as a Factor in the Problem-Solving Performance of Males and Females," *Journal of Personal and Social Psychology*, 5 (1967), 304-10.

Manis, Melvin, "The Interpretation of Opinion Statement as a Function of Message Ambiguity and Recipient Attitude," *Journal of Abnormal and Social Psychology*, 63 (1961), 76-81.

Manis, Melvin, "The Interpretation of Opinion Statements as a Function of Recipient Attitude and Source Prestige," *Journal of Abnormal and Social Psychology*, 63 (1961), 82-6.

March, J.G., "An Introduction to the Theory and Measurement of Influence," *American Political Science Review*, 49 (1955), 431-51.

March, J.G. and Simon, H., *Organizations* (New York, Wiley, 1958).

Marek, Julius, "Information, Perception, and Social Context. II," *Human Relations*, 19 (1966), 353-80.

McGuire, William J., "Persistence of the Resistance to Persuasion Induced by Various Types of Prior Belief Defences," *Journal of Abnormal and Social Psychology*, 64 (1962), 241-8.

McGuire, William J. and Papageorgis, Demetrios, "Effectiveness of Forewarning in Developing Resistance to Persuasion," *Public Opinion Clinical*, 26 (1967), 24-34.

Melton, Arthur W., "Present Accomplishment and Future Trends in Problem-Solving and Learning Theory," *American Psychologist*, 11 (6) (1956), 278-81.

Meltzer, Bert, Crocket, Walter H., and Rosenkrantz, Paul S., "Cognitive Complexity, Value Congruity, and the Integration of Potentially Incompatible Information in Impressions of Others," *Journal of Personal and Social Psychology*, 4 (1966), 338-43.

Menzel, H., "Public and Private Conformity under Different

Conditions of Acceptance in the Group," *Journal of Personal and Social Psychology*, 5.

Miller, N.E.,"Experimental Studies in Conflict," in J. McV. Hunt, ed., *Personality and Behavior Disorders* (New York, Ronald, 1944).

Miller, Norman and Campbell, Donald T., "Recency and Primacy in Persuasion as a Function of the Timing of Speeches and Measurement," *Journal of Abnormal and Social Psychology*, 59 (1959), 1-99.

Miller, Louis and Meyer, David E., "Decision Effectiveness as a Function of the Structure and Number of Alternatives at a Choice Point,"*Proceedings of the 74th Annual Convention of the American Psychological Association* (1966), 25-6.

Mills, Judson and Jellison, Jerald, "Avoidance of Discrepant Information Prior to Commitment," *Journal of Personal and Social Psychology*, 8 (1968), 59-62.

Morlock, Henry, "The Effect of Outcome Desirability on Information Required for Decisions," *Behavioral Sciences*, 12 (1967), 296-300.

Nahemow, Lucille and Bennett, Ruth, "Conformity, Persuasion and Counternormative Persuasion," *Sociometry*, 30 (1967), 14-25.

Newcomb, T.M., "An Approach to the Study of Communicative Acts,"*Psychological Review*, 60 (1953), 393-404.

Nisbett, Richard E. and Gordon, Andrew, "Self-Esteem and Susceptibility to Social Influence," *Journal of Personal and Social Psychology*, 5 (1967), 268-76.

Osgoode, C. and Tannenbaum, P., "The Principle of Congruity," *Psychological Review*, 62 (1955), 42-55.

Papageorgis, Demetrios, "Anticipation of Exposure to Persuasive Messages and Belief Change," *Journal of Personal and Social Psychology*, 5, 490-6.

Rabbitt, P.M., "Learning to Ignore Irrelevant Information," *American Journal of Psychology*, 80 (1967), 1-13.

Restle, F., *Psychology of Judgment and Choice* (New York, Wiley, 1961).

Richey, Marjorie H., McClelland, Lucille, and Shimkunos, Alimantes M., "Relative Influence of Position and Negative Information to Impression Formation and Persistence," *Journal of Personal and Social Psychology*, 5 (1967), 202-10.

Rokeach, M., *The Open and Closed Mind* (New York, Basic Books, 1960).

Rosenbaum, Milton E. and Zimmerman, Isabel M, "The Effect of External Response to an Attempt to Change Opinions," *Public Opinion Quarterly*, 23 (1959), 247-54.

Rosenberg, Leon C., "Conformity as a Function of Confidence in Self and Confidence in Partner," *Human Relations,* 16 (2) (1963), 131-40.

Rosenberg, M.J., "An Analysis of Affective-Cognitive Consistency," in M.J. Rosenberg and C.I. Hovland, eds., *Attitude Organization and Change* (New Haven, Yale University Press, 1960), 15-64.

Rosenberg, M.J. and Abelson, R.P., "An Analysis of Cognitive Balancing," in M.J. Rosenberg and C.I. Hovland, eds., *Attitude Organization and Change* (New Haven, Yale University Press, 1960), 112-63.

Schroder, H., Driver, M., and Streufert, S., *Human Information Processing: Individuals and Groups in Complex Social Situations* (New York, Holt, Rinehart and Winston, 1966).

Sears, D.O., and Freedman, J.L., "Effects of Expected Familiarity with Arguments upon Opinion Change and Selective Exposure," *Journal of Personal and Social Psychology,* 2 (1965), 420-6.

Shepard, Herbert R. and Blake, Robert R., "Changing Behaviour Through Cognitive Change," *Human Organization,* 21 (2) (1961), 88-96.

Sherif, M., ed., *Attitude, Ego Involvement and Change* (New York, Wiley, 1967).

Sherif, M. and Hovland, C.I., *Social Judgment* (New Haven, Yale University Press, 1961).

Shrader, Elizabeth G. and Lewitt, David W., "Structural Factors in Cognitive Balancing Behavior," *Human Relations,* 15 (1962), 265-77.

Shrauger, S. and Altracchi, J., "The Personality of the Perceiver as a Factor in Person Perception," *Psychological Bulletin,* 5 (1965), 289-308.

Simon, Herbert A. and Newell, Allan, "Information Processing in Computer and Man," *American Scientist,* 52 (1964), 281-300.

Smith, William A., "Cognitive Complexity and Cognitive Balance," *Sociometry,* 26 (1963), 66-74.

Smith, William A., "Cognitive Complexity and Cognitive Flexibility," *Sociometry,* 25 (1962), 405-14.

Steiner, Ivan D., "Receptivity to Supportive Versus Non-Supportive Communications," *Journal of Abnormal and Social Psychology,* 65 (1962) 266-7.

Steiner, Ivan D. and Johnson, Homer H., "Authoritarianism and Conformity," *Sociometry,* 26 (1963), 21-34.

Tannenbaum, Percy H., Macaulay, Jacqueline R., and Morris, Eleanor L., "Principle of Congruity and Reduction of Persuasion," *Journal of Personal and Social Psychology,* 3 (1966), 233-8.

Taylor, Richard L., "Differences in Accuracy of Public and Private Judgments," *British Journal of Social and Clinical Psychology*, 5 (1966), 241-3.

Tajfel, Henri and Wilkes, A.L., "Salience of Attitudes and Commitment to Extreme Judgments in the Perception of People," *British Journal of Social and Clinical Psychology*, 3 (1964). 40-9.

Triandis, Harry C., "Cultural Influences Upon Cognitive Processes," in Leonard Berkowitz, ed., *Advances in Experimental Social Psychology* (New York, Academic Press, 1964), 2-48.

Triandis, Harry C. and Fishbein, M., "Cognitive Interaction in Person Perception," *Journal of Abnormal and Social Psychology*, 67 (1963), 446-53.

Vannoy, J., "The Generality of Cognitive Complexity- Simplicity as a Personality Construct," *Journal of Personal and Social Psychology*, 2 (3) (1965), 385-96.

Vidulick, Robert N. and Karman, Ivan P., "The Effects of Information Source Status and Dogmatism on Conformity Behavior," *Journal of Abnormal and Social Psychology*, 63 (1961), 639-42.

Wallach, Michael A. and Kogan, Nathan, "Aspects of Judgment and Decision-Making: Interrelationships and Changes with Age," *Behavioral Sciences*, 6 (1961), 23-6.

Walton, Richard E. and McKersie, Robert B., "Behavioral Dilemmas in Mixed-Motive Decision Making," *Behavioral Sciences*, 11 (1966), 370-84.

Ware, Robert and Harvey, O.J., "A Cognitive Determinant of Impression Formation," *Journal of Personal and Social Psychology*, 5 (1967), 38-44.

Wasserman, Paul and Silander, Fred S., *Decision-Making: An Annotated Bibliography* (Ithaca, Cornell University Graduate School of Business and Public Administration, 1958).

Whittaker, James O., "Cognitive Dissonance and the Effectiveness of Persuasive Communication," *Public Opinion Quarterly*, 28 (1964), 547-55.

Wilkins, L. and Chandler, A., "Confidence and Competence in Decision Making," *British Journal of Criminology*, 5 (1965), 22-35.

Wolf, Eleanor P., "Research Data as an Element in Decision Making," *Social Problems*, 6 (1958-9), 362-6.

Zajonc, Robert B., "The Concepts of Balance, Congruity, and Dissonance," *Public Opinion Quarterly*, 24 (1960), 280-86.

Zajonc, Robert B. and Bernstein, Eugene, "The Resolution of Cognitive Conflict under Uncertainty," *Human Relations*, 14 (1961), 113-9.

Index